Mass. Committee on Public Health

Evidence and Arguments

on petitions of Cambridge and Boston, for leave to take water from Shawsheen

River before Committee on Public Health of the Massachusetts Legislature

Mass. Committee on Public Health

Evidence and Arguments
on petitions of Cambridge and Boston, for leave to take water from Shawsheen River before Committee on Public Health of the Massachusetts Legislature

ISBN/EAN: 9783337302337

Printed in Europe, USA, Canada, Australia, Japan

Cover: Foto ©Andreas Hilbeck / pixelio.de

More available books at **www.hansebooks.com**

EVIDENCE AND ARGUMENTS

ON

Petitions of Cambridge and Boston,

FOR LEAVE TO TAKE WATER FROM

SHAWSHEEN RIVER,

BEFORE

COMMITTEE ON PUBLIC HEALTH OF THE MASSACHUSETTS LEGISLATURE.

J. W. HAMMOND, } *For Petitioners.*
J. L. STACKPOLE, }

GEO. A. TORREY,
R. M. MORSE, Jr.,
GEO. H. POOR, } *For Remonstrants.*
E. G. LOOMIS,
CHARLES COWLEY,

————•◆•————

BOSTON:
PRESS OF ROCKWELL AND CHURCHILL,
No. 39 ARCH STREET.
1881.

HEARING.

OPENING STATEMENT OF J. W. HAMMOND, ESQ.

Mr. Chairman and Gentlemen : —

I appear here in behalf of the petitioners, prepared to show you our absolute necessities in this matter, for I think before the hearing closes you will come to the conclusion that it is a matter of necessity with our city ; and while I do not desire to take up the time of the committee, yet perhaps a few words, showing you what we want, and why we want it, may shorten the hearing.

I regret to say that the city engineer came in here without his plan, and I am obliged to rely upon a plan, which, while substantially like that which we have, is not quite so large, and was not made for the purposes of this hearing, although it was made for a purpose which was near enough to the purpose of this hearing to make it of use here.

We desire authority to take water from the Shawsheen river, in quantity not exceeding 8,000,000 gallons a day, and carry that water by pipes to the City of Cambridge, there to be used by the inhabitants for domestic and other purposes.

We desire to take this water where the Shawsheen river crosses the old Middlesex canal, and to lay the pipe along the Middlesex canal until we come near the Mystic pond, and there branch over from the Mystic pond, through Arlington and part of Belmont, to Fresh pond in Cambridge. It is a distance of somewhere about 13 miles. For the purpose of gathering the water we desire to build a dam at the point where we take the water across the river, which would be from 1,800 to 2,000 feet long, — the exact figures I do not pretend to give, but only approximately ; also to make storage basins above that dam, taking perhaps 800 acres of land for that purpose.

The CHAIRMAN. — At what point did I understand that to be?

Mr. HAMMOND. — That would be where the Shawsheen river crosses the bed of the old Middlesex canal. It is near the line of Billerica. It is just south of where the Shawsheen crosses the Lowell Railroad, as I understand it.

Mr RAND. — Where do you propose to take your 800 acres for storage basins?

Mr. HAMMOND. — Almost exclusively in Billerica, — three-quarters of it in Billerica, and the rest in Bedford. In a word, we desire to take a quantity of water not exceeding 8,000,000 gallons a day at that point from Shawsheen river, for the use of the city, and to build the works which are necessary to do it. That is what we want.

The reason why we want it is because there is no other way in which our city can be supplied with water. We have the right to take water from Fresh pond, from Little pond, and from Spy pond, in Cambridge, Arlington, and Belmont, and also from Wellington brook. Fresh pond is in Cambridge, Spy pond is in Arlington, and Little pond is in Belmont. I have here plans which were prepared for another purpose, but which will indicate perhaps better than any words can what rights we now have. The whole of Fresh pond is in Cambridge. That pond contains about 185 acres; Little pond contains about 19 acres; Spy pond contains 116 acres or thereabouts. By the Statute of 1875, Chapter 165, Cambridge obtained the right to take water from those ponds. It was believed that that right was a valuable right, and under it certain canals were made between Spy and Little ponds and Fresh pond; but it was soon ascertained that Spy pond and Little pond were not proper sources of water-supply for the City of Cambridge, and in 1878, on account of a wide-spread dissatisfaction among the people of Cambridge, the City Council of Cambridge appointed a committee, consisting of the Mayor and other city officers, to fully investigate the matter, — the quantity and quality of the water which we had a right to take. That committee employed as one of their experts Mr. E. S. Chesbrough, of Chicago, who has been intimately connected with the water-supply of Boston, has an extensive and accurate knowledge of this section of the State, and is probably as conversant, perhaps more so, with the whole sub-' ject of water-supply of cities than any other engineer in the country. We had him examine thoroughly the matter. We also secured the services of Prof. Wood, connected with Harvard Medical School, who has had great experience in these matters, who stands second to none on this question of water-supply, in all its chemical and sanitary relations. This committee, after investigating the subject for nearly a year, making extensive explorations there concerning the character of the soil and concerning all the matters which pertain to the quantity and quality of that supply, made a report to the city government; and in that report they substantially say, that the waters of Spy pond and of Little pond are unfit for use and cannot be relied upon; that the waters of Wellington brook can be relied upon only in certain seasons of the year; so that our water-supply now is reduced to Fresh pond, which is situated wholly within the limits of Cambridge, and to such temporary, and we might call it spasmodic, use of Wellington brook as the laws of nature will permit us to make. This supply we have relied upon for the last year. Fresh pond can only be relied upon to furnish about 1,750,000 gallons a day. That is the report of all the engineers who have ever had any occasion to examine it; it is the opinion of our own city engineer; it is the opinion of Mr. Chesbrough; it is also the opinion of Mr. Crafts, formerly an engineer of the City of Boston,— a man eminently qualified to judge of the matter, who made a report in which he estimated the quantity of water we could get from Fresh pond at 1,600,000 gallons a day. That is the daily supply of Fresh pond. We have considered it perhaps worth 1,750,000 gallons a day for the year.

The City of Cambridge contains between 52,000 and 53,000 inhabitants. Assuming a supply of 50 gallons a day to each inhabitant, which is less than the average by far in American cities, we should need 2,500,000 gallons a day. This is the amount which we would absolutely require. Of course there are days when we pump from 3,000,000 to almost 4,000,000 gallons a day. We are now so situated with regard to Wellington brook that we do not expect that we shall be able to draw from that source scarcely at all. There is a slaughter-house near that brook, which was put there while it was a part of the town of Belmont, which has a large muck-heap, where it deposits much of its filth; and, without going into detail, I will simply say that Wellington brook is so situated that we cannot rely upon that, we believe, for any length of time. We have been obliged to shut the water off from Wellington brook during this past rainy season, because it was not safe to let it go into our pond.

Now, it does not need any particular argument to show this committee that a pond from which only 1,750,000 gallons a day can be drawn, is an inadequate supply for a city which needs at least 2,500,000 gallons a day. These are plain figures, and, without any ornament or attempt to enlarge upon the matter on my part, they show that our water-supply is entirely inadequate. It is absolutely certain that we must go elsewhere for a supply, We are not situated as towns are that never have had a water-supply, where every man has a well; but for years and years the City of Cambridge has relied, not upon wells, but upon water conducted to the houses by pipes. I don't suppose that there are 20 wells in Cambridge that are used to-day; I don't know of one. That is to say, it is a large community, which has adapted itself to the use of water through pipes. It has no way to get it, — there is not a place from which it can take water, — except the Shawsheen river. So I say that is why we want it. Our necessities require it.

I judge, from the appearances here. that we shall meet with opposition from the various towns and corporations interested in the water of that river. It is the opposition which is met always, at all times. It is the question whether the water which comes from the clouds and runs on the ground shall be used for domestic purposes or for manufacturing purposes ; and I take it that this Legislature, whenever the question has come to that, have always decided that the use of water for drinking and domestic purposes is superior in right to the use of water for manufacturing purposes ; and especially when, as in this case, the parties taking the water will be obliged to pay any man or any town who may be damaged what a jury shall say they have fairly suffered. Of course no bill would be presented without that clause in it, and anybody who has had anything to do with defending suits before juries on these questions of water-rights knows very well that the land-owners do not suffer by that mode of procedure. If anybody has property which is involved here, that property will be paid for. So it is really a question whether a city which stands in absolute need shall be allowed to take water, which it cannot get in any other way, from people who do not suffer in the eye of the law by the taking of it.

I forgot to state, that, as you would expect where the water-supply is inadequate, we have been reduced to great straits during the past season. Our pond has actually gone down so low that we were obliged to put upon the banks of the pond a pump to pump water into our conduit, from there to be pumped into our reservoir. The pond has been very low, unprecedentedly low, and we were obliged to take some temporary measures to connect for a certain season with Boston ; but we were not obliged to use that connection, and we do not want to be obliged to use it.

Testimony of George P. Carter.

By Mr. Hammond. — You are President of the Water Board of Cambridge?

A. Yes, sir.

Q. And have been connected with that Board for how many years?

A. About 10 years.

Q. As a member of that Board have you had occasion to consider the wants of Cambridge on this water question, and how those wants may be relieved?

A. I have.

Q. Will you state to the committee, in your own words, your views about the adequacy of the water-supply from Fresh pond?

A. It will be mostly a repetition of what Mr. Hammond has already said. The City of Cambridge purchased the water-works of an incorporated company, which was then supplying the city with water, in 1865. The amount of water that the city was using at that time was 1,461,048 gallons a day. With the same experience as all other cities, of course this quantity has increased all the time ; and, like the experience of all other cities, we began too small. Our works, which we thought perhaps would supply us for a great many years, have virtually given out this last season. In 1875 the level of the pond was reduced to 7 feet 4⅝ inches below high-water mark. In that year we got permission to unite Spy pond and Little pond, and Wellington brook, with Fresh pond.

Q. Wellington brook is a brook that runs between Fresh pond and Little pond, does it not?

A. Yes, sir.

Q. And crosses the conduit that connects Little pond with Fresh pond?

A. Yes, sir.

By Mr. RAND. — What does Wellington brook flow into?

A. Wellington brook naturally flows into Little pond and empties into Alewife brook. That is the natural course of it ; but our conduit intercepts it.

By Mr. HAMMOND. — Intercepts it before it reaches Little pond?

A. Before it reaches Little pond.

Q. It crosses the conduit?

A. Yes, sir. Connections were made with the expectation that the waters of these different supplies would be fit for domestic use. They were at the time the conduit was constructed, or at the time that it was arranged to be constructed. The conduit was to run from Fresh pond to Spy pond, intercepting Wellington brook on its way, with a gate-house there, so that the water at any time could be shut off or let on. The waters of Wellington brook are not always, as was known at the time, in a fit condition to let into Fresh pond.

Q. Well, why?

A. The water was contaminated in its flow along the brook.

Q. There were dwellings upon the banks, were there not?

A. There were. So this gate was designed so that we could let on that water when it was supposed to be fit to be used for domestic purposes. We did use it in the year 1875, when the level of the pond was reduced more than it had ever been before. In the year 1878 a slaughter-house was erected within 400 or 500 feet of Fresh pond, running very near this conduit, against the most strenuous efforts of our city and people, knowing, as we well did, and as all the experts informed us, that it would be a great detriment to our water-supply; and it has so proved.

During this last season, which every one knows has been an extremely dry season, our pond reached the lowest level ever known, which was 9.12 feet below high-water mark. At that time we were obliged to use our centrifugal pump, which we had established on the border of the pond for pumping into the conduit that takes the water into the engine-house. It had got below the reach of our main pumps. At the same time, we seemed to be in so much danger of a water famine that it was thought advisable, if permission could be obtained from the City of Boston, to connect with the water-supply of that city. Permission was obtained, and a connection was made with the City of Boston by a 16-inch pipe across Brookline bridge.

Q. I will ask you whether, in your judgment, looking out reasonably for the interests of the city, you believed that was a necessary precaution in that state of the water-supply?

A. I certainly did. I recommended the adoption of such a course to the Water Board. It was done at an expense of over $20,000. I certainly should not have advised the expenditure of so much money had I not felt the extreme necessity, and the very great danger of a water famine. When I recommended this project of connecting with Boston we were only 23 inches above the top of our conduit. At that time the weather was extremely hot and dry, and we were pumping 4,000,000 gallons a day. I suppose every gentleman of the committee understands fully that in extremely dry weather the consumption of water increases. It doubled with us. It is the same in very cold weather. Our average pumping is about 2,400,000 gallons a day, which doubles in these extreme times of cold and hot weather.

By Mr. RAND. — How much water did you draw from Boston at that time?

A. We have never drawn from Boston. After the connection was made, we consulted with the Water Board of Boston, and they were equally short with us. They were then pumping into their conduits on the Mystic, and had made arrangements to do the same with the Cochituate; and they thought that we ought to do the same thing in regard to pumping into our conduit at Fresh pond.

By Mr. HAMMOND. — This connection was not with the Mystic supply, but with the Sudbury supply?

A. Yes, with the Sudbury or Cochituate. So that, for that reason, we had to erect a centrifugal pump on the borders of the pond; and when the water got at the lowest point we used it until the rain came on, which it did very soon afterwards, — the late heavy rains, — which we have been obliged to use to fill up the pond in a way which I will explain to the committee if I can.

Q. As I understand it, we pump the water from the pond by means of a pipe that runs out into the pond some feet from the bank, do we not?

A. The centrifugal pump was erected on the border of the pond.

Q. The water went away down below the pipe that connects with the well-room, did it not?

A. Oh, yes; the water was 15 inches below the top of the conduit that supplies the pump in our well-room.

Q. So you had to pump it into that?

A. Yes, sir. Owing to the erection of this slaughter-house, we found, upon examination, that the water of Wellington brook, which we had relied upon after the heavy rains, had got contaminated; that the water from the muck-heaps, that this slaughter-house has constructed near by, had contaminated it. These muck-heaps are on a hill which has a slope directly to our water-supply.

Q. You call them " muck-heaps." They are muck-heaps; but what does the slaughter-house put there?

A. In the first place, they put muck, which they get from the swamp, on this hill, and then they pump what is called their " soup " on to it. This soup, as I understand it, is .what the hog is immediately put into after he has been stuck. He is immediately put into this, with all the blood, etc., and he is there cleaned. One of your committee can tell much better than I can how that is done, but it is pretty poor stuff to drink when put into water, evidently; and for that reason we have lost a large supply of water that we could otherwise have taken from Wellington brook. The waters of Spy and Little ponds have never, since we constructed the conduit, been in a condition that was fit to use.

Q. Have you ever used the conduit from Spy pond?

A. We never have.

Q. Because the water was not fit?

A. The water was not fit.

Q. How is it with regard to Little pond?

A. Little pond has never been in a condition to use.

Q. Will you state the surroundings of Little pond, with reference to whether the land is highly cultivated about there or not?

A. It is very low. It is pretty nearly on a level with the meadows, which overflow in heavy rains, and everything in the nature of manure that is used for the cultivation of the soil comes in contact with this water, and it is contaminated in that way. We have made an exception this year in our extreme necessity, and have opened this gate at Little pond. From the fact that there was such an amount of water

from the rain and the melting of snow and ice, we, after consulting
with our most eminent citizens, Dr. Walcott and Prof. Wood, have,
in our extreme necessity, taken this water. I do not think it is what
they would recommend should be taken for domestic use if it was not
for the dire necessity. The fact is, the whole surroundings of our
water-supply are contaminated. If we want to furnish our citizens
with pure water, we must be confined entirely to Fresh pond — we
ought to be — not taking anything outside of it that is within our
reach. That is the sum and substance of the whole matter.

Prof. Wood will, in his testimony, give you the facts in relation to
the quality of the water, which will be more authentic and be of more
weight than anything I could say. He has been our chemist, and
has analyzed these waters and knows exactly their condition.

Q. Mr. Carter, I will ask you whether the periods in which the
waters of Wellington brook can be taken are not growing less and
less every year?

A. I think they are.

Q. Have you caused the water of Wellington brook, even during
the last rainy season, to be shut off because you did not dare to let it
enter into the pond?

A. We have done that more than half-a-dozen times. We have
had a constant watch on the water; and by its color and by its flow
from the muck-heap have decided when it was best to open the gate
and when to shut it; and we have opened and shut it perhaps twice
in a day, the conditions so frequently change.

Q. Your idea is to take the water of the Shawsheen, as much as we
need, into Fresh pond, as a natural reservoir, is it?

A. Fresh pond must be used as a natural reservoir. Everything
else will be shut off.

Q. Shut the water off from all other sources, and use that as a
natural reservoir, and take the water from the Shawsheen and carry it
into the pond, so much as may be necessary to keep the pond in a
fairly full condition?

A. Yes, sir.

Q. Do you know the average amount of water which has been supplied in Cambridge during the past year?

A. I have it here. The average daily supply in 1865, as I have
stated before, was 1,461,048 gallons. In 1868 (we have no record
for 1866 or '67) it was 1,732,755 gallons; in 1869, 1,677,481 gallons; in 1870, 1,739,869 gallons; in 1871, 1,747,704 gallons; in 1872,
1,626,206 gallons; in 1873, 2,124,884 gallons; in 1874, 2,298,953 gallons; in 1875, 2,718,484 gallons. There was a severe drought that year,
and there was more water used than in any other year on the list.
In 1876, 2,438,564 gallons; in 1877, 2,631,732 gallons; in 1878,

2,257,190 gallons; in 1879, 2,432,386 gallons; in 1880, 2,429,500 gallons. I would like to state here what I meant to have stated before, that we have made great efforts to reduce the consumption of our water to the minimum. We reduced it last year to 46 gallons and a fraction *per capita.* I think the consumption in Boston is 97 gallons *per capita.* Owing to the scarcity of our water we have made every effort to reduce consumption by stopping leaks, by shutting off the water into sections, and by pressure-gates, to ascertain where the leaks are and stop them. A great deal of time and money have been spent in that direction.

Q. Is it a fact that the water is very generally taken by the citizens?

A. I think it is, very generally.

Q. Your conduits run all over the city, do they not?

A. They do.

Q. Do you believe that Cambridge can have water at all unless it can get it from the Shawsheen river or from Boston?

A. I know of no other source. The experts' testimony is before the committee.

Q. Have you examined the matter in all its bearings to ascertain that fact?

A. I have.

Cross-Examination.

By Mr. Poor. — Have not the rainfalls for the last two years been exceptionally light?

A. The average rainfall is about 48 inches. The rainfall of 1879 was 38.80 inches. The rainfall of 1880, last year, was very light,— 33.31 inches.

Q. Whether, in reducing the consumption of water, you restricted your manufacturers in any measure? Have you cut off from them any water-supply?

A. We have not. We have cut off the city from water for sprinkling the streets this past season.

By Mr. Torrey. — What is the trouble with the water of Spy pond and Little pond?

A. I should prefer that our chemist should answer that question.

Q. I suppose so; but, if you will, answer it generally.

A. Generally, in reference to Spy pond, that is so situated that it takes the drainage of everything around it, more than Little pond or Fresh pond. More surface water runs into that. We have no surface water running into Little pond of any consequence. And in Spy pond there appears to be a green vegetable growth, that has troubled other ponds in the neighborhood, particularly Horn pond. We have the same there.

Q. When did you make connection with Spy pond?

A. In 1875.

Q. Has the quality of the water changed since that time?

A. It changed about that time.

Q. Changed about the time you took it?

A. About the time we took it. We had a complaint from the Gages, who were collecting ice from the pond, — a large establishment. They maintain that our shutting up the pond had made this sudden change in the water. They cut no ice the next year after we constructed our conduit, I think; the ice was not fit to be used. I think there is no question that the water of Spy pond is not fit for domestic use.

Q. What is the amount of flow of rain-water into Wellington brook?

A. That is variable.

Q. Suppose you took it all, what would be the average supply?

A. We do not take the water at all when the ground is not frozen; we are restricted to that by our expert scientific men. One year — I think it was in 1876 — we took in some hundred millions in about a week.

Q. From this brook?

A. From this brook. Last spring we did not get anything.

Q. Was that because the water was injured?

A. No, sir; because there wasn't any there.

Q. Is there any trouble with this water except that caused by this slaughter-house?

A. Yes, sir, there is.

Q. What other difficulty is there with that water?

A. It takes the drainage. The amount of it is, it is a small brook; it overflows the meadows, and on those meadows are the manure-heaps of the farmers there, — the soil is highly cultivated, — and it gets contaminated in that way.

Q. Where are these meadows that are overflowed?

A. They are all in the neighborhood of these three ponds.

Q. In Cambridge?

A. They are in Belmont, Arlington, and Cambridge.

Q. Where is the slaughter-house you speak of?

A. It is now in Cambridge; it was in Belmont at the time it was erected.

Q. Have you ever taken any means to have that slaughter-house removed?

A. No, sir. We have taken means to have this matter of the muck-heap done away with, and " soup" has been forbidden to be put on there.

Q. You have a Board of Health in Cambridge?

A. We have.

Q. Has their attention ever been called to this slaughter-house?

A. It has.

Q. Have they been asked to take any action about it?

A. Not about the slaughter-house, I might say, directly; but about these muck-heaps more particularly.

Q. They are connected with the slaughter-house?

A. Yes, sir.

Q. Have they been asked to take any action about that?

A. They have.

Q. Have they done so?

A. They have.

Q. Does the difficulty now continue?

A. It does. The muck-heaps are there; they have not been moved.

Q. What action did they take about it?

A. They forbid them to put any more " soup" upon the muck-heap.

Q. Do they continue to do that after this prohibition?

A. I don't know, sir.

Q. You have not investigated to see?

A. I have made inquiries; I am watching them all the time. Of course it is a constant source of annoyance. We keep men watching and taking records all the time.

Q. Isn't it a fact that, no matter to what source of water-supply you go, it will take more or less drainage from the surrounding country?

A. I don't think it is, sir. I don't think any drainage of any importance gets into Fresh pond.

Q. I don't mean sewage, or anything like that; but the natural flowage coming from the surrounding land, — as you say of these ponds, the water flows over some meadows. Is it not a fact that, to whatever water-supply you go, the same thing will be true?

A. We have, on the west side of the pond, some drainage that goes in there, that the City Council have already provided for taking care of. Outside of that, I know of nothing that goes to the pond.

Q. What pond?

A. Fresh pond.

Q. Have you personally examined Shawsheen river?

A. I have not.

Q. You don't know whether, above the point where you propose to take water from that stream, it receives, at various places, large surface drainage?

A. No, sir.

Q. Have you investigated to see if there is any other source of water-supply available besides the Shawsheen river?

A. Yes, sir; we have been some five or six years about that.

Q. Did you find any?

A. No, sir; we did not.

Q. Was your attention ever called to Concord river as a source of supply?

A. No, sir.

Q. Never paid any attention to that at all?

A. No, sir.

Q. Have you ever made any investigation as to the amount of damages that will probably result from taking this Shawsheen water?

A. I have not.

Q. What investigation has been made by the City of Cambridge before they came here with this petition?

A. Investigation has been made through the city engineer as to the facts in regard to the case, and they have been reported to the Water Board.

Q. Can you tell, approximately, the amount of water that is wasted in Cambridge? — I mean by the takers; water that passes through the service-pipes and runs away, without doing any good to anybody?

A. No, sir, I cannot.

Q. Haven't you ever made any sort of estimate in reference to that?

A. No, sir.

Q. Do any of your reports contain any statement in regard to that?

A. They might, in a general way, have stated what my opinion was.

Q. What is your opinion about it?

A. I think that with water-works, generally speaking, there is about 50 per cent. of waste. I don't think there is so much waste as that in our works.

Q. What do you think it is cut down to?

A. I think we have cut it down to the minimum. I don't think we shall ever be able to reduce it any lower.

Q. What is your opinion as to how much is wasted with your works?

A. I can't tell, sir. It would be entirely guess-work.

Q. What steps have you taken to reduce the waste?

A. I presume we have done more than any other system of water-works I know of. Our superintendent every year divides the city into sections, particularly in the night-time, and then with a pressure-gauge goes round and tests the pressure, and in that way he discovers leaks, and by examining the sewers to see how much water there is running in the sewers. I believe we have the best system, and do the most work in that direction, of any water-works I am acquainted with.

Q. You have stated what your superintendent has done to ascertain the amount of water wasted, — what have you done to prevent it?

A. If we discover any leaks we stop them.

Q. I refer now to the waste by takers.

A. If they run the water to waste to prevent freezing, which is against the law, and we catch them at it, we fine them; and if their fixtures are leaking, which we examine once or twice a year, we direct them to repair them; and, if they do not do it, we do it ourselves, and shut off the water.

Q. To what extent do you fine water-takers for wasting water? How many water-takers have been fined within the last two years?

A. Very few.

Q. Not more than half a dozen within a couple of years?

A. That is the registrar's business; I can't say — I can't say directly. I should not think there had been a great many more than that. The reason that they are not fined is, that the leaks are found, and the takers are ordered to repair them without any fine; and they do it. That has been done to a great extent. There have been hundreds of such cases.

Q. Have you ever investigated the subject of the use of water-meters?

A. Somewhat.

Q. What is your opinion about that?

A. My opinion is that the water-meters would probably save a large waste of water.

Q. Is there any meter that you know of that is fit for use?

A. Yes, sir. I know of a number of meters that are fit for use.

Q. What should you think of the expediency of the City of Cambridge, instead of going to this great expense to obtain a further supply of water, trying the other system of preventing the waste, which you say is so large, by adopting a system of meters?

A. I should not believe in it at all.

Q. Why not?

A. It is too expensive, to begin with. I do not think our waste is so great as to cause much anxiety about that. I think, in a sanitary view, there should be a certain amount of waste water.

Q. Why?

A. For the purpose of keeping clean. I don't believe, if you attached meters to your houses for domestic purposes, there would be, in many cases, enough water used to flush the water-closets properly.

Q. Supposing you should allow each family to use so much water, which would be an ample quantity for all family purposes and for purposes of purity, flushing water-closets, etc., allow them that quantity at your regular water-rates, and then charge them for any excess; would there be any objection to that system except the expense?

A. I don't know. I have not considered it enough to answer that question.

Q. Has any particular consideration been given by your Board to this question of stopping the waste of water, instead of obtaining an additional supply?

A. It is a matter that has been discussed off and on for years.

Q. But no systematic investigation has been made, has there?

A. No, sir.

Q. I see that in your petition you speak of obtaining water for the City of Cambridge " for domestic and other purposes." What do you mean by " other purposes "?

A. Manufacturing purposes.

Q. Can you tell the committee what proportion of the water of Cambridge is used for manufacturing purposes and what for domestic purposes?

A. Yes, pretty nearly. It would be governed by what water we sell through meters. We should charge that to manufacturing purposes and the rest to domestic purposes, and also fire purposes. Our metered water amounts to about $30,000 a year only. It is not quite that, I think.

Q. How much water would that be?

A. It is two cents a hundred gallons. I have not figured it.

Q. Is all the water that is used for manufacturing purposes metered?

A. Pretty much all; it is not all.

Q. What is this water used for, — to supply boilers or for power?

A. Yes, sir, for power; and there is a sugar-house that uses it.

By Mr. MORSE. — Can you give us the statistics showing the population of Cambridge approximately at the time you took your water-supply and the present time?

A. I had that in my mind at one time to ascertain; but I came away this morning without it. I have made inquiries this morning, in order to be able to answer that very question, and I could not ascertain.

Q. Can you state from memory about what it was?

A. I don't dare to trust my memory on figures; I am very poor at it. We have now 52,000. When we took the water I should think we might have had 35,000. I ought not to attempt to give any answer to that question, because I don't remember.

Mr. HAMMOND. — We took our water in 1866. I think our population in '65 was a little less than 35,000.

By Mr. MORSE. — Is this increase in the use of water due to the increase of population chiefly or to the increase of manufactories?

A. I should say the increase of population.

Q. Is not the increase in the use of water much in excess of the increase of population?

A. If you mean the natural increase from year to year, it is not.

Q. So that you really had enough for your own use last summer?

A. Yes, sir.

Q. You have stated the amount you now furnish at about 2,500,-000 gallons a day and the amount which you furnished the first year was about 1,500,000. Is not that increase due more to the increase of manufactories than to the increase of population?

A. I think not, sir. I don't know that our manufactories have increased very much there. And, besides that, I ought to say that our manufacturers, to a considerable extent, bore for water. They use wells on their own premises, — quite a large number. We do not supply any water to some of them.

Q. I suppose you desire to supply them with water?

A. If we had water enough we should supply them, the same as every city does.

Q. If you could supply it cheaply enough?

A. It is about as necessary for a city to be able to supply water for manufacturing purposes as it is for domestic purposes. We do not want to drive our manufacturers out of town because we cannot supply them with water.

Q. To what extent do your manufacturers supply themselves from wells or from other sources than the city supply?

A. It is quite large, comparatively.

Mr. MORSE. — I understood Mr. Hammond to say in his opening that there were not more than 20 wells in Cambridge.

Mr. HAMMOND. — I meant for domestic purposes.

Q. Then there are wells from which manufacturers supply themselves with water?

A. There are wells from which they do supply themselves with water.

Q. In what part of the city are those?

A. Those are in the part next adjoining Boston, — nearest to Boston.

Q. Is that a good quality of water?

A. I don't know what the quality is, sir.

Q. Are there any manufacturers who supply themselves with water independently of the city?

A. I don't know that there are. I think that the Dover Stamping Company supply themselves without the city water.

Q. Where is that?

A. That is on Pleasant street, Cambridgeport.

Q. Any other company?

A. I have none in my mind that do not patronize us at all.

Q. Then is there a large number of manufacturers who supply themselves in part from their own wells?

A. Yes, sir; there is quite a number of them.

Q. You have a manufacturing establishment in Cambridge?

A. I have.

Q. Where is that?

A. That is in the port.

Q. Do you use the Cambridge water, or have a supply of your own?

A. We use both.

Q. To what extent do you use the Cambridge supply?

A. I guess our tax averages about $300.

Q. How much is that a day?

A. It is two cents a hundred gallons.

Q. How much water do you use a day from the Cambridge supply?

A. I should have to figure that up.

Q. I didn't know but you might know.

A. Oh, no; it varies.

Q. Suppose that your manufacturing establishments in Cambridge were not supplied from the Cambridge water-supply, would there be any difficulty in supplying the water for other uses now?

A. The same difficulty there is now.

Q. Wouldn't you have water enough for other uses?

A. No, sir.

Q. How much water do you estimate is needed for domestic purposes?

A. I never estimated it. The water-supply for manufacturing purposes in our city I think is very small, comparatively.

By Mr. Loomis. — You speak of the water of Spy pond having been contaminated by vegetable matter growing in it, and of complaints having been made by the Gages. Is it not a fact that that vegetable growth has ceased, and that the Gages have been able to take ice from the pond the past season?

A. I don't know that they have been able to take ice for domestic use. They took ice two years ago for cooling purposes; they could not use it for domestic purposes.

Q. Is it not a fact that they cut over the whole pond this winter?

A. I don't know, sir; they have been cutting ice there for a long time. I don't know for what purpose they use it. The water is not fit for domestic purposes; there is no question about that. If we had it, it would not be a supply such as we ought to have. All the water of Spot pond, with Little pond, would not be a sufficient source of supply.

Re-direct.

By Mr. Hammond. — Do you supply any water to manufacturers, to run their wheels by?

A. No, sir.

Q. The water that you supply to manufacturers is for boilers and drinking purposes, is it not?

A. For boilers and drinking purposes, and to the sugar-house, I suppose, for refinery purposes. That is only one establishment, however.

Q. And, as I understand you, the water used for manufacturing purposes is measured by meters generally?

A. Generally; yes, sir.

Q. And you think that the amount you collect by meters would be a fair representation of what is used for manufacturing purposes?

A. Yes; but while nearly all the meters are for measuring water used for mechanical purposes, there is still some water used for mechanical purposes that is not metered. They are small manufactories, however.

Testimony of Prof. Edward S. Wood.

By Mr. Hammond. — You are Professor of Chemistry, and connected with the Harvard Medical College?

A. Yes, sir.

Q. Did you, at any time, have occasion to look into the Shawsheen river, as a source of water-supply for cities?

A. I have, for the City of Boston.

Q. When was that?

A. I was appointed one of a Medical Commission, in 1874.

Q. How many were there on that commission?

A. Three.

Q. For the purpose of seeing whether it could be used for the supply of Boston, was it?

A. Yes, sir.

Q. As a member of that commission did you examine into the character of the supply which could be obtained from that source?

A. I did.

Q. What did you personally do about it? Will you detail what examination you made about it? Did you go up there?

A. Our information was entirely gained by personal inspection of the brook, or river, and its surroundings, and chemical examinations of the water; and in reference to certain points we obtained assistance from the city engineer of Boston.

Q. Did you personally go on the ground?

A. I did.

Q. Will you describe to the committee what sort of a place that is for a water-supply?

A. The water was found to be superior in regard to quality to any of the other sources of water-supply that we investigated.

Q. What waters did you investigate?

A. Charles river, Sudbury river, and the Mystic.

Q. And this was found to be the best?

A. It was found to be the best in regard to quality, chemical composition, and best in regard to present pollution (that is, pollution at that time), and probability of any future pollution; and that was determined by a calculation of the rate of increase of population in the drainage area of that river. It was also determined by calculating the rate of increase of manufactories upon that river and throughout the entire drainage area. Those figures are all given in the report of the Medical Commission of the City of Boston.

Q. Did you go over the ground?

A. We did. We went over the ground very thoroughly, and collected samples from points which might serve as the location of the reservoir, provided the City of Boston had taken that river as a source of supply. The samples were taken at the locations where it was proposed to build the different dams.

Q. (Referring to plan.) One there and one here?

A. Yes, sir. If I remember rightly, it was calculated that those reservoirs would hold about 3,000,000 gallons.

Q. The blue line shows where you would have had the reservoirs?

A. Where the water would flow after building the dams.

Mr. HAMMOND. — I will say that we desire to build reservoirs exactly where that commission recommended that land should be taken for reservoirs or storage basins, if Boston finally decided to take water from Shawsheen river.

Q. Do you believe that that would be a proper source of supply for any city, as to its purity and the chances of contamination in the future?

A. Yes, sir. The chances of contamination in the future are very slight indeed. We considered them so, according to our calculations at that time, at any rate.

Q. I will ask you if you have, since that time, made analyses of waters that are used by cities for domestic purposes?

A. Yes, sir, I have; a great many.

Q. Have you had occasion to consider the purity of the supply which Cambridge now relies upon?

A. I have.

Q. Will you state when your connection with that began, and what opportunities you have had to know about it?

A. In 1879, I reported to a committee on the water-supply of Cambridge in regard not only to the character of Fresh pond and the sources of pollution that were flowing into it, but also the character of the water which was at that time, or might at that time be used as a source of additional supply, namely, Wellington brook, Little pond, with its tributaries, and Spy pond.

Q. That was done in '79, was it?

A. Yes, sir.

Q. You were employed for that purpose?

A. Yes, sir.

Q. Did you try to ascertain whether Little pond, Spy pond, and Wellington brook might be relied upon as sources of water-supply?

A. I did.

Q. Did you make analyses of the waters from those sources?

A. I did.

Q. Did you come to any conclusion upon those investigations?

A. I did.

Q. Did you make a report?

A. I did.

Q. You have seen this pamphlet since you have been in here, have you not?

A. Yes, sir.

Q. Does your report in that pamphlet state the result of your investigations?

A. Those are my conclusions as I gave them at the time. I will state, in addition to that, that those conclusions have been realized since.

Mr. HAMMOND. — I will state that I hold in my hand a pamphlet which contains the report of the committee appointed in 1878, the report being made in 1879, which is entitled, " Report of the Special Committee on the water-supply of the city." Appended to this report are several documents, the first of which is the report which Prof. Wood, who was employed by that committee, made to the committee with regard to this source of water-supply. I desire to put that in and I will furnish the committee with copies of the report.

Q. Now, will you state what conclusion you came to with regard to Spy pond as a source of water-supply?

A. Spy pond is totally unfit for a supply of water for domestic purposes.

Q. Will you state to the committee your reasons for that conclusion?

A. In the first place, there are steep slopes on one side of the pond, these slopes being occupied entirely by dwelling-houses or kitchen-gardens, where a great deal of manure is used and where a great deal of night-soil is used, and the sub-soil holds water; even though there be no direct sewage, the flow is very rapid, and the water is very much more impure than in Fresh pond.

Q. Did you analyze the water of Spy pond?

A. I did not at that time.

Q. Have you since?

A. I have.

Q. Have you found your analyses confirm your opinion?

A. Yes, sir.

Q. Is it fit for domestic purposes, in your opinion, from the results of your analyses?

A. It is not fit; and in the summer time it is filled with growths which have been very disagreeable, at any rate.

Q. What is your conclusion about Little pond?

A. Little pond is fed chiefly by two brooks which have their rise in Arlington Heights, upon the hills, and at the sources of those brooks the water is very pure and very nice,— ordinary New England brook water, which is very good water indeed. But on flowing down, it flows down a side-hill upon which there are now situated quite a number of farms, and then flows through flats which are covered with market gardens which are very highly manured, highly cultivated, so that they get two or three crops a year from them, and during that flow the water is contaminated to a considerable extent. At one time specimens were collected at the source, and as soon as I could go from the source to the mouth of the brook in Little pond, the water, upon examination, proved to have taken up on the voyage more than double the impurities by flowing through this highly manured district, and it became, from colorless, pure-looking water, brown, turbid, and evidently colored with manure. Little pond receives a very large amount of water from those brooks, and, in addition to that, it is surrounded by market gardens, from which it draws its sub-soil supply of water, and that is very great.

Q. What is the sort of manure which is used on those gardens?

A. Night-soil, as much as they can obtain; but, of course, they cannot obtain their whole stock of manure of that quality by any means.

Q. Did your analyses of the water of Little pond confirm your views about it?

A. Yes, sir.

Q. Is it fit for domestic use?

A. It is not, at certain times, at any rate. I think that occasionally, before the period of the cultivation of the soil, storm water could be admitted; but during the whole year I should not think it advisable or safe.

Q. Did you make this examination of Little pond for the purpose of taking the water if it could be taken?

A. Yes, sir.

Q. Was it the desire of the Board, as you understand it, to take that water if it could be done safely?

A. It was.

Q. Did you report to them that it was safe?

A. I reported to them that they could take a portion of it; that is, I mean, for a limited period.

Q. Now as to Wellington brook. You have examined that brook, have you not?

A. Yes, sir.

Q. Been upon the ground?

A. Yes, sir.

Q. Looked it over for the purpose of ascertaining whether it was a proper source of water-supply?

A. Yes, sir.

Q. What do you say of Wellington brook?

A. I would make about the same statement in regard to that that I did about Little pond and its tributaries. It collects a great amount of drainage and sewage indirectly from the town of Belmont. It rises in Belmont, and flows in the midst of highly cultivated territory, so that the spring which forms the head of Wellington brook really has the same character as a well sunk in a highly manured field; and it then flows side of the Fitchburg Railroad track, taking the excretions from a great many houses in Belmont; and then through the flats, where it is exposed to the same sources of contamination as the tributaries of Little pond, namely, night-soil, manure from market gardens, and also, lower down, it receives the sewage from Richardson's piggery; and still lower down it receives the washings of the slaughter-house muck-heap, which has been mentioned before. I visited it the other day, Friday, and a very large amount of brown-colored water was flowing in, which, upon collection, you could distinctly perceive an odor in. That water was flowing directly into the brook.

Q. Now take Little pond, Spy pond, and Wellington brook, what do you say as to the probability of contamination in the future,—whether it is greater or less than now?

A. Greater. The market gardening certainly will not diminish, and it cannot be stopped. It is impossible to stop it without buying the whole town of Belmont.

Q. Now among your conclusions you state "that the water of Little pond and Wellington brook is at times polluted to so great an extent, and with material of so dangerous a character, that those waters are totally unfit to be used as sources of water-supply." Is that your view now about it?

A. Yes, sir.

Q. "And since this pollution is of such a nature as to render it impossible to prevent it from entering these waters, their use should be discontinued, and they should be prevented from entering Fresh pond." Do you believe that now?

A. Yes, sir.

Q. What source of water-supply has Cambridge now that it would be prudent to rely upon?

A. Fresh pond alone.

Q. Now, will you explain to the committee why it is that at times you think perhaps it might be reasonably safe to take water from Wellington brook? What times do you mean?

A. I mean to take the storm water, which does not have an opportunity to wash the manure from the ground; that is, in the spring of the year, when the ground is frozen. I think water collected in that way — only storm water — might be used.

Q. That is a quick brook, is it not?

A. Yes, sir, very quick.

Q. In freshets the water runs down in large quantities, and then in summer time how large a brook is it?

A. I don't know how much the flow would be. I don't know that it has ever been measured.

Q. It is a small brook, is it not?

A. It is a small brook, but still it carries a great deal of water at certain times. It is a quick brook, like any country brook.

Cross-Examination.

By Mr. MORSE. — Have you ever examined Concord river as a source of supply?

A. I have made some examinations of the water of Concord river, but I have never formed any opinion about it, because I did not know where the samples came from.

Q. What examinations have you made?

A. I have made them for the State Board of Health, — simply analyses of the water.

Q. You have not personally examined the river?

A. No, sir, I have not.

Q. Do you know the fact that Concord river is nearer to Fresh pond by some two miles than Shawsheen river is?

A. I don't know how that fact is.

Q. How happens it that Concord river has not been considered in this investigation as a source of supply?

A. That I am unable to say.

Mr. MORSE. — I believe, as a fact, Concord river is some two miles nearer Fresh pond than the Shawsheen.

Q. Concord river is larger than Shawsheen river, is it not?

A. Yes, sir.

Q. Much larger?

A. That is a question for engineers. I am not sufficiently familiar with the ground to say anything about it.

Q. At the time you acted as one of the Medical Commission for the City of Boston, was your attention called to Concord river at all?

A. Not that I remember. Not particularly, at any rate. It may have been mentioned in conversation with the city engineer at that time.

Q. At that time you were looking for a source of supply for Boston?

A. Yes, sir.

Q. You have never made a special investigation, with a view to determine upon a new source of supply for the City of Cambridge?

A. I never have. I was only directed to examine certain waters at that time.

Q. So that you do not undertake to say that the Shawsheen river is the most desirable source of water-supply?

A. No, sir, only that it is the most desirable place I have examined.

Q. You simply say that the quality of the water is suitable, and the chance of pollution is less than any other source of supply that you have examined?

A. Yes, sir; that I have examined.

Q. But you have never been requested to make any general investigations as to the proper source of supply for that city?

A. No, sir; I have not. I have this impression as the result of my labors for the City of Boston, that the bed of the old Middlesex canal is already created, and it would be much easier to run pipes along the bed than anywhere else.

Q. You think it would be cheaper to obtain water from that river than from any other source?

A. That was my impression about Boston in 1873. Of course it would hold good in regard to the City of Cambridge.

Q. Does not that canal cross Concord river?

A. That I cannot tell you. This is a mere matter of recollection. It may be an erroneous impression.

By Mr. TORREY. — I should like to ask you one question about Wellington brook, — where did you say that brook takes its rise?

A. It takes its rise in Belmont, near the so-called Cushing estate.

Q. How far does it run before it is materially polluted from any source?

A. It is polluted at the source by farmers manuring there. The head of Wellington brook is a spring, and that spring is boxed up, and always upon the side of the box is a mug for people to drink from, they considering it to be perfectly pure spring water. But my examination showed it to be very bad water, and to be contaminated with manure from the neighboring fields.

Q. That contamination at the source could be easily avoided, could it not?

A. I don't know how, sir. They must manure the fields, I suppose, to get crops.

Q. Is there a large extent of territory around there?

A. Yes, sir; the Cushing estate and the Alvin Adams estate.

By Mr. MORSE. — You said you made some analyses of the water of Concord river?

A. Yes, sir.

Q. When were those made?

A. I should have to refer you to the reports of State Board of Health. They were published, I believe. I don't exactly know when that was. It may be two or three years ago.

Q. What was the result of that analysis?

A. That I don't remember. The State Board of Health investigated into the condition of a number of river basins and other waters; I don't remember the year. Prof. Nichols made most of the observations.

Q. Whatever you did appears in their reports?

A. Yes, sir.

Mr. HAMMOND. — I now desire to call the attention of the committee to the report made by Mr. Chesbrough, which is the second document appended to the report of the committee in this pamphlet, which I have handed to the committee. I will read the third and fourth conclusions, on the 57th page of this pamphlet: —

" *Third,* That to provide against future probabilities it will be necessary to take constantly into Fresh pond sources of supply now admitted to but a limited extent because not sufficiently pure ; or,

" *Fourth,* It will, as I believe, be found best, ultimately, to abandon the attempt to make and keep all the present available sources of supply pure, on account of great expense and impracticability ; and for an additional supply to take a part of the Shawsheen river ; or go to the City of Boston."

These are the recommendations of Mr. Chesbrough.

Dr. Henry P. Walcott.

By Mr. Hammond. — Are you a member of the State Board of Health?

A. No, sir ; I am the Health Officer of the Health Department of the State Board of Health and Charity.

Q. You are the executive officer of the Board, are you not?

A. Yes, sir.

Q. Have you had occasion to examine the water-supply of Cambridge?

A. Yes, sir. I was a member of the commission that made the report to which Prof. Wood referred.

Q. Have you in your present position, or in any other way, had occasion to consider the question of the sources of water-supply for cities?

A. Yes, sir.

Q. Do you know anything about the fitness of the Concord river for that purpose?

A. Yes, sir. There is no point at which the Concord river is a fit source of water-supply. I need not remind this committee that the town of Concord is already before it, in order to get rid of the pollution of the State Prison, which now directly enters that river. The whole drainage from the State Prison, with 700 or 800 human beings, is now carried directly into the Concord river, or into one of the branches of the Concord river, above the town of Concord.

Q. Have you witnessed the pollution of the water of Wellington brook this year?

A. Yes, sir.

Q. Have the waters been so polluted that we have been obliged to shut them off ?

A. Yes, sir.

Q. Have you made a personal inspection of that brook?

A. Yes, sir.

Q. I will ask you whether you think that is a safe source of water-supply for the city?

A. No, sir, I think that at least eight months of the year it is utterly unfit as a water-supply.

Q. It can be used only under what conditions?

A. It can only be used under the conditions of a frozen soil, when there is a freshet and the water flows over the ground without touching it, without coming in contact with the cultivated ground.

Q. Is there anything outside of Fresh pond upon which we can rely now?

A. No, sir; I think there is not.

Testimony of William S. Barbour.

By Mr. Hammond. — You are the City Engineer of Cambridge, and have been for how many years?

A. Five years.

Q. Have you had occasion in that capacity to examine the question of the water-supply of Cambridge?

A. Yes, sir, somewhat.

Q. And the practicability of obtaining water from the Shawsheen?

A. Yes, sir.

Q. Where do you propose to put the dam?

A. Near the location of the old Middlesex canal.

Q. Is that a plan prepared by you?

A. Yes, sir.

Q. Does this colored place indicate the water-shed of the Shaw-sheen river?

A. Yes, sir.

Q. Will you point out upon the map where you intend to take the water? [Witness indicated the place upon the plan.] In what town is that?

A. In Billerica.

Q. And at the junction of the Shawsheen with the old Middlesex canal, is it?

A. Yes, sir.

Q. What does that space upon the plan indicate?

A. It represents the flowage after building the dam.

Q. That part of the meadows which will be overflowed after the dam is built?

A. Yes, sir.

Q. How much space is there there?

A. About 800 acres.

Q. Is there any house there?

A. Not in the flowage area.

Q. What is the minimum capacity of the Shawsheen river as concerns the water-supply at that point?

A. We call it about 20,000,000 gallons in 24 hours.

Q. There are times when a much greater quantity passes by, are there not?

A. Yes, sir.

Q. Have you made observations, or caused them to be made, when a much greater quantity passed?

A. I have.

Q. What have you observed?

A. The largest gauging that we have made at any one time was 200,000,000 in 24 hours.

Q. You have caused it to be gauged when it indicated a flow at that rate, have you?

A. Yes, sir.

Q. Now your plan is to build a dam how long?

A. 1,600 feet.

Q. How many basins do you intend to have?

A. Only one for this purpose.

Q. When that basin is filled, the rest of the water will pass over the dam?

A. It will.

Q. Have you, during the past year, been upon this ground and made surveys, etc.?

A. We have, to some extent.

Q. What is the character of the neighborhood there as to probable pollution of the water?

A. I think the probability of pollution is very slight.

Q. Can you see any house after you get where you propose to build the dam, for three or four miles?

A. There are very few houses. I don't recollect that there is any house in sight, from the site of the dam.

Q. Your idea would be to take these 1,800 acres of land, clear it of brush, by burning or otherwise, and build a dam and flood it?

A. Yes, sir.

Q. And keep the water there, and use from it 8,000,000 gallons a day, and let the rest flow over the dam?

A. Use what we wanted.

Q. How much would be wanted?

A. We should not want 8,000,000 gallons a day for a long time.

Q. How much do you think we should need from that source?

A. We should not need more than 2,000,000 gallons a day, at the outside.

Q. Your purpose is to convey it by pipes, open or shut?

A. My plan was to have a closed pipe, an iron pipe.

Q. If more is taken, it would be done by an open pipe?

A. If more is taken — if the whole river were taken — the probability is that a conduit would be built a certain portion of the way; and a certain portion of the way it might be run in an open channel, and the rest of the way by an iron pipe to Cambridge.

Q. You would take it on the bed of the old Middlesex canal?

A. Yes, sir; in part, and by highways in part.

Q. In what towns would you take it in the highways?

A. We should follow the canal bed down to Wilmington, certainly, and there we might leave the canal bed and take the highway for a part of the way down to North Woburn; then we should take the canal again part of the way in North Woburn and part of the way in Woburn Centre, and a portion of the way the streets, until we reach the head of Mystic upper pond; there we should branch off and strike over towards Cambridge, through Arlington and Belmont.

Q. There you would have to go through private property?

A. Yes, sir; part of the way.

Q. And part of the way by the highways?

A. Yes, sir.

Q. Then, in substance, it is by the Middlesex canal most of the way, — at times, however, in the highways, — from the Shawsheen until you get to the lower Mystic?

A. That is it.

Q. And then from the lower Mystic by a pretty straight route to Fresh pond, through such property as you need to go?

A. Yes, sir.

Mr. TORREY to Mr. HAMMOND.—Would you object to putting it the other way in your bill, — that you should take what you want?

Mr. HAMMOND. — It would be easier to measure what went through the conduit than what passed down the stream. Perhaps we should prefer to say what we want, because we know that, and we do not know what other people want.

Mr. MORSE. — And don't care.

Mr. HAMMOND. — Yes, sir; we do care. If we injure anybody, we shall have to pay him.

Q. You have, as I understand, made a calculation yourself of the amount of water which the Shawsheen river could be relied upon to supply, haven't you?

A. Yes, sir.

Q. And you fix the minimum at 20,000,000 gallons a day?

A. Yes, sir.

Q. Have you examined the present source of supply for Cambridge?

A. I have been familiar with it for the last five years. I was connected with that committee or commission.

Q. You were a member of that commission?

A. I was a member; yes, sir.

Q. Did you consult with Mr. Chesbrough about that matter?

A. I did.

Q. Did you see him in Chicago?

A. I did.

Q. See him here?

A. I did.

Q. After consulting with him and making such examinations as you could, what conclusion did you come to as to where Cambridge must go for its present water-supply?

A. We came to the conclusion that we could not get a full supply from Fresh pond, and we must look to some other place; and the Shawsheen river and the City of Boston were the two points that seemed to us to be practicable.

Q. Do you know the Wellington brook?

A. Yes, sir.

Q. Travelled over it a good many times, haven't you?

A. Yes, sir.

Q. Can the waters of that brook be used to any great extent?

A. I think not, only under the conditions which have been stated by previous witnesses.

Q. When the water is running over frozen ground, then you may take some of it?

A. There are certain seasons of the year when we may take a portion of the waters; but they have to be watched very carefully indeed, and shut off or let on as the case may seem to warrant.

Q. Have you made an estimate of the probable expense to the City of Cambridge of taking water from the Shawsheen river?

A. I have, with the exception of mill damages.

Q. What is your estimate of the cost?

A. $600,000.

Q. Does that include the land damages?

A. It includes damages for flowing and for right of way.

Q. How did you get at the land damages there, for flowing the land you are going to take for that purpose?

A. By inquiring and getting the best valuations I could, and then doubling them.

Q. You got what everybody said would be a fair price, and then doubled it? Is that the way you did it?

A. Yes, sir.

Q. And in that way you got up to about $600,000?

A. Yes, sir.

Q. Exclusive of mill damages?

A. Exclusive of mill damages.

Q. Have you looked into the mill damages somewhat?

A. No, sir.

Cross-Examination.

By Mr. MORSE. — I want to know, Mr. Barbour, whether you personally made any examination in regard to Concord river?

A. No, sir.

Q. Why has not Concord river been considered by the City of Cambridge as a source of supply?

A. I cannot answer for the City of Cambridge. For myself, I have had the impression for a long time that the Concord river was not a suitable source of water-supply. My impression has been that the water was impure.

Q. Well, scientific men do not act on impressions, do they?

A. No, sir.

Q. They make investigations?

A. I say I never made any investigation in regard to Concord river.

Q. Then you have made no investigations, because you have the impression that it is not a suitable source of supply?

A. That was one reason.

Q. Have you ever considered the question whether it would be practicable to take a sufficient supply there, and do much less injury to manufacturing establishments, than you would do by going to the Shawsheen?

A. No, sir.

Q. Do you know the distance from Concord river to Fresh pond?

A. It would depend upon what point you took the water.

Q. I will say, the point where you propose to take it.

A. I don't know. I cannot give you any figures upon that.

Q. Do you know what the comparative cost of bringing water from Concord river to Fresh pond, and bringing it from Shawsheen river to Fresh pond, would be?

A. I have made no examination upon that.

Q. Then, if I understand you, your passing by Concord river as a source of supply is not due to any engineering difficulties in bringing the water from the river to the pond?

A. I don't know as I can answer that. There may be engineering difficulties. I should think from my knowledge of the country that there would be engineering difficulties; and there is no point that I carry in my mind from which water from Concord river could be taken and brought to Cambridge under as favorable conditions as we can bring water from Shawsheen river.

Q. But you have never been over the ground for the purpose of forming an opinion?

A. No, sir; but I have a general knowledge of the ground.

Q. Have you ever looked at the reports of the State Board of Health to see what they report in regard to the quality of that water?

A. I have usually read the reports of the State Board of Health, but I don't remember at this time having my attention especially called to Concord river.

Q. Do you know whether the State Board of Health report that that water would be suitable for domestic purposes, or not?

A. I don't remember; no, sir.

Q. You say you have not paid any attention to what might be the mill damages on the Shawsheen, and you propose to have the city come in here without any regard to those?

A. All my reports have been submitted to the city government, and they go into it with their eyes open, certainly.

Q. Have you ever made any report as to what damages would be caused by taking the mill privileges and the other privileges on that river?

A. No, sir; I have not.

Q. Do you understand that the plan of the City of Boston is to take the water which you do not take from the river?

A. I think that is their plan; yes, sir.

Q. So that you propose between you to take the whole river?

A. Yes, sir.

Q. Then have you considered that that will result not only in damages to the mill owners, but in damages to everybody who has any rights on the stream?

A. Certainly.

Q. You have not figured on those?

A. I have not figured on the damages in that respect.

Q. Don't you think that before recommending this plan to the City of Cambridge it would have been better to have taken Concord river into account and ascertained if you could not get just as good a supply there, cheaper?

A. Well, not having considered it, I don't know how I could answer that question.

By Mr. POOR. — At what season of the year did you make the investigation as to the quantity that could be obtained from the Shawsheen?

A. In July, last.

Q. July, 1880?

A. Yes, sir.

Q. Do you undertake to say that there were 20,000,000 gallons flowing there every 24 hours then?

A. No, sir, I didn't say any such thing.

Q. What did you say, then?

A. I said that the minimum capacity of the river, with suitable storage, was 20,000,000 gallons in 24 hours.

Q. How much water was running through the river, in your judgment, when you made the examination?

A. Some days when I made gaugings there was no perceptible flow at all; I could not get any results from my gauges or from my floats. On other days there were 10,000,000 or 12,000,000 gallons; sometimes even less than that.

By the CHAIRMAN. — That was in 1880?

A. Yes, sir. I accounted for that in this way : that there were two small mills above the point where I took my gaugings, and it was probable that the mills had used the water from their ponds and had shut down and were filling up, and for that reason I got no flow in the river.

By Mr. POOR. — Have you ever contemplated the possible sanitary effect of this scheme to take the whole river upon the towns below, especially where there are villages, as in Andover, for instance? In making your recommendations to the City of Cambridge, have you considered whether or not the carrying out of this plan would expose people to the danger of pestilence?

A. I had not thought of that. But in speaking of the whole river, we mean the minimum flow. A great deal of the time there would be a large amount of water wasting. I think there would be enough to keep the river in a good sanitary condition. I should not anticipate any trouble on that score.

Q. Do you think there would be any flow in the summer time over this dam, judging from your observations of last summer?

A. Well, that would depend on certain conditions. There might be times when, if we were drawing large quantities, there would not be any flow over the dam.

Q. Did you examine the river below this point where you propose to have your dam, to know whether any brooks enter it there?

A. I did not make any particular examination below our pond. I had no occasion to do that. It did not seem to me necessary.

Q. If the City of Cambridge and the City of Boston join together in this matter, and take all this water, would it not practically dry up that river?

A. I think not.

Q. Would it not dry it up in the summer season?

A. There would be times when there would be a very much smaller flow in the river; but I don't know that it would dry up entirely.

Q. Should you say, from your observations of last summer, that there would be any flow in a dry season over your dam?

A. I think there would be times when there would be no flow. That would depend upon whether the rains were abundant or not.

By Mr. STACKPOLE. — It would depend upon the conditions of the act, would it not, as in the case of the act authorizing the taking of Sudbury river, as to how much should be left in the river?

A. Probably some would be retained.

By Mr. TORREY. — Have you any knowledge whatever of the amount of water power or mill property below your dam which would be injured or destroyed by taking this water?

A. I have not made any examination in that respect.

Q. Did you recommend this project to the City of Cambridge without making any examination whatever in this respect, and also without making any examination of Concord river?

A. I have stated that I made no examination with regard to the mills. I have stated to our people that there would be mill damages, and they would probably be heavy.

Q. You have recommended this scheme to the city for adoption?

A. Yes, sir, I have.

Q. And you have made no examination whatever as to the amount of mill damages? That is so, isn't it?

A. Yes, sir.

Q. And you have made no examination whatever of Concord river?

A. No, sir.

Re-direct.

By Mr. HAMMOND. — You have stated that 20,000,000 gallons was the minimum supply; that is, there would be that quantity after the reservoirs were filled; then, whatever came down, less the 20,000,000 gallons, would go over the dam?

A. Yes, sir.

Mr. HAMMOND. — Of course I need not state that any bill which should be prepared would provide for some flow down that river all the time. We should expect that.

Mr. STACKPOLE. — There is such a provision in the Sudbury bill, for instance, that a certain amount must always come down.

The CHAIRMAN. — Provided the bill will make it come.

Q. There is one question I forgot to ask you: considering the sources of supply from which water for Fresh pond can be derived, how many million gallons a day can we get from Fresh pond?

A. From a million and three-quarters to two millions, according to the season.

Q. Whatever Cambridge uses above that must be taken from the pond itself, or from this precarious source, Wellington brook?

A. Yes, sir.

Q. You know Mr. Crafts who made this report for the town of Watertown?

A. Yes, sir.

Q. Is he a competent engineer?

A. He is.

Mr. HAMMOND. — I desire to show that Mr. Crafts, who is, of course, a disinterested man in the matter, in making his report to the town of Watertown (page 37), estimates the supply from Fresh pond as follows : —

" From the foregoing discussion, I should estimate the average daily supply of Fresh pond at (in round numbers) 2,000,000 galls. And the minimum daily supply at (in round numbers) 1,600,000 galls."

Q. Have you considered how much water Cambridge uses *per capita* compared with other American cities?

A. I have some figures that give those facts.

Q. Will you state to the committee how our consumption compares with other American cities?

A. Our consumption is generally lower. Our average *per capita* for the last year was 46 gallons and a fraction ; for the year previous it was about the same, and it has rarely exceeded 54 gallons, while some of our larger cities are very much in excess of that.

Q. Have you looked over this table which is on the 29th page of Mr. Crafts' report, containing estimates of population, etc. ?

A. I have.

Q. Do you believe it to be fair?

A. I see no reason why it is not fair.

Mr. HAMMOND. — I desire to read from Mr. Crafts' report, page 29 : " Report of a committee appointed by the town of Watertown on the subject of water-supply and drainage in 1874. Printed by Rand, Avery & Co., in 1874." On the 29th page there is a table containing the population of Cambridge from 1870 to 1925, and the daily supply of water at 50 gallons per head for those years, and the daily supply at 60 gallons per head for those years, the population being given for every five years. It is wonderful to see how near this man has estimated the population for the year 1880. Population in 1870, 39,634 ; 1875, 45,574 ; 1880, 51,514. This estimate was made in 1874, and we have a population of a little over 52,000. We have exceeded his estimate, but he comes reasonably near. He estimated that we should use 2,575,700 gallons a day, at 50 gallons a head; and it is a remarkably close estimate. Of course it would be a little more at 60 gallons a head. According to this estimate, which time, as far as it has expired since it was made, has shown to be a reasonably accurate one, in 1890, which will be nine years from now, the population of Cambridge will be 76,968, and in 1900 the population will be 100,000 and some odd. We shall then need 5,002,900 gallons a day, if we do not use but 50 gallons a head, and 6,000,000 if we use 60 gallons a head. I desire to put in this table, and I shall quote from it in what I have to say at the close. I put it in as the statement of a very capable man, and a disinterested man, who was for a great many years an engineer for the City of Boston.

Re-cross.

By Mr. TORREY. — You have read this report of Mr. Crafts', have you?

A. Yes, sir.

Q. You endorse him, I believe, as a reliable man?

A. Yes, sir.

Q. Have you read what he says on page 44 about Bell brook and Kendall's pond?

A. Yes, sir.

Q. What do you think of them?

A. I don't think they would answer our purpose.

Q. Why not?

A. Because there is not enough water there, in the first place.

Q. How much is there there?

A. It would not exceed 2,000,000 gallons.

Q. 2,000,000 gallons for how long?

A. 2,000,000 gallons a day for a year.

Q. Mr. Crafts says that Kendall's pond, in Belmont, is a source of water-supply capable of furnishing 2,654,356 gallons a day, which can be obtained at very small expense. Is that true or not? What is your opinion about it?

A. We did consider that at one time, and asked for it, and had leave to withdraw. That is my recollection about it.

Q. Do you confirm that statement?

A. I think his estimate of the quantity is correct.

Q. It is good water; is it not?

A. I think it was then; I don't know anything about it now.

Q. You have not investigated this source at all?

A. Not in this connection.

Q. That could be very cheaply obtained?

A. At much less cost.

Q. How far is it from Fresh pond?

A. I don't recollect. I should think about two miles, or about two and a half.

Q. You made no report upon that subject whatever to the City of Cambridge?

A. No, sir, I did not consider that. I stated that we have considered that in previous years, and we have not been encouraged that we could have it in any way. The town of Belmont has wanted it when we looked for it.

Q. I suppose, if you have leave to withdraw on this petition, you will come back and try to get that, won't you?

A. I don't know. We shall look around then and see what is best under the situation.

Q. Is there any objection to going to that source of supply and taking in this 2,500,000 gallons a day, except that you don't think that will be enough?

A. And that we cannot get it. We have had leave to withdraw upon it. I have considered it out of the question.

Q. When did you have leave to withdraw on it?

A. I don't remember the year.

Q. In this estimate does not Mr. Crafts allow that, after supplying Belmont with all the water they will need, you can still take 2,000,000 gallons a day from that source?

A. I don't remember what he says about that. If he says so I should not dispute it.

Q. Now, Mr. Barbour, was not the reason you received leave to withdraw because the town of Watertown had previously obtained the right to take this same water within a certain time, and that time had not expired?

A. Possibly. I know there was some good reason why we could not get it.

Mr. TORREY. — That was the case. The Legislature had given the right to Watertown before you applied.

WITNESS. — Possibly. I have considered that source as out of our reach. At any rate, we couldn't get it for the reason either that it had been given to some one else, or was reserved for the town itself.

Q. If there is nothing to hinder your getting 2,000,000 gallons a day from that source at a small expense, why should not the City of Cambridge adopt that plan?

A. I should think we ought to look for a larger source of supply than that.

Q. Is not the testimony here, that all you will want for a long time to come is 2,000,000 gallons a day additional?

A. In looking for a source of supply it is always customary to look for a larger amount than you want at the present time. That would be very short-sighted, I think.

Q. That is the testimony here, is it not, that all you will want for a long time to come is 2,000,000 gallons a day additional to what you have now?

A. Yes, sir; I think that was the testimony.

Q. Now, did you not make this application to take water from the Shawsheen river because you were afraid that the City of Boston would apply for leave to take that water and get it, and you thought you had better come at once?

A. No, sir, I think not. That is not my understanding of it at all.

Q. You testified yourself, didn't you, a little while ago, that the city would not need, for the present, more than 2,000,000 gallons a day?

A. Yes, sir; I think I did.

Q. What did you mean by "for the present"?

A. Several years.

Q. How many?

A. Possibly five years.

By Mr. HAMMOND. — Do you think it would be good judgment to come here for Kendall's pond, for the purpose of getting water for five years, and go to the expense of building dams, storage-basins, and water-works?

A. No, sir, I don't.

Mr. HAMMOND. — Mr. Chairman, and gentlemen of the committee, I could put on other witnesses, but their testimony would be cumulative; and, as I suppose the committee do not desire to have us put on witnesses, as we sometimes do before juries, to swear to a lot of things that everybody knows are true, and as you do not desire to have cumulative evidence, I think we will rest here. We understand that these various reports are in. We can show, if the committee desire it, the efforts which are made by our city to stop the leakage of water, and reduce the consumption to the lowest possible limit. If my friends upon the other side want to know what measures we take for that purpose, we will show them. I do not suppose, however, that they will argue that a city which has reduced its water consumption to less than the average is open to the charge of wasting water. If they propose to argue that, I should like to know it.

Mr. TORREY. — That is the testimony of Mr. Carter. He said there was a large quantity of water wasted there.

Mr. HAMMOND. — Under the circumstances, I will put on Mr. Nevons.

TESTIMONY OF HIRAM NEVONS.

By Mr. HAMMOND. — You are Superintendent of the water-works of Cambridge?

A. Yes, sir.

Q. Is it part of your duty to examine the pipes, and see whether they are sound or not, and to detect leaks?

A. Yes, sir.

Q. State what portion of your time you devote to that matter, to stopping leaks and seeing what you can find out about them.

A. That would be pretty hard to determine, sir, as we divide the time up. Part of it is devoted to that.

Q. Do you watch carefully the pipes to see if there is any waste?

A. We do, sir.

Q. Do you observe the pressure from time to time in the pipes?

A. Yes, sir.

Q. Have you anything at the reservoir which assists you in doing this?

A. We have a chronograph, that records the fluctuations during the night, which we use particularly to ascertain the consumption after all the day consumption is supposed to cease.

Q. Can you tell by that whether there is leakage anywhere?

A. Yes, sir; we can. We record and keep the average, and if anything unusual takes place it at once makes a record of the same, and shows the difference.

Q. Have you been directed to watch carefully the pipes, and see about leaks?

A. Yes, sir.

Q. Have you taken pains to reduce consumption to the lowest point?

A. Yes, sir. We have adopted a method in the fall of the year, take it along after the use of hose has ceased, of shutting off different sections during the night, and testing for leaks. Wherever we find leaks on that particular section, we send inspectors around into the houses to inspect all the fixtures, and wherever there is a leak found, the parties are notified to make repairs, and given so long a time to make them.

Q. If the leaks are not in the houses, then you search for them in the streets, I suppose?

A. Yes, sir.

Q. Have you a gang of men for that purpose?

A. Yes, sir; that is, my regular gang.

Cross-Examination.

By Mr. Poor. — How long have you been Superintendent of the water-works?

A. Three years.

Q. What has been the dryest year you have seen?

A. This last year.

Q. Didn't you have water enough then for all the needs of Cambridge? Did you draw from any other source? You didn't take any from Boston, did you?

A. No, sir.

Q. So that you really had enough for your own use last summer?

A. Yes, sir.

Q. Which was the dryest year you have seen?

A. Yes, sir.

Q. You have lived in this part of the country how long?

A. About 25 years.

Q. And it was the dryest year you have seen?

A. It was the dryest year I have had any occasion to notice from my position.

By Mr. Torrey. — Didn't your reservoir in Cambridge leak very badly at one time, so that you were afraid it was going to injure the people living below it?

A. Yes, sir.

Q. When was that?

A. I discovered the leak first in the fall of 1877, I think it was.

Q. When was it repaired?

A. We repaired it in '78.

Q. Has it leaked since then?

A. No, sir, not to amount to anything. I don't know as I should say that the reservoir leaks at all, — the main reservoir; but it leaks from the foundation, which we think is legitimately accounted for.

Q. Have you any idea how much water is wasted now from all sources, including leakage proper, and waste caused by the leaving of faucets open to prevent the water freezing?

A. I don't know. That is a pretty hard thing to say. I have thought that if the water-closets alone could be thoroughly controlled there might be a saving of 150,000 to 200,000 gallons every 24 hours. I have thought so at times; but I don't know how accurate that is. It is pretty hard to find out.

Q. Is there not a great deal of water wasted by leaving faucets open during the night?

A. There is during cold weather; I don't think there is a great deal at any other time?

Q. That would amount to a good deal in the course of a winter, wouldn't it?

A. Yes, sir. The coldest weather we had, I think our consumption increased somewhere about 2,000,000 gallons, and we accounted for it solely on that ground. It only lasted while the cold weather lasted. The consumption came back almost as soon as the weather changed.

A. What is the consumption at night, after the ordinary consumption ceases?

A. We have four hours in the night that we make a special record of, which is from one until four o'clock. In the fall of 1873 I got the consumption down to 27,000 gallons — I think it was — during those four hours. Up to that time the consumption keeps falling until about one o'clock, and then it holds along very steadily until four, when it commences to increase.

A. That consumption between one and four is nearly all waste, is it not?

A. Well, that is doubtful; because you will see people up, more or less, all through the city. And there are some establishments that run all night, — the sugar refinery and the Boston & Lowell Railroad; their tanks are generally running at that time. J. P. Squires' establishment runs through the night.

Q. What is the consumption of water in cold weather during those hours, the worst times you have noticed?

A. We intended to have a perfect record this winter; but it was so awful cold that the chronograph froze up, and we lost the record right in the time when we were in hopes to have got it; but, by measurement, somewhere from 40,000 to 50,000 gallons.

Q. During those four hours?

A. Yes, sir.

Q. We understood you to say something about 2,000,000 gallons being added to the amount used at one time.

A. Then I was speaking of the particularly cold weather we had this winter.

Q. That is the time I am inquiring about.

A. Our consumption increased 2,000,000 gallons on account of that cold weather.

Q. That 2,000,000 gallons was nearly all waste, was it not?

A. Yes, sir, we considered it all waste. But that was only for a few days; the moment the weather moderated, the consumption came back to its legitimate standard.

Q. During which season is more water used, winter or summer?

A. Just about alike. The winters compare just about with the warmest weather in the summer time.

Q. Is not that because in the winter there is about as much water wasted as there is used in the summer on account of warm weather?

A. Yes, sir.

Q. If no water was wasted, there would be much less water used in winter than in summer?

A. Yes, sir.

Mr. HAMMOND. — I now desire to call the attention of the committee to the 25th page of Mr. Crafts' report, which gives the amount of water consumed by American and foreign cities in different years. Of the cities in this locality, Boston, in 1850, consumed 42.6 gallons daily per head; in '55, 66 gallons; in '61, 100 gallons; in '66, 62 gallons; in '70, 60 gallons; in '73, 65 gallons. Charlestown consumed, in 1867, 42 gallons daily per head; in 1870, 70 gallons. Cambridge consumed, in 1873, 46 gallons daily per head, which is about what we consume now. In foreign cities the consumption is less, on the average, than in American cities. You will find that, in the earlier history of water-works, the consumption per head is less than in later years, in any given city, arising, of course, from the fact that there are more water-takers as time goes on.

I do not care to detain the committee any longer in putting in our case.

[*Adjourned to Wednesday, March 16, at 10 o'clock.*]

The hearing was resumed.

OPENING STATEMENT BY J. L. STACKPOLE, ESQ., FOR THE CITY OF BOSTON.

Gentlemen, I shall call the Chairman of the Boston Water Board, and the City Engineer of Boston, in a minute or two, but I desire to say to the committee a few words in introducing this case to them, this being a question of so great public moment. I need hardly advert to the circumstance, which is apparent to everybody in this city, that the subject of Boston's water-supply has become a serious matter of concern, not merely to the city government, not merely to the Water Board, and persons especially entrusted with the care of that supply in the city government, but to all the citizens, and this not only with respect to quality but to quantity; and it is a matter which concerns not merely the citizens of Boston, but the citizens of the whole State, who come to Boston on their various matters of business, politics, or what not, that there should be on the statute books of the Commonwealth sufficient power for the City of Boston, at whatever expense, to supply themselves with an ample supply of pure water. I say with an *ample* supply in the first place and of *pure* water in the second place. It should be ample. The power that should be given should not merely be for the present, but looking with a wise regard at the exigencies of the future. Looking back at the past, and even at those years of comparative depression which have been in the immediate past, we see that the Boston of to-day is but a small city in comparison with the Boston of the future. We see that Boston is rapidly becoming the great metropolis, not merely of Massachusetts, but of New England; and is steadily increasing, from year to year. It is not merely that the building of these reservoirs and these conduits will take time, but it is the duty of the City Government and the Water Board, with a wise provision, to look forward and procure water at that place where it is probable that they can obtain a sufficient supply for the future increase of the city. It would be the utmost folly to construct works for the present supply, at a large cost of money, which would have to be abandoned in the future. That would be a waste of the people's money. So much for the *amount* of supply as a matter of general principle.

With reference to the purity of supply, I trust the time will come when you will not see in apothecary shops about the city advertisements that they sell spring water, and that the citizens will not have to buy it by the gallon because the impurities in the regular source of their water-supply are so great; when it will not constantly be a constant subject of conversation, and a subject of debate at meetings of physicians, whether the present water can be drank without danger to health, and when so many citizens will not be obliged, in addition to paying water-rates, to obtain for their families water from the country springs brought in by the gallon, in tanks or in demijohns, for the purpose of domestic use. That state of things exists in the city, and we know it from the daily prints, and from personal experience; and we are asking power from the Legislature for the purpose of seeing to it that this shall not occur in the future, and that we shall have a supply of water adequate to the growth of the city; that we may begin by spending money where it is necessary to-day for the present wants, and that this money shall not be thrown away, so far as the future wants are concerned.

Now, gentlemen, with reference to the immediate matter. Probably most of you are aware that this question of resorting to the Shawsheen river, as Boston's water-supply, was a question considered in connection with the taking from Sudbury river in 1874. A very carefully prepared report exists in the city documents of that year, with reference to its quantity and quality; that its quantity, as has already been stated, at the present day is at a minimum of 20,000,000 gallons per day; that its quality, as it has been tested by experts, is excellent. The condition of things with reference to the city is exactly this: for the purpose of water-supply, Boston is substantially divided into two districts; Boston proper, including also Roxbury, West Roxbury, Dorchester, and Brighton, is supplied from Lake Cochituate and from the recent addition to that of the Sudbury river. It is believed by the Water Board and the City Engineer that even if it were possible, which it is not, except at a very large expense to transfer any portion of this water to the other district of the city, it is not wise, considering the future needs of Boston, to do so, for that source of supply must be used by the former district of the city, and not by the latter; and that, considering the growth of the city, it must be applied solely to the former district in the future; so that we have substantially this state of things: the first district, if I may so call it, is to be supplied from Cochituate and Sudbury river, and in the future this source of supply may be regarded as applicable to that, and that only.

Now, what is to be done with reference to the other district, which consists of Charlestown, Somerville, Chelsea, and Everett, and, sometimes, East Boston, that is to be supplied from the Mystic? In the first place, take the Mystic under its most favorable circumstances and it is not probable that, as a source of water-supply, it will be possible, owing to the various impurities and the growth of the population along its banks, to resort to it for a period of over ten or twelve years. Even if that were to be done, it would be necessary, in order to meet the present wants of the city, to construct reservoir basins for storing the water there, at an expense estimated at $400,-000; and even then, if the seasons were as dry as some we have, it would be doubtful whether the water would fill those basins. The fact is notorious that this supply has only been made available by pumping during the last season, and that those portions of the city, together with Somerville, Chelsea, and Everett, supplied from the Mystic have been in danger of conflagration should that pumping happen to give out, or become defective, at the period of any fire. Such a state of things cannot continue.

Then, if the committee should not grant us this privilege of taking water from the Shawsheen, all we could do would be to construct these basins at an expense of $400,000 on the Mystic, of doubtful utility, in the first place, and undoubtedly to be abandoned, and the money to be wasted, at a period of less than ten years. In this case I have not adverted to the question now before the committee, with reference to the Mystic sewer, because on that question no bill has been reported; but under some circumstances should the report of the committee be such as to render the continued use of this source of supply expensive and detrimental to the interests of the city (which I trust will not be the case), — should the result of that bill be adverse to the city's interest, the abandonment of the Mystic would become a question of the immediate present, and not of the future.

Therefore, I say, gentlemen, that we come in here with a pressing exigency asking for this bill. I need not say that the water cannot be poured into the dwelling-houses immediately. It will be necessary after getting the bill, to prepare carefully the plans and estimates. At least three years must be occupied in constructing and building the necessary conduits, reservoirs, supply-basins, and pumping-stations, which the bill will authorize us to build. We, therefore, have come here, at this Legislature, and not at a subsequent one, owing to the length of time which it is necessary to take in constructing these works, and making the surveys, to ask for a bill authorizing us to take the Shawsheen under proper regulations and provisions, and with every regard for private rights, with ample provisions for the payment to every mill owner, and every real estate owner, for all the damage done to him. We ask that such a bill may be reported at this session; and in that we are in accord with the City of Cambridge, it being agreed between us that what water can be taken — I state it roughly at 20,000,000 gallons a day minimum, — shall be divided between the City of Boston and the City of Cambridge, at the rate of three-fifths to the City of Boston, and two-fifths to the City of

Cambridge. We believe that the bill, or, if need be, two bills, side by side, may be prepared and passed at this session.

And, now, a single word with reference to such objections as may be made. It fell to my lot, as counsel for the city, to appear before this committee, or the predecessors of this committee, on the petition to take the Sudbury river. That was resisted with great spirit by the large number of mill owners who owned property upon the river. It is to be expected that in this case, as well as that, such persons should take care of their rights, and I dare say that they feel it is their duty, knowing that the question of damages is likely to arise, to begin by saying, "This is a matter which we protest against." They can, therefore, upon the trial for assessment of damages, repeat that it was against their will, and therefore that their damages are not to be decreased in any way, because it is a thing which they always protested against; and it is very proper that they should do so. It is a matter of policy. But I apprehend it has been the policy of the Legislature of this Commonwealth, in granting authority to great towns and cities to take a supply of pure water for their citizens, to regard the wants of the cities for supplying an ample source of the purest water to their citizens as superior to the claims of persons owning mills which are worked by the water upon those rivers; to regard their possession in the same way as that of persons situated upon lands where it is necessary to lay out highways for the public interest; and the exigency with reference to water is even stronger, as it is in the interest of health and is, therefore, a greater necessity than the highway in the analogy I have suggested. It is to be remembered that the bill must contain and reserve the most ample right of these parties to appeal to a jury of their own neighbors, together with such provisions of various kinds as the Sudbury river bill contains, which will always permit and constrain these two cities to leave a sufficient amount of water in the river that will prevent any injury to the health of the towns through which the river runs when the water is drawn away. On those subjects the cities taking the water must be liberal, and those provisions must be introduced.

Now, gentlemen, we desire at this session of the Legislature — and I submit to you that it is necessary for the exigencies of the City of Boston — that the committee should report, and the Legislature should pass, a bill of this kind which I have intimated.

I will ask Mr. Wightman, the City Engineer, to state his views to the committee.

STATEMENT OF HENRY M. WIGHTMAN.

By Mr. STACKPOLE. — You are the city engineer of Boston at present?

A. Yes, sir.

Q. And you were chief assistant for some time before?

A. Yes, sir.

Q. How long a time?

A. Eight or nine years.

Q. Now, Mr. Wightman, I wish, in your own way, you would give to the committee your views with reference to the needs of the City of Boston for this bill authorizing it to take the water of Shawsheen river?

A. I think you have stated the case to the committee about as well as I could. I don't know as I could add very much to what you have already said. Of course there is the question of figures Mr. Stackpole has not gone into, that is, the question of quantities; but the general statement he has made to the committee is simply one I should indorse. For instance, on the Mystic supply without storage, we used last year 9,387,000 gallons. Excepting in a dry year, the Mystic is adequate for that supply; but, in a dry year, as shown last year, it is not adequate for it. From the 1st of October until the 17th of January that entire district which comprises Charlestown, Everett, Chelsea, and Somerville was entirely dependent upon temporary pumping machinery; and, in case of accident, we would have been entirely out of water, and nothing could have helped us. That machinery is of a very temporary nature. I think the committee are familiar with it, because they have seen it. That is not the condition in which the city's water-supply should be in; and there are only two ways of remedying it. One is by building a basin on the upper reaches of the Abbajonna, and one above Horn pond. These two are the ones we have proposed to build. These two basins would increase the supply about 4,000,000 gallons, and they would cost about $400,000. As Mr. Stackpole has stated, it is doubtful whether that would be a judicious expenditure of money. In any event it is an open question whether the purity of the Mystic supply can be maintained; and, in fact, it may be acknowledged it cannot be maintained for any long period of years. It may be for the next ten years, and may not be for five. It depends upon what action the Legislature take now in the matter of the sewer; and, in that case, it would be very foolish for the city to spend $400,000 on a supply which it must eventually abandon. The other source of supply in that direction which can be used to the best advantage, if not the only one, is the Shawsheen river. This is a source of water-supply which is undoubtedly free from contamination, and will be as free from contamination in the future as it is certainly free from contamination now. It is ample to meet the wants of the city, and, if Cambridge pays two-fifths of the whole cost, and Boston pays three-fifths, which is the present arrangement between the two cities, the cost of taking it to the City of Boston will not very greatly exceed the cost of building the two basins on the Mystic, which will eventually have to be thrown away; that is, the whole cost would be about $700,000, and $420,000 is what would be the cost of the works on the Shawsheen. That includes building the lower basin and a conduit in the Middlesex canal, the conduit to be about 11,500 feet long, and to be an open canal, 19,200 feet. The basin and conduit to become eventually a part of the system of supply from the Shawsheen, entirely independent of the Mystic system, if it becomes necessary; but at present that is all that it is proposed to do. That does not represent the cost to both cities. That represents the whole cost as far as Abbajonna river. Cambridge has got to run a pipe to Fresh pond, and that additional cost is to be charged to it.

Q. What do you estimate to be the cost to the City of Boston, exclusive of mill damages, which, of course, cannot now be stated?

A. It would be three-fifths of $700,000; the cost to the City of Boston, about $420,000.

Mr. STACKPOLE. — How long, Mr. Wightman, would it probably take to construct these works in the ordinary way, using reasonable despatch?

A. Three seasons — three years.

Q. That is, if the bill was passed by the Legislature this session, it would be three years before this water could be utilized by the city?

A. Yes, sir.

Q. That would be using all due despatch for the purpose?

A. I think that would be doing it as quick as it could be done.

Q. Whether or not it would be wise economy to expend this money for basins upon the Mystic river?

A. No, sir, it would not.

Q. And would it not, in your judgment, before a very long time, be, substantially, money thrown away?

A. That is my opinion.

Q. Now, I want to ask you, with reference to the water-supply of what I termed the district of the city proper, from the Cochituate and Sudbury river, whether or not, in your judgment, that water is, considering the future exigency of the city, more than sufficient to supply that portion of the whole city, the city proper, Dorchester, Roxbury, and West Roxbury, and so on?

A. Well, from present developments in the way of water consumption, I should say it is insufficient; — that is, with all the basins built on Sudbury river, in the next ten years, probably the entire supply will be utilized, and we shall have to be looking for some other source of supply than those works.

Q. So that, so far as supplying that part of the city with water which is now supplied by Mystic is concerned, if this bill is granted, it will hereafter be supplied by the Shawsheen ; so that the Cochituate and the Sudbury river may be regarded as entirely out of the question?

A. Yes, sir. It could be done, of course, by building basins on the Sudbury river, and by connecting the works with the Mystic pumping-station by a pipe ; but it would cost at least $800,000 to do it, and that money would, eventually, be thrown away, because those basins would have to be used for the supply of that district, or the district on this side of Charles river, and then the cost of laying the pipes to the Mystic pumping-station would have to be, practically, thrown away. The cost of laying the pipes alone would be $400,000, and the cost of basins $400,000 more.

Q. So that would result in throwing away about $800,000?

A. About half that, because the basins would be just as good.

Q. Is there, in your judgment, any practical method of furnishing a proper supply of pure water to the City of Boston, except by taking the Shawsheen river?

A. Well, there are other practical ways. We could take the Concord river, or the Merrimac ; but, at the same time, we shouldn't consider those as practical ways, because they are not within the limit of expenditure which would be allowable.

Q. Why not?

A. If we took a small supply from the Concord river, we should have to pay for the whole river ; and it would not therefore be economy for the City of Boston to take a small amount of water from that river and pay the damages that might be awarded. If it was going to take any, it would be because its need required a large amount, for the cost of the works would be very large, in addition to the damages. The cost would be at least $2,500,000, and I don't think that would be a judicious expenditure for the city, because it don't need the water at the present time, although it may need it in the future.

Q. Now, with reference to the Merrimac?

A. Just the same reasons exactly.

Q. You have no question about the purity of the Shawsheen?

A. No, sir. I have examined the basin, the river, and the country, and I think there is no question about the purity of the water from such a source.

Q. How about the pollution of the Concord river?

A. Well, the Concord river, so far as it has been considered by the City Engineer's department, and it has been considered in previous years, and within the last five years, has never been considered a very desirable source of supply. It was considered a source that the city might eventually be forced into taking if it couldn't get water any-

where else ; but, at the same time, it is a source that it wouldn't use
until it was actually forced to.

Q. And how has that objection been increased since the State
Prison drained in there?

A. Well, it has been very largely increased. In fact, that river
of itself is very undesirable. It is a long, low, flat, sluggish river,
and runs through long meadows above Billerica, and is not increased
in purity by so doing.

Q. Somerville, Chelsea, and Everett have no other method of
supply?

A. No, sir.

Q. They have no other supply than that; so if the supply should
be cut off, which the city now provides, they would be entirely without water?

A. Yes, sir.

Q. By Mr. R. N. MORSE. — Mr. Wightman, I saw the statement
in the "Advertiser" this morning that 300,000,000 gallons of water
were running to waste over the dams of the Cochituate and Sudbury
river; is that so?

A. Yes, sir. There were 460,000,000 gallons running to waste the
other day on the Sudbury alone.

Q. And for how long a time has that state of things continued?

A. Well, it may continue sometimes for two or three weeks ; that
is, in such amounts as that ; we usually waste for a number of months
in the spring usually until the first of May.

Q. Supposing that waste of water for those three weeks could be
stored, or even a small portion of it, wouldn't it be sufficient to furnish the additional supply that Boston needs?

A. No, sir. That is to say, if there was storage sufficient to save
that water on the Sudbury river, of course the Sudbury-river supply
would be worth more than 40,000,000 gallons a day, but as it is now,
that is all it is worth.

Q. My question is, if it could be stored, wouldn't it be sufficient for
all the needs of the city, including Charlestown, Everett, and Chelsea?

A. I wouldn't say that for a long series of years, but it might be
sufficient for a considerable number of years.

Q. Well, this little Shawsheen is going to give the city of Boston
12,000,000 gallons a day, isn't it, at the outside, that you can depend on?

A. Yes, sir.

Q. You think it is worth while to go after that 12,000,000 gallons
a day when there are three or four hundred millions running to waste
for weeks here?

A. I certainly do, sir. You can't keep the water that is running
to waste ; you can't stop it, and you can't hold it.

Q. You can build storage-basins?

A. You can if you have sites for them; but if you have no sites for them —

Q. I thought you said you could build basins, only it would cost too much money?

A. The Sudbury supply is nominally about 40,000,000 gallons a day. That storage is all the storage that can be got on the river, because there are no more sites for basins on the river. There can be built eight basins; there are now three; there can be built five more. We have got to build one more to make the supply good for the city alone. That leaves four basins only, and if we were going to use that water now to do what you speak of doing, we should have to build two of those basins at once, and, consequently, use the Sudbury supply to that extent, and then, in addition to that, we should have to expend $400,000 for the pipe line leading across to the Mystic.

Q. Now, you have three basins, and you are proposing to build another; that will be four?

A. Four.

Q. And it is entirely practical to build four more?

A. Yes, sir.

Q. And when you build the four, you then have a storage capacity to get the 40,000,000 gallons a day?

A. Yes, sir.

Q. How long would it take to build those five additional basins?

A. Probably four years.

Q. And at what cost?

A. Well, the four basins I haven't made any estimate on, but they would cost probably $600,000.

Q. And does that $600,000 include all the expenses?

A. Yes, sir.

By Mr. STACKPOLE. — Do you mean it includes getting the water over to the other district?

A. It is simply the cost of building the basins alone — nothing else; then you have got to spend $400,000 to get that water over to the Mystic.

By Mr. MORSE. — Now, when the Sudbury river was taken by the city, was it not contemplated to build basins enough so that the Sudbury-river supply should be ample for the needs of the city for a long time to come?

A. Simply for the city proper; never for Chelsea, Everett, Charlestown, and Somerville.

Q. By building these basins the city would be amply supplied?

A. You would simply meet the legitimate wants of the city and reach the capacity of the Sudbury-river works sooner than you would otherwise. .

Q. What is the daily consumption in Boston?

A. Thirty-six million gallons.

Q. What does that include? How much do you include under the head of Boston?

A. That includes the Mystic, Cochituate, and Sudbury supply.

Q. Then, you are including not only Boston, but Chelsea, Everett, and Somerville?

A. Yes, sir.

Q. And you say that all those places together use 36,000,000 gallons a day?

A. Yes, sir; they use an average of 36,000,000.

Q. Now, how much of that comes from the Sudbury river and the Cochituate?

A. Twenty-six million five hundred thousand.

Q. And the rest comes from the Mystic?

A. Yes, sir.

Q. So that you could increase the supply from 26,000,000 up to 40,000,000 from the Sudbury?

A. Yes, sir.

Q. And you could get that additional supply about as soon as you could get the supply from the Shawsheen?

A. Yes, sir.

Q. And you would get a little more than what you would get from the Shawsheen, wouldn't you?

A. Let me see: 36,000,000 — yes; 14,000,000.

Q. You expect to get 12,000,000 from the Shawsheen, and you get 14,000,000 from the Sudbury?

A. Yes, sir; but it will cost $1,000,000 to get it.

Q. But, as to the quantity, you get more water from the Sudbury than from the Shawsheen?

A. Yes, sir.

Q. And in about the same time?

A. Yes, sir.

Q. Now, when you come to the question of the cost, you have not taken in the amount, have you, of the cost of land damages, the mill owners' rights, and all that, on the Shawsheen?

A. Yes, sir; everything except mill-damages.

Q. So that when you come to figure the question of cost, it might turn out more expensive to take the Shawsheen?

A. Yes, sir, it might; but we have been over this question pretty often, and know pretty well what it will cost. There are certain general principles on which such matters are based.

Q. Have you had any experience in entirely destroying a town, as you propose to do here?

A. We don't propose to destroy any town here.

Q. Well, you understand it will practically destroy it, don't you?

A. No, sir, I don't, by any means. We have not destroyed the town of Saxonville, nor any town on the Sudbury; and, in fact, if it wasn't for the amount of water we are obliged to run through it, there wouldn't be any water in the river at times.

Q. So you really give more water to the river than there would have been in it at times?

A. Yes, sir, on account of the storage-basins.

Q. Now, your land-damages and your mill-damages on the Sudbury have been settled?

A. Yes, sir, so far as the three basins are concerned. The mill-damages have been settled for the entire river.

Q. So, if you built any more basins, you wouldn't have any damages to pay, except land-damage?

A. Yes, we would, because there are mills above where these sites for the basins are. There are mills that are above the point where we have paid for the water, and, of course, on those we have got to pay mill-damages.

Q. There are not many, are there?

A. Yes, sir. There are Jordan & Marsh's Mills at Ashland, and mills at Hopkinton, and Cordaville; there must be half a dozen, — not large mills.

Q. Now, you say that of the present supply, 26,500,000 gallons a day come from the Sudbury, and about 10,000,000 from the Mystic?

A. Yes, sir.

Q. How much of that daily supply of 37,000,000 do you estimate runs to waste?

A. Well, they use on an average 87 gallons per head, in that entire district; that is, counting the population 412,000 on the basis of last year. They use an average of 87 gallons. I think 60 gallons is ample.

Q. Isn't 42 gallons considered a fair amount?

A. No, sir; I don't think it is, not for an American population.

Q. Isn't that what they allow in Worcester?

A. I don't know. I could tell by looking over the reports. That is the estimate of the best engineers.

Q. What cities have you taken into account in arriving at that average?

A. If you want to go into that, Mr. Morse, there are reports and various tables of the cities of the United States. It is a pretty large subject, and I should want to go into it very carefully.

Q. My understanding is, that the City of Worcester considers 42 gallons an ample supply?

A. Yes, sir; and in the City of Providence they don't use over 50, and in Boston it has run up over 100, and last year it averaged 87.

Q. Well, taking your own estimate, assuming 60 gallons a head a proper allowance, that would make out how much runs to waste?

A. Well, it would be about 30 per cent.

Q. That would be in round numbers something like 10,000,000 gallons?

A. Yes, sir.

Q. About 10,000,000 gallons run to waste every pay?

A. Yes, sir, that is the average for the day. Probably some days our consumption runs up to 40,000,000 gallons a day. Take it a cold day, our consumption runs up to 40,000,000 in the city proper.

Q. Because they leave their faucets open at night?

A. Yes, sir.

Q. And there isn't any attempt made to stop it, is there, in these places?.

A. Well, I don't know exactly what you call an attempt.

Q. I will ask you whether you think there has been any attempt made to stop it?

A. I don't think there has been any serious attempt made of late years.

Q. Now, take the City of Somerville; is there any system of meterage there in use?

A. I presume they have the same system that we do in Boston.

Q. Do you know whether there is?

A. I do not know. That is out of my department.

Q. Who would have the knowledge?

A. The Water Registrar of Boston, Mr. Davis.

Q. And do you know how it is in Everett and Chelsea?

A. I don't know.

Q. Or in Charlestown?

A. Charlestown I am more familiar with, but even that I don't know the detail of.

Q. How is it in the city proper?

A. I can't tell you the number of meters in the city proper. It is all in that annual report. I don't carry those matters in my mind. The City of Boston, as a rule, isn't what you would call a metred city; the number of meters is comparatively small.

Q. From such observation as you have given it, have you any doubt the system of meterage could be adopted here?

A. No, I haven't any doubt it could be adopted, but I don't think it would be wise for the city to adopt it.

Q. Why not?

A. On account of the expense, mainly.

Q. Are you aware that in the City of Worcester, where there are 5,000 services, 3.700 are metred?

A. I think very likely there may be. I am not aware of it.

Q. Well, I will state that to you as a fact. Now, is there any difficulty in applying to the City of Boston the same system of meters that is applied there?

A. Simply the increased expense, that is to say, the expense of putting on the meters. I shouldn't say wholly the increased expense, but the expense of putting on the metres would be very large, and the cost of maintenance would be still larger; and, then, another question that comes into that system is the question of water-rates; that is to say, if you put metres on every house, the probability is you would have to charge it to the houses at water-rates; and if the consumers paid for it at the metre-rates, the income would not probably pay over a quarter of the interest on cost of the works, whereas now it does very nearly pay the interest on the cost.

By Mr. STACKPOLE. — What about the public sentiment?

A. I don't think the public sentiment would sustain the meter system and it is so in every city in the United States; the same question is raised, and, except in the very small cities, they have not been able to use the meter system.

By Mr. MORSE. — It has been testified by the city officials of the City of Worcester before this committee that that system has been used with great success, and they have saved money. One thousand consumers have apparently paid for the cost of the meters, not only of the manufacturing establishments, but the small domestic services.

A. That may be so in a small city. It has only 3,700 meters out of — I don't know what population Worcester has, but it cannot be over 100,000.

The COMMITTEE. — It is 62,000.

The WITNESS. — Boston has got 350,000 at least, which makes a good deal of difference.

Q. Isn't it a political thing at City Hall very largely, this matter of introducing meters?

A. I don't think it is; as far as my experience goes I think the sentiment of the people —

Q. You think a free and independent Bostonian won't stand a meter?

A. I think he don't want it.

Q. You think he drinks too much water?

A. I don't think he wants his water measured out to him any more than he does his air; that is my idea of it.

Q. Do you know any reason, Mr. Wightman, why the same rule wouldn't work here that works in other places in regard to meters?

A. Well, I have told you, Mr. Morse, this question is a very complicated one, in regard to rates, even if you put meters on; and even if it were a possible thing to adjust those rates, it would be almost impossible to make them generally satisfactory. For instance, a large consumer pays at the rate of $2\frac{1}{2}$ cents a hundred gallons. Now, if a house did not pay more than at that rate, the income that would be derived from it would be very small.

Q. Haven't you rates now that are satisfactory?

A. Yes; that is, they are partly satisfactory. The fact is, the meter system has never been made to work in any large city. It has been talked of in St. Louis and New York.

By Mr. MORSE. — I wish to call the attention of the committee, as a part of this examination, to the fact, that in the last annual report of the Water Board, it appears that the whole number of meters in this district is 1,097.

The WITNESS. — I think it is fair for me to state to the committee that the City of Boston is now about to try what are called Deacon meters, which they have recently imported. It is a kind of meter in use in England, which is simply to prevent waste, and not like putting a meter on every house, but by measurement of the waste in the houses in a street, and then by inspection preventing it. The only place that this meter can be tried in is the Charlestown District. An experiment is going to be tried there, and if successful, would probably be applied to the whole city; but to do that involves an expense of $300,000, that is, to change the service stop-cocks in the city proper. The service stop-cock has got to be changed from the street to the sidewalk. When that system is in operation I have no doubt we shall be able to reduce our consumption; but while doing that we have got to provide for the present consumption, and what will be required until we accomplish it.

Q. Now, in regard to the Mystic supply, what is the capacity of that river?

A. The Mystic supply, with storage, is good for about 17,000,000 gallons.

Q. And, in point of fact, you get now about 7,000,000?

A. Without storage it is good for about 7,000,000.

Q. There is a very large quantity running to waste?

A. Two hundred millions a day running to waste at present.

Q. And there is no doubt the storage capacity can be increased?

A. Yes, sir; it can be increased.

Q. Suppose you were to stop the waste of the water by the citizens, by the water-takers, and suppose you were to store all the water you can store on the Sudbury and on the Mystic, for what length of time do you think that would provide water for the city?

A. That is a complicated question, sir, to answer right off. I don't know.

Q. You say the present supply for the city is 37,000,000 a day, and according to your figures 10,000,000 can be saved?

A. I think so.

Q. That would bring the present supply down to 27,000,000; and, then, the capacity of Sudbury river can be increased to 40,000,000 a day, and the capacity of the Mystic to 17,000,000, making a total of 57,000,000 a day?

A. Yes, sir.

Q. And how long do you think 57,000,000 gallons a day would be sufficient to supply the city, and this district?

A. I shouldn't want to express an opinion on it.

Q. If 27,000,000 are sufficient for the present, don't you think 57,000,000 would be sufficient for 50 years?

A. I don't think it would.

Q. Do you think we will double our demand for water in 50 years?

A. I do. I think the city of Boston is going to be double its present size in 50 years. I shouldn't be surprised if it was.

Mr. MORSE. — I hope you will live to see it, Mr. Wightman.

Q. Now, you say that this little Shawsheen, with its 12,000,000 gallons a day, is only to be a temporary supply. How long will it last?

A. How long that will last will depend upon how long the purity of the Mystic will last. If you can tell me how long the Mystic will be pure, I can tell you. You must answer that question yourself.

Q. It is entirely with the city to keep it pure, is it not?

A. No, sir.

Q. Assuming the Mystic supply can be kept pure, you can get water enough from Sudbury river to supply the city for an indefinite length of time?

A. No, sir. Not for an indefinite length of time.

Q. Well, for a period of years beyond what the Shawsheen will cover?

A. Well, we could get along without the Shawsheen for a considerable time, probably.

Q. Now, has this matter of taking the Shawsheen, do you remember, been presented to the City Government, and acted upon by the City Government, at all?

A. It has, so far as petitioning the Legislature for the right to take it.

Q. When was that action taken?

A. The order was passed by both branches of the City Government to petition the Legislature, in January, I think.

Q. Was that after it was known the City of Cambridge had applied?

A. I don't know about that.

Q. Isn't it a fact, that the petition to take the Shawsheen is wholly an after-thought?

A. No, sir; that is not so. This matter of taking the Shawsheen river, and I state it exactly as it is, has been brought to the attention of the City Government on account of the Mystic-valley sewer. I don't think the city government has realized the condition that valley is in, and I think they do not wholly now. Experts have told them that it is impossible, for a long series of years, to preserve the purity of the Mystic, and for that reason they think it is wise to try to get another supply to use when that is abandoned; but I don't think that it had anything to do with the City of Cambridge.

Q. Isn't this particular application to the Legislature rather a sudden move?

A. Well, sudden, simply in this way, just as I have stated; I don't think the City Government realized the condition that the Mystic was in until this agitation about the Mystic-valley sewer. They have been told of it. It has been reported upon, and they have visited and looked at it; but I don't think they actually realized it until the matter was brought prominently to their attention in connection with the Mystic-valley sewer.

Q. Don't you think it has been the opinion of the press and citizens, that getting the Sudbury supply was the thing that was going to make us all contented, on the matter of water-supply, for years to come?

A. I think so, sir; but if you will read this annual report you will see what time has done in the way of reaching the capacity of water-supply. That was ten years ago, and the City of Boston has increased both in consumption and population very largely since then.

Q. Now, Mr. Wightman, one single point further. I understand you to say that, even if you should abandon this idea of building additional basins upon the Sudbury and Mystic, and go on to the Shawsheen and get your 12,000,000 gallons, that even then that would only be for the temporary needs of the city, and that the city would have to go to the Concord river, or Merrimac, or Lake Winnipiseogee, or some other source of supply?

A. I think they may come to that.

Q. Within what time?

A. There again, sir, I can't answer.

Q. Don't you think they would come to a larger supply sooner if they take the Shawsheen than if they build these storage-basins on the Sudbury and Mystic?

A. No, sir; I don't see any reason why they should. In fact, if they are successful in reducing the consumption by the means we are now proposing to use, it might last longer than I have any idea of.

Q. Supposing that at some time or other the city will double its population, say in 50 years?

A. Then they might.

Q. If they should, probably the Shawsheen wouldn't last very long, would it? 12,000,000 gallons a day wouldn't supply the city as a whole?

A. Well, it isn't intended to supply the city as a whole, but only the district which is now supplied by the Mystic.

Q. My point is this, when it proves insufficient where is the city to go next after taking Shawsheen?

A. I should have to leave that to the engineers of the future.

Q. Well, you are going to be in office probably a long while.

A. I hope so, sir.

Q. Now, my question is, if you were asked, to-day, to give your opinion as to where the city was to get its next supply, after taking the Shawsheen, what would you say?

A. I should decline to answer it, because I have no sufficient data to form an opinion; and I think I should want at least a year, and quite a large corps of engineers, to examine every available source of supply for the city.

Q. You don't expect any new lakes or rivers are going to be discovered in 50 years?

A. No, sir; but whether it would be better for the City of Boston to take the Merrimac river or go to Lake Winnipiseogee, or go to Lake Quinsigamond at Worcester, I could not now say which would be best.

Q. Isn't it one of those sources of supply?

A. Well, I am not prepared to say that even.

Q. Well, just think of it. You don't propose to go up to the St. Lawrence?

A. Well, probably not; but I don't know how far we might in the future have to go to get a supply. Much would depend upon the amount of mill-damages we would have to pay for any near source of supply.

Q. I don't understand that you take mill-damages into account?

A. Well, we have a general idea of the amount.

Q. Now, sooner or later, the City of Boston will have to go to the

Concord or Merrimac, or Charles, or Lake Winnipiseogee; isn't that a reasonable proposition, in case these supplies turn out to be insufficient? It is one of those four sources of supply?

A. I should think so; although, on the Sudbury side, I think the Charles river would be the next source of supply.

Q. Now, the sooner the city takes one of those large sources of supply the better it will be, so far as the question of damages is concerned, won't it?

A. I don't know about that, either; the future of mill powers I don't think anybody can foresee. Without storage they are not going to be of any great value, and with storage they are going to approximate, in cost, the power of steam; so I don't want to express an opinion on the matter now.

Q. Do I understand that you have recommended the city authorities, or Water Board, that it is proper economy for the city, to-day, to build no more additional basins, except the one on Sudbury river; and to think of no other source of water-supply, but simply to get this Shawsheen?

A. No, sir.

Q. Have you made any such recommendation?

A. No, sir.

Q. Then this application is not made on your recommendation, is it?

A. Yes, sir.

Q. How so, unless you recommended to the Water Board that it is a prudent and economical thing to do this?

A. I have recommended it to the Water Board as being the best for the interest of the city; I haven't recommended it as the only way of getting a water-supply. But it is the best and cheapest way of getting an additional water-supply for the Mystic system.

Q. What do you allow for mill-damages on the Shawsheen?

A. I haven't made any estimate.

Q. Then how can you say it is the cheapest source of supply?

A. Because I have my opinion.

Q. What is your opinion?

A. I don't think that is hardly a fair question to ask me. I don't think it is a question I ought to answer, either. Your clients are coming into court, and I do not think I ought to commit myself.

By Mr. MORSE. — You don't want to give the city away?

By Mr. TORREY. — I understand your testimony to be, that, at no very great period of time in the future, the city will have to abandon the Mystic source of supply; am I correct?

A. Yes, sir; that is an opinion of mine and other experts.

Q. Which is now about 9,000,000 a day?

A. It has supplied 9,500,000 a day; but the supply is only good for 7,000,000 in a dry year like last year.

Q. Now, have you any doubt that, when that time arrives, a few years hence, when you are obliged to abandon the Mystic, the demand of the population supplied by the Mystic will be 12,000,000?

A. I think it will, sir.

Q. And when that time arrives — immediately when that time arrives — you will then have to go to work, won't you, and get an additional supply to the Shawsheen, — the Shawsheen supplying 12,000,-000 — as soon as you abandon the Mystic, there being no margin there?

A. That will depend upon the use you make of the Mystic. There probably will be portions that we can use in connection with the Shawsheen.

Q. On the theory that you abandon the Mystic entirely, then the use of the Shawsheen will be of no practical value to you at that time; so far as saving you from going to one of these larger streams is concerned?

A. Well, it simply comes back to the question of judgment how long the Shawsheen will last. That is a question which I cannot answer.

Q. Have you any doubt that within a few years the population will be using 12,000,000 gallons a day?

A. That depends upon what you call " a few years."

Q. Ten years?

A. Well, I think it will.

Q. Then in 10 years, if the city abandons the Mystic entirely, the city will have to get some additional supply from the Shawsheen?

A. I think they are liable to.

By Mr. STACKPOLE. — I understand, Mr. Wightman, if you should abandon the Mystic partly, that you think you could supplement the Shawsheen by taking some portion of the Mystic?

A. Yes, sir. I haven't studied the question of what should be done with the Mystic, but I think even if we abandon a portion of the Mystic supply, it is still possible to utilize the remaining portion of it.

Q. So that would add to the 12,000,000 — how much?

A. 3,000,000 or 4,000,000. There is one branch of the Mystic supply that is specially contaminated. We shall have to abandon it. There is another part that might continue 15 or 20 years. The part I should say that might be abandoned would be about one-third of the supply.

Q. Which would give you 18,000,000 a day for this district, and it would be a long time before it would reach that limit?

A. Yes, sir.

Q. Now, what do you call "waste;" what does that include? 10,000,000 waste—is it wholly waste, or does it apply to the Fire Department, and things of that sort?

A. Well, I think it may be called "waste" simply.

Q. I suppose that in the spring, when the snow melts, there is the largest amount of water going to waste over the dam. Now, how far is it practicable to store water for future use in these rather extraordinary times?

A. It isn't practicable. There isn't usually half storage capacity enough on any stream to save all that water; that is, it is extremely rare.

Q. Now, I understand you to say with reference to this question of Mr. Morse, as to building the basins on the Sudbury — in the first place, it will cost you $600,000 to build these additional basins?

A. Yes, sir; that is, to build all the basins. I have made an exact estimate of the number of basins to make the Mystic supply good. The cost of those would be about $600,000.

Q. Then, in order to take that water from these basins over to the district now supplied by the Mystic, would cost $400,000 more?

A. Yes, sir.

Q. That is, $1,000,000?

A. Yes, sir.

Q. Then, you say there are large mill-owners to whom you would have to pay damages, by reason of building these basins, so it would cost $1,000,000 plus the damages that would have to be paid to these large mills?

A. Yes, sir.

Q. And, then, when you get the use of the water by this district including the city proper, up to the full capacity of the Sudbury river, you then would lose this $400,000 which you have spent in getting it over to the other district? You would have to lose that in time?

A. Yes, sir; less the value of the pipe dug up.

Q. That would be practically very small?

A. Wouldn't be of any particular value. The money would be practically thrown away, because then you would have to get a supply from the Shawsheen, or Concord, or Merrimac, for this portion of the city.

By Mr. TORREY. — Isn't it an advantage to have such a pipe as that, so that both sections could be supplied from either source?

A. Not at that cost. The pipe is of no use unless you put water behind it to supply it in case of emergency. In case you do that, you have got to spend your money upon the Sudbury at once.

Q. You supply East Boston with it?

A. Yes; sometimes on the Mystic, and sometimes on the Cochituate.

By Mr. E. G. Loomis. — Have you made estimates of the flow of the Shawsheen?

A. Yes, sir.

Q. On what do you base your statement that the yield will be 12,000,000 gallons a day?

A. Based on the survey of the water-shed.

Q. But this water must be stored in the storage-basins. How many storage-basins have you estimated for?

A. Three.

Q. Do those appear on your map?

A. They do, sir.

[Map explained.]

By Mr. Morse. — Does this map show the proposed tapping of Concord river?

A. Yes, sir. That was a map made to show how a supply could be had by going beyond the Shawsheen, from the Concord.

Q. How far beyond the Shawsheen is the Concord?

A. About four miles.

Testimony of Leonard R. Cutter.

By Mr. Stackpole. — You are the Chairman of the Boston Water Board?

A. Yes, sir.

Q. I wish you would, in your own way, state to the committee your views of the necessity that Boston is under for the legislation asked for here, to take the Shawsheen river as a source of water-supply?

A. Mr. chairman and gentlemen, the ground has been so thoroughly gone over, there is not much for me to say, unless I repeat what has been said.

The Chairman. — I would not do that.

The Witness. — Therefore what I have to say will be very brief.

Q. Whether or not you concur in what has been said?

A. The Water Board has considered this subject very faithfully. It is their duty to keep the supply ahead of the demand, and they have been just able to do it, with these additional works, for the last 10 years. We thought, when we got them completed, we would have a rest, but we must not be idle. We find the demand is about equal to the supply, and we find we must be looking around for an additional supply for the Mystic division; and in looking the ground over, as far as examination is concerned, for the city and otherwise, we have believed it to be judicious and practical to take the Shawsheen, and the Board recommended the city government that they petition the Legislature to take the waters of the Shawsheen. The Mystic we have had considerable difficulty with. You gentlemen are pretty well posted in regard to the impurities that run in it. In fact, we haven't been able to get more than half of the impurities out, and hardly that; and that has troubled the town of Medford a good deal, by running half of it round our water-basin; and it seems to us, that pure water is what we ought to get, and what we ought to advocate, and seek for. In considering that to be our duty, we have gone to the Shawsheen, and we think if we get the Shawsheen, that we can get everybody out of the difficulty, and get ourselves good, pure water, and which will last for some time to come. I can't say how long, but it will keep up the supply, and when that becomes short again, it may become our duty to look round for additional sources; we have got to keep up the supply.

Q. Have you any question, Mr. Cutter, considering the whole subject as you have considered it, as to purity, economy, and supply; but that this is the best plan for the city? Is that your deliberate judgment?

A. That is the judgment of the Water Board. We recommended in our last report, additional facilities would have to be sought for on the Mystic division.

Q. This is not an after-thought at all, as has been suggested here?

A. No, sir. The question is, whether to build additional basins on the Abbajonna, or go to the Shawsheen?

Q. Would building those basins, in your judgment, be a wise economy?

A. I prefer to go to the Shawsheen, on account of the purity of the water, and expense also.

By Mr. TORREY. — Were you a member of the Water Board in 1874?

A. Yes, sir.

Q. Well, I find in your report of 1874 this statement, speaking of the Sudbury-water supply: " Our citizens will, with it, beyond all question, secure what they all desire, — *an adequate supply of pure water for the next fifty years.*" Your name is signed to that report, and I suppose at the time you made it that was your opinion?

A. I suppose it was.

Q. Is it your opinion now, that the supply of water from Sudbury river will be adequate for the City of Boston for 50 years after 1874?

A. With my experience of the past two years, I should change my mind.

Q. With the exception of that abnormal dry season, would you say so?

A. I should hardly think so.

Q. How long?

A. In your question do you cover all the Mystic division?

Q. Whatever you say there.

A. That is the Cochituate division there.

Q. I read it precisely. I don't know what it means.

A. That is the Cochituate report you are reading there. It hasn't anything to do with the Mystic.

Q. Won't you tell us what you meant when you said this?

A. We meant that the City of Boston, at that time, that portion of it that was supplied with Cochituate water would probably be able to get a supply from that source for the next 50 years. We were then supplying East Boston by the Mystic. We are now supplying East Boston by the Cochituate.

Q. What is the proportionate consumption on the Mystic route, and on the Sudbury?

A. The consumption per day?

Q. Yes; the proportionate consumption from each source; how much of one kind is used, and how much of the other?

A. It is all down in the report, — 26,500,000 on the Sudbury, and 9,387,880 on the Mystic.

Q. Then if it had been true, Mr. Cutter, that Sudbury river would supply what you call the Cochituate service for 50 years, it would have answered the purposes of the whole city for 30 or 40 years, wouldn't it?

A. Well, as I said before, we hadn't experienced the dry seasons we have for the last two years, and I should change my opinion. I shouldn't make a report the same as that. My experience would teach me that I shouldn't sign a report in that way. At that time we were correct about it, I supposed; we were honest.

Q. What should you say now, with your personal experience, how far ahead would you say the Sudbury would supply the district which you refer to here?

A. I think the Sudbury is calculated to supply 40,000,000 a day. We are now using 28,000,000.

Q. It is simply a question of increase of population, I suppose, how soon they will get up from 26,500,000 to 40,000,000?

A. Not altogether so. The cheaper we offer the water the more will be used, I suppose.

Q. Now, haven't you expressed your opinion officially several times that at least one-half of the water that was consumed in the City of Boston was wasted?

A. No, sir; my opinion on the waste is a little different from the engineer's.

Q. Were you a member of the Water Board of 1879?

A. Yes, sir.

Q. The City Engineer makes this statement in this report: " There is plenty of evidence to prove that one-half this quantity is a liberal supply for all useful purposes." That is Mr. Davis, your City Engineer?

A. Yes, sir.

Mr. STACKPOLE. — I think you ought to say that was when there was 100 gallons per person.

Mr. TORREY. — I ought to say what is in the report. I am reading from page 45. Let me call your attention to this sentence. I cannot tell from this document whether it is the report of the City Engineer, or the report of the Board itself. It is headed, " Report of the Water Board." It says: " The waste in Boston, though not so great as in a number of other cities, and, in fact, not so great, proportionately, to the population as it was in this city 15 or 20 years ago, is, nevertheless, enormous. We are now using nearly 80 gallons of water per inhabitant, and there is plenty of evidence to prove that one-half this quantity is a liberal supply for all useful purposes." Now, can you tell me whether that was the report of the Board itself, or the report of the engineer?

Mr. STACKPOLE. — The report of the Board, Mr. Torrey, ends on page 26.

A. That is the report of the engineer, signed by Mr. Davis.

Q. He was a very excellent man for that position?

A. Yes, sir.

Q. A man whose opinion was entitled to respect?

A. Yes.

Q. And you published his report as part of the report of the Water Board?

A. Yes, sir.

Q. And there is no comment upon or dissent from, that part of the report by the Board, is there?

A. No, sir.

Q. Now, apart from these reports, I ask you what is your own opinion as to the amount wasted in the City of Boston?

A. I don't think there is so much wasted as our engineer states it; that is my opinion. He, perhaps, knows better than I do; but I call it excessive use. There is an excessive use of water, but I don't call it all waste. If a man lets water run in his water-closet to sweeten it, I don't call it waste; I call it excessive use. The engineers probably put it down as waste.

Q. Assuming that it is waste, for the purpose of this question, what do you think is the amount of water wasted that might be used for other purposes?

A. I can't state. The way they get at the waste is, they take the amount of water that comes in the conduit and comes into our reservoirs, and they subtract from that the amount that is measured by the water-meters, and then they attribute the balance as so much for the day; and, of course, if the reservoir leaks, that goes into the day's use; then there is its use at fires, public fountains, etc., which is called waste, and I call it excessive use.

Q. Make all the deductions you please; but I would like to have you tell the committee how much water is wasted, meaning by the word " waste " a greater use than is proper for the amount of people in the city.

A. I don't know as I have estimated that close enough to answer very specifically.

Q. Have you any opinion about it?

A. I have a general opinion about it; yes.

Q. What is that?

A. I have a general opinion for these reasons: Last fall we found our water-supply getting short, and we didn't know but what if the winter came on us without the fall rains we would be in a state of water famine, and we issued notices to the people, and called their attention to the fact, that unless they used the water more carefully there would be danger of the water-supply becoming almost exhausted; and we found, by sending out those notices, that we saved about 2,000,000 gallons a day, and I suppose that would be about what I should consider excessive use, or waste.

Q. That is all you think is wasted?

A. I think I should base my judgment on that.

Q. You signed this report of 1879?

A. Yes, sir.

Q. Have you altered your opinion any in regard to waste since that time?

A. Yes, sir, I have.

Q. You don't think there is much wasted now?

A. I don't think there is; on account of our circulars last fall, I think the people considered it and saved the water, and in so saving, we saved 2,000,000 gallons every 24 hours; and I think that is about what they used uselessly.

Q. Then your opinion is based upon the assumption that the waste was entirely stopped by your circular?

A. Oh, no; but it had that effect.

Q. I understand you to say the amount was reduced 2,000,000 a day after your circular?

A. Yes, sir.

Q. And you understand that to be the amount of waste?

A. I think it was some over 2,000,000 a day.

Q. Then that comes to this, don't it; you state to the committee you think your circular stopped substantially all the waste there was?

A. I think they had regard to our circular, and that they didn't use water so wastefully as they did before; so excessively. I think if we should put meters into every house in Boston, we would have the Board of Health after us. Already they come to us if we allow a water-closet to be supplied by a faucet that is in direct connection with the sink of the kitchen; they come to us when the water-closet is inadequately supplied with water; and, in a sanitary point of view, they need a good deal of water in water-closets.

Q. Do you mean to say that the policy of the city is to allow every man to use just as much water as he wants?

A. I think he ought to have water enough to make his water-closet clean, and have pure air.

Q. Whether you think there should be any limitation whatever put upon the water, or each man should be left to use precisely what he pleases?

A. I think there should be a limitation put on to prevent its waste.

Q. Now, assuming for the purpose of this question, not as a fact, that the use of water-meters in Worcester, Fall River, and other cities of that size, has been found to be successful, and largely reduced the amount of water wasted, still leaving as much water as the proper demand requires, is there any reason why the same system could not be adopted in Boston in your judgment?

A. I am not very sure that Boston people use any more water than they do in those cities.

Q. They use a great deal more per head?

A. Yes, sir; but you must take into account the Fire Department. I don't think Boston people are more wasteful than other cities.

By Mr. STACKPOLE. — Do you allow anything for the floating population?

Mr. TORREY. — They don't float in the water.

Q. The use of water in Boston is about 80 gallons a head a day?

A. Yes, sir.

Q. And in Worcester it is about 42?

A. You say so.

Q. Now, is there any reason why, if the meters work well in other cities, like Worcester and Fall River, they won't work well in Boston?

A. The objection to meters is the cost of them.

Q. But the same objection exists in Worcester to the cost of meters as in Boston, don't it?

A. Perhaps it would *pro rata;* but when we undertake to meter the whole city of Boston, it would cost more money than it would to take two such places as the Shawsheen ; and our people, instead of paying for meters, had rather expend their money for water in another direction.

Q. My question comes to this precisely ; if the meterage of water is successful in a city of 30,000 inhabitants, is there any reason why it should not be successful in a city of 850,000?

A. I don't think the people of Boston use any more water than the people of Worcester do. There are a thousand ways which the people use it : the Fire Department, fountains, etc., and it all goes into what the engineer calls " waste." Fountains are used a great deal.

Q. If you don't answer the question, I shall consider it can't be answered.

A. What is your question?

Q. Suppose the use of meters is a beneficial thing, and that they work well in Worcester and Fall River, why won't they work well in Boston?

A. Do you mean as to saving water, or expense?

Q. Both.

A. I think they would work well to save water, and not expense.

Q. Suppose the system works well in both those respects? I understand there is evidence before the committee that it does save —

Mr. STACKPOLE. — I want to object to this examination. This witness has not heard this evidence. He does not know how it works in Worcester, and how can he compare it?

The CHAIRMAN. — He wants to know why they cannot work as well in Boston as in Worcester, assuming they are successful in Worcester.

Mr. STACKPOLE. — If he had been there and examined them, and saw how they work, it would be a very proper question to ask why they could not be used here. It seems to me it is, on the whole, a useless and improper question, and is needlessly taking up time. There are plenty of people in Worcester who could be brought here to testify to it.

Q. Do you know any reason why the system of meterage wouldn't work substantially in the same way in the City of Boston that it would in the City of Worcester or the City of Fall River?

A. I think it would work the same as the prohibitory law does. I don't know as I have anything further to say, only the law in a large city works different from what it does in a small city.

Q. Don't you think the same thing would be unpopular to the City of Boston, — that they would rather have their water by paying for it, than to be restricted in its use; and that such a law would be unpopular in Boston, and officers would not enforce it?

A. The people that don't pay any taxes don't pay for the water.

Q. But a man who pays no tax but a poll-tax would rather have the city supplied by Shawsheen river, and have it put in here, than have the expense in his own house?

A. I think, as a citizen of Boston and a tax-payer, I had rather spend my money for a more liberal supply of water than spend it for a meter; because, if you have meters on dwelling-houses, you can't raise revenue enough to run the works at the rate we are selling at, — 2 cents a hundred gallons. There would be a very small revenue, and we are obliged to raise a certain amount of revenue to meet the expenses of our department and interest on our debt, and if we don't do it, at the end of two years the Supreme Court can take it out of our hands.

Q. But can't you make the rate for a dwelling-house the same as you do now, for instance, and then charge for the excess of water used over a certain amount; that is, allow a certain amount for the regular water-rate which is sufficient for the purposes of the family, and then, if the meter shows a greater use, charge for the excess?

A. You can't make that work with any safety. You can't make the distinction without a good deal of trouble.

Q. Have you investigated it yourself?

A. I have been an advocate of meters this last dry season. I believe in having it where it won't injure the Water Department.

Q. You mean the Water Board?

A. I mean the Water Department, — the whole system.

Q. Have the Water Board investigated the meterage system in any city in Massachusetts? Are you prepared to state, to-day, what the result of meters is in the City of Worcester, or Fall River, or any other city in Massachusetts?

A. I have in my desk — I think I can give you information; I can't here.

Q. Have the Water Board examined that subject so as to pass an opinion on it, and advise the city in regard to it?

A. We have examined it with a view to reducing our tariff.

Mr. MORSE. — Mr. Cutter, I want to call your attention to one or two paragraphs in the last report of the Water Board, the report made in 1880, the last published report, I understand. After speaking of the daily consumption, on the second page of that report, you say, "This excessive use of water has caused the Board no little anxiety, and it is evident that steps must be taken, at once, both to stop its wanton waste and to supply works to meet legitimate and largely growing demand." You then go on to say in that report it was contemplated, in the beginning, to building additional basins on the Sudbury river; and then the report of the City Engineer, which you will find referring to this subject, on pages 30 and 31, says, "If the waste of water is not stopped, it is clear that, in case of a dry season, the present supply would soon fall short of the wants of the city; and, as two years, if not more, would be necessary to build those reservoirs and have them in readiness to supplement the supply, I believe it advisable to take action towards securing the necessary lands for building at least one of the storage reservoirs contemplated in the valley of the Sudbury river." Now, what I call your attention to, Mr. Cutter, is this : that as late as the report that was submitted in April, 1880, when you were contemplating the state of things as it then existed, all that you proposed as necessary was to build one at least of the additional basins on the Sudbury river; is that not so?

A. You will see, if you read that report, that we recommend an additional quantity on the Mystic division, either by an additional storage-basin on the Abbajonna, or " otherwise." I believe that is the word we use : this " otherwise " contemplated the Shawsheen.

Q. But you didn't, in your report, make any mention of the Shawsheen?

A. No, sir.

Q. Has the Water Board ever made any report to the City Government recommending the taking of the Shawsheen?

A. I don't think they have.

Q. Or has the engineer ever recommended the Water Board to take the Shawsheen?

A. I beg pardon. We sent a communication to the City Council to petition for the Shawsheen.

Q. Have you a copy of that report here?

A. I have not.

Q. Did you recommend, at that time, abandoning the building of basins on the Sudbury river?

A. No, sir.

By Mr. Looms. — Has there been any attempt made by the City of Boston to obtain water, for mechanical purposes, by driving wells, and other supplies, than the Sudbury river?

A. We drove some wells out near the Mystic — 19 wells — and put on pumps, to see what they would give us.

Q. Are there not wells within the city limits from which water is used for mechanical purposes, and isn't that supply one which can be largely increased?

A. I presume there are wells in the city limits.

Mr. STACKPOLE. — Mr. Chairman, I do not think it necessary to duplicate this evidence. We could probably go on in the same way, but we have stated the case to the committee, and therefore I shall call no other witnesses. I want to make a single suggestion which occurs to me with reference to the rate per gallon of Boston's supply. Of course when the estimate is made per day it includes simply the citizens of Boston who live there. There are many thousand people who come into the city and use our water, the great number that live in surburban towns and do business in the city — strangers, at the hotels, or visiting-places of amusement, and on business. It is impossible to estimate that number. There is no account of it kept anywhere; but were that amount estimated it would very much reduce the amount used per day *per capita*.

Mr. HAMMOND. — Mr. Chairman, at the hearing the other day, I judged from the question put by the counsel for the respondent that they intend to claim that the water of the Concord river may be taken by the City of Cambridge instead of the Shawsheen, and at a shorter distance from Cambridge. I understand that the pollution of the Concord river by the State institution has been before you, and I should like, if any friends upon the other side intend to argue, either that the Concord river is a more accessible place to take water from, or that it is a proper source of water-supply, — then I want to introduce a little evidence here; but I should not suppose they would argue the last proposition, at any rate, that it is a proper source of supply. I understand the drainage from the whole State Prison, a few hundred feet from the banks of the river, goes into it. Those are matters that we have not considered much; we are not prepared to say much about the Concord river. We presumed that, it is so greatly polluted, no reference would be made to it; but now it seems to me entirely unnecessary to take up the time of the committee to show either that the river is polluted, or that we cannot get it as well. I put on witnesses who swore that the river is not a suitable source of supply, — the executive officers of our State Board of Health, — and I will let it rest there, unless further testimony is desired. I do not wish to accumulate it, but I have witnesses who can testify.

Mr. MORSE. — Mr. Chairman, before any opening is made by the remonstrants, I wish to make a single inquiry of our friends on the other side, which ought to be answered before we proceed, and that is as to the form of the bill to be presented to the committee, whether or not this is an application on the part of the two cities for one bill, or whether they desire two bills; and if so, what the nature of those bills is? It may make considerable difference in the action we take if we could see what the measures are that they ask for.

Mr. HAMMOND. — I see my brother Stackpole is gone, being engaged in the trial of a case in court, which he left for the purpose of coming here, and I will state that it is the desire of Cambridge to avail ourselves of the opportunity of obtaining a water-supply in conjunction with the City of Boston ; and we have substantially made an arrangement with the City of Boston, if authority is given to the two cities to take the waters of the Shawsheen, by which the expenses are to be shared by the cities, and as to the manner in which they are to be shared, and as to the amount of water which each city shall have. The expense of the dam and the storage-basins will be substantially the same whether we act alone or whether we build them in conjunction with Boston ; and we also believe that, practically, if Cambridge takes 8,000,000 gallons from that river, we would have to pay about as much mill-damages as Cambridge and Boston would for the whole ; not because it is worth it, but because our brothers here upon the other side are pretty able men, and would make a jury think that 8,000,000 is as great a loss as 20,000,000 ; so, practically, it would be a saving of a large expense to our city to take this water in conjunction with Boston, and we desire to do it. We have made an agreement with Boston. At the same time, it is my duty to say that the exigencies of the case are such that we should feel bound to press our claims on the part of Cambridge even if the claim on the part of Boston should not be sustained ; but we do not want to resort to that method ; we rather act with the City of Boston. Whether there should be one bill or two bills depends, of course, somewhat upon the issue to which the committee shall come ; but whether in one or two we cannot yet say. Whether in one or two, it will, in substance — if the petition of both cities is granted — take the waters of the Shawsheen, and build those dams which I spoke of ; and whether it is in one or two bills, if the petition of the two cities is granted, and they are allowed to take the water, I cannot see how it can make any difference. Of course the legal rights asked for are that Boston and Cambridge may take the water, and build storage-basins, carry the water down the Abbajonna river, there let it be divided, and Cambridge take part, and Boston take part. That is what we ask for.

Mr. MORSE. — I suppose it is understood that before the arguments are made, the bill or bills will be presented to us.

The CHAIRMAN. — I think they ought to be.

Mr. GEORGE H. POOR. — On behalf of the Town of Andover, it has been assigned to me the duty of opening the defence, if I may call it so, to this proposition. I am to be followed by my brother Loomis, who represents manufacturers higher up the stream ; and, therefore, gentlemen, I shall confine myself principally to the objections which we shall urge against this petition, so far as it relates to the Shawsheen river, below the proposed dam ; and we shall endeavor to show that this ~~proposed~~ scheme which is proposed, is one which is fraught with the most ruinous consequences to all the mill-owners, inhabitants of the villages, farmers, and everybody below this proposed dam. I very much question the accuracy of the statements of the petitioners here, with reference to the capacity of the Shawsheen river. I have grave doubts about its being able to furnish any such quantity of water as they have told you it will furnish; but assuming it to be true, that it will furnish as much as they say, we shall claim that, practically, it is an annihilation of the stream, if they do all that they say they will do for us, to wit, that they will permit a certain quantity (they have not stated the amount, except perhaps inferentially) to run.

Now, I propose, in the first place, to call you attention to the topography of the country below the proposed dam, because that is where our interests are affected, and for that purpose I have brought a map of the Town of Andover as it existed previous to the division, which was about 1864 or '5, and which shows the Shawsheen as it runs through the town. You will observe, gentlemen, that it enters Andover from Tewksbury, and I should judge the part of Tewksbury which it crosses, after leaving this dam, is not more than four or five miles wide; I have never been to the point of the ~~old~~ dam; but it is but a comparatively short distance. The Shawsheen enters Andover at this point, and very soon strikes the village of Ballardvale. Now, Ballardvale is a village of some 600 inhabitants, wholly dependent upon Captain Bradley's mill, which is a woollen mill wholly run by water-power, and is the only industry in the place. If that mill-power is destroyed, that village is destroyed; its people must seek other homes. Many of them have been there from the earliest settlement of that village, in 1836, I think; many of them English families which came there from the old country. You all know, gentlemen, the attachment which people have for their homes, and it will be a very cruel thing to compel those people to seek other homes.

You follow down the stream, and you come to Abbott village, as it is called, which is about at this point. It is a little below, or within a quarter of a mile of Andover Centre. Abbott village has a population, strictly connected with the mills, of 400 or 500 people. The mills there are the upper mills of the Smith & Dove Manufacturing Co., a very large linen and twine concern. That is a very ancient mill-site; and I ought to say that Capt. Bradley's mill, as a mill-site, has existed for more than 130 years. It has been improved as a mill there for that length of time. Here is a saw and grist mill, one of the early ones; that privilege is very ancient. As early as 1689, our records show that encouragement was given to establish a fulling-mill there, and the records further show that a mill was established, and there has been a mill-power there to this time. The Smith &

Dove Co. occupy the whole stream, and more in the summer, because there is not sufficient water in the dry season. They must have a very large water-power here, too, for bleaching purposes. In the winter time, when the stream is very low, as this last winter, the water is very scarce, the flow very slight, and in an extraordinary season they are put to inconvenience for want of pure water for their purposes; and if this scheme is carried out, matters will be made much worse.

Then, we follow along the stream, not more than a quarter of a mile directly down the stream, and we come to Marland village. There is a woollen mill there, and a population dependent upon it of somewhere from 200 to 300, perhaps more than that, 400; that is an ancient mill, too. In fact, before 1700 there were iron-works there, and in 1775, by encouragement of the General Court, a powder-mill was established there, and much of the powder that was used by the Continental Army was made at that mill.

Then we come on down the stream about a mile, and we come to Frye village, where there have been mills from 1718, and there is a very considerable population, several hundred, dependent upon the mill there. That is Smith & Dove's lower privilege.

COMMITTEE. — What do they manufacture?

Mr. POOR. — Twine, shoe-threads, etc., the same as the upper Smith & Dove mill. Those are the manufacturing interests on the stream; but while I represent the manufacturers, I also speak for a greater interest, — the town of Andover.

This stream, if you will observe, gentlemen, is the only stream in the town of Andover. This little stream over here is in the town of North Andover, and this stream runs through the village of Andover. The bulk of the population of Andover may be said to be upon the two sides of the valley. It is the natural drainage of the town. Take away that drainage, and you expose the river bed — muddy flats — to breed pestilence in the summer, and destroy the health as well as the beauty of the town; for if these flats are uncovered they will be very unsightly; and we have, it seems to me, certain rights in that stream which are not to be taken away without very grave necessity, which we shall claim that our friends have not shown here to-day. The town of Andover, too, has no means of sewerage apart from this river, and that is a very important question, quite as important as the public health of Cambridge or Boston. We are to have a system of sewerage before long, and it must necessarily be into the valley of this stream; and every drop of water that comes down there will be needed to wash and scour it out, and carry the sewage off into the Merrimac. The town of Andover is, perhaps, not quite so energetic in some matters as some of the other towns, — newer towns in our

Commonwealth. We do not move swiftly in the matter of public improvement; we are a conservative people, very cautious about using public moneys. We do not rush into water schemes, or sewerage, or anything else without due consideration; but in the course of time the sewerage must come, and the water must come. Whether we shall be able to utilize the Shawsheen for water is a question we have not much discussed. The full amount of the stream is very considerable. I suppose we could by pumping.

COMMITTEE. — What is the population of Andover?

Mr. POOR. — A little over 5,000. I should say 5,200 or 5,300. If we shall need the stream for water, as we are liable to, we certainly ought to have the prior right to these people outside, who, by their own testimony, have got other water already in abundance, and certainly the testimony for the City of Boston cannot lead one to think that they have any need of the Shawsheen river at the cost of the destruction, not only of the private interests, but of the public interests of Andover. We are the parties most affected by it. There are no towns or villages above where any considerable number are affected, save private interests, which can almost always be compensated for by money; but, as I have endeavored to show you, the stream is vitally important to the town of Andover as a municipality, not alone to the people confined to its banks, and engaged in business there; and, in a sanitary point of view, we should object to this scheme with all our might. We have sent the remonstrance of the town, which was adopted in a remarkably well-attended meeting, considering that it was a special meeting, — adopted unanimously, and I think that you may well pause before giving away to these petitioners our property, our health, and all our interests, which are so dependent on this stream. You may well pause, gentlemen, and ask them whether this is wise, whether for a temporary relief, as they claim it is (they do not say it is anything more than temporary), they shall be permitted to take away that from us which we can never replace in the nature of things. We cannot replace it, and we must not lose it. Gentlemen, we cannot appear before the General Court; we have no voice there, except through you. It is an appeal to your discretion. We shall endeavor to show you by evidence which we shall bring here that the best exercise of that discretion on your part will be to report leave to withdraw.

Mr. E. G. LOOMIS. — Gentlemen, the time of the Committee is brief, and I shall be brief. I appear for Mr. Chas. E. Clark, whose property is situated on the stream, and who owns part of the property which it is proposed to flood by erecting the contemplated dam. The property, I shall show to you, has been a valuable property ever since the country has been settled. As long ago as the time of

King Phillips' War the property was occupied as a mill-site, and we find in the records that in its early days soldiers were stationed there, and, ever since that time, it has been used as a mill-site, and as a great and indispensable public convenience for the inhabitants of the towns of Lexington, Bedford, and Billerica. It is the only privilege which is large enough and adapted to the use of the people within a circuit of five miles, which can be used for sawing logs, pressing apples into cider, and grinding corn. We appreciate the needs of the city of Boston, perhaps, as much as they do. We shall prove to this committee that no case has been made out of any such crying need of any additional water-supply for Cambridge or Boston as will justify an interference by them with our rights in this property. We shall most earnestly deprecate any bill being brought authorizing the City of Cambridge or the City of Boston to interfere with our rights in the premises. There are water-privileges, it appears, which they have not yet exhausted, but they prefer to go out in the country, and seem to think, as a matter of course, we shall be ready to give up to them our rights whereby we live rather than have them pay for the slight expense of being a little careful in the use of water. The Cambridge people have almost demonstrated, from their own report, the feasibility and advisability of taking the water from Kendall's pond instead of Shawsheen river, and no better evidence can be offered to your committee than the evidence on record of the very officials of Boston who have testified in favor of Sudbury river.

Mr. J. R. REED. — Mr. Chairman, it is an unpleasant thing for the town of Lexington to oppose the wishes of the good old City of Cambridge, or even the City of Boston, for our welfare is entirely dependent upon the prosperity of this city ; but there are some points in which we are greatly interested, and it seemed best to the town, at our meeting last week, to appoint a committee to appear at these hearings to explain their feelings. Our committee have asked me to be their spokesman in introducing the matter.

The town of Lexington, as most of you are well aware, is situated quite high. Where Vine brook, one of the sources of the Shawsheen, crosses our main street, it is at a level of 220 feet, I believe, above the sea level.

Several other little branches of the headwaters of this stream also start in the town, and if these are taken away from us, all power of getting water in the future will be gone. There is no other available supply for us. The town has not at present any water works. Whether it will need them for some years or not, is an open question ; but it certainly desires to reserve the right of any future use of the waters within its own limits.

Mr. HAMMOND. — We do not object to that. We are willing to

make ample provision in the bill that the town of Lexington or the inhabitants of Lexington may take water from any stream which is a tributary to the Shawsheen.

Mr. REED. — Well, sir, there is one other point upon which we also ask the protection of the committee. Our town is situated on high land, and a very large part of it is on the highest land, and if we ever introduce a system of drainage and sewerage where can we send this drainage and sewerage if not downhill? I doubt if the town ever grows to be a large town. There are no factories in it or manufactories. It is a town where the farming interest is chief; and as many residents do business in the city, it will never be a large town probably, but it will need sewerage. Now, this Vine brook, which goes through the town, is an impure stream at present; that is, its water is not fit to use for domestic purposes, not even for washing clothes; but in the course of two or three miles Vine brook becomes clear. Down below Burlington its waters are good and clear, and it might be polluted somewhat by our sewerage. We simply ask that our inhabitants be saved from the expense of defending suits which might possibly be brought against them, by having some provision made to hold them harmless in the matter. I can speak from a knowledge of the waters on this stream, and I believe for that reason the gentlemen of the committee have asked me to be their spokesman, because I am rather fresh from a fishing experience in it. Our trout will only live in clean water. Vine brook, in the centre of Lexington, will not keep trout; they will not live there; but in Burlington, two or three miles below, the water becomes pure, and they live down there; the water draining through several large swamps and meadows which, I suppose, act as filters to it.

I believe I have stated the position of the town of Lexington in the matter.

Mr. HAMMOND. — You want the privilege of draining into that brook?

Mr. REED. — Of sending our sewerage and surface-draining off as it runs now. From Vine brook we should never take water probably, because it is not good. Our drainage would go into Vine brook, which, if you will observe the map, flows several miles before going to the Shawsheen. Its course as the brook turns would be nearly 10 miles; 4 or 5 in a straight line. Where we would want to take water would be from one of the other branches.

COMMITTEE. — Then you do not propose using the water of Vine brook for drinking purposes, but for drainage?

Mr. REED. — Yes, sir; I believe I am representing the committee in saying that, or for watering the streets. It is not to be used where it flows through the centre of the village.

Committee. — And when do you want to use it for drainage?

Mr. Reed. — There is a bill before the committee now, I think, to incorporate a private company.

Mr. Hammond. — What is the population?

Mr. Reed. — About 2,500, — the whole town.

The Chairman. — Are the people of Lexington, as far as you know, looking to a water-supply from that corporation?

Mr. Reed. — The people of the village are, I think.

The Chairman. — Do you think they want it incorporated?

Mr. Reed. — I should think a large number of people in the village want a water-supply of that sort.

The Chairman. — Do you hear anything said against it in the town?

Mr. Reed. — I have heard nothing said against it. They do not wish the town to incur any liability on account of it at present. We merely want to secure our future rights.

Committee. — You want a provision in the bill that you can drain into Vine brook?

Mr. Reed. — Yes, sir; and that we can take our water from other branches if we ever wish to have anything to do with it.

Mr. Loomis. — I am a member of the committee of the town of Bedford, on the queston of water-supply. If the city is to be allowed to take the brook which flows through our town I think a provision ought to be in the bill for the town of Bedford to tap the stream in the same way the town of Lexington desires to be allowed the privilege.

Mr. Hammond. — What is the population of Bedford?

Mr. Loomis. — 800; a small town; but they have been troubled about a water-supply, and they appointed a committee last year to consider the question of getting water, because they have never had good water in the village; otherwise I should not have mentioned the matter.

Committee. — Do you want to drain down on to Lexington?

Mr. Loomis. — We do not care where we drain.

Testimony of Chas. E. Clark.

By Mr. Loomis. — You are the owner of a mill-property, are you, on the Shawsheen river?

A. Yes, sir.

Q. Will you please describe the property, giving your estimate of its usefulness to the community, and also the amount of business done there?

A. I have a grain-mill, saw-mill, and a mill for making cider, to which people of that vicinity come more or less.

Q. Do you use the power of the river through the season?

A. Yes, sir.

Q. What quantity of business have you done in the course of a year, as near as you can estimate?

A. About $25,000.

Q. Is there any other mill where corn can be ground within a circuit of a number of miles?

A. There is none that grinds but a very little, — off seven or eight miles, I should think.

Q. Do you grind corn, and saw logs, for the people of Billerica, Bedford, and Lexington?

A. Yes, sir.

Q. To what extent?

A. Well, there are people come from — I don't know; people from Burlington, Lexington, Lincoln, Concord, Carlyle, Billerica, and Chelmsford, all more or less come to my mill. The amount of grinding for individuals, I should think might be $2,000 or $3,000 a year. I can't state so very accurate as I could some other parts of the business.

Q. Can you give an estimate of the value of your property for the purposes for which you use it? There is no other property, as I understand you, in the town that can be used for these purposes. Will you give some estimate of its value?

A. I should estimate it about $20,000.

Q. Is there any substitute that could be used for this water-power, as far as you know? Would it be practicable, without great expense, to bring coal for the purposes of fuel?

A. I don't understand the question.

Q. Could you put in steam machinery there, and use coal without a very great expense?

A. I couldn't compete with water-powers that are near me. It couldn't be done by steam-power.

COMMITTEE. — Do you mean, Mr. Clark, if they used water-power, and you used steam-power, you couldn't compete with them?

A. Yes, sir.

By Mr. HAMMOND. — How long have you owned the mill? Not from King Philip's time, have you?

A. Not quite so far back as that, — a little more than 6 years.

Q. Do you own it now?

A. Yes, sir.

Q. What did you pay for it?

A. I paid $6,500.

Q. Paid it when?

A. 1874, I think.

Q. How much land is there that you bought?

A. I think about 2 acres.

Q. Built any new buildings?

A. I have built a house, and started the foundation of another building.

Q. I would like to know how you get at $20,000 as the estimated value of that property?

A. When I purchased it, it was in a run-down condition, owned by an administrator, who had run it several years so that the business had almost left it entirely, and about that time the Middlesex Railroad came into the town, which brought up the value of the mill.

Q. How?

A. Because we could handle Western grain there. Before that it was never done.

Q. Did you ever run a saw-mill on steam?

A. No, sir.

Q. Don't you know they do run saw-mills on steam, getting heat from the refuse lumber?

A. Yes, sir.

Q. Then how do you know the cost of it, if you never run one?

A. I have had a little experience with a grist-mill.

Q. What was your property assessed at last year, — houses, lands, and everything?

A. I think about $7,000 or $8,000. I won't be positive.

Q. That includes the mill and buildings?

A. Yes, sir.

Q. What is the fall you have there?

A. From 10 to 13 feet.

By Mr. LOOMIS. — I understand you use two turbine wheels a good part of the time?

A. Yes, sir.

Q. And 60-horse-power wheels, each of them?

A. No, sir; the two combined.

Q. Is it a fact that you do a large business in Western corn, that is, buy corn in the West, grind it up, and sell to families in the neighborhood?

A. I do considerable in that way. That is my principal business, — the chief part.

Q. And that is entirely a new business, and built up by you since you bought the property?

A. Yes, sir.

Testimony of Dr. W. H. Kimball.

By Mr. Poor. — You are a practising physician in Andover?

A. Yes, sir.

Q. How many years?

A. Thirty and more.

Q. Have practised in all these villages along the stream?

A. Yes, sir.

Q. What would be the sanitary effect if the waters of the Shawsheen were materially diminished so as to expose the flats there?

A. My observation has been that when the water has been drawn off, and left the flats exposed through the hot weather in the summer, that sickness has materially increased in the villages there. This has been done since my residence in Andover two or three times, and I remember the old physician who practised there before me said he always expected half the children to die when they drew off the water, and let the flats remain exposed.

Q. In your judgment, as a professional man, you think it would be very injurious, too?

A. I think it would be very injurious to the health of the villages situated immediately on the stream. The houses are built very near the water, and there is a large surface of flats exposed when the water is drawn off; and if those flats are left exposed during the heats of summer, the result is exceedingly injurious to the health of the people.

Q. Is the natural drainage of the bulk of the population of Andover into that stream?

A. It must be if there is any drainage at all. There is no other way. It has got to be drained into that stream ultimately, I suppose.

By Mr. Hammond. — Were these flats bare last fall, doctor?

A. They were to a degree.

Q. How long?

A. I can't tell how long. I speak in regard to the injury resulting during the heats of the summer.

Q. You don't know how long a time they were bare last fall?

A. No, I don't. I think a month; but it was later.

Q. Was it remarkably sickly there then?

A. No, sir, it was not.

Q. Is there anything peculiar about this river different from any other river in that respect?

A. Not that I know of, except that the flats are usually covered by the back water from the dams.

Q. But I want to know whether there is anything peculiar in that river so that it would be any worse to take water out of that river than any other river?

A. Not under the same circumstances.

By COMMITTEE. — Did you say half the children died in Andover?

A. No, sir, not in Andover; that was the remark of an old physician, that half the children in the two villages there usually died when the water was drawn off early in the season.

Q. Do you mean half the children under two years of age?

A. Yes, sir.

Q. Has that been your experience, doctor, or anything like it?

A. I think when the flats have been exposed, there has been a very great fatality in those two villages; dysentery has prevailed there to a very great extent.

Q. Didn't that strike you as a very extravagant statement?

A. It did at the time.

By Mr. HAMMOND. — If you have sewerage from Andover go into the river, and the flats get dry, would it be any better?

A. It wouldn't be so good.

[Adjourned to Thursday, at 10 o'clock, A.M.]

THURSDAY, March 17, 1881.

The hearing was resumed at 10 o'clock.

TESTIMONY OF MR. SIMEON BARDWELL.

By Mr. POOR. — You are one of the selectmen of Andover?

A. I am.

Q. And have been such for a good many years?

A. Quite a number of years ; yes, sir.

Q. Lived in the town most of your life?

A. I was born there, sir.

Q. And are familiar with the Shawsheen river?

A. I am.

Q. You are also a member of the Board of Health there, are you?

A. I am.

Q. What are the industries of Andover aside from the mills along the river?

A. Farming, mostly, besides the mills.

Q. There are no mechanical or manufacturing industries, aside from the mills, on the river?

A. No, sir.

Q. And Ballardvale, do you know that district?

A. I do, very well.

Q. Is that village wholly dependent upon Mr. Bradlee's mill?

A. Wholly dependent ; no other manufacturing interest whatever there.

Q. And Abbott village, is that dependent upon the Smith & Dove mill, and Marland village upon the Stevens' mill?

A. Yes, sir.

Q. And also Frye village, is that dependent upon the mills?

A. Yes, sir.

Q. Do you know the population in those villages?

A. I have no means of stating the exact population.

Q. Well, about?

A. I should say some 600 or 800, sir.

Q. And Ballardvale, — do you know about that; do you know whether it is about 600, as I stated yesterday?

A. I should think it was about 600 in Ballardvale.

Q. And what for Abbott village?

A. I couldn't state with any accuracy.

Q. Mr. Abbott informed me about 400 ; is that correct?

A. About 400, I think.

Q. Then Marland village?

A. Some 200 or 250.

Q. And, then, also, lower down, Frye village?

A. Frye village, I couldn't say, sir, with any accuracy.

Q. What is your judgment?

A. Three hundred. That is the lower village, — Smith's Mill.

Q. What is the character of the river along there? Are these mills pretty near together?

A. Yes, sir ; they are very near together.

Q. Would taking away the water expose the flats there?

A. It would very much, above the fall. There is a large amount of flats there, I should suppose from 140 to 150 acres, perhaps, that are flowed by Bradlee's dam. It is mere guess-work. I haven't accurate means of knowing. It flows nearly up to the Burt mills. It must be some 3 miles up.

Q. What would be the effect on those villages if these industries were taken away?

A. I should think it would have a most ruinous effect.

Q. Whether the town would lose its population?

A. It would lose population, and very much in taxable property, and it would be a great detriment to the town in many respects.

Q. How is public sentiment in Andover on this subject, — unanimous?

A. I should say it was, judging from the town meeting we had. There seemed to be but one mind.

Q. The bulk of the property in Andover is in the Shawsheen valley, on both sides?

A. Yes, sir ; I should think it was.

Q. The hill drains that way?

A. Yes, sir ; there is no other drainage.

Q. Do you know of your own knowledge whether the water of the Shawsheen was used last summer for domestic purposes?

A. It was, to a very large extent. I know some teams kept drawing water for weeks there.

Q. Is there any other source of supply anywhere within some miles of the village?

A. I don't know of any other nearer than Haggett's pond, and that is 4½ miles from the village.

Q. Do you know, Mr. Bardwell, about Tyer's factory, where it gets its water?

A. From the Shawsheen.

Q. How?

A. By being drawn there by teams.

Q. It is a fact that the Shawsheen is resorted to very frequently in dry years, isn't it, at low water?

A. Yes.

Cross-Examination.

By Mr. HAMMOND. — It is pretty good water, isn't it?

A. Yes, sir, called good water for the purposes it has been used for.

Q. I mean, for drinking?

A. I never knew it to be used for drink.

Q. What did they use it for?

A. Washing, and family purposes. I should hardly think it was used for drinking.

Q. Where is the rubber mill?

A. In South Andover, in the centre of the town, or near the centre.

Q. Is that on the river?

A. No, sir ; half a mile from the river.

Q. Does that go by steam-power?

A. Yes, driven by steam-power entirely.

Q. Are you a mill owner?

A. No, sir.

Q. Interested in mills?

A. No, sir.

Q. Know anything about how to run a mill?

A. Nothing more than by observation, and living in the town that length of time.

Q. Do you know where Foster's pond is?

A. I do, sir.

Q. Don't that run into the Shawsheen?

A. Yes, sir, at certain times of the year it does, when there is anything to run in.

Q. Do you know how far it is from where the Shawsheen river crosses the Boston & Lowell Railroad to Andover village?

A. I don't think I could tell you.

Q. About ten miles, as the river runs, or more?

A. I shouldn't like to say.

Q. You have always lived there?

A. I have always lived in Andover. I don't live near Foster's pond.

Q. How far do you think it is from Andover village to where the Shawsheen river crosses the Boston & Lowell Railroad?

A. Which village in Andover? There are three villages.

Q. The one called on the map " Andover village," where the theological seminary is?

A. That is not on the Shawsheen river. The village is some half a mile or quarter of a mile from the river. It is in the valley.

Q. How far is it?

A. Well, I shouldn't like to give any figures as to that, sir.

Q. Ten miles isn't any too short a distance to call it, is it?

A. I should hardly think it is ten miles; still it may be.

Q. Then, the village in Andover where the theological seminary is isn't situated upon the Shawsheen river, is it?

A. Not directly.

Q. Where are these flats you speak of?

A. Above Ballardvale. Ballardvale is some two miles from the centre of the town, — the post-office.

Q. How far above Ballardvale are these flats?

A. Directly above them. They come down very near, — right in sight.

Q. And they are usually covered by Bradlee's pond?

A. Yes, sir.

Q. And when he draws it down they are exposed?

A. If he draws it down very much they would be.

Q. And he has drawn it down so they were?

A. Oh, yes; there have been times when it was drawn down.

Q. Any other flats in town?

A. There are flats all the way down from Ballardvale, between all the villages; not so extensive flats as there are above Ballardvale.

Q. I suppose you know that between where we propose to take this water and Ballardvale, on the Shawsheen river, there are various ponds and streams that run into the Shawsheen, don't you?

A. I don't know any of any amount, except Foster's pond, and that is below where you will take it.

Q. This map shows as many as a dozen little streams?

A. There may be little streams. I am not familiar with those little streams.

Q. And you don't know how much water runs into the Shawsheen from these little ponds between where we propose to take it and Ballardville?

A. I don't.

By the Chairman. — How many miles above Ballardvale is the point where you propose to take it?

Mr. Hammond. — Measuring on the map here, I should say that it was certainly five, and perhaps six, miles from where we propose to take the water to Ballardvale.

By Mr. Poor. — Wasn't the Almshouse supplied last year from the Shawsheen?

A. Yes, sir. The Shawsheen runs very near the Almshouse.

By Mr. Nettleton. — How many town paupers are there?

A. We have 38 — 39; one came yesterday. About 37 or 38 is our average.

By Mr. HAMMOND. — They drink the water, don't they?

A. No, sir; I don't think they do. We give them better water than that to drink.

By Mr. POOR. — Do the farmers along the Shawsheen use it to water cattle in the summer?

A. Yes, sir, they do.

Q. To a considerable extent?

A. Almost entirely, those living on the river.

By Mr. HAMMOND. — What you mean to say is, that people through whose land the Shawsheen runs use it when they want to?

A. Yes, sir.

TESTIMONY OF THE REV. G. F. WRIGHT.

By Mr. POOR. — You are a clergyman settled in Andover?

A. Yes, sir.

Q. Given considerable attention to scientific pursuits?

A. To a small degree.

Q. Are you familiar with the Shawsheen valley?

A. I am familiar with the lower part of it, below where the Boston & Lowell Railroad crosses.

Q. Do you know the Shawsheen in relation to Andover, through its entire length and course in the town?

A. Yes, sir.

Q. As to these flats, Mr. Wright, that have been spoken of here, are you familiar with them?

A. Yes, sir.

Q. How many acres of flats do you think there are?

A. I don't know as I am proper authority on the number of acres. I know that there are flats upon either side of it, some two or three miles above Ballardvale, down as far as Frye village.

Q. And when the water is low, or if it should be drawn off, they would be exposed, wouldn't they?

A. Yes, sir; the flats back of my house are peculiarly of that character. The flats bound the river all the way from 2½ miles above Ballardvale as far down as Frye village, except a very short distance. The flats just back of my house are exposed even now in dry weather, so that they are very troublesome to me and the neighbors about there.

By Mr. MORSE. — Where is your house, Mr. Wright?

A. Between Abbott village and Marland village.

By Mr. Poor. — Some question has been made here as to streams entering the Shawsheen below this proposed dam. Do you know of any considerable water-supply for the river below that dam?

A. From where the Boston & Lowell Railroad crosses, which is very near the dam, about five miles to Ballardvale, there is a stream, — the outlet of Long pond, — that comes in below, which is in Tewksbury.

Q. That is a small pond, is it not, Mr. Wright?

A. Yes, sir; it is somewhat larger than Foster's pond, however.

Q. Do you know whether that affords any considerable water-supply?

A. The water is there all the year round, that and Silver lake, which runs into Ipswich river.

Q. Do you know Strong Water brook?

A. I don't know it by that name.

Q. The brook up at Tewsbury?

A. There is a tributary in Tewksbury that comes in to supply some water, I know.

Q. Have you seen that to know what sort of brook that is?

A. I have not paid special attention to it. I know something of the brook in dry weather.

Q. It isn't a large brook, is it?

A. No, sir; it is a small brook.

Q. And Foster's pond — you have examined all that region, I suppose?

A. Yes, sir, I have.

Q. What sort of a pond is that?

A. In summer it isn't any pond at all.

Q. It is simply a storage-basin?

A. Yes, sir; the water is drained off before dry weather. There is no drainage-basin to supply it.

Q. After leaving that, there are no other tributaries to the Shawsheen, that you know of?

A. No, sir; the north-western part of the town drains into the Merrimac, and the south-eastern into the Ipswich; so after it reaches Ballardvale, there are no tributaries at all.

Q. Isn't the Shawsheen the natural drainage of the most of Andover.

A. The populous part of it, it is.

Q. What would be the effect upon Andover to take the water of the Shawsheen away, in your judgment?

A. There are two aspects in which you can view the effect. If, as I suppose it will, it destroys the manufacturing interest, it will ruin the hopes of 2,000 people; they will have no redress. But that is a matter that I am not a judge of, although I should apprehend serious results.

Q. That is one effect, and the other effect is what?

A. The other effect would be upon the sanitary condition. I live in the parsonage upon the banks, and probably a hundred families of my church, largely workmen, live along the banks of the river, within a mile of where I am. I should apprehend serious results from any large diminution of the water on account of their health.

By Mr. COWLEY. — Can you tell us the water-shed?

A. The-water shed above Ballardvale is about 60 miles.

Q. How much below?

A. Perhaps 10 miles below.

Q. Have you given any consideration to the subject of the public policy of the city on this question?

A. That is the only interest I have in it, as it touches us.

By Mr. HAMMOND. — Which side of the public policy, the Andover side or the Cambridge side, have you given attention to?

Mr. COWLEY. — The Cambridge policy is a local policy; that is, not public policy.

By Mr. POOR. — What is your opinion as to the feasibility of supplying Boston from the Merrimac?

A. That is a question of a little increased expense, only. This any one could see. The Concord river is only four miles, and the Merrimac but seven or eight miles, from the point where they propose to cut off the Shawsheen.

By Mr. COWLEY. — You think it desirable to supply Boston from the Merrimac, rather than from the Shawsheen?

A. I should think that before they decide to sacrifice so many innocent parties entirely, the public policy of the State should be to make Boston respect the laws of nature. We have gathered about the Shawsheen, expecting the laws of nature would not be interfered with without public necessity; and I take it that is a principle applicable to all the small towns of the Commonwealth.

Q. Have you given any attention as to the capacity of this Shawsheen, Mr. Wright?

A. Yes, sir, I have.

Q. What is its capacity?

A. The drainage-basin, as I said, is about 60 square miles above Ballardvale. That would furnish with storage, in dry weather, something like 20,000,000 gallons a day, probably, according to their estimates made of the upper part of it.

Q. You estimate that the entire volume of water in the Shawsheen is 20,000,000 gallons a day?

A. I estimated the square miles and drainage, and I took the estimates of the engineer, yesterday, — 40 square miles. Two-thirds of this drainage is above the proposed dam.

Q. I thought you said 60?

A. Sixty is the whole, and that leaves about 20 square miles for Andover.

Q. Hasn't the volume of water diminished there perceptibly since the cutting away of the forests, in your judgment?

A. I haven't been in Andover long; I have only been there about nine years.

Mr. HAMMOND. — What forests do you mean?

Mr. COWLEY. — The forests that formerly stood on the water-shed.

Mr. HAMMOND. — Cut away when?

Mr. COWLEY. — Cut away within the time of history, sir.

Mr. HAMMOND. — Have you got a witness whose memory extends back to that?

Mr. COWLEY. — We have a scientific witness whose computations perhaps extends back to that.

Q. Isn't it the view of the scientific men that our water-shed has diminished about 50 per cent. since the cutting away of the forests?

A. That would take us back about 200 or 250 years. As to this past century, I do not know as there has been any change.

Q. Well, there has been a diminution in the capacity or the volume of water of all our rivers in this settled part of New England in consequence of cutting away of the forests, is there not?

A. That is somewhat theoretical.

By the CHAIRMAN. — You don't know anything about it, do you?

A. I don't know.

The CHAIRMAN. — Then I would not testify on that.

Cross-examination.

By Mr. HAMMOND. — Mr. Wright, if I understand you, you think that if Cambridge wants water, they better go to the Concord or the Merrimac?

A. I say that before they destroy us, they should give diligent attention to three or four other sources of supply.

Q. And if anybody is going to suffer, you would rather it would be the people on the Concord and Merrimac than on the Shawsheen?

A. No, sir. I haven't said that. What would be the destruction of us wouldn't be the destruction of them.

Q. Now, don't you know that there are two streams, three or four miles long, in Tewksbury, that enter into the Shawsheen below the point where we propose to take the water?

A. Yes, sir. I have said there are twenty square miles of drainage basin above Ballardvale.

Q. Have you made any estimate of the amount of water that would come into the river from that area?

A. Taking your estimate, yesterday, as the basis for the 40 miles above, it would, under the same conditions, supply about 7,000,000 gallons a day, alone.

Q. Then, you think that the water-shed, between the point where we propose to take and Ballardvale, would give about 7,000,000 gallons a day?

A. It is just about one-third of the whole water-shed.

Q. Now, these flats you speak of consist of the mill ponds, I suppose, and what else?

A. The water sets back.

Q. The difference between the high-water and low-water mark, do you mean?

A. The water sets back from one mill to another. When the water is shut off at Ballardvale the pond doesn't fill up in all day. If two-thirds of the water were shut off the pond would be three days in filling up.

Q. That is, the lower man's mill pond isn't full; that is the substance of it, isn't it?

A. Yes, sir, the lower mill ponds are not full.

Q. That has been so about all the summer, hasn't it?

A. This last summer it has been more so than usual.

Q. Well, they have been bare all summer, substantially, haven't they?

A. They have had longer intervals of being bare than usual.

TESTIMONY OF J. PUTNAM BRADLEE.

By Mr. TORREY. — You reside in Boston?

A. Yes, sir.

Q. Always have?

A. Yes, sir.

Q. And you are the proprietor of the Ballardvale mills?

A. Yes, sir.

Q. And in the village of Ballardvale, in Andover, what do you manufacture?

A. Fine white flannel.

Q. To what extent? What is about the extent of your annual product?

A. My annual product ought to yield between $400,000 and $500,-000, at the market price, a fair season.

Q. At what other places in this country are those goods manufactured?

A. I know of but one place, at Ware, — Mr. Gilbert's.

Q. What is the proportion of your manufacture to his?

A. Mr. Gilbert's place is larger than mine, but he manufactures other goods. Our mill has only that one specialty.

Q. What proportion does he make of your class of goods?

A. We make four-fifths of all the fine flannels manufactured in this country. My impression is he is running three sets, and we are running thirteen.

Q. The population of the village has been testified to as about 600?

A. Between 600 and 700.

Q. What is their occupation?

A. If my mill wasn't run there would be no work there. I can set about 180 a day at work. I employ between 180 and 200 men, women, and children.

Q. Now, won't you state, generally, to the committee, when you use the water of the Shawsheen river, and your method of managing it?

A. Well, sir, in the first place, making nothing but entirely white goods, I must have good water, and I must have head. If the water is taken away from me, my supply is gone, and there must be some compensation for me to scour and finish my goods. I must be compensated in water, not money. I can't live without it. If we have a good wet season we can get along; but in order to carry on my work successfully I have been obliged to put in two engines, so that when the water begins to leave the river, I have to use the engine, and put one-half of the mill on steam to keep my head up so I can wash my goods; and, then, when it is still going away from me, I put the other half on, and so I keep my head on, and in that way I am able, in ordinary seasons, to get along with my scouring. I have had to do it in that way right straight along, when there has been a season like the last one, and everybody else has been troubled in the same way, that wasn't on some big river. I know nothing, gentlemen, that would compensate me if you take the water. If you take that river and don't give me a sufficient quantity of water, I consider my specialty is dead at Ballardvale.

Q. Do you know how much water you use at Ballardvale?

A. I don't know. That is not my part. I am not superintendent. I never had it measured. We have to take it as it comes, and we have to work with just what water we have. The mills were established there in 1836, and we had to do the best we could.

Q. Could you run your mills with steam alone, without any water?

A. I could not, sir. I could make my cloth, but I could not finish it. I want good water. I don't want muddy water. I don't know how the City of Boston can compensate me for the water.

Q. Does this village depend upon this river for a water-supply at times?

A. I have seen people lead their horses down there to drink. I am only there twice a week.

Mr. HAMMOND. — If it will shorten things any, you may let it be assumed that farmers let their cattle drink this water.

Q. Do you know where these parties propose to take this water?

A. I have heard them state. I was never up there.

Q. Now, do you know what tributaries there are to the Shawsheen between where they propose to take the water and your mill?

A. I think there are some above Burt's dam ; but between Burt's dam and ours I think it is all gone.

Q. Is there any amount of money compensation that would satisfy you for having this water taken away from your mill?

A. No, sir. I must have an equivalent in water.

Q. Now, suppose you should stop your works entirely, take your money consideration, and go off somewhere else, and go into the manufacture of fine flannels — would that removal be an injury to your business?

A. Yes.

Q. How?

A. Because the goods are known throughout the whole country as "Ballardvale flannels." I should have to take the name with me if I went anywhere else. Ever since 1836 those goods have been known as "Ballardvale flannels ; " and the people have been educated up to making them, and it would be a serious injury to them.

Q. You think the fact that the goods are manufactured in that place is a great advantage?

A. Yes, sir. The trade-mark of any man well established in business is a great thing.

Q. Suppose they should allow, as suggested, a million gallons a day to pass their dam, would that be of any material value to you?

A. One-half would evaporate in the summer season, and it would ooze along through the mud at the dam, and it would be thick and slimy. I could not use it. I can't use anything but the best water. When the pond gets down, as it has this season, I have had to stop, it comes so slowly.

Q. I understand you to state that you use steam to a great extent when you might use water, for the purpose of saving this water for scouring?

A. As soon as the water begins to drop I begin to save. I have got the mills fixed so I can run the mills by one engine or both, and I can regulate the matter.

Q. That is done for the purpose of saving the water for scouring?

A. Yes, sir, and to keep my head up. I must have a head to drive that water right out from the flume and scour the goods.

Q. Are there very many streams that you know of that are adapted to make as fine goods as you make? That is, is the water pure enough that is used in any of these mills for your work?

A. I never looked at it in that way; never had occasion to. Mr. Gilbert and myself have always made all that is wanted; but I should not think anybody would start a mill of that kind where there was no pure water.

Q. What do you think the effect upon your village will be as to the health of the inhabitants?

A. I think it would be very injurious. The people live right round the pond, close around the mill; and there are a good many parties there that own their houses. There are some widows whose husbands used to work in the mill who get along very comfortably, but they are close on the banks of the river.

Cross-Examination.

By Mr. HAMMOND. I understand you to say that you require pure water?

A. I do, sir.

Q. Do you know anything about the mills of Saxonville?

A. I do not, sir.

Q. Do you know what they make?

A. I know something of what they make.

Q. They make a pure white flannel, don't they?

A. Not to my knowledge.

Q. You don't know they don't?

A. I don't know they do not. I never saw any.

Q. You never saw the blankets they make?

A. Yes, sir, I have seen them.

Q. Weren't they pure white goods?

A. They don't require so much scouring as my goods.

Q. I ask you whether they were not pure white goods?

A. Well, they can get along with less pure water than I can.

Q. How do you know?

A. I judge from the cloth they make, — what is on the market, — that is all.

Q. What is the title of your Ballardvale goods?

A. " Ballardvale flannels."

Q. They are sold all over the world?

A. Sold, not all over the world, but all over the United States.

Q. Do you suppose one man that buys them knows whether they are made in Ballardvale, or where they are made?

A. Yes; a great many know.

Q. Can't you go somewhere else, and carry that work with you?

A. I shouldn't carry a fraud with me.

Q. Would you regard it as a fraud to take a trade-mark with you? Didn't you say that if you moved away you would have to take the name with you? Did you mean it?

A. I mean the Ballardvale name is worth money to me, — the name itself.

Q. You stated to the committee, if I remember right, that if you moved you would have to take the name " Ballardvale " with you ; did you make that statement?

A. Well, I probably did. What I mean by it is, that the name " Ballardvale " is very valuable to me. If I went away from Ballardvale I should have to carry that name with me.

Q. Fraud or no fraud?

A. I don't say that. Perhaps I should do it. To get the mercantile value out of my goods I should have to.

Q. Do you mean you would or wouldn't?

A. My impression is, when I am driven away from Ballardvale, that is the last I shall have to do with making white flannels. My mind is this, that if you drive me away from my mill at Ballardvale, it is very likely it is the last I shall have anything to do with any mill. I don't want to go round the country, and carry my mill somewhere, and then assume a name that my goods are made in a certain place, when they are not.

Q. Now, sir, how many gallons a day went down by there this last summer?

A. I don't know, sir.

Q. In the dry times?

A. I have no means of knowing.

Q. Do you know the capacity of your pond?

A. No, sir.

Q. Doesn't water run over it now in great quantities?

A. It has been running over there pretty lively this last week.

Q. You don't begin to use the water that runs by there?

A. No, sir. We stopped two days, Friday and Saturday, because there was back water, — too much water.

Q. How much water do you use of this pure water a day?

A. I don't know.

Q. How do you get it into your mills?

A. It comes over the wheels.

Q. Well, what do you do with this water that must be so absolutely pure?

A. Why, I scour the wool and finish my goods, — wash the goods out, rinse them out.

Q. Wash the goods in this water?

A. Yes, sir.

Q. Where is the wash-room?

A. In the basement of the mill.

Q. And you don't know how many gallons you use?

A. No, sir.

Q. Is it put into tanks?

A. Put into the washers.

Q. Is it the same water that runs over the wheel?

A. Yes, sir; comes from the flume.

Q. Now, how do you get water from the Shawsheen to your flannel?

A. Why, I put the flannel into these rollers, and have the water go into washing-machines.

Q. Right in the river?

A. No.

Q. How do you get it from the river to the flannel?

A. By these wash-boxes.

Q. You have a stream running from the Shawsheen?

A. Why, certainly; right from the flume; get the head from there.

Q. Is there any reason why you can't store that water that you wash these flannels with?

A. I store all I can.

Q. Well, you have engines there. Now, if it were not for the fact that you need this pure water, the factory could be run by steam, couldn't it?

A. I could make the goods by steam.

Q. If you should make, then, a class of goods not quite so good, you could get along by using steam?

A. I don't know, sir. I couldn't judge for anybody else.

Q. How much did you run by steam last year?

A. About nine months, one machine, on the average, I should think. In 1879 we run about 11 days with steam.

Q. Then, if that mill should be devoted to a business that didn't need this water, it wouldn't make any very great change in the method in which it is run, would it?

A. I don't know anything about it.

Q. I hold in my hand, captain, a statement of the assessors' valuation of the real estate in Andover for 1880. It puts your mill, the brick mill and shop, at $28,000, the wooden mill at $10,000, and then some other buildings, making $7,000 or $8,000, besides, and all your buildings and about 8 or 10 tenement-houses and the land that goes with them, at $77,550?

A. Yes, sir.

Q. You suppose that to be their valuation, don't you?

A. No, sir, I don't.

Q. Well, I don't ask you whether it is your valuation, but it is the valuation of the assessors?

A. Yes, sir.

Q. Now, you have machinery in that mill, have you?

A. Yes, sir.

Q. Will you tell me how much you paid for that?

A. No, sir.

Q. Can't you tell?

A. No, sir.

Q. Can't you guess?

A. No, sir.

Q. Well, captain, do you mean to say that you haven't any idea what that machinery is worth?

A. Yes, sir.

Testimony of George H. Torr.

By Mr. Morse. — You are the treasurer and selling agent of the Smith & Dove Manufacturing Co.?

A. I am.

Q. And they have two mills on the Shawsheen river?

A. Two mill privileges ; four mills.

Q. Where is No. 1?

A. Abbott village.

Q. And Abbott village is how far below Capt. Bradlee's?

A. I think between two and three miles. I am not sure.

Q. That is where you have your upper mill privilege?

A. Yes, sir.

Q. Your lower one is at what place?

A. About a mile below there.

Q. And, then, the Marland mill comes between your two mill privileges?

A. Yes, sir.

Q. This is a corporation, as I understand, that carries on those mills?

A. Yes, sir.

Q. Does the corporation own the real estate?

A. They own the real estate at Abbott village and part of the real estate at Frye village.

Q. Who owns the rest of the real estate at Frye village?

A. Mr. Smith.

Q. What is the capital of the corporation?

A. $500,000.

Q. What is its business?

A. The business is flax-spinning. The goods manufactured are chiefly shoe threads, sewing twines, and carpet yarns. We manufacture various other goods.

Q. Do you manufacture all these goods at all the mills, or are certain mills devoted to certain of the manufactures?

A. The flax goods are spun principally at Abbott village; what we call tow goods at Frye village, mostly.

Q. How long have the mill privileges been used?

A. The privileges at Abbott village have been used ever since the settlement of the town, I believe.

Q. And the one at Frye village?

A. That was purchased by our president, I believe, in 1823 or 1824.

Q. How long has your company carried on business at these mills?

A. The flax-spinning business has been carried on about 46 years; I think since 1835. Previous to that, John Smith carried on the business of manufacturing cotton machinery.

Q. How many men are employed in all these mills?

A. They employ from 300 to 350 persons. About half are men.

Q. What proportion of the population of those two villages is dependent upon your mills?

A. Well, I think the whole of Abbott village.

Q. Which consists of how many?

A. I am not able to state the number.

Q. I understand the population is 400. Is it all dependent on your mill?

A. Almost every one, I think. We employ at Abbott village people who live over at Andover, that don't live in Abbott village, are not able to get tenements in Abbott village; so there is rather more than the population of Abbott village dependent upon those mills.

Q. And at Frye village?

A. Nearly all the population there.

Q. How much do you understand that to be?

A. I [think that more than one-third of our operatives are there. I can't state the number.

Q. What proportion of the people in the village are dependent on your mill?

A. Nearly all. There is no other business carried on there except the stores, and the stores are supported entirely by the people there.

Q. What use do you make of the water of the river?

A. We use it for running our water-wheels as far as it will go, and piece out with steam.

Q. For what other purpose?

A. For washing our goods at our bleachery.

Q. Can you give the committee, Mr. Torr, an idea of how much water per day is used in your mills for bleaching purposes?

A. I will say, in the first place, that the water used for bleaching purposes has to be clean, and for that purpose we are obliged to draw it below the head, so as to get rid of the scum. The water from Stevens' mill comes down and covers the water with an oily scum, which we can't use. I think we use at Frye village about 2,000,000 gallons a day in bleaching ; what we call gray bleaching.

Q. Do you make white bleached goods there?

A. We make what is called for. If there should be a demand for those goods we should have to supply it.

Q. Then you would need at least 4,000,000 gallons a day at those two places for bleaching purposes alone?

A. Yes, sir.

Q. Do you use the water at the upper mills for bleaching purposes?

A. No, sir.

Q. Do you make any other use of the water at the upper mill except for power?

A. No, sir ; that is all.

Q. Now, is there any substitute that you can make for the river water for bleaching purposes?

A. No, sir.

Q. Supposing that the water of the river should be taken away, whether you could continue your manufacture there?

A. I think our bleachery would have to go. I don't know where else we could get water to supply 3,000,000 or 4,000,000 gallons a day, and if our bleachery goes, all the other business will have to go with it, because it is absolutely necessary to have the bleachery connected with the mills.

Q. In regard to power, do you have steam-engines at your mills?

A. We have three.

Q. In all, three?

A. Three in all ; two in Abbott village and one at Frye village.

Q. What part of the year have you been obliged to use those engines?

A. We use the engine at Frye village all the time, except in the spring when the water is very high.

Q. How is it at the other mills?

A. There we use it when the water falls short. Last year we used it nine months, I think.

Q. Suppose that you could use steam for power, where could you get water to make steam if the water of the river is taken away?

A. Nowhere except from the Shawsheen.

Q. Supposing the Shawsheen is taken away, is there any source where you could get water enough to make steam?

A. I think not.

Q. So that, practically, taking away the river would require the removal of your establishment?

A. It would.

Q. Whether or not, aside from the effect upon the people of the place, and the pecuniary interests there, the establishments have acquired a reputation as identified with that place?

A. Our goods are known all over the United States as "Andover Goods," "Andover Shoe Threads," "Andover Twines." That is not our trade mark, but that is the name the goods are known by in trade.

Q. And whether it would be a serious injury, even if you were to go elsewhere and set up your establishment, and lose that name?

A. It would be a serious injury.

Q. What is the amount of your manufacture a year?

A. Last year we used 2,700,000 pounds of flax and tow.

Q. Where do this tow and flax come from?

A. It is imported, about nine-tenths of it.

Q. What is the amount of your sales?

A. It is from $500,000 to $800,000 a year. In regard to a small supply of water, I think if the water was diminished, we should be entirely at the mercy of the man who owns the Ballardvale works, because he could hold it back, and keep the water entirely away from us. As I understand, that whole pond at Ballardvale has a capacity of 40,000,000 gallons, and, if he should run that off over his wheel to save steam, and then undertake to hoard up water, we should be entirely out of water until his pond was full again, and it might be thirty or forty days before there was rain again, and, during that time, I don't know where we could get any water. We should be entirely at his mercy. He could stop our works, if our business was good and his business was poor, and make us share with him. We should be continually subject to vexation. Even now, with the water as it is, we have to put on our engines when we want more power. When his water comes down in the morning when he begins to run, it drains down on us, and it takes some little time for it to drain down from Ballardvale to us. Our pond is small, and, in running, we run it down very quickly, and when we have lost our head, we have lost a great part of our power.

Cross-examination.

By Mr. HAMMOND. — This property is owned by the Smith & Dove Manufacturing Co.?

A. Yes, sir.

Q. How long have they owned it?

A. They bought the Abbott village property in 1846, I think.

Q. And have been operating it as a corporation ever since?

A. Not as a corporation. Smith, Dove & Co. was the first firm that run it.

Q. I asked how long the Smith & Dove corporation have operated it?

A. It was turned into a corporation about 15 years ago. The members of the firm became members of the corporation.

Q. That was the Abbott village mill?

A. Yes, sir.

Q. Is there more than one mill there?

A. Two.

Q. With one dam?

A. One dam; yes, sir.

Q. And one at Frye village?

A. Yes, sir; one dam there.

Q. Let us see if I remember the geography right. Abbott Mills village dam is nearer than the other?

A. About one mile nearer.

Q. You have been bothered a good deal this summer by the Ballardvale mill keeping back the water, haven't you?

A. We are bothered almost always in summer time when the water is short.

Q. Have you used 2,000,000 gallons of water a day for bleaching purposes at Frye village this season?

A. I can't say that we have done that every day. That is the capacity of our bleachery; and sometimes we run it full and sometimes we don't.

Q. Have there been 2,000,000 gallons a day there to use?

A. I can't say.

Q. Haven't you any idea about it?

A. I have no idea of what has been running in the river.

Q. Have you any idea whether 2,000,000 gallons have been used?

A. 2,000,000 have been used some days, I think. We are crowded with work sometimes. We have orders for our goods, and we have to put them through.

Q. When you say you use 2,000,000 gallons a day, do you mean you use it on an average, or 2,000,000 gallons when you use it?

A. We have no means of keeping back what we don't use.

Q. How many days in a month do you use 2,000,000 gallons a day?

A. It depends upon the orders we get. If we get orders, we run our bleachery full, and if the orders fall off, we run less.

Q. Is that the most definite answer you can give?

A. Yes.

Q. Your mind don't fix itself upon any number of days?

A. No, sir.

Q. And that is the best information you can give the committee about it, is it — that you don't know?

A. No, I am not able to say. I don't say that we do it all the time. That is the capacity of our bleachery, and a good deal of the time we run it at its full capacity.

Q. What you mean is, your mill is capable of running or using 2,000,000 gallons a day?

A. Yes, sir.

By the CHAIRMAN. — Do you think you use that amount half the time every month?

A. I should think that the past year we had nearly half the time. I am not quite sure of that. I wouldn't make any definite statement, because it is not a matter that comes under my observation.

By Mr. HAMMOND. — Is your station at the mill?

A. My business is at the office.

Q. At Boston?

A. We have no office at Boston. We sell our goods in Andover. We have an office there.

Q. So you can't state much from observation, personally, about it, but only what you have been told?

A. I have been about there a good deal, and I have a general knowledge.

Q. Is your general knowledge on other matters any better than it is on this?

A. The point I make there is, we are obliged to have 2,000,000 gallons to bleach our gray goods, and when we don't do that, we don't save the water for future use. It don't help us at all We have no way of storing what we fail to use for future use, and if the quantity is diminished, the capacity of our business is diminished.

Q. Isn't it a fact that 2,000,000 gallons a day didn't run down that river this summer?

A. Not without being used by us in some shape.

Q. Suppose you used it all, was the capacity of the river 2,000,000 gallons a day there this last summer?

A. I don't know how large a quantity 2,000,000 gallons is, spread over the river.

Q. Your mill at Frye village is entirely operated by steam now?

A. No, sir. The steam is used to piece out the water.

Q. Can you give me the relative horse-power furnished by the water and by the steam at Frye village?

A. No, I am not able to do that.

Q. I should like your best judgment?

A. The power of our water-wheels, all of them, I think, is about 370 horse-power; the whole of them at both villages; five wheels at Abbott village, and, I think, four at Frye village, — nine wheels.

Q. What is the water-power at Frye village, do you know?

A. It is not so large. The fall is only six feet, so we use a larger quantity of water to get the same power.

Q. I didn't know but you could tell me the horse-power at Frye village?

A. The horse-power is in the neighborhood of 75 horse-power, if we run it all in our engine.

Q. You require in your factory about 75 horse-power?

A. We have an engine capable of 100 horse-power?

Q. Do you think your water is equal to 20 horse-power?

A. I really don't know.

Q. Then you can't tell the committee whether the engines that you have there now are sufficient or not to run the mills without any water, can you?

A. I think somewhere between 75 and 100 horse-power will run our mills.

Q. As a matter of fact, don't you run them for days without any water-power, and haven't you the last summer?

A. Entirely?

Q. Yes, sir.

A. I think we have.

Q. Then the machinery which you have in there is sufficient to run the mills?

A. To run the mills; yes, sir. I think we might run the mills.

Q. The only trouble, then, at Frye village is water for bleaching purposes? That factory could be used substantially as it now stands for any other purpose that don't need water?

A. I don't know how you could get power without water. We could not make steam without water.

Q. How do you suppose mills get along that are not on the banks of a river?

A. They get water from somewhere. I understand it is proposed to take away this river, so that in the summer time there will be no water running there to amount to anything.

Q. Do you know how much water you use a day for your boilers?

A. I do not.

Q. Now, at Abbott village, you don't use the water for bleaching purposes?

A. Yes, sir.

Q. Whether you suppose you would use a million gallons a day in your boilers?

A. I won't undertake to say, because I am not a steam-engineer, and never gave any attention to the subject.

Q. Now, at Abbott village you run your engines, as I understand you, nine months in a year, substantially?

A. Yes, sir. We did last year; nine months in the year. We don't usually do that.

Q. And can you give me the relative amount of steam and water used there?

A. I cannot.

Q. Have those mills been run some days entirely by steam?

A. I am not quite sure about that. I think that some days they were run almost entirely by steam.

Q. Then, it is your belief, isn't it, although you are not sure about it, that there is steam-power there sufficient to carry the machinery already in the mills?

A. I don't think we have steam-power to run the mills quite as full as if all the machinery was on.

Q. The only inconvenience you would suffer there would be in getting water for your boilers?

A. The inconvenience would be that, after we got the goods manufactured, we couldn't sell them until they were bleached; and if we couldn't bleach them, we would have to go out of the town. The goods that are bleached are made entirely at Abbott village.

Q. Then the mills in Frye and Abbott villages are in condition, if you could get water for the boilers, to manufacture goods that don't require bleaching?

A. Yes, sir. You might do that; but our business couldn't be carried on there without plenty of water for bleaching.

Q. I should like to have you give an idea of the inconveniences you have suffered the past season from the Ballardvale mill.

A. I won't undertake to relate those inconveniences.

Q. You have suffered inconvenience from lack of water?

A. I won't undertake to say how much. I know, as a general thing, or at least I have heard it said, until the water gets down from Ballardvale, sometimes we are bothered a little. We keep it back, and use steam until we get sufficient.

Q. Is there any deed or contract, or anything as to the relations between your mills and the Ballardvale mills on this water-power question?

A. There is a contract so far as Foster's pond is concerned. Foster's pond is the place where we store up spring water. There is a contract in regard to the use which shall be made of it, and the proportions that the mills shall pay in regard to keeping it in order.

Q. Now, does Foster's pond run into the Shawsheen?

A. Yes, sir.

Q. By its natural outlet?

A. Yes, sir. That is not very large now. The water damage was divided by the contract. Then the Ballardvale folks have substantially the control of that, and they hold it up when they want to.

Q. That is not in the contract, is it?

A. The contract is that it shall be used as agreed upon by the different parties ; but I don't know that they ever met to talk it over.

Q. Then, in all other respects, your rights and the rights of the Ballardvale mills, so far as the water-supply is concerned, and water-power, are determined by the natural riparian rights, are they, on the river?

A. As far as I know.

Q. I have here a statement which purports to be a valuation of the town of Andover, and I find there is assessed to Smith, Dove, & Co., "new brick mill," "stone factory," "saw-mill," "brick store-house," "Jones house," "Abbott house," "Foster house," "Skinner house," etc., amounting in all to $84,700. I suppose that is their valuation, so far as you know, isn't it?

A. That doesn't include the lower falls.

Q. It includes all but Frye village?

A. Yes, sir. Some of those houses named there are at Frye village.

Q. Frye village is assessed to John Smith?

A. Yes, sir.

Q. Well, the first thing that is assessed to John Smith is house, barn, and corn-house, and ice-house ; is that the mill property?

A. No ; we don't use that.

Q. I see the assessment of the mill property at Frye village is $30,200. Is that what you suppose it to be assessed?

A. I don't know. I am not posted on Frye village property.

Q. It is a part of the Smith & Dove Co. property, isn't it?

A. The Smith & Dove Co. holds part of the property, and John Smith owns the falls. He is the original proprietor there, and is president of the company.

Q. All the real estate which you own there is assessed to John Smith, of the Smith & Dove Co. ?

A. Yes, sir.

Q. Now, can you give us the value of the machinery?

A. No, sir.

Q. That is not in your department?

A. I am not able to give you the value of the machinery.

Q. Don't it stand for something on your books?

A. Yes.

Q. What does it stand for on your books?

A. I have forgotten about that. We reduce it on our books so as to wipe it out. Machinery wears out very fast.

Q. You try to make an honest showing there, don't you; try not to get things too low?

A. Try not to get them too high.

By the CHAIRMAN. — Mr. Torr, does the machinery in your mill have a peculiar value to use that it wouldn't have as salable property, suppose you should sell off your property to-morrow?

A. There are very few mills in the country that could use to any advantage the machinery. There is one concern starting up at Grafton, by a Scotchman, who has recently come over here. They wouldn't buy our machinery. There is another firm in Patterson; that is an Irish house. They are the chief competitors in the business, and besides them there are some small concerns in the neighborhood of Troy, N.Y.; but there is no market for second-hand machinery in this country.

Q. If your mill was stopped, and you were to sell off the machinery, what proportion of its value to you, as now located, would it bring to you?

A. Nothing. I don't know of any parties that would buy it. There might be some machine company here and there, or some small firms on the Hudson; but I don't think these branch houses, these Scotch and Irish concerns, would buy second-hand machinery at all.

Q. Do assessors usually assess machinery at its value in the market, or its value to you?

A. I don't know.

By Mr. HAMMOND. — There is no valuation of your personal property in that list?

A. No, sir.

By COMMITTEE. — On what stream is the Grafton mill?

A. It has recently started there. I am not acquainted with the neighborhood. It is a little village called "New England Village." It is some six miles from Worcester. I have never been there at all.

Q. Do you say that you wipe out the value of your machinery on your books after a while?

A. We reduce it so as to exterminate it after a while. We don't want to value our machinery, when we can't sell it. In one sense, it is worth only what it would sell for; in another sense, if we continue to use it, it is worth more. We are constantly putting in new machinery.

Testimony of G. W. W. Dove.

By Mr. Morse. — You are interested in this same company?

A. Yes, sir.

Q. Where do you live?

A. In Andover.

Q. Have you given any attention yourself to the question as to how much water you use for bleaching purposes?

A. Yes, sir; somewhat.

Q. Will you tell the committee what your opinion is about it?

A. Well, I think we use about 2,000,000 gallons a day for bleaching and washing.

Q. Do you state that after some consideration of the question?

A. Yes, sir. I have been calculating somewhat.

Q. Have you any opinion how much you use for boiler purposes?

A. I don't remember that. The whole thing was about 2,000,000 gallons, aside from the wheels.

Q. Can you give the committee any idea of what proportion of that 2,000,000 is used for boiler purposes and bleaching purposes?

A. The largest part of it is for bleaching.

Q. Is there any other source of supply for water for your boilers except the river?

A. Not now.

Q. What is the chance of your getting water except from the Shawsheen?

A. I don't know of any chance within our means. A little manufactory there uses an engine, perhaps 15 or 20 horse-power, and during last summer they drew water from the river into two large hogsheads. It took two horses and a man every day to draw water enough for that small engine. That will give you an idea of the trouble in getting water for larger engines. We have three large engines, and if the water was taken away from the Shawsheen, we don't know where we could get water. It would be entirely impracticable to haul it.

Q. Could you get water for your bleaching purposes from any other source?

A. We could not. We should have to move away.

Q. Now, in reference to this stream, are you personally familiar with this river?

A. Yes, sir; somewhat familiar with the lower part of it.

Q. How have you made yourself familiar with it?

A. Well, I have been up and down the river in a canoe several times ; way up to Lexington and Vine brook, as far as you can go in a canoe.

Q. You have been up to where the proposed dam is to be?

A. Yes, sir.

Q. And above it?

A. Yes, sir.

Q. Will you tell the committee what tributaries there are to this river below the proposed dam?

A. Well, there are two or three little brooks there running a portion of the time ; during the summer, almost entirely dry. This last summer especially I have been over the river three or four times, and they are so insignificant it is very hard to find them. You couldn't see them unless you made an absolute hunt for them.

Q. Is there any stream that runs all the year round into the river below the proposed dam?

A. I don't remember any now. I think there is one, a little stream that runs from a little pond in Tewksbury. It may have a very small flow in dry weather in summer, but I don't know of any other. I think that one is never dry. I think there is always a little water. The other brooks that are running full now, in summer, that is, during July, August, and September, are practically dry ; so that at the time when the water is needed most, there is nothing to come from those streams, and, for manufacturing purposes, the minimum flow of the stream is what we must consider.

Q. Does any water come from Foster's pond into the Shawsheen?

A. The territory there is located in such a way that by building one or two dykes we can dyke in a large territory, and in the spring that fills up with water.

Q. How large a pond is it?

A. I don't know how may acres it measures.

Q. Is it a large or small pond?

A. A mile or two long altogether ; and then, during the dry seasons, the water is let out during the ten hours the mill is running.

Q. How much water do you get from that?

A. The gate is perhaps two feet square, and that is hoisted half way up, perhaps, or more, and when that is let out, we get it some times.

Q. Would the water that comes from that pond alone be sufficient for manufacturing purposes?

A. Oh, no, sir. That is exhausted now in a month or six weeks. We use only a small amount of it in a day of ten hours.

Q. Is there any difference in the waste of the stream and the apparent quantity flowing at the proposed dam, and at Ballardvale?

A. Very little when you get above the influence of the mill-dams, because the mill-dams cause the water to flow back a distance; but when you rise above that flow, of course the quantity of water is about the same away up above that.

Q. So that, substantially, the water that runs into the river comes into it above the proposed dam?

A. Yes, sir; almost entirely. There are some places on the river, away up, where the river appears deeper and wider than below. I have noticed that in paddling up, but there was very little addition to the water up two or three miles above this point. In fact, the two principal brooks that unite with the Shawsheen unite at this place in Lexington, one called Vine brook and the other is the Shawsheen; the branch is called Vine brook. There is no other place where you could paddle a canoe.

Cross-examination.

By Mr. HAMMOND. — Were you here when Mr. Wright testified?

A. Yes, sir.

Q. You heard Mr. Wright say that he should think there were 6,000,000 or 7,000,000 gallons went into the Shawsheen below?

A. I don't think he said that. He said there would be about that amount. I don't think he said it goes into the river. I am very sure he didn't say so, because it doesn't.

Q. Do you think he didn't say so, because you don't remember it, or because you know it does not?

A. I know it does not.

Q. How do you know it?

A. I have been over the river so many times. I was born in Andover, and have lived there all my life.

Q. And having been born in Andover, and gone over the river frequently, you are willing to state to the committee that you know the water from the water-shed of 20 square miles of the Shawsheen don't come into the Shawsheen?

A. No; that I do not say.

Q. What would be a fair statement of what you do know about it?

A. I know this: we use water that flows through an aperture of a certain size, and you can easily calculate the number of gallons that flows into the river; that is, all that passes by us. It cannot get by in any other way. Of course that is a fair measure of the quantity in the river.

Q. But is it a fair measure of where it comes from?

A. No, I think not.

Q. Now, will you tell me that you don't know that a considerable part of it comes from below where we propose to make the dam?

A. Well, the dam that you make will cut off about two-thirds of the water-shed.

Q. Suppose it does, that leaves one-third?

A. Yes, that sheds its water during a certain season of the year.

Q. It sheds its water as often as any other water-shed, and no oftener, and in about the same way?

A. About the same way.

Q. Is there any difference between the time that one-third of the water comes down and the time the other two-thirds come down?

A. I don't know that there is.

Q. Now, will you state how you know that that one-third don't get into the river?

A. I don't say it don't get into the river.

Q. Well, it does, does it?

A. I suppose it must.

Q. How much is it?

A. I don't know what the water-shed ought to yield.

Q. Mr. Wright says he has calculated it at 6,000,000 or 7,000,000 gallons a day; do you know whether that is right or wrong?

A. I don't know anything about it.

Q. Well, if that is right, you would say that got into the river, wouldn't you?

A. I don't understand you.

Q. There is about one-third of the water-shed below the dam where we propose to take it, according to your statement?

A. That is Mr. Wright's statement.

Q. Of course, you don't mean to say that the river contains more water above where we propose to put the dam than it does below?

A. No, I don't think I stated that, did I?

Q. No, but you stated that at some places above it was wider and deeper?

A. Well, the river comes to places where there are rapids, and then gets where it seems to spread out, and it would seem as if it increased, although it don't really increase, but the same quantity flows up there as down further.

Q. Now, you stated that you made a calculation of what you use for bleachery purposes?

A. Yes, sir.

Q. And that you thought it would average 2,000,000 gallons a day?

A. Yes, sir.

Q. Can you explain to me how you calculated that?

A. Yes, sir.

Q. Please do so?

A. Well, we measure the aperture through which the water flows, and the head that is above the aperture, calculating the water flowing from those dams.

Q. Well, sir, what was the aperture?

A. One aperture about a foot square, with a foot head on it. There is another pipe, about four inches in diameter, with a three-foot head upon it. Those two made, according to. my calculations, about 2,000,000 gallons a day. I wasn't very accurate about it; but that was it, in round numbers.

Q. What theory did you proceed on? Will you please state, so I can ascertain whether you are wrong in any respect?

A. Shall I go back to the beginning, and repeat the multiplication table?

Q. Such part as you think I won't understand without your repeating it. I desire to get at the manner in which you made this calculation, so if you are wrong I can ascertain it.

A. Those are the data : The wooden pipe that leads the water to the bleachery is about a foot square, I think, or a little less, and there is about a foot of head on it. The pipe that leads the water to the boilers in the bleachery is four inches in diameter, with three-foot head on it; one pipe a foot square, and one-foot head, and a four-inch circular pipe, and three-foot head.

Q. How long does it run?

A. It runs ten hours a day.

Q. Every day?

A. Every day ; six days in the week.

Q. That water is used for all the purposes for which you use water in the mill, except the wheel?

A. Yes, sir.

Q. Well, you use water for washing purposes, aside from bleaching goods?

A. The yarn is washed three or four times during the process of bleaching.

Q. For what purpose do you need this pure water, and must have it?

A. To wash the chemicals out of the yarn. Linen, in order to be bleached properly, must be treated with acids and alkalies, and then they are washed out with clean water. If any portion was left in there, it would, of course, rot the fabric, and we have to use enough clean water to wash out all the chemicals.

Q. Have you any idea how much of this water you have described is used for this process of washing out acids?

A. It is all used for that purpose.

Q. Part of it goes into the boiler, don't it?

A. Oh, for making steam, do you mean?

Q. Yes.

A. Yes, that is included in the 2,000,000 gallons.

Q. Do you know how much goes into the boiler?

A. I calculated it, but I don't remember ; a few thousand gallons a day. It is easily attainable. We know how much coal we use, and how much water a pound of coal will evaporate. I base my calculation on the amount of water that a pound of coal will evaporate ; and we know how much coal we use during the year.

Q. You have forgotten that?

A. I don't remember.

Q. Are you familiar enough with the subject to know whether 700 gallons a day is about right for a 100 horse-power engine, we will say?

A. It will depend somewhat upon what boilers you use. We use the old-fashioned boilers.

Q. Would you think that would be enough for 100 horse-power?

A. I should think that would be enough.

Q. How many horse-power have you?

A. We have about 260 in the engines.

Testimony of Moses Stevens.

By Mr. Poor. — You are the proprietor of the Marland mills, in Andover?

A. Yes, sir.

Q. How large a mill have you there? How many sets of machinery?

A. Fourteen sets.

Q. How large a production of goods do you turn out in a year?

A. About $400,000 worth.

By Committee. — What kind of manufacture?

A. Flannels.

By Mr. Poor. — And you make flannels exclusively?

A. Yes, sir.

Q. Your mills are run by water-power from the Shawsheen, principally?

A. Yes, sir.

Q. Do you use water for any other purpose than power?

A. For power and for washing, as Capt. Bradlee does.

Q. Use a good deal of water for washing?

A. Yes, sir; a good deal of it.

Q. Must you have clean water?

A. It is necessary to have clean water to wash flannel.

Q. You have an engine there, I suppose, to supplement your water-power?

A. Yes; we have two.

Q. And your mills are about half a mile below Smith & Dove's mills, at Abbott village?

A. Yes. About half-way between them and Abbott and Frye village.

Q. You are one of the proprietors of Foster's pond, are you not?

A. It came to me with that property.

Q. What do you think of that as a source of supply?

A. It is a good storage-basin; but I don't understand there is any stream running there.

Q. Is it a fact that you draw it all out at once when you do use it?

A. Well, yes; draw it out within say two or three weeks.

Q. And then is it done for the season?

A. There is no water there then. It is merely a storage-basin.

Q. How many hands do you employ in your mill?

A. One hundred and fifty.

Q. And they live in the village about your mills?

A. They live on the banks of the river.

Q. And are dependent on the mill the same as the other villages?

A. Yes, sir.

Cross-Examination.

By Mr. HAMMOND. — You are prepared to run by steam?

A. Partly.

Q. What part?

A. About one-half; perhaps a little more than one-half.

Q. Do you know the horse-power you have by steam and that which you have by water?

A. No, sir; I don't know. The whole power of our wheels is from 120 to 130 horse-power.

Q. Now, how much steam power?

A. We have got about 70 horse-power in steam-power. What we should do with it, I don't know. I don't know how steam-power is rated exactly.

Q. You have run your mills entirely by steam, I suppose, at times?

A. No, sir.

Q. You have not steam-power to do it?

A. No, sir.

Q. What do you do when there isn't water enough?

A. Well, we have generally got water enough on one side of the river to run the mill, and when there isn't, we stop two or three days.

Q. I hold this valuation of your property. Will you please look at that page, and see if I may state that to the committee as what it is valued at?

A. That is the real estate valuation.

Q. Does it include other property besides your mill property?

A. That includes nothing but real estate; no machinery.

Q. Can you tell me about the machinery?

A. The machinery probably would be valued at about $50,000.

By COMMITTEE. — How much is it assessed for in your town?

A. Much of it has been put in since the last valuation was made. I think it was assessed $15,000 last year. It was assessed $40,000 this year; $15,000 last year; and $40,000 the year before.

Mr. POOR. — I do not know but I ought to say that the assessors of Andover, in assessing all property, assess it very light.

Mr. HAMMOND. — Are they aware of the law that it is to be assessed at the full market value?

Mr. BARDWELL. — I think the law says we shall not assess on less than three quarters.

Mr. HAMMOND. — I do not know that law.

Mr. BARDWELL. — I think I have seen it.

Mr. HAMMOND. — I should like to have that, if my brother Poor is going to argue that it is right.

Mr. MORSE. — If they assess upon their view of the law, whether it is a correct view or a mistaken view, it has the same bearing upon this question.

TESTIMONY OF N. H. CRAFTS.

By Mr. TORREY. — Where do you reside, Mr. Crafts?

A. Boston.

Q. What is your occupation?

A. Civil engineer.

Q. How long have you been civil engineer?

A. Since 1849.

Q. Were you the city engineer of the City of Boston at one time?

A. Yes, sir.

Q. For how long?

A. About nine years.

Q. Have you given special attention to the source of water-supply, and schemes of supplying water for the use of cities?

A. Yes, sir; more or less, while I was connected with the department. Perhaps I have taken more or less interest in the matter since then.

Q. You are the gentleman who made an examination of the source of water-supply for the town of Watertown, and made a report in print, which has been referred to before?

A. Yes, sir.

Q. In 1874, among other sources that you mentioned in this report, is Kendall's pond. Where is that pond, Mr. Crafts?

A. It is partly in the town of Belmont, and partly in Waltham. The stream that feeds it runs out into Lexington.

Q. How far is Kendall's pond from Fresh pond?

A. I should think it was three and a half miles or four miles.

Q. Is it higher than Fresh pond?

A. Oh, yes. It is 160 feet higher at least. I have forgotten the exact figures. I think we called it 160 feet above tide-water.

Q. You estimate here, I see, that the yield of that pond would be about two and one-half millions of gallons a day, a little over that?

A. Yes, sir, upon a certain supposition.

Q. Well, you may state what you mean by that.

A. That was reckoning a certain number of inches of rain-fall in the year on the average. I think it was 15 inches, or it may have been 20. That was the common standard at the time that report was made, and it was generally indorsed by most engineers. In fact, the engineer of the City of Boston and the consulting engineers adopted that standard in regard to the Mystic basin; but Mr. Davis, who was engineer for the "additional supply," considered that 12 inches was the amount that would be used in a year of excessive drought; and I think the experience of last year showed that he was right in that respect; but, taking an average, there wouldn't be probably but one year in twenty when the amount would be as low as twenty inches.

Q. What is the average, do you think?

A. It has been common to reckon about a million gallons to a square mile. That would be somewhere in the neighborhood of 20 inches.

Q. Now, is it perfectly practicable for the City of Cambridge to secure a supply from this pond of 2,000,000 gallons a day, in your opinion?

A. Take this year and last year, and I think it would fall a little below that; but with proper storage it would probably exceed that.

Q. I believe it has been testified here that the Cambridge Water Works are connected now by a pipe with the Boston works?

A. I have understood so.

Q. Now, do you see any difficulty in the City of Cambridge procuring a supply of two or three million gallons a day from the City of Boston for several years to come?

A. I see no difficulty so far as the amount of water is concerned, and connections and appliances. If there is any difficulty I suppose it relates to the terms of the contract.

Q. It is practicably to be done with the consent of both cities, is it?

A. Yes, sir.

Q. You have heard our testimony in this case, haven't you?

A. I was here present yesterday, during the hearing, and to-day.

Q. Were you here the first day?

A. I was not.

Q. You know what the scheme is of taking the water of the Shawsheen river and carrying it to Cambridge?

A. I know it in a general way. I haven't even seen the report of the engineer of Cambridge. I understand substantially that it was proposed to take about 30 square miles of the water-shed as the source of supply, and they reckoned that it would yield a certain amount of water sufficient for Boston and Cambridge.

Q. You heard the testimony put in yesterday by the City of Boston?

A. Yes, sir.

Q. I wish you would state to the committee, in your own way, your view of these respective schemes, the practicability and advisability of them, considering other sources of supply that are available.

A. Well, my own judgment is, that the City of Boston has water enough at its command to-day, without seeking for any new sources, providing they will make a proper use of it; but if the present waste is continued, that is another question. It seems to me this whole matter hinges upon what is a legitimate supply for all ordinary and useful purposes. I think that the standard of what constitutes a liberal supply of water among engineers to-day is less than what it was five or ten years ago. That is, I think it is being demonstrated by the experience of such cities as Providence, Fall River, Lowell, and Lawrence, and other cities of that character, that from thirty to forty gallons to an inhabitant is an ample and liberal supply, and I find from the testimony introduced yesterday that Mr. Joseph P. Davis, formerly city engineer, has given that as his opinion, although when he made his estimates for the Sudbury river, I think he reckoned upon sixty gallons per person. That has been the common practice, to reckon from sixty to seventy gallons a person as the basis; but, as I said before, the experience of the cities which have introduced metres to a considerable extent, or encouraged their use, has shown that an average of a less amount than that is ample for all useful purposes; and if you look at the experience of European cities, you will not find a single city in Europe that goes up to anything like the American standard; and my judgment is that forty gallons is an ample supply, and if you take fifty gallons as the amount, Boston has got a supply for over fifty years; and if we take Cambridge, we have a supply for that city certainly, it seems to me, sufficient for fifty years to come.

Q. Now, can you give the committee the amount of water used per inhabitant in some other cities? [Showing witness a table of statistics.] Is that supposed to be correct?

A. Yes, sir; I have no reason to doubt that.

Q. I see by this table, Mr. Crafts, the amount of water used *per capita* varies from twenty gallons in Taunton to 119 in Chicago. Boston is given at from seventy-five to eighty-one. Now, do you know any reason why the City of Boston requires more water *per capita* than the City of Philadelphia?

A. No, sir; I don't.

Q. The City of Philadelphia used sixty-two gallons *per capita* with a population of 850,000, in 1878. Isn't that quite a large manufacturing city?

A. I am not enough acquainted with Philadelphia to say. I think the city has not so large a number of manufactories, in proportion to the population, as the City of Boston. I couldn't say as to that.

Q. What experience have you had, either practically or from investigation, with the use of metres?

A. I have had no practical experience in regard to the different styles of meters in use. I learn from cities and places where they are generally used, from their reports and from conference with parties interested in them, that they are regarded as entirely practicable, and they wouldn't do without them. It is a matter of great importance, where a city has to pump its water, whether they pump forty gallons to an inhabitant or eighty, and it is important in many repects. The City of Providence, and I think, perhaps, the City of Fall River, have as large a percentage as any, and in Fall River their consumption per head of their population is not up to thirty gallons, I think. It was not a year or two ago. Twenty-six was the last I saw, I think, and reckoning the amount per consumer, I think it only runs up to about thirty-five.

Q. Now, do you know any reason why a meter system cannot be as well applied in the City of Boston as in any other cities where it is generally used?

A. I see no reason why it cannot.

Q. Do you know any case where some citizens of Boston tried the water metres as an experiment, to see how much water was used in their families?

A. While I was city engineer, at the time the water works were under the management of the water board, there were seven members of the board had metres attached to their houses, with a view to ascertaining what was a fair and legitimate use for domestic purposes, and I kept the records of the metres for about sixteen months, and the average of those families was about 24.6, say 25 gallons to a person, and it would be even less than that if the highest had been thrown out. That was in the case of Mr. Norcross; and it very much surprised him that he led all the rest of the board in the consumption per head. His ran up to forty gallons. It was investigated, and it was found that there was a leak. When that was fixed, it ran down to about as low as the rest. Probably twenty-three or twenty-four gallons would be the average.

Q. While they were using metres, did they try to economize particularly, or did they use the ordinary amount of water?

A. I can't say as to that. I presume all the families kept servants, and the matter was left to their discretion. I think the lowest was eighteen or nineteen gallons. That was Mr. Wadsworth's. Mr. Thorndike's was about twenty-one. That, it seems to me, is a fair measure of what would be required; and, in fact, estimates made by engineers give it as a lower amount than that. I think Mr. —— puts it at twenty gallons per person for strictly domestic uses. Then all the hotels, manufactories, etc., are metred. For 1879, the average daily amount of water metred was three million gallons, and that, divided by the number of population, would amount to about seven gallons per person, which should be added to the domestic use. Then, aside from that, there are some public uses, some fountains, street watering, fires, and so on; but it seems to me that eight gallons a day ought certainly to be a liberal allowance to cover all those things.

Q. Shouldn't you, then, as an engineer of experience in these matters, advise the City of Boston and the City of Cambridge, before going to this large expense of taking Shawsheen river, to investigate this question of metres, and see if a great amount of water cannot be saved without interfering with the good of other people?

A. Certainly I should. In fact, I understand that the City of Boston is an applicant now to the Legislature for permission to put on a system of metreage; and, in fact, it appeared yesterday in the testimony that they have been to great expense in putting on Deacon metres, which are in use, and reducing the consumption thirty or forty per cent. I think it is unwise, too, for the city to embark in any new undertaking for a water-supply, until they see what can be done in regard to saving the waste of water. There is no question in my mind but one-half, or more than one-half, this last year, has been wasted. I won't say entirely. I don't mean to say maliciously wasted, or that in all cases it is negligence, but owing to defective fixtures, the pipes being improperly put into the houses to avoid danger of freezing.

Q. That was the opinion of Mr. Davis, wasn't it, when he was city engineer in 1879?

A. That was what he expressed in the report he made.

Q. Considering the amount of water which Boston has now on hand, and that Cambridge is connected with the Boston supply, and all other existing facts in the two cases, do you think there is any danger in allowing both those cities to wait another year in order to try the experiment of saving water? Is there any danger in allowing them to wait another year before they get additional water, and letting them try the experiment of saving what they now have?

A. I don't think there is any danger. In fact, I think it is the wisest thing to do.

Q. Mr. Crafts, something has been said in this case about allowing a million gallons a day to run down the Shawsheen river. I should like to ask you if a million gallons a day couldn't run through a 12-inch pipe?

A. Yes, sir.

Q. At what elevation? With what fall?

A. Well, a fall of one foot in 560 or 565 ; or, perhaps, one foot in 500.

Q. If there is any other suggestion you would like to make to the committee, you can do so.

A. I don't think of anything more.

By Mr. NETTLETON. — Mr. Crafts, is there any way of saving except by metres?

A. You mean metres on private houses?

Q. Yes. You spoke of waiting a year in order to give Boston an opportunity to see what could be done in the way of saving water. Is there any way of saving except by the use of metres?

A. Well, perhaps a system of inspection. I don't know how rigidly that is kept up at the present time. I think in 1864 or '65, the Water Board put on inspectors, who cautioned the people against extravagance in the use of water, and exercised what authority they had to prevent waste, and they reduced the amount from 16,000,000 to 12,000,000, or nearly that.

Q. For aught you know, that same system of inspection is now carried on?

A. I don't know. I think not so rigidly.

Q. What opportunity have you had for observing that? Have you observed the difference in the mode of inspection?

A. No, sir.

Q. Then, apart from inspection, is there any other method, excep by the use of metres?

A. I think by the use of these district metres which is proposed.

Q. I will include the whole system. Is there any method of saving except by metres?

A. No, sir; metres and by inspection.

Q. Now, in the cities which you have cited, where the metre system has been used, are they not cities where they have recently introduced water, and where the metres have been put on as the works were constructed?

A. Yes, sir; except Worcester. I don't know whether Worcester is included in that statement or not.

Q. What would be the cost of the metre to each taker?

A. I presume that would depend upon the metre used. I am not familiar with the prices. I think there are metres furnished now at Pawtucket and Providence at about $15 apiece.

Q. Proper metres?

A. Yes, sir.

Q. Proper for the head of water in Boston?

A. The head in Pawtucket is three times what it is in Boston.

Q. For the quantity of water running in Boston?

A. Yes, sir. I may be mistaken in the price; it may be $20.

Q. What would be the cost of putting those on?

A. That I can't say.

Q. How long time would it take to put metres on 40,000 service-pipes, with the pipes now laid in the ground?

A. I don't think it would be necessary to put them on to every house, or all at once. I think the fact that they were put on in cases where there was reason to suppose there was waste, would do a great deal toward checking the waste.

Q. Then you would discriminate, would you? If you found one family using water wastefully, you would put it on there?

A. I think that is the authority asked for.

Q. And that is the way you would have them discriminate?

A. Yes, sir.

Q. Do you know whether they can use the same metre with the water we have here that they use in Fall River with the water they have there?

A. I know no reason why not.

Q. Do you know anything about the different corrosive effects of the water between here and there?

A. No, sir, I don't.

Q. Now, do you know that we have to use brass linings where metres are used?

A. I know we do use them.

Q. And whether or not this would increase considerably the expense?

A. Yes, sir, I should suppose it would. It depends, I presume, upon the nature of the metre used. I am not prepared to say which metre I should approve, or to go into the relative merits of the meters; but I do know it has been found practicable in other cities to introduce them, and it has effected a great saving in the use of water, and I see no reason why Boston can't do it. If they can't do it all at once, they can do it gradually.

Q. There are 41,000 takers in the city. Now, what in your opinion would it cost to put on these metres through the city?

A. I presume, if put on all at once, it would cost something over $1,000,000.

Q. Now, if we could get a supply of 12,000,000 gallons for from $400,000 to $500,000 expense, which do you think would be the more satisfactory to the users of the water, — to have that additional supply at that expense, or to have a limited supply with the metres, where it would cost $1,000,000 to put them in?

A. I think, looking at the future interests of the city, in the point of economy, it is exceedingly desirable to reduce the waste of water to the lowest possible degree. I think it is not fair to look at the matter of first cost. As you keep adding to the supply, the inducement is to waste, and so we have been going on making additions to the supply, and with every additional supply, the rate of water has gone up, and I think the future interests of Boston require that it should be stopped. A million dollars spent for metres to-day would be of greater advantage to the city than $400,000 for the Shawsheen river.

Q. The cost of repairs would be something added to the cost?

A. The cost for repairs would be no greater than under the old method.

Q. You don't see any reason why Boston should use any more water than those other cities?

A. I don't know as I said that. Yes, I will say that I see no reason why Boston should use more water per head than the city of Providence.

Q. Now, does not the amount of water used depend upon the miles of pipes and number of takers in the various cities?

A. It depends upon the number of takers; it don't depend upon the miles of pipe.

Q. Very well; call it the number of services.

A. That is not an absolute guide. Take a city like Fall River: one service there may answer for a whole tenement-house. In manufacturing villages one service supplies a whole boarding-house. In a city made up chiefly of single families there is a larger proportion of services. If you can get at the actual number of consumers, that is the fairest basis.

Q. The population of the City of Boston at 12 o'clock in the day time, and through working-hours, is nearly double what it is at 12 o'clock at night, on account of the several hundred thousand people, I suppose, who come into Boston as workmen and workwomen, etc., during the day, merchants and others?

A. I think the number is not so great now as it was before annexation.

Q. It is very much larger at 12 o'clock, noon, than it is at 12 o'clock at night?

A. Yes, sir.

Q. And would it, in your opinion, be an unfair estimate to say the population is at least 150,000 greater in the day time than it is at night?

A. Perhaps not.

By the CHAIRMAN. — How much do you know about that?

A. I have no more means of knowing the increase of the population at 12 o'clock at noon than any member of the committee or anybody else.

By Mr. NETTLETON. — Had your attention been called to that when you said you had been able to discover no reason why Boston should use any more water than other cities and towns?

Mr. MORSE. — Your question assumes that the population of other cities and towns is the same at noon as it is at night.

Q. You have drawn your illustration from Fall River?

A. Providence and Fall River. Providence is one of the most marked instances.

Q. Now, take the population of Providence, — do you know whether the working population of Providence comes from outside the city, as in Boston?

A. No, sir, I don't.

Q. You spoke of tenement-houses in Fall River. Isn't it the fact that nearly all the employés in the mills in Fall River live right there in the corporation blocks?

A. I presume it is.

Q. And that the additional number of population in Fall River per day is very much less, proportionately, than the increase in Boston? and isn't it the fact that the increase in Boston is very much larger than that of any of the other cities in the Commonwealth to which you have referred?

A. I think it is somewhat larger.

Q. And wouldn't that account, then, for the increased amount of water used in Boston per day?

A. It would account for a very small fraction, because these people who come in, — what may be called the floating population of Boston,

— people who are coming in and passing through the city, and staying a short time, or who come in every day and go out at night, — the amount of water that should be charged to that population, it appears to me, is included in the amount of metred water; for that population, so far as they make use of the water, make use of it at hotels, restaurants, and places of that sort, and all those places are metred.

Q. Are you sure of that?

A. Certainly. It includes a great deal more than that, for that includes shipping and other uses, and there is only 3,000,000 for that. Now, you may take that whole 3,000,000 and then deduct your floating population, and you will get a fair statement. You may deduct the amount of metred water, and charge that to the floating population. That is all they use.

Q. Now, the water is used during the working-hours of the day most largely?

A. Yes, sir; but it is wasted by night in a ratio that is certainly up to three-quarters of the day consumption. That has been proved by experiments of the Water Board here in Boston.

Q. In the winter time?

A. No, sir: at other times in the year experiments were made. I have forgotten the exact figures.

The CHAIRMAN. — That is in testimony before the committee, fully as strong as that.

WITNESS. — That is the consumption after everybody is supposed to be in bed. Certainly there cannot be a very large population around town, after all those out-of-town people are at home and asleep.

Q. Now, you say that Cambridge might be supplied from the Boston water-supply. You mean from the Sudbury river and from Farm pond?

A. Yes, sir.

Q. And the town of Framingham might also be supplied in your opinion?

A. Yes, sir.

Q. And all the towns along the Sudbury river might be supplied in the same way, and still Boston have plenty of water?

A. I don't see why not.

Q. What is the supply from Sudbury river?

A. About 60,000,000 gallons a day.

Q. What do you take as the average daily consumption per individual for Boston?

A. Eighty gallons in 1879. I think eighty-seven last year.

Q. You would reduce that by metres from 80 to what per person?

A. I have said that 40 gallons is a liberal supply. I don't mean to say that in an old city like this, by the use of metres it can be reduced 40 gallons. I think there should be a distinction there. Although that is a liberal supply, I think probably it wouldn't be practicable to reduce it below 50, but I think it would be possible to reduce the consumption to 50 gallons a person.

Q. Are you familiar with Sudbury river and Farm pond?

A. Yes; with Farm pond somewhat. The upper part of the. Sudbury river I am not.

Q. With the present facilities that Boston has for the storage of water, can Boston go on and supply all the towns along its sources of water-supply?

A. Certainly, if you are using only 50 gallons to an inhabitant. If you are using 80 or 100, that is another thing.

Q. Well, during this summer you have had occasion to notice that all the ponds and reservoirs were very low, I suppose?

A. Yes, sir.

Q. And that the City of Boston, without furnishing Cambridge or Framingham, had reached the limit of the supply?

A. Yes; I have understood that to be the case, the basins were drawn down low.

Q. And you would cure that all by the use of metres?

A. I think so.

Q. At a cost of something over a million dollars, to say nothing of the repairs that would be required?

A. It wouldn't be an immediate outlay of a million dollars, but that, together with the reduction of waste by the district metres, and finding out where it is, and what it is, and what would remedy it, would do a great deal of this work.

Q. How many years would it take you to carry through this system?

A. Well, I should say it could be effected in as short time as you could build your storage-basins.

Q. How many years?

A. Three or four years; three years, possibly.

Q. Then you would consider, as an engineer, the wiser course for the City of Boston would be, instead of building any new storage-basin, to put in a system of metres?

A. I think that would be the wiser.

Q. And you have no interest in metres at all?

A. No, sir.

Q. And haven't advocated their use in the City of Boston?

A. No further than in a general way. I have always considered it for the interest of the City of Boston.

Q. Have you not advocated their use in the City of Boston and other cities?

A. Not in any public way that I know of.

Q. Haven't you been before city governments for the purpose, in a public or private way, of urging the introduction of metres?

A. No, sir.

Q. Nor any particular metre?

A. No, sir.

Q. Haven't you been consulted as an engineer in regard to that matter?

A. I have.

Q. And by owners or parties interested in the metres?

A. Yes, sir.

Q. Weren't you advertised as consulting engineer of one of those companies?

A. I think my name was appended to a circular to that effect.

Q. Was that done without your authority?

A. It was, sir, and against my request. I desire to state simply in regard to that, an inventor in the City of Boston owned a patent for a metre which he claimed had peculiar advantages over other metres, and he applied to me to make certain drawings, which were in my line of business. He had already got out a patent for the metre, but he wished a working-drawing of it made, if possible, to experiment with, and I made this drawing. He also requested me to make some examination with regard to the accuracy of the metre, which I did, and I did it simply in the ordinary transaction of my professional business. As to using my name, the gentleman who did it was kicked out of the concern in three weeks after, as being a sort of adventurer. That is the only connection I ever had with any metre of any kind or nature.

Cross-examination.

By Mr. HAMMOND. — I would like to read a few lines from this Watertown report, pages 26 and 27 : " With a view to ascertain the legitimate requirements for household uses among a class of people who use the water freely, — having all the modern appliances, set wash-tubs, bath-tubs, water-closets, and bowls in every chamber, with hot and cold water, — metres were attached to the dwellings of each member of the Cochituate Water Board in 1865-6, and a record kept of the amount," — and that you have stated in substance here : " In 1866, the amount of water used in the City of Boston for manufacturing purposes, hotels, saloons, and all large establishments where it is measured by metre, was, in round numbers, 2,000,000 gallons per day, while the whole amount consumed was a little over 12,000,000, showing that the ratio of the domestic and miscellaneous smaller requirements, to the manufacturing and larger requirements, is as six to one ; so that, if we assume, say 30 gallons per day for each inhabitant, and add one-sixth for manufacturing and miscellaneous uses, we should have 35 gallons per head per day as a liberal supply. If large quantities are used, as in Cambridge, for watering the streets, and for sprinkling lawns and gardens, operating fountains, etc., there should be a still further allowance; and to cover all such requirements, and any unforeseen contingencies, I should, for the purposes of a town like yours, estimate the requirements at from 40 to 45 gallons per day for each inhabitant; and, in measuring the capacity of any proposed source of supply, I should go still further, and assume a maximum requirement of 50 gallons per day per head." Is that your view now?

A. I think if I were selecting a source of supply, I should not put that down as being what I should call a liberal supply, but I think there are many things that enter into a decision as to a source of water-supply, — many unforeseen things that should be provided for.

Q. Now, would you recommend a city which has its consumption reduced down to 40 gallons per day to use metres?

A. No, I should not.

Q. Don't you think that is about as low as it ought to go?

A. In a city like Boston I should, or a city like Cambridge.

Q. Don't you think that shows an economical use of water there?

A. I think it shows a very liberal use of water. I don't think it shows an economical use.

Q. But there is no waste in the sense in which you properly use the term?

A. I should say there is not much waste. I suppose it is a common practice to make allowance for unavoidable waste.

Q. Now, you stated that you thought Kendall's pond would be good, as I understand you to calculate, for not quite 2,000,000 gallons?

A. I think about 1,800,000 gallons. That is based on 12 inches. You can get the proportions.

Q. I am informed that the Cochituate water-shed didn't yield but 10,500,000 last year?

A. Well, that is one year in 40 or 50. I think it is within the power of most cities and towns to curtail to cover such an extraordinary year as that.

Q. But you reckon at 12 inches?

A. Yes, sir. I don't think we should take into account such an exceptional year as the last one.

Q. Do you know the character of the meadows upon which the reservoirs would be placed, if the Kendall's-pond scheme should be carried out?

A. I think there is more or less depth of peet. I think it is stated in that report.

Q. Is it certain in your mind, that that water would be good stored there over that peet?

A. The storage there would be precisely as the storage you get on the Sudbury river and other places.

Q. It isn't certain that it will be good water, is it?

A. I don't know why it shouldn't be.

Q. Well, it is objectionable, isn't it?

A. What, sir?

Q. The character of the soil upon which the reservoir must be built?

A. The reservoirs here would be simply built by forming a dam. I think that matter has been very fully discussed in various places, and decided that flooding the land one or two years will get rid of all the objectional features 'in the characteristics of the soil.

By COMMITTEE. — Do you know anything about the water-supply at Arlington?

A. I know that they get their supply by damming up a stream somewhat smaller in size, of the general characteristics of Kendall's pond.

Q. The character of the water?

A. No, sir, I don't.

By Mr. HAMMOND. — There was another question I wanted to ask you. In this table, which I suppose both sides will use, the names of Taunton, Newton, Fall River, etc., appear. I suppose, as a matter of fact, it is not exactly a fair thing to estimate the number of gallons to each inhabitant, unless we take into account the number of years in which the water-works have been in existence, is it?

A. I don't think that is a sound way of getting at it. Where it is possible, I have generally adopted this plan: if the water reports which come to me give the number of families supplied, I think that is the better way to get at it; to take the number of families, and multiply by five, and you will get at the actual consumers very nearly.

Q. Do you know how long water-works have existed in Newton?

A. Two or three years.

Q. And in Fall River?

A. Six or eight years.

Q. In Cambridge we have had water-works for 15 or 20 years?

A. Yes, sir.

Q. I suppose you would expect the longer water-works existed the greater the percentage of people who take the water, wouldn't you?

A. Certainly. I think in the case of Cambridge we must have 90 per cent., perhaps 95; probably as high as that in Boston. I think in the towns of Brookline and Arlington they have in five years since their works were built about seven-tenths, something less than three-quarters.

Q. Do you think, considering the probable growth of Cambridge, that it would be advisable for Cambridge to expend money to take Kendall's pond for water?

A. Not unless that basin could be used afterwards as a receiving reservoir in connection with any further extensions; certainly not as permanent.

Q. Assume it to be a fact that Fresh pond is liable to be so diminished that we could not use it, and that Cambridge is looking around for water to meet that contingency as well as others, would you say it was advisable for her to go to Kendall's pond?

A. I don't think I have the information to answer that question.

Q. What information do you mean?

A. Well, I should, in the first place, want to know whether that basin could be available as a part of a future supply. I estimated the cost of the land and basin there to be somewhere from $37,000 to $50,000 in the case of Watertown. If Cambridge should take its supply, if there should be a supply taken from the Merrimac river some future day, or from some more distant point, with a view to supplying the towns and cities along the line, the reservoir might be of advantage in that case as a receiving reservoir.

Q. Assuming that Cambridge needs 3,000,000 gallons every day, and takes that from a supply which is rather precarious, and so reported by those who examine it, and it seeks a good supply, would you recommend Kendall's pond?

A. No, sir.

Q. Well, where would you go?

A. Until I was fully satisfied as to the best course, I should get a supply from the City of Boston, if I had the means of doing it.

Q. Suppose the City of Boston told you they hadn't got it, and wouldn't give it to you, what then?

Mr. MORSE. — Apply to the Legislature.

A. I don't think they could say that they haven't got it.

Q. Suppose they did, is there any other place that you know of except the Shawsheen?

A. I havn't looked into the merits of the Shawsheen.

Q. Suppose there is a report that the Shawsheen is good water, and Mr. Chesbrough, whom you well know, says it is a proper place of supply, do you know of any other.

A. There may be others that would cost more. There is the Concord river and the Merrimac.

Q. Do you think the Concord is fit?

A. I can't answer that question.

Q. Do you know why it is not as fit as the Sudbury? Wouldn't it be more expensive?

A. I don't know. I am not prepared to say even what the expense of the Shawsheen project is.

By COMMITTEE. — What town is Kendall's pond in?

A. Partly in Belmont and partly in Waltham.

Q. What is the area of the pond?

A. The ponds now are small. Their dams are in such a condition they don't hold water. Their present area is seven or eight acres.

By Mr. HAMMOND. — It can be made available from the fact that you can put a dam across there somewhere and make a pond?

A. Yes, sir.

By COMMITTEE. — Where does it empty now?

A. Charles river. This is called, in my report, "Beaver brook." There has been some confusion as to names. It is known in that vicinity now as Clematis brook.

G. W. W. DOVE. — *Recalled.*

By Mr. MORSE. — Mr. Dove, will you tell the committee whether there is any difference in the character of the water-shed above and below where this proposed dam would be on the Shawsheen?

A. Well, the character of the soil at Tewksbury, on both sides of the river, is sandy and open. Up in Lexington and Concord there is more marshy meadow land. Referring to the water-shed question again, as I understand it, if all parts of the water-shed yielded the same amount of water per square mile, if you cut off two-thirds of it, you might assume that the other third would give you a proportionate amount of water. If the whole water-shed gave you 2,000,000 gallons, and you cut off two-thirds, the other third would give you 700,000. But I have noticed that after a heavy rain we never get the whole of the water until about three days after the rain has fallen. The water continues to rise for three days after the rain has fallen, until we get the highest water, and then it gradually goes down. We know that the water in the upper part is held in reserve, and given out slowly; but that which falls in the lower part sinks into the ground, and doesn't go into the river.

Q. Then you think that while, as a matter of theory there may be one-third of the water-shed below this dam, yet, as a matter of fact, you wouldn't get one-third of the water?

A. Yes, sir.

By Mr. HAMMOND. — Wouldn't that be the same if the water-shed were exactly the same, that you would get more water after a day or two than along at first?

A. I should think on the upper parts of the water-shed you would notice the difference quicker than the lower.

Q. Do you know whether this river is different from any other river in that respect?

A. I should think it is different, but I don't know by comparison ; but that is a fact, that the water doesn't come down until three days after it has fallen.

By COMMITTEE. — Are those three streams above Ballardvale dry in the summer?

A. I think there is one of them, a little brook, running all the year, but the others are dry. The bottom of the brook is so dry a cow could not get water enough to drink, and that is the time that the manufacturer must take his measure for water.

[Adjourned to Friday, at 10 o'clock, A.M.]

Friday, March 18, 1881.

Closing Argument for the Remonstrants.

By George A. Torrey, Esq.

Gentlemen of the Committee: —

My brother Morse and myself have divided between us the task of presenting to you the case for the remonstrants, taking no more time than either would have taken had he performed this duty alone.

I desire, in the first place, to thank you for the attention which you have paid to this case. It may have been somewhat tedious to you, — perhaps some of it consisted of repetitions; but you must remember, that when a party is defending his property, which is very dear to him, to which he is attached, and which he is in danger of losing, a little prolixity may be excusable. When I look around me in this spacious apartment, so "fearfully and wonderfully made," with every possible contrivance to add to the discomfort of its occupants, and to deprive every man who comes here of the happiness to which the constitution entitles him, it seems to me, Mr. Chairman, that it is a very fit place for the hearing of this petition. If there ever was a place which was adapted to dark designs and evil deeds, this is one; and, if our clients are to be deprived of their property, there can be no place more appropriate than this in which to do it.

The constitution of Massachusetts contains these provisions: "All men are born free and equal, and have certain natural, essential, and unalienable rights, among which may be reckoned the right of enjoying and defending their lives and liberties; that of acquiring, possessing, and protecting property; in fine, that of seeking and obtaining their safety and happiness." . . . "Each individual of the society has a right to be protected by it in the enjoyment of his life, liberty, and property, according to standing laws. . . . And whenever the public exigencies require that the property of any individual should be appropriated to public uses, he shall receive a reasonable compensation therefor."

Now, for many years, when anybody has tried to do an unconstitutional thing; when he has tried to do an unjust thing, an unlawful thing, he has been very apt to call these provisions of the constitution mere "glittering generalities," of no particular meaning; well enough in their place; a rhetorical flourish which our forefathers adopted, but of no substantial meaning or value. Now, that is by no means true. You will perceive that the constitution specifies only one contingency in which a person can be deprived of his property; that is, "whenever the public exigencies require." Now, there is some confusion of ideas, it seems to me, in regard to that provision of the constitution, and I submit to you that a great part of the petitioners' case has been put in upon the assumption that that provision means this and nothing more, viz.: That if three hundred and fifty thousand men would like to take the property of one man, they have a perfect right to do it by paying for it. If the City of Boston, or the City of Cambridge, large cities, desire to despoil the town of Andover, a small town, they have a right to do it by paying the damages. That is not the law of this Commonwealth, Mr. Chairman. It is only when the public exigencies require that you can do this thing, not when several people desire it. It would undoubtedly add to the happiness of a great many individuals, if all the property in the town of Andover were confiscated and divided among the people of Boston. Three hundred and fifty thousand people would be made happy, perhaps, if they could be happy in the reception of money from such a source; but the Legislature could not do it under any conceivable circumstances, so that the question for you to determine is not whether it would be convenient for the City of Boston or the City of Cambridge to have this water, but whether they show such a public exigency for it, that no man has a right to come here and say, "This water shall not be taken, although I am paid for it."

Now, sir, ideas have been advanced in connection with these cases which are nothing but rank socialism, when we come to follow them out to their extremes. The newspapers have reported, undoubtedly erroneously, — it cannot be true, — that a legal gentleman stated on the floor of the House, that the time had come when manufacturers must give way and give up their water for domestic purposes without compensation. Of course, that is an erroneous statement. No man would have said it, much less a lawyer, as such a statement is directly in contravention of the provisions of the constitution. That, of course, is socialism, nothing else; every many who has property which the public wants must be deprived of it, and it must be divided among the public. Now, that is not a doctrine which is to be applied to this case. The rule which we have laid down must be the only one for you to apply here, viz.: has such an exigency been shown by these two cities for this water that the people who have a right to use it, and the poor people who live upon the banks of this river and are entitled to its benefits, and can receive no compensation if it be taken from them, must give it up for these purposes? If this has been proved, I am authorized to say for my clients that nobody would more readily yield to that demand than they will. Dear as their property is to them, there is not one of them who desires to keep it.

If the City of Boston and the City of Cambridge actually need more water for domestic purposes, and cannot obtain it anywhere else without doing more damage than by taking it from this source, they are willing to give it up without criticism, without question. But it is because we say there is no such exigency shown, and because we claim that every member of the committee, although some of you live in these very cities, will be satisfied, when they come to consider this case, that no such exigency has been shown, that we confidently ask you to give the petitioners leave to withdraw.

Now, let us see, in the first place, what they ask to do. They ask to take all the water of Shawsheen river, — the whole of it. Now, they may say to you, in reply to that, "Very true ; our bill gives us leave to take all the water of this river, but everybody knows that, practically, we shall not do it." But I may say in the outset, Mr. Chairman, that it would be much better for every manufacturer on that stream to have them take every drop of water the year round, than to have them take every drop of it, as they will do, in the dry time, when we need it most and must have it, and drown us out and overflow the flats in the spring, when we do not need so much water, and when the excess is simply a nuisance. It would be better for these manufacturers if the whole stream were diverted, rather than to have a large quantity of water thrown upon then in the spring, flooding their lands, and then, in the summer, have these cities, as they will do, take every drop of it. They propose to deprive these towns of all this water for the uses which are now made of it ; they propose to stop the mills upon that stream ; they propose to deprive every agriculturist on its banks of the opportunity to use that water for watering his cattle and for domestic purposes. I am speaking the literal truth in this matter ; and the committee will see, as we proceed in the presentation of this case, that I am correct.

Now, should that be done? should these industries be annihilated? The testimony before your committee from one of those manufacturers, Capt. Bradlee, who manufactures an annual product of half a million dollars, is, that if this petition be granted, he shall undoubtedly abandon his works, rather than move to some other place. It may be said, " What does the City of Boston care if he does?" Perhaps the petitioners do not care ; but you and I care, Mr. Chairman, and every public-spirited citizen of the Commonwealth cares. Take this industry alone. Four-fifths of the fine flannels which are made in this country are made upon that spot. Do you desire those flannels to be made abroad? Do you wish them made in New Hampshire, or New York, or some other State? Do you wish to deprive the State of Massachusetts of that manufacture? Do you desire, from time time, as these cities need more water, to take it from the mill-streams, until

one after another, the mills disappear from the Commonwealth and go
to some State where they are encouraged, and where the doctrine is
not proclaimed that manufactures must give way? If you do, what
will become of the City of Boston and the Commonwealth? What
makes the City of Boston to-day? It is not agriculture; it certainly
is not commerce; it is manufacturing industry. Every mill you destroy in the country, injures the City of Boston, and injures the City of
Cambridge.

At least one-fourth of the population of the town of Andover is to
be deprived of its means of support if these mills are abolished.
Now, my friends upon the other side say, "Why, they can put in
steam-engines and draw their coal and run those mills." That is very
true. Perhaps they can, but will they? What are those mills there in
the valley of the Shawsheen for? They are there because the water is
there, and for no other reason. The mere money value of the land,
deprived of its water-power, the mere money value of the buildings,
without the machinery, is not an important item. You dry up that
stream, and the real estate is of very little value. It is not of sufficient
value to induce these manufacturers to remain on that spot, rather
than to go somewhere else where they can have water-power; and
they will be certain, gentlemen, not to locate within such a radius of
the City of Boston or the City of Cambridge, that these cities can
come and take their stream away from them a few years hence.

Now, it is said that this will not be the result. It is said that they
have taken the waters of the Sudbury river, and still there are mills
running on the Sudbury river below where they take the waters. But it
is very dangerous, Mr. Chairman, for the consumers of water to-day
to say, "Five or ten years hence we shall not need all the supply which
we are entitled to take."

In 1874, the Water Board of the City of Boston, in its annual report, used this language: —

The act passed by the Legislature, granting Sudbury river to the city, is a
very favorable and valuable one; the water-shed is singularly free from sources
of pollution, and, if any are found to exist, can be easily controlled; the water
is excellent, and the storage facilities very favorable, while the cost — predicated
upon actual and intelligent surveys — is not large, considering that our citizens
will, with it, beyond all question, secure what they all desire, — an adequate supply of pure water for the next fifty years.

And yet, in 1881, they come in here and say that they are suffering
for more water. In the face of that testimony, will these gentlemen
tell me that, in the summer time, the only time when this water is of
such immense value to us, they will not take every drop that flows
down the Shawsheen river? Will they tell us that every land owner

on that stream, below their dam, will not have an action for damages against these cities for being deprived of his water? You understand the law in that respect, Mr. Chairman and gentlemen. When this act is passed, and this water is taken, we must come for our damages. We cannot wait five, ten, fifteen, or twenty years to see whether they are going to take all that water or not. They have a right to take it all, we have a right to assume that they will take it all, and they must pay us damages for taking it all, because we have to apply for our damages within a short time after the water is taken. I say every land owner on that stream will have his action against these cities for damages, and this sum which they have testified to here as the cost of these works is a mere trifle compared with the sum which they will have to expend, if the plan of taking this water is carried out. I understand the law to be, that every man who owns land on the borders of that stream is entitled to damages. A man who owns land two rods from the bank of the river, and who is employed in one of these mills, who has no legal right of access to the river, will receive no damages, although the diversion of this water will not only deprive him of his means of subsistence, but will subject his family to sickness and death.

I thought there was some little attempt at merriment when that aged physician of Andover came here and testified to the fact that drawing down the water on the meadows would be injurious to the health of the town ; but I should like to ask the gentlemen from Boston and Cambridge two questions : In the first place, is there any practical doubt that sickness and death, to some extent, will result from depriving the meadows of the water which covers them? And if not, do they think that the exigency of these two cities to-day is sufficient to justify the taking of the life of a single individual? Would the executive officers of Cambridge or Boston slaughter one child to-day for the purpose of supplying their cities with more water if they could not get it in any other way?

But they tell us, "All this is imaginary, because we propose to allow a million gallons a day to escape over that dam, and we are willing you should put that in the bill." What is a million gallons a day? That is an amount that would flow through a twelve-inch pipe with a fall of one foot in 565, and with a greater fall it would flow through a much smaller pipe. There is no doubt that that water would pass through a six-inch pipe, with sufficient head.

How is it going to benefit the town of Andover to have a million gallons a day pass over a dam some eight or ten miles above that village? How much of that water will ever get down to the town of Andover, or to the mills of the remonstrants?

Perhaps the petitioners will go further. They might agree to allow us this million gallons a day, and, in their kindness, lay a cement or iron pipe through Andover down to the Merrimac river and supply it with faucets, so that we can draw the water for our use. Then the future historian, perusing the annals of this Commonwealth, will read, " Andover, — once a flourishing manufacturing town, situated on the Shawsheen river, is now located on a cement pipe, twelve inches in diameter, and occasionally a little water reaches the town, although most of it is lost before getting there." That would seem ridiculous, but it would be a great deal better than what is proposed, because, if the water were to run in a pipe, some of it might reach the town of Andover ; but, as the proposition now is, a great deal of it would be lost by evaporation and waste before it reached the first privilege on this stream.

They say, again, that there is a large water-shed below the proposed dam, covering a great many square miles, and, theoretically, there would be considerable water running into the Shawsheen river from that source. If theory is to govern this case, we have no objection to a theoretical taking of the water ; but, if we are going into practical questions, let us see what the fact is. As everybody knows who has investigated the matter, below where they propose to put their dam there is no water flowing into the Shawsheen of any amount ; there is no tributary that is not entirely or substantially dry in summer ; there is no perceptible water running into the stream below this dam. Why is that ? You all know what a water-shed is. They tell you such a stream or such a pond has twenty square miles of water-shed. That is, there are twenty square miles of territory, the natural inclination of which is such that the water, if it flows anywhere, will flow down into the stream. If that territory is composed of solid rock, every drop of the water will flow into the stream ; but if the soil is light, porous, sandy, only a small proportion of the water will flow into the stream, because most of it will sink into the earth before it reaches the river ; and that is the condition of the territory below the site of the proposed dam. Mr. Dove testified to you that above the dam the sub-soil is largely composed of clay, impervious to water ; but below the dam, the soil is light, porous, sandy, so that very little water in the summer time passes into that stream.

There is no escape from our position, that they ask to take, substantially, the whole of this stream away from us. There is no escape from our position, that that will substantially destroy all these man-ufacturing industries. There is no escape from our position, that it will be an almost irreparable damage to the town of Andover.

Now, how long will this supply last ? They talk about abandoning the Mystic supply, because the drainage into that river is injuring the water for domestic purposes. How long before the drainage of Lexington and Bedford and the other towns above this dam, will injure this water for domestic purposes? I do not stand here to advocate the right of anybody intentionally or wilfully to cast filth into a stream of water, but dirty water will run down hill just as clean water will. The drainage of Lexington and the other towns around this dam must go into this valley; it can go nowhere else; and in time it will pollute that stream to a great extent. What is going to be done then? Then, I suppose, the petitioners will take Concord river, or some other river, and repeat this process of coming to the State House and asking for the right to destroy private property.

Now, what is the necessity for this work? Because, as I said before (I say this without any consultation with my associates, though I know they will agree with me), we stand here unhesitatingly to pledge every client whom we represent to this statement, that we shall cheerfully give up our rights if there is a public exigency shown for it. If the City of Boston and the City of Cambridge are suffering for water for domestic purposes, and can obtain it nowhere else with as little damage as by taking ours, we are ready to give it to them, with proper compensation.

I say. with all due respect, that the case which the City of Boston has presented here is ridiculous. I do not know any other adjective to apply to it. The reservoirs of the City of Boston are overflowing with water; its supply is practically limitless; water which has been bought and paid for, and which they are bringing into the city. And what becomes of it? Fifty per cent. of it passes through the pipes into the Atlantic ocean, without doing any individual any more good than if it did not flow within a hundred miles of this city. I propose to show this to be a fact by the testimony of the officials of the City of Boston themselves. Fifty per cent. of the water which they have bought and paid for, which they have brought into the city at an immense expense, might just as well, and much better, have stayed on the Sudbury marshes; and yet, without any attempt to use what they have, they come here and ask you to give them more. What would you say of a miller who, when his hopper leaked at the lower end above the mill-stone, instead of stopping the leak continued to buy more corn to pour into the hopper so as to keep it full? That is what the Boston Water Board proposes to do. The fact that they are public servants, looking out for the public interest, renders their action rather more objectionable, perhaps, than if they were doing it on their private account. But that is what they are doing to-day.

We say to the City of Boston, before you take our river, or anybody's else, in the first place, stop your waste; use the water you have now as far as practicable. In the second place, when you need

more water, abandon this miserable make-shift policy of taking a little brook here, and another little brook there, until you have gathered
in all these small streams. Go to some source that is sufficient to
supply Boston for the next hundred years; take it, and end the question.

Now, in the year 1874, I propose to show you that it was demonstrated beyond all doubt that one-half of the water-supply of that time
was wasted. It was not a matter of opinion; it was a matter of
demonstration. In that year some very careful experiments were
made. The city officials selected one portion of the City of Boston
and disconnected it from the rest of the service, and made experiments to see how much of the water was wasted. The time chosen
was Sunday morning, between the hours of one and three o'clock, at
the very time of all the week when there was no call for any appreciable quantity of water. It was found that there was drawn from
the reservoir during two hours, 386,857 gallons of water, equivalent
to 4,600,000 gallons in twenty-four hours. They say, "This enormous rate of night consumption indicated either a heavy leakage or
great waste." They did not stop there; they determined to investigate and find out which it was; and so they took the utmost pains to
stop the leaks. Now, at the expense of being a little tedious, let me
give you the number of leaks which they found. They found that
there were 4,111 leaks, which they stopped, every one of them. They
stopped every leak they could find. What was the result of that?
You would say, of course, that that would make a very appreciable
diminution of the quantity of water wasted. But after all these leaks
were stopped, they say this: "Although a considerable saving must
have resulted from the stoppage of so many leaks, yet the quantity
thus saved was so small in comparison to the immense waste through
fittings left open wilfully or carelessly, that it proved of no appreciable value in diminishing the daily consumption." That is, although
they had stopped over 4,000 leaks, there was, practically, as much
water wasted as before. So far as they could ascertain, the amount
saved was not appreciable. What became of the rest of it? It went
into the sea, and did no good to anybody.

Mr. Cutter, of the Boston Water Board, tells you to-day that he
does not think there is much waste of water, — perhaps two million
gallons a day out of thirty millions. He does not think it amounts to
a great deal. In 1879, this is what Mr. Cutter said, as a member of
the Water Board: "There can be no question that the quantity of
water wasted is very large, and that something should be done to
prevent it. The Board have never been unmindful of this fact, and
have felt that it was one of their most important duties to seek out a
remedy for the evil. Waste is never justifiable, not even in the use

of water. Within a few months the City Engineer has called the attention of the Board repeatedly and specially to the subject, and emphasized his fears as to the result if some preventive measures are not soon taken. In his report will be found an elaborate statement of the case, with diagrams and figures to illustrate and show the correctness of the position which he takes.

"The large expense already incurred for an additional supply of water could have been postponed," he thinks, "for a number of years longer, if the fact of enormous waste had been appreciated by the public eight or nine years ago; ' and, unless it be appreciated and acted upon now, heavy additional outlays will be required in the near future to enlarge the distributing system of the Cochituate works, and to increase the storage capacity of the sources of the Mystic supply.'

"The use of improper fixtures and bad plumbing," the report says, "are largely the cause of the waste, and are, at the same time, among the enemies to the public health against which it has to contend."

That is what Mr. Cutter said in 1879. To-day he tells you that there is not much waste, — perhaps 2,000,000 gallons a day; and a good deal of that is not waste, for it is a very good thing to allow the water in water-closets to run all the time, with a view to the public health.

Now, the Water Board may contend: "We know this was very bad several years ago; but the waste is decreasing, and, probably, in time it will remedy itself." But listen again to the report for 1879: "Particular attention is called to the sudden rise of the profile line during the last year, as it indicates a great increase of waste, and shows the present tendency."

This is what the Water Board said in 1879, when they were not before the Legislature asking for more water: —

"While asking for the special attention of the City Council to these statements of the city engineer, the Board feels called upon to add their decided opinion that the time has fully arrived when active measures should be taken to check the growing tendency to waste among water-takers, and to save the treasury from excessive and unnecessary expenditure. All the demands of health, comfort, and luxury can be fully met by the present water-supply; but deliberate waste should not be encouraged, and ought to be prevented. Exactly how this is to be done has not yet been determined; but some rule must soon be adopted to limit and control the use of water, and wasteful water-takers must be preparing for its operation."

Compare Mr. Cutter's statement before this committee with the following from the report of the city engineer for 1879: —

"The waste in Boston, though not so great as in a number of

other cities (and, in fact, not so great, proportionately to the population, as it was in this city itself fifteen or twenty years ago), is, nevertheless, enormous. We are now using nearly 80 gallons of water per inhabitant, and there is plenty of evidence to prove that one-half this quantity is a liberal supply for all useful purposes.

"Had this fact been generally appreciated by the public eight or nine years ago, it is natural to suppose that the Water Board would have been granted the power and means to so control the consumption of water that the large expenditure which has just been made for an additional supply might have been postponed for a number of years longer; and, unless it be appreciated and acted upon now, heavy outlays will be required in the near future to enlarge the distributing system of the Cochituate works, and to increase the storage capacity of the sources of the Mystic supply.

" For this reason, if for no other, it merits the careful study of those to whom the management of the city's finances is entrusted.

" The statement which is frequently made that, on account of sanitary considerations, the use of water may be unrestricted, may, perhaps, when properly qualified, be defended; but it is generally put forward to defeat any attempt to prevent leakage and unlimited waste. These result largely from the use of improper fixtures and bad plumbing. Water-closets that require a constantly-running stream of water to make them even tolerable, and pipes that render the soil and walls damp by leaking and sweating, so far from promoting the public health, are, on the contrary, among the enemies against which it has to contend."

I have marked several other passages, with which I will not trouble the committee; in fact, the literature of the City of Boston on this water question is full of just such statements as I have read. Now, can this committee say that the public exigencies require the City of Boston to take more water, when one-half of the water which is brought into the city to-day runs to waste, and not the slightest attempt is made to stop it? — excuse me; an attempt was made. The honorable Water Board published a notice in the daily newspapers of the city, saying that, for a few days during the cold weather, they trusted the citizens would be rather economical in the use of water; and Mr. Cutter, of the Water Board, says he thinks that accomplished its purpose, and that that was an efficient means to take to stop the waste of water in the City of Boston! Has he read of Mrs. Partington's attempt to stay the Atlantic with a broom?

Now, you will find another very interesting passage in one of these reports, where Mr. Davis, formerly city engineer, was speaking of this waste. He says: " Several years ago measures were taken to stop it, which resulted successfully for a time, but they were finally abandoned." Now, why do you suppose they were abandoned? " Because they were a serious annoyance to some of the citizens *and to the Water Board.*" There is the rub, in the last sentence. It annoyed the Water Board to stop the waste of water by the citizens of Boston! Mr. Cutter stated it correctly, as you would expect from him, when he said, " The citizens of Boston will not stand being controlled in their use of water any more than they will stand a prohibitory law." Now, why has a prohibitory law never been enforced in the City of Boston? Because the first officer of the City of Boston who attempts to enforce it will lose his position. So with the Water Board. If they attempt to stop this waste of water, they fear they will lose their heads. That is perhaps a very proper consideration to enter into their minds, but is that a public exigency such as is referred to in the constitution? Is it a public exigency that Mr. Cutter and other gentlemen should retain their positions? It may be desirable and gratifying, but is it such a public exigency as to demand that the town of Andover should be deprived of its only source of water-supply?

When a man comes up here and tells this committee that the system of meterage which is good enough for the City of Worcester, for the City of Fall River, for the City of Salem, for the City of Lowell, and every other city in the Commonwealth except the City of Boston, will not do for the City of Boston, one of two things is true : either his statement is incorrect, or else it is time for the Commonwealth to take hold and see if it can govern the City of Boston. One of those two things, I say, is true, and I prefer to think the former is true rather than the latter, because I think the City of Boston can govern itself; and I say to you the first man who comes out publicly and asks the question, " Why should there be this reckless waste of water, and this reckless expenditure for the purpose of getting an increased supply, instead of an attempt to prevent the waste?" will inaugurate a reform which is sure to succeed. And when this question is ventilated on the floor of this House, it will be seen that it is one of the most important questions that can come before the Legislature.

My friend, Mr. Wightman, says that the people here think their water must be as free as air. But it is not as free as air to-day. What water a man can get upon his premises to-day is free. He can set out a tub and catch all he can. In the same way, the air is his that comes on his premises. But the City of Boston does not go up into the country, collect pure air, and transport it to the city for the people to breathe. Neither does it go up into the country and bring in water and furnish it to its citizens without price. The petitioners say we must take the Shawsheen river to-day ; we must take the Concord river to-morrow ; we must take Lake Quinsigamond on the third day, and bring the water into Boston, because the citizens of Boston — in which respect they differ from the citizens of Worcester, and Fall River, and Salem — must have their water as free as air, to waste at pleasure and without restraint!

That is the position the City of Boston takes here to-day. But I ask you, not only as counsel for these remonstrants, but I ask you as a citizen of Boston, who has an interest in the city, to stop this reckless mismanagement of the city affairs, and signify to the Water Board that they had better use that which they have before they come here and ask your assistance to enable them to tax the City of Boston for taking that which they do not need.

I see that I have used up very much more time than I intended, and should be trespassing upon the time of my associate if I said much more. But I have not begun to argue this case to you. I was going to suggest to you that the uncontroverted testimony is (I need but allude to it), that to-day the water of Sudbury river and Mystic river is running to waste by millions of gallons. Further than that, upon the Sudbury supply, there are but three reservoirs, where there can easily be eight or nine, at a moderate expense. The Mystic supply is equally extensive. If it be said the Mystic source is so polluted that it must be abandoned, we reply, the Shawsheen will not supply the territory that is supplied to-day by the Mystic. Mr. Wightman says that in a few years the population of the district now supplied by the Mystic will be such that 12,000,000 of gallons a day will not supply them. So, if the Mystic fails, the petitioners must come to the Legislature again, whether you give them this stream or not. So that in that respect you will not help them.

Now, the City of Cambridge does not present a case which is so utterly without foundation as that of the City of Boston, but still it is not a strong case. The testimony of Mr. Carter shows that even in the City of Cambridge the waste is very great, although not great in comparison with the City of Boston. They have not established any meterage system there, — a system which is in very successful operation in several cities of the Commonwealth. They have, within a few miles of their city, Kendall's pond, which will supply them for many years, and the taking of which will do no damage to anybody, so far as appears. They have a connection, to-day, with the City of Boston, which has millions of gallons of water which can be sent over to Cambridge if they wish it. The City of Cambridge can get along very well with its present sources of supply until it has time to experiment, in order to save the water it already has. There is no exigency which requires that you should supply more water this year or next. The citizens of Cambridge are well enough as they are until these experiments are tried with regard to the saving of water, and by that time

Boston and the adjoining cities and towns should come together and
devise some comprehensive plan for taking the water of the Merrimac,
or some other source, where there is plenty of water beyond all question, and where one system of aqueducts will supply everybody, instead of continuing this make-shift policy of having ten or a dozen
aqueducts leading from ten or a dozen separate streams, and involving an immense expenditure to keep them in order.

Mr. Crafts tells you that the system of meterage is not only practical, but in use in very many cities. He tells you that the Water
Board of the City of Boston tried it several years ago. What did
they find ? They found that such gentlemen as then composed the
Water Board (and they were the *élite* of the city, — men who went
neither dirty nor dry) used a trifle over twenty gallons a day for each
member of the family. They were not trying to stint, but put the
meters on to see how much water they were using habitually from day
to day. And yet the City of Boston, to-day, uses 87 gallons per
head !

There are several other considerations which my associate will
undoubtedly address to you, and many which will occur to you without any suggestion from us. I desire simply to state, in closing, as I
did at the outset, that the question for you to pass upon is : Does the
public exigency demand this thing? To illustrate how strictly the
courts apply that rule, let me take the case of the great fire in 1872.
There, you remember, $100,000,000 of property in Boston were
swept out of existence in a single day. No such misfortune ever
happened in this Commonwealth as happened at that time. The
Legislature was called together, and an act was passed authorizing the
City of Boston (whose credit was unlimited and unbounded, notwithstanding this calamity) to borrow money to be loaned to the
owners of real estate upon the Burned District, at a proper rate of
interest, to enable them to restore the buildings on that district which
had been destroyed by fire. The City of Boston would not have
risked a single cent under the provisions of that act. They could
borrow money at three or four per cent., and lend it at an increased
rate. It was actually a source of profit. But the Supreme Court
said, " This act is unconstitutional. You have no right to tax the
whole City of Boston for the benefit of owners of property on this
burned district. Every man in Boston has an unalienable right to his
property, unless the public exigency requires it to be taken from
him." They said that even a case as strong as that was not a case of
public exigency.

Now, I ask you, Mr. Chairman and gentlemen, to compare the
situation of the City of Boston on the morning after that great fire
with its situation to-day in regard to water-supply, and with the

situation of the City of Cambridge to-day, and say, if there was no such public exigency then, if there be any existing to-day, so that you have the constitutional right to take from us our property, to which, rightfully or wrongfully, we are attached, and which we do not desire to sell, and to give it to these gentlemen for the purposes for which they ask it.

Closing Argument of Hon. R. M. Morse, Jr., for the Remonstrants.

Mr. Chairman: —

The City of Boston was originally supplied with water from Jamaica pond. A private aqueduct company now owns the right to take water from this source, and, in fact, takes it from that pond to supply a portion of the inhabitants of the city. The city then got from the Legislature an act authorizing it to take the waters of Lake Cochituate, and used those waters until it found them insufficient. The Legislature then passed the act of 1872, chap. 177, which authorized the city to take Sudbury river. The City of Charlestown had originally taken the water of Mystic pond, under an act of the Legislature, and in 1874, by the act, chap. 400, of that year, which was passed after the annexation of Charlestown to Boston, the City of Boston was authorized to take the entire water-shed of Mystic-river valley. The town of Brookline was authorized to take so much water as it needed from Charles river, and by the act of 1875, chap. 127, Brookline was authorized to sell water to the City of Boston. The Act of 1880, chap. 126, authorized the City of Boston to sell water to the City o Cambridge, the City of Cambridge already having the power to take the waters of Fresh pond, of Spy pond, of Wellington brook, and of Little pond. I call attention to these acts for the purpose of showing to the committee that the Legislature has given to the City of Boston the right to take Jamaica pond, Lake Cochituate, Sudbury river, Mystic pond, the entire water-shed of Mystic valley, and, if these prove insufficient, to buy from the town of Brookline the water of Charles river ; and that the City of Cambridge is authorized to take these several ponds that I have named, and if that supply proves insufficient, to buy water from the City of Boston. The pipes of the City of Cambridge are connected to-day with the pipes of the City of Boston, so that, practically, except in the matter of adjusting the terms of the bargain, — which, between parties who agree so entirely as do our friends here representing these two cities, would be a very simple thing to do, — except as to adjusting the terms of the bargain, the City of Boston and the City of Cambridge, between them, practically, control four or five great water-supplies. Those supplies, Mr. Chairman and gentlemen, are not only adequate for present needs, they are adequate for all the needs, for all the population that our most sanguine imagination can picture as living here a hundred years from now. Why, the skilful and experienced engineer of the City of Boston testifies that the storage capacity upon the Mystic is 17,000,000 gallons a day, and on the Sudbury, 40,000,000 of gallons a day, making a total of 57,000,000. So that, if the City of Cambridge were entirely without water to-day, the City of Boston alone is able, by spending $1,435,000, which is the total cost of building all the basins on both these rivers, to supply 57 gallons a day to every individual in a population of one million people. The City of Cambridge is using to-day only 46 or 57 gallons a day per head. Then, allowing 57 gallons a day to every inhabitant, the city has to-day, using these two water-sheds alone, it has water sufficient to supply 1,000,000 of people, and all that is needed is an expenditure of a million and a half of dollars. Of course, we do not assume that any such expenditure would be made at once ; works of this kind are not all done at once ; but that is the entire limit of cost of utilizing the whole of the storage capacity of those two rivers. One million and a half of dollars will furnish 40,000,000 gallons a day from the Sudbury, and 17,000,000 from the Mystic. This 40,000,000 supply is only the Sudbury river, the Cochituate is an entirely independent supply. I accidentally omitted it in stating the figures, but that, of course, should be added. And I desire to call attention again to what I said in regard to Charles river. The town of Brookline has authority to take the water of Charles river. Is it conceivable that the town of Brookline, which also is likely to become a part of Boston before long, — is it conceivable that the town of Brookline would hesitate at any time to take such additional quantity of Charles-river water as might be needed in order to furnish it to the City of Boston, if that was really required? Practically, the City of Boston has to-day the right to take Charles river.

Now, Mr. Chairman, I wish to put this case in regard to the needs of this community upon the ground that, for purposes of water-supply, Boston and Cambridge are to be treated as one. I think the Cambridge Water Board have made an excellent showing here, so far as utilizing their present water-supply is concerned. Although not using a system of meters, they have unquestionably reduced the amount used by each individual to a very small figure as compared with Boston. I have no doubt that the City of Cambridge needs additional water, but the City of Cambridge is connected with the Boston water-supply ; it has that supply at its command, subject only to making proper terms; and I will venture to say, that if our friends should not be able make a bargain as to the terms on which the water should be sold by the City of Boston to the City of Cambridge, the Legislature would have no difficulty in providing that the City of Cambridge might take the water and might pay the City of Boston whatever it was fairly worth. The two cities, in this connection, are to be treated as one. The City of Boston and the City of Cambridge in all probability will be united within a few years; and the City of Cambridge, I will venture to say, would not to-day, if it had the power, go into the expense of obtaining an unlimited supply of water, not knowing whether annexation is to take place or not. But whether the city is annexed or not, for such purposes as the supply of water, the City of Cambridge is to be treated as part of the City of Boston. It is all one great community. It is just as much part of the City of Boston as the City of Somerville, or the town of Everett, or the City of Chelsea; and those municipalities are all embraced within the district for which the City of Boston undertakes to provide a water-supply.

A single word in reference to what is a reasonable amount of water to estimate for the demands of the individual consumer. The table of statistics from different cities has been called to your attention. The committee will find it, if they desire to examine it, on page 57 of the report of the Boston Water Board for 1879. I have looked that table over with some care, and without reading all the statistics to the committee, I wish to say there is not a city in the United States, with the exception of those that pump water out of the great lakes or the St. Lawrence river, that uses as much water per day as the City of Boston; not one. The cities of Detroit, Cleveland, Chicago, Toronto, and Montreal use large quantities of water, although the City of Montreal, that takes its water from the St. Lawrence, only uses sixty-nine gallons per day per head. The City of Chicago and the City of Detroit use water in very large quantities, but, of course, their supply is unlimited, and it makes no difference how much they pump out from the lake, it all goes back shortly afterwards. But when you come to the cities that have to pay for their water-supply, that have to take it from streams or from ponds, and have thereby to infringe upon the rights of private persons, you will not find a city in this country that uses the quantity that Boston does. They talk about what small towns can do. The City of Philadelphia, with a population, as stated in this report, of 817,500 — almost as large a population as that which my friend, Mr. Wightman, anticipates for the City of Boston fifty years hence — uses only 58 gallons a day per head; while we have the City of Providence using 25 gallons, the City of Lowell 33 gallons, the City of Fall River 26 gallons, the City of Lawrence 44 gallons, the City of Cincinnati 57 gallons, the City of Columbus 43 gallons, and so on. Now, Mr. Chairman, is it not an extraordinary fact that the City of Boston is using the enormous quantity of 86 gallons a day per inhabitant?

I had the curiosity to go through another set of statistics; that is, those which show what the City of Boston has done in regard to meters. It has been suggested here, in the examination of witnesses, that it would do very well for a city just introducing a water-supply to put on meters, but it would not do for a city that had an old-established water system, that would have to subject the water-takers to the inconvenience and expense of meters. I should the more readily believe that that was the true explanation of this trouble if I found any evidence that the new customers of the city for a supply of water were required to put on meters, or that any movement was made to inaugurate the system.

Mr. STACKPOLE. — Perhaps you do not know that we have applied for legislation in regard to the use of meters by certain classes of customers.

Mr. MORSE. — I do. I am glad you have. I want to call the attention of the committee to certain facts about meters. I find that in 1875 there were 44,676 takers of Cochituate water. That is the number of takers who were supplied from that system. At that time the whole number of meters in the City of Boston on the Cochituate service was 1,092. In 1876 there were 46,885 water-takers, and the number of meters had increased to 1,120; that is, the water-takers had increased 2,200 and the meters had increased 28. In 1877 the number of water-takers was 48,328 and the number of meters 1,082, which was ten less than two years before, the water-takers then having increased 4,000 and the meters decreased ten in number. In 1878 there were 49,970 water-takers and 1,079 meters; that is, three less meters than there were the year before, although the water-takers had increased 5,500 from 1875. In 1879 the number of water-takers was 51,523 and the number of meters 1,089, three less than there were four years before, although the water-takers had increased in number 7,000. In 1880 there were 52,268 water-takers and 1,097 meters, the water-takers having increased nearly 8,000, the meters having increased five. Five meters for the 8,000 water-takers.

Then, take the statistics of the Mystic. In 1877 (the reports I have do not go back prior to that time), on that special supply there were 17,890 water-takers and 180 meters. In 1878, 18,730 takers and 185 meters. In 1879, 20,025 takers and 202 meters. In 1880, 20,566 takers and 216 meters. In four years the number of water-takers had increased nearly 3,000, and the number of meters had increased 36.

Now, Mr. Chairman, I do not hesitate to say that such statistics as those are disgraceful to the City of Boston. I say, when it has been demonstrated by the experience of other cities — I mention Worcester particularly, because the committee have had the benefit of hearing from the officials of Worcester, and in a way that nobody can question the statement as to the entire success of the water-meter system — out of 5,000 services in that city they have more than 3,700 meters, and the testimony was that it was found a matter of economy not only to the city but to the water-taker, so that consumers were glad to have the meters put upon their services, — I say that in the face of facts like these, which cannot be questioned, it is disgraceful to the City of Boston that they should be up here asking for legislation to take this little Shawsheen river away from these people who need it, and use it, and give it to a city which has deliberately set its face against what experience and science have shown to be practical in the matter of measuring water and stopping waste. And without dwelling further upon that point, I wish to emphasize all that my brother Torrey has so well said in regard to it. I would rather see the Legislature vote for a bill making it obligatory upon the City of Boston to put a meter on every service in the city than give it one gallon of additional water-supply. The City of Cambridge, as I said, presents a very much better showing, because, although it is a manufacturing city, and a considerable portion of its water is used for that purpose, and although it has not introduced a general system of metering, it has reduced consumption. I am free to admit, upon the testimony here, that it is not probable that that consumption can be very largely reduced.

So much, then, for the principal points. First, for the proposition that there is already legislative authority sufficient to give to the City of Boston, and through that to the City of Cambridge, all the water that is needed, and at an expenditure that is not disproportioned; and further to the point, that in estimating how much is needed, the committee are to be governed by the experience of other places as to what is to be a fair allowance to each inhabitant.

But, if the committee should come to a different conclusion upon either of these propositions, if they should think that there was an exigency shown in regard to either of these places, there would still remain a question as to whether this act should be granted. The committee will notice that the act itself is not presented, and it may be quite important, if the act ever should be seriously considered by the committee, that we should be heard again upon the mode in which any rights here should be exercised, because there are two petitions. One is for the City of Cambridge to take a portion of this river; the other is for the two cities to take the whole. I shall address myself to it, however, upon the assumption that one course is as objectionable as the other. Although the two cities combined would take the entire supply, yet I apprehend that an act that would authorize the City of Cambridge to take 8,000,000 gallons only a day, would, in the times of the year when the manufacturers and the people along the banks particularly need water, deprive them of the water; that is to say, in the dry times I do not suppose that 8,000,000 gallons pass through the river per day, and, of course, if they do not, then the entire supply is taken, and this at a time when it is particularly needed. Nobody objects to having the water taken from any of these rivers in the spring. There is great waste, of course, from all rivers at that season of the year. But you are to look at the minimum supply; you are to look at the minimum quantity that runs through the river, and say whether or not an application that seeks to take that away is not practically an application to take the entire river.

The committee are so familiar with this class of questions that I need not dwell upon it. I merely suggest to them that where a small river, which furnishes only a limited amount of water, is to be drawn upon to supply a certain amount, like 8,000,000 of gallons a day, it is, practically, to be exhausted at the most critical time. As was suggested in another hearing before this committee, it would be a kind of partnership that would be extremely uncomfortable. A city owning a certain portion, and the people along the banks owning another portion, it would be very difficult indeed to adjust the matter between them and determine how much water they were taking. The question of damages would be a hard one to settle. There would be constant annoyance and friction between the parties, and as my brother Torrey has said, it would be far better, if the committee were inclined to give any portion of the river to these parties, to give the whole of it to them, and let them take it once and for all.

Without further argument upon the question, whether or not there is any distinction between the cases of taking the whole and taking a part, I submit to the committee that whatever needs the City of Boston or the City of Cambridge may have, their need is not great enough to induce the committee or the Legislature to take away this river. It is a river, which, as has been testified here, is the natural drainage for this town of Andover. It is the natural drainage for towns above Andover, which cannot be stopped up and its water diverted without making a very serious change in the condition of things in that vicinity. It is needless to say that the health of the community, if any community would remain when the river is taken away, must be seriously affected by such an important change. The river, in its way, is just as important in that view as a larger river, like the Mystic or the Charles, is to the inhabitants along its banks. There is, therefore, as the first objection to any such measure as this, the unanimous opposition of the town of Andover, of it officials, of its citizens, of its physicians, of persons who have given atttention to the subject and know very well what they speak. There is the opposition that has been presented here from the town of Lexington, which I need not dwell upon, as they have presented their own case. Besides that there is the manufacturing interest. And here again I beg to reaffirm what my brother has said in reference to the importance of that interest. I represent particularly the Smith & Dove Manufacturing Company, which the committee heard from yesterday, a company with a capital stock of half a million dollars invested in real estate, in machinery, and in business at Abbott village and Frye village. The testimony is, that that manufacture cannot be carried on unless they can have the water of the Shawsheen river for the purpose of bleaching. No damages will give them that water; no damages will enable them to carry on their manufacture there without it; therefore, so far as they are concerned, an act of the Legislature authorizing the cities of Boston and Cambridge, or either of them, to do what they ask permission to do here, would be an act to drive that manufacture from this State; to throw out of employment hundreds of people who are dependent upon that manufacture; to send them to another State, or, perhaps, to wander over this State without employment. It would be an act to deprive this town of Andover of a large amount of revenue; it would be an act to take from this State a manufacture which has given additional credit and distinction to the manufactures of this State, and to transfer it, if transferred at all, to some other place, where it would have to begin under a new name and without all the advantages which this old establishment gives to it.

I was struck by what was reported in the newspapers as having been said in the House in reference to the rights of manufacturers, that the time had come when they must give way without compensation to the demands for water-supply. Of course, no such sentiment could possibly, it seems to me, have been expressed. If such a sentiment should be acted upon, there would be no occasion for any water-supply in any city or for any action before the Legislature. The City of Boston could not exist if it destroyed the manufactures about it. It must do everything it can to-day to meet the competition from other States. So far as agriculture is concerned, the State long since ceased to hold any preëminence. The tide of emigration has set West. The tendency of manufactures to-day is to the West. Manufactures are being established in New York, in the West, and in the South, and our manufacturers are finding close competition under circumstances unfavorable to them in all the markets of this country and of Europe. Now, Mr. Chairman, the State Legislature, so far from driving out a single one of these industries should do

153

what it can actively and positively to promote them. So far from encouraging such a sentiment as was reported to have been uttered in the House the other day, every committee that has a matter of this character before it should take the earliest opportunity to stamp such a proposition with its disapproval. We need every one of these industries. We need to give them all the encouragement that can consistently be given.

Closing Argument of J. L. Stackpole, Esq., for the City of Boston.

Mr. Chairman and Gentlemen : —

There are two sayings, which have passed into proverbs in our language, which occurred to me during this hearing. One of them is, that " history repeats itself ; " the other is, that " history is philosophy teaching by example." The first saying occurred to me in connection with the hearing in reference to the Sudbury river, in which I participated as counsel for the City of Boston some eight or nine years ago ; and the second in connection with the duty which this committee will, I hope, perform in connection with this hearing and other similar hearings which have taken place before this committee and its predecessors. I remember well, gentlemen, that when we came here for liberty to take the Sudbury river, we were opposed with the greatest vehemence by a large number of private interests and by some public interests, such as the towns. I counted one day, up in the green-room, as opponents of that measure, — I did not have the assistance of Cambridge then, either, or of my friend, Mr. Hammond, whose intelligence and skill always assist in determining any question ; • I was there by myself, — I counted seventeen counsel sitting in a row at the table ; and, as was said by a boy who threw a stone out of a window at Willard's, during the war, and struck three brigadier-generals, it was not a very good day for brigadier-generals, nor was it for lawyers, that day. There was nothing that was not prophesied as to the evil that would result from the city's taking Sudbury river, and there was nothing left unsaid that the ingenuity of counsel could devise as to the awful violence to the constitution, the terrible result that would come to the manufactures of New England, — their utter prostration. I felt very badly to-day when my brother Torrey read that extract from the constitution which he fears you are about to violate, until I remembered that at that time the whole constitution, article by article, and section by section, was read by the various counsel, who claimed that the whole of it would be violated ; and when I remembered the result of the action at that time, — that the constitution has not been even stretched by the taking of Sudbury river, — I feel a little better. It was then calculated by gentlemen, and figures were presented in the most able way by the statisticians of the time, that the supply of Lake Cochituate would be ample for any time within the expectation of man. The arguments on this subject were presented with an eloquence almost equal to that of my brother Morse. It was pointed out that the industries situated on that river, which are very much larger than those on this Shawsheen river, would be entirely destroyed, and it would be substantially shutting up and destroying those manufactories, of which New England is justly proud. It was pointed out that the town of Framingham would become a deserted village, to which that of Goldsmith would afford no parallel ; that there would be a sort of desert of Sahara there ; and that same simile of the little pipe (it shows how the same great ideas occur to great minds, even at periods somewhat distant from each other) — that same simile of the little pipe going through there, and containing the solitary remnant of the river, was, I remember, used by one of the counsel at that hearing ; I do not believe my brother Torrey heard it ; but that same simile was used, so I did not feel so badly when I heard it from him. But we took that river, and the constitution still remains, and citizens are still sworn to support it ; the town of Framingham is still there, and

Health and plenty cheer the laboring swain.

The people of the town are still engaged in cultivating their fields and working in the mills, and they enjoy the additional agreeable recreation of recovering damages from the City of Boston, and spending the money upon their mills and their pastures. I believe it to be a fact (it has been so stated to me), that not a single mill has stopped, except where there were large dams, which actually covered their sites. Not a single mill of all those great establishments has ceased manufacturing. In that case, it was testified that they needed the fresh flow of the river for purifying their wool for the purpose of making blankets ; but the act was passed, the water was taken, and they are just as well off as they ever were. They recovered damages from the city (which we are perfectly willing to pay in this case), and the town of Framingham goes on, everything goes on, just as well as before. More than that, it appears, in regard to this Sudbury river, as will be the case with the Shawsheen, that the very necessity of storing a supply and the obligation of the city to allow a flow of 1,500,000 gallons a day, actually gives them what they did not have before, that is, a steady stream in periods of drought; because, before that, there was never water enough in the river in such seasons. To-day we are obliged to let a million and a half gallons go down the river daily, and they are supplied with it. And so far from freshets injuring the river, it is a notorious fact that before the water can go down the river so as to stop the machinery of the mills, the storage-basins must first be filled, so that the force of freshets is broken, and mills get notice beforehand of them, and there is in some seasons an actual benefit by reason of this management of the river.

Now, we must expect, wherever we should go for a supply of water, if we go to any river or stream within reasonable distance, that private persons will object, and, of course, they employ eminent counsel, and they come forward and they tell you not merely about their own interest, but they talk about sickness and death, and matters of that sort, in a way that is calculated to be pathetic, if your fair reflection does not show you that such results are highly improbable. They are very proper suggestions for counsel to make, if they think they will have force, but they are suggestions prompted by the interests of their clients, which are purely monetary. Unless we can go to some pollysyllabic Indian lake, like the Moosetockmoguntic or the Mollychunkamaug, or to some pond situated in a remote region of this or some adjacent State, where the only creatures entitled to damages would be the solitary heron or the leaping trout, I do not know that we could go anywhere where private interests will not be disturbed, and I do not know any way of paying them except by money, and that we are willing to do; and if counsel will state what amount they desire to be retained in that river, if that amount appears reasonable to the committee, we are willing to have that put into the bill. In the Sudbury-river bill, for instance, a flow of 1,500,000 gallons a day is provided for. Suppose you should put 2,000,000 of gallons into this bill. That is a larger amount per day than now suffices to supply the whole City of Cambridge for all their domestic and manufacturing uses.

There is, naturally, a deterioration of water-power as woods disappear near cities. It is comparatively a wild region at the Shawneen river, but the woods will be cut down in course of time, and the water-power will naturally decrease, and it is necessary that steam should, to a certain extent, take the place of water-power, as it has already done on the Sudbury. And here I desire to call attention to one or two facts which somewhat militate against some of the statements made by my friends on the other side. I am told that it appears as a physical fact (if I am wrong my friends will correct me), that there are twenty square miles of water-shed between where we propose to take the water and Andover, and that that is good for

500,000 gallons at least a day, and if stored would be good for 10,-000,000 gallons a day. This water-shed is much larger than the number of square miles of water-shed between our lower dam and the Saxonville mills, which is only thirteen square miles.

Now, Mr. Chairman and gentlemen, how does this matter stand? We are not here for our private advantage. We are not a private corporation, a manufacturing or monetary corporation, that petitions for something for its private benefit. Public corporations and private corporations differ in this respect: The public corporations, cities, and towns are purely political divisions of the community, which are separated for the purposes of government, and are really political parts of the entire whole, the powers being divided. The legislative power, the main power of the State, is the only one that possesses that power of giving to these various parts the right to act, in certain cases, under the right of eminent domain, and take private property for public uses on paying a fair compensation for it. And here I would say, that the case of Lowell *v.* the City of Boston, which was cited by my friend on the other side, which merely decides that a law authorizing a city to borrow money at wholesale, and lend it to a certain number of its inhabitants to build private stores or houses, is unconstitutional, has no connection whatever with this case. The power to give to a city or town the right to take pure water for its citizens is undoubted, and is constantly exercised every year that the Legislature meets, and it has no connection whatever with the right of a city to borrow money to enable a portion of its inhabitants to build private stores or houses. There is no sort of connection, I repeat, between the two.

Now, gentlemen, let me say this: You know perfectly well that probably the most unpopular thing that can be done by any public officer of the City of Boston is to suggest to the city that it is necessary to spend more money for any purpose. We are very close on the limit of our municipal indebtedness; our taxes are very heavy; and I can assure you, gentlemen, as probably you know without any assurance, that no official or board of officials of the city would undertake to advise the expenditure of any money by the city for any public purpose unless they were well satisfied that that purpose was necessary. There is, moreover, nothing which the water board or the city engineer can gain. They have no private purpose in coming before you and suggesting to you that this bill is necessary; they simply do it as a matter of public duty. And it appears to you in this case that the city engineer, who is an able and accomplished officer, who has been in the service of the city a long time, after having looked over the matter, deems it his official duty to advise the Water Board that, in his judgment, a further supply of water is necessary.

Considering the time it will take to build new works ; considering the impurities which already exist ; considering the want of economy that there would be in building new reservoirs on the Mystic river. he. as a part of his official duty, advises the Water Board that it is their duty to take it into consideration, and that this Shawsheen river is the best source from which water can be had ; that the water is pure, that it is comparatively near, that the matter has been thoroughly investigated by other engineers in former times, and that the expense will be moderate. Well. gentlemen, that is taken into consideration by the Water Board, consisting of three gentlemen selected for their special knowledge on the subject, who, considering the exigencies of to-day (and I do not care what their view may have been five or six years ago on this subject), have come to the conclusion that it is their duty to advise the City Council to make this application, and the City Council are here, by petition of the mayor, made in accordance with a vote of both branches, saying to you that they desire, and that they believe it to be necessary for the City of Boston, to take the Shawsheen river. Well, gentlemen, they are merely representative men ; they are persons elected by the citizens of Boston, and in doing this they undoubtedly have public sentiment behind them. There is no subject upon which the public mind is so much exercised to-day, as I told you in the opening, as having an ample supply of pure water for the city. The City Government has public sentiment behind it, and it comes here and tells you that in its judgment this division of the whole political system of the State should have authority to take the Shawsheen river in addition to its present supply ; it lays the case before you, it brings in the city engineer and other witnesses, and after that, gentlemen, the responsibility rests with you. They are but public officers ; they have nothing to gain in this matter ; they have performed their duty. I am sent here by the city to assist these gentlemen in stating their case to you, and, having performed that duty, the responsibility then rests upon you. We lay the case before you, and if you say that the water we have got to-day is sufficient for our 350,000 people to drink ; if you say that this water is not needed to take the place of or supplement the Mystic, not only now, but considering what is probable to occur in the future ; if you say that it is not the part of prudence, looking forward to the time that will be taken up in building these works ; looking forward to the fact that it is necessary to increase that portion of the city's supply, that the building of those reservoirs on the Mystic will cost some four or five hundred thousand dollars, and then may not give us a pure source of supply, and that that money will be thrown away in the end, — why, gentlemen, that rests upon you. These gentlemen have done their duty and I have done my duty in presenting the case to you.

Now, gentlemen, the matter stands just here, — I do not wish to repeat at much length what I said in my opening, but the matter stands exactly here : The city engineer and our other witnesses tell you that, considering the probable growth of the city, — I believe it has doubled itself twice in the last fifty years, and is very likely to do at least that in the next fifty years, — that considering the probable growth of the city, considering the interests of a wise economy, and considering what it will cost to take the water which now supplies this portion of the city, — the city proper, including Roxbury, West Roxbury, Dorchester, and Brighton, — from the Sudbury and the Cochituate, — they tell you they believe that those sources should be left to supply the district which they now supply, and that the water should not be carried away to supply other districts at an expense of, in round numbers, about half a million of dollars. We leave it to you, gentlemen, to say if they are right in that proposition. They tell you, further than that, that the only way of utilizing this water would be to build at once these basins on the Sudbury, which it is not now necessary to build, at an expense of $600,000, not counting mill damages, and to carry the water over to the other district at an expense of $400,000, making $1,000,000 to be spent immediately, — $600,000 of which it is not necessary to spend at once, and $400,000, that is to say, the expense of carrying it over, which would become utterly useless when the demand reaches to the extent of the supply of the Cochituate and the Sudbury on this side ; and they say that, in their judgment, it is much better to spend this $400,000 for the permanent gain of 12,-000,000 gallons a day by taking the Shawsheen river, where nothing would be thrown away.

Now, if you are of that opinion, — and that is an opinion based upon careful study, and I do not know any scientific man who has been called here (they have called Mr. Crafts, but they did not ask him any questions on that subject), or anybody who has investigated the subject, who denies that those figures are correct, and that wise economy demands keeping Lake Cochituate and the Sudbury for this district, — if you are of that opinion, then you may lay that whole question aside, and you are brought face to face with the demands of the other district. Now, that is supplied by the Mystic river and its tributaries. We took from that river, last year, an average of over 9,000,000 gallons a day, the calculation being that it is competent to supply, on the average, but a little over seven millions. All last season, the City of Charlestown, the safety of its inhabitants, was at the mercy of one piece of machinery. Had a single cog broken there, which would have stopped the pumping-apparatus, its operation during the pendency of an ordinary fire, more money would have been lost to the inhabitants, ten times over, very likely, than the whole expense of these works, and I dare say, ten times over the value of any of these mills along the Shawsheen river, not to speak of the loss of life and suffering that such fires cause. There can be no question that even considering our present wants, the Mystic is not sufficient. Then, looking forward to the future, shall we go on and build these large reservoirs upon the Mystic, when we may be forced to abandon this as a source of supply within a few years? Is that prudent, gentlemen? Because, remember, if we do not get this bill, that is what we must do. Shall we say to those people, we are going to invest another half million dollars in this Mystic supply. The water may be impure, very likely will be impure, but we have invested this half million dollars here and we cannot spend any more money." Take three or four years hence, gentlemen, if you please. Suppose we do not get this bill, the City Government say, " We went to the Legislature ; we stated to them our case ; they would not give us the bill we asked for ; we adopted the only other alternative, we went to work and we have built these storage-basins on the Mystic. When we built them, we knew they would not last ; we should have to abandon the Mystic as a source of supply ; we knew we could not furnish an ample supply of pure water to the inhabitants of Charlestown and Somerville and Chelsea and Everett ; we knew that was the case, but what could we do? Could we leave that district to the danger of conflagration again? We were obliged to build these basins. We have put half a million dollars into that work ; we knew it when we started, but we could not do anything better ; we were forced into that, and what were we to do?"

Now, if that is not a public exigency, I do not know what it is. I admit that there must be a public exigency, but if this is not a public exigency, tell me where, in any petition, to take water for any city or town, a public exigency has arisen. More than this, gentlemen, here is this question of the Mystic sewer. I do not desire to argue that question again, but it stands now in this way : In 1875. in order not to have any further trouble with these tanneries, we tried, as a matter of compromise, to see what we could do. The City of Boston said, " Rather than fight it, and in order to keep the water pure, we will build a sewer at an expense of $100,000, and let the sewage run out into Mystic Lower pond," supposing it would run out there and go on its way to the ocean without troubling anybody. This plan has not succeeded. In dry seasons, offensive odors arise, which disturb the neighborhood. Now, the City of Boston are in this position : It endeavored to compromise this matter ; it was willing to spend $100,- 000 in building this sewer, but it is not willing to look after the whole drainage of that valley, right or wrong. Now, should the Legislature see fit to pass a bill, making us look after the entire drainage and sewage of that valley at our own expense, I cannot tell what the consequences will be. A possible result is that the tanneries then may discharge their pollutions into that water-supply, and it is going to take years of litigation to stop them. Are we to make the people of Charlestown and Somerville, and the rest of these cities, continue to drink this Mystic water while this litigation goes on? But, independently of that, I have pointed out to you that the supply to-day is inadequate for the purpose, and that the building of these extra reservoirs on the river is impolitic and uneconomical. We are using from that source to-day 9,000,000 of gallons, and it is probable that within a short period of time the demand in that district will increase. But Mr. Torrey argues that the supply from the Shawsheen will be insufficient, and will be soon exhausted. Now, mark you, suppose we get these 12,000,000 from the Shawsheen, and are enabled to supplement that from the less polluted districts of the Mystic, — it is estimated that we are to have two-thirds from there, or perhaps a half, say 4,000,000 gallons more, — then, instead of having, as we have to-day, a supply of 7,000,000 gallons a day, we shall have 12,000,000 from the Shawsheen, and say 4,000,000 more. That is to say, we shall have 16,000,000 of gallons a day with which to supply our citizens. We are using 9,000,000 now. Is not that an adequate and ample supply for the coming future? I say this to answer the argument used by my friends on the other side. They say that this supply — 12,000,000 of gallons a day — is not enough,—will not last any time. I say that, with the supplement from the Mystic, which we can probably use, is sufficient, and it is the wisest policy to do this. Why, gentlemen, look at it. We want to get on in the cheapest way. We can get this 12,000,000 gallons a day for $400,000. Are you going to send us to the Concord or the Merrimac? The Concord, a river which is so sluggish as to be unfitted for water-supply anyway, and which is likely to be deteriorated by other pollutions. Are you going to send us there, which would cost double or 'treble what it will cost to get the water of the Shawsheen? Or are you going to send us to the Merrimac, at an expense, I suppose, of two or three million dollars, when we can get all we want from the Shawsheen for less than a quarter of that sum? Gentlemen, I cannot believe it.

Now, gentlemen, I desire to say a word in reference to this talk about waste and about supplying the whole city with meters. In the first place, you have been told that the citizens of Boston use more water than should be used per day. Well, I admit it, to some extent. They do use rather more, but not a great deal more. Let me tell you that the amount used now by Worcester and Cambridge, some 40 gallons a day per head, is not, in the experience of the best experts, a sufficient supply to be used by the inhabitants of a large city, everything considered. Then, gentlemen, remember this with reference to the City of Boston, which does not obtain with reference to the smaller cities : that, in addition to the population which you find down on the census table, which is confined to those who actually reside in this city, rembember that, in addition to that, there is a population which we cannot estimate, but, perhaps, you may have some idea of, who come into Boston and pass half their lives here regularly, and use the water. I think it would be fair to say that there are 100,000 men, women, and children, coming into Boston every day, and passing the day time here. I do not know but I am underestimating in that statement. It is a matter of common experience. There is no way of counting these people. Then, there is a certain number that come to our hotels. Now, when you calculate the amount of water used per head, you take merely the census returns. If you add to those census returns a third, you do not make our 80 gallons on the census population a day so very large. But we are trying to reduce it by putting on metres where metres are allowable, on the large buildings. But I tell you, gentlemen, that this talk about metering a great city is prac- tically useless. My friend on the other side talks " reckless extrava- gance " of Boston, and because our officers do their duty in calling attention to any abuse that they see from time to time, not concealing it, but calling the attention of the people to it, he chooses to charge them with " reckless extravagance." I supposed " reckless extrava- gance " to be committed by the thoughtless ; our people are certainly thoughtful on this subject. Undoubtedly, there can be some diminu- tion made in the consumption of water, and that has been in the minds of the City Government in coming forward and making the application to you for legislation authorizing meters on large build- ings ; but they are still of opinion, that using meters as far as they can, using this Deacon meter, which will prevent waste without measur- ing the water, it is necessary for them to have the Shawsheen river.

Now, look at it for a moment. There are 44,000 takers of water in the City of Boston. It is said, " Put on meters." Well, gentlemen, meters cost on an average about $30. There is an expense of $1,200,000 ; three times the expense of taking the Shawsheen river, without the mill damages.

Mr. TORREY. — The testimony was, yesterday, that they cost $15 or $20 apiece. That is the only testimony there is about it.

Mr. STACKPOLE. — I am told that they cost $30. But take it, if you please, at $20 ; it costs something to put them on. I don't sup- pose they will go on for nothing. Without mentioning the expense of repairs and renewals, that is $880,000. That is double the cost of taking the Shawsheen ; and, meantime, you have violated public senti- ment. Well, hadn't we better have our full supply of water when we say we are willing to pay for it, than to metre the city at double the expense, under the protest of its most intelligent citizens? It seems to me that it is a mistake to compare the City of Boston with the City of Worcester, and urge that, in a large city like Boston, you can do this; that because in the City of Worcester they have consented to it, you can do it in the large cities. I was reminded, Mr. Chairman, when that idea was presented by my friend on the other side, — with whom I had the pleasure of traversing the pleasant plains of knowledge on the other side of the river, — of the shepherd in the Eclogue, who tells his companion that, when he was a young man, he used foolishly to compare the town of Mantua, to which he drove his tender lambs, with the great City of Rome. My friend still adheres to his mistake, whereas the shepherd acknowledged that he was wholly wrong. Will he allow me to suggest to him that his rustic pipes, whether containing music or water, are unsuited to our people, and that rustic metres are not in accord with the music of the city. No, gentlemen, his talk about metres is all very pretty on paper, but it does not amount to anything. You know, gentlemen, — for you are practical men, — that it would not go down in the City of Boston. You know we are asking for a bill, to-day, to enable us to put metres on these large houses, that are occupied, to a large extent, by business people. But even there, where metres are highly proper, we are meeting with some opposition; and I undertake to say (and in this I agree with my friends on the other side), that any water board that undertook to carry that policy out would have to leave their places in a very short time; and very justly so, because public officers are bound to know the sentiments of their constituents and to carry them out.

We are also told that we ought to get water from Brookline, which, I believe, takes the vast amount of 1,500,000 gallons a day, which is about a twentieth or thirtieth part of what we use.

Mr. MORSE. — There is no limit to the amount they can take.

Mr. STACKPOLE. — I know it; but how can we oblige them to take it and let us have it? I do not know any principle of law by which we can oblige the City of Brookline to take any more water than they want, and sell it to us. It is possible my friends on the other side, who are admirable lawyers, know some principle of law by which we can call upon the town of Brookline to take 20,000,000 of gallons a day and sell it to us. At present, Mr. Healy has not advised the city that it can do it. No, gentlemen. There is a general law, I believe, on the statute-book, which allows towns and cities to sell water to one another. It is a very sensible law, because it enables one town or city which has a surplus to sell it to another town or city; but if you are to rely upon it, if you are going to aggregate all this water, and say that the needs of Boston will be supplied because Brookline has power to take water which she will not take, or that Cambridge has power to take water which she will not take, the proposition is absurd. We have power to sell water to Cambridge, but they cannot make us take water for that purpose. We can cut it off at any moment if we have not got a large supply; and so it is in other cases.

Gentlemen, I find I am within a few moments of the limit of time which we have agreed to take, and I believe I have said everything I thought of saying. Something has been said about this being an afterthought, but I think there is no evidence of that. You will find in the city engineer's report of this year, made or written before this Legislature was in session, a recommendation that a new source of supply be obtained. We feel that this is a public exigency. If we do not get this bill, we feel that we shall be unable to perform our duty to our constituents; and we see nothing here but these private interests, these private monetary interests, which will be found everywhere, which came up ten-fold stronger when the proposition to take the Sudbury river was before the Legislature, and must come up everywhere; and those interests we are willing to pay for all property taken. And if gentlemen are here representing those towns who desire to have a special provision in the bill allowing a certain quantity of water to remain in the river for the benefit of the health of those towns, Mr. Hammond and myself (I believe I am authorized by him to say so) will be happy to meet those gentlemen, or their representatives, for the purpose of making a bill that will be fair to all, because we ask nothing else.

Closing Argument of J. W. Hammond, Esq.,

For the City of Cambridge.

Mr. Chairman and Gentlemen: —

I am sorry to be under the necessity of asking you to consider this matter any longer; but perhaps the better way will be to proceed with what I have to say, without expressing any regrets that I am under such necessity.

As I took up the Boston *Herald* last night, I saw an article there headed " The Shawsheen River — what will be the effect if it is drawn upon for a water-supply?" signed by " G. Frederick Wright," who, I suppose, is the same gentleman who appeared before us yesterday. As showing the state of mind into which honorable gentlemen may get when they consider a matter of this kind, I desire to read an extract or two from it.

" To cut off the Shawsheen, as the present proposition contemplates, is the practical confiscation of the little all of hundreds, and the destruction of the vested rights of thousands of the citizens of Andover. A principle is at stake which it behooves our legislators to be wary of breaking wholly down. It is but two or three months since the citizens of Andover came together, at the instigation of Boston philanthropists, to hear Mr. Tibbles and Miss Bright Eyes rehearse the wrongs of the Poncas. Little did we think that within so short a time our own rights would be in as imminent peril from Boston as those of the Poncas have ever been in from the Indian ring. This small band of Indians was driven from its home at the point of the bayonet. But a company three times as numerous as the Poncas is likely to be driven from the homes its ancestors have occupied in Andover for seven generations by a process as irresistible and a force as implacable as has ever been employed against the savages on our Western plains. Where are Senator Dawes and Mr. Walter Allen, and the host who have been so ready to champion the cause of the oppressed, and to defend the rights of the weak against the encroachments of the strong?"

That made me feel badly. I felt wicked. I got over it, however, somewhat, until I came in this morning and listened to the dismal remarks of my ordinarily cheerful brother, Mr. Torrey. Knowing the generally sanguine nature of his temperament, and the cheerful disposition which he has always heretofore shown under the most calamitous circumstances, I was surprised at the state of mind in which he was, and I began to think that I was wicked. I began to feel as I used to feel when my good old parents used to tell me that I should not play cards. I could not see why, but as they were so strenuous upon it, I supposed there must be something wrong about it. But as my brother Torrey went on, and began to give the reasons why we should all feel so wicked, and why we were all so wicked, I felt as I used to feel when my parents used to give me reasons why I should not play cards. I continued to play cards then, — perhaps to my detriment; perhaps they were right about it; I suppose they thought they were. But certainly, the reasons which my brother gives why Cambridge should feel so wicked do not impress me at all as the dismal character of his remarks, and the piteous appeal contained in this paper, made me feel.

I may say, before proceeding, that Boston is ably represented here, and I shall confine my remarks simply to the Cambridge side of the question.

We desire to take eight million gallons of water a day from the

Shawsheen river at a point near where it crosses the Middlesex canal, and build storage-basins there sufficient for that purpose ; to take that water by the way of the Middlesex canal until we come to the Mystic lower pond, and then from there to Cambridge ; and we desire such provisions in the bill as will give us the right to do this.

Now, I gladly accept the issue which my brother Torrey has tendered to this committee. Do the public exigencies require that Cambridge should have that eight million gallons? I am willing that this matter should be decided upon the answer to that question. I believe we have shown to you that if ever there was a proper occasion for the exercise of the right of eminent domain, it is this of giving the City of Cambridge eight million gallons of water.

What are " public exigencies"? When is this right of eminent domain exercised, and under what circumstances? Under every principle of jurisprudence which is at all adapted to the wants of civilization, this right of the public at certain times to take private property for public uses is recognized, and must be recognized. No road can be built without it. Year after year you give railroads the power to exercise this right. You have now a general law authorizing any individuals, in the exercise of what they consider to be a profitable right, to take any man's house and any man's lands for public uses — the uses of a railroad. So of canals. What does this mean, this " public exigency"? It means simply and solely this : that where the public reasonably need certain powers, those powers shall be granted, notwithstanding private property is taken thereby. Our constitution does not *give* us the right of eminent domain ; it *recognizes* it ; and the provision which my brother read is only a provision providing for the giving of compensation where it is exercised. And if there is any class of cases in which the Legislature have freely and ungrudgingly exercised this right of eminent domain, and have granted it to others, it is where requests have been made for pure water to drink and for domestic purposes. This very year this committee are considering whether they will give a private corporation in the little town of Lexington a right to take water, which involves giving to that corporation the right to take private property for public purposes. And will you say that the owners of the little land which is needed for that purpose are not as much under the protection of the Legislature as these mill owners are? Why, I do not believe a legislature has been in session for years without granting this right of eminent domain for the purpose of taking water. My brothers here must concede that at least the subject-matter which is asked for is one in regard to which the right of eminent domain may be exercised.

Now, *the necessity.* Why, as I reflect upon the evidence which is before this committee, it seems to me that the necessity under which

Cambridge is here is perfectly indisputable. We have our consum: tion now reduced so low that our friends upon the other side concede that we have done about all that can be expected. Nowhere else in the Commonwealth has there been such an economical use of water, so strenuous efforts made to confine its use to those purposes to which it ought to be put, as in Cambridge. The result is, that notwithstanding the boasted situation of Worcester, we are lower than Worcester in the consumption *per capita*, and stand so upon the tables which have been introduced here. We have been driven to this by the severe necessity of our situation; and that record, of itself, is the best evidence you can have of the stress in which Cambridge to-day stands in reference to water.

What is our position? Needing 2,500,000 gallons a day, and more than that at fifty gallons a head, we have only Fresh pond, capable of supplying 1,750,000 gallons, with an opportunity to catch Wellington brook when we can, — and that is at rare intervals, — and carry the water into the pond. Spy pond is useless, Little pond is useless — the ponds that we once supposed would supply us. As our city engineer says, "Spy pond is not fit, Little pond is not fit, and Wellington brook is fitful."

I will read to you from the report of the commission from which I quoted in the beginning a few sentences, to show where we stand with reference even to Fresh pond. I read from page 10: —

"Fresh pond is exposed to certain dangers to which all ponds in the midst of rapidly-growing centres of population are subject; and these dangers are to a great extent inevitable. That our pond must at no very distant day fail to be an acceptable source of supply for this reason is, in our opinion, to be expected."

Then it goes on and says, in speaking of the capacity of Fresh pond: —

"The abandonment of the water from Wellington brook is only a matter of time, and the time may come in the near future, and we shall then be left to the Fresh pond alone. Even with our present population, this, of itself, is an entirely inadequate supply. Whether we protect the pond or not, it is as clear as the noon-day sun that we must soon look elsewhere for a supplemental supply at least."

Nowhere else in the Commonwealth — I challenge contradiction — nowhere else in the Commonwealth do all the circumstances indicate such an extreme necessity for more water as in the City of Cambridge. It is not the ordinary case of a village coming here which has plenty of wells, and has never used water from a public service, but it is a city of 52,000 inhabitants, all of whom must have water through pipes, or they cannot get it at all, so situated that it cannot get water enough through its pipes to supply its inhabitants. Are you not satisfied on that point? Is there any clearer case of necessity for an additional supply of water than Cambridge has shown? Can we economize any further? Our friends upon the other side do not ask that. Then, the question is, where shall we go? That is the only question, and it is the only question with Cambridge. We must come to this Commonwealth for authority. We must come to you. We are powerless without further legislation. We must get the right from the Commonwealth to take private property and pay anybody who suffers. Can we go to Concord river? I will not argue it. It is not a fit supply, and we all know it. My brothers on the other side have not seriously said anything about it. Can we go to Kendall's pond? Fresh pond, with 1,750,000 gallons per day; Kendall's pond, with less than 2,000,000 gallons — both supplies not equal to 4,000,000 gallons a day — shall we go there? Will it answer our purpose? Is it a reasonable expenditure of money to do it? No, we propose to adopt the rule which my brother Torrey said, a moment ago, Boston should adopt: "abandon the plan of taking every little stream, and go to some source which will furnish an adequate and permanent supply." The same rule which he applies to Boston with regard to Shawsheen river, we apply to Kendall's pond. I do not care to argue that any further. No city authorities would do it. It would be an unreasonable thing for us to do. The water might not be fit when we got it, but it is certain it is not sufficient; we must go elsewhere.

Now, can we go to Boston? Can we get our water from Boston? Well, there has been a great deal said here about the wasteful extravagance of Boston on this water question, but Boston, they say, has plenty of water. That may be true; I do not know anything about that. My brother who speaks here for Boston has taken care of that city, so that there is no need of my saying anything about it. But one thing is true — Boston uses that water; we cannot control it. If Boston says she has not water enough, how in the world can Cambridge make her do any differently from what she does? If a child goes to his mother and asks for a glass of water, is it any answer for her to say, "John has got a bucket-full; go out and see if he won't let you have some," when John is so much larger than the little child that he cannot get it unless John is willing he should have it? That is the condition here. Tell Cambridge to make terms with Boston, when Boston says she has not water enough! We supposed Boston could supply us; it was so reported. The commission appointed in Cambridge a year or two ago told us we could get water from Boston; we all supposed we could get it from Boston, and a connection was made with the water-supply of that city by a 16-inch pipe. I don't know as it is any worse or any better for Cambridge to rest upon a 16-inch pipe than it is for Andover, but that is what we did. We were in this condition : our pond was reduced nine feet below high-water mark ; our conduit, that we had run out into that pond for the purpose of taking the water, was laid bare ; we had to pump water into the conduit for the purpose of having it run into our well-room, so that we could exercise our pumps and distribute the water through the city. We did this for several days this last year. Our pond, which has 187 acres at high-water mark, was reduced in area to 152 acres.

It is uncertain how long you can draw from a pond where you lower it nine feet below its high-water mark ; you cannot tell what is the nature of the water below, or how soon you will stir up mud from the bottom. You may soon find that you have water there which is not in a condition to be used. It is uncertain ; it has troubled us very seriously. In that condition of things, the City Council were called together in vacation last summer for the purpos of making this connection with Boston. Our authorities did not fee easy, and they say in their report for 1880 : " It was decided to seek connection with the Boston water-works as the best thing for us to do, and our president obtained from the Boston authorities the permission to connect with their pipes at Brookline bridge. No price was agreed upon, for we did not know that we should want any water from them. On their part, they only agreed that they would give us a supply in case of necessity. On our part, we at first thought if the pond should fall below the reach of our pumps, that we could arrange with Boston for a partial supply until the fall rains came to our relief. But when September came, and there were no rains of any account, a committee of the Cambridge Water Board waited on the Boston Water Board to see what terms we could make with them for water. We found that they were no better off in some respects than we were ; that already they had commenced to pump into their conduit, at the Mystic works, with the prospect that unless rain should come before sixty days, they would have to do the same thing at Cochituate lake. Under these circumstances, we could not reasonably ask them to supply us until we had exhausted all our means to supply ourselves. This made it necessary to arrange to pump into our conduit as soon as possible." That is, to pump from the pond into the conduit which was laid bare, so that the water could run from the conduit into our well-room, from which it could be pumped to the reservoir, and then distributed throughout the city.

Now, you may say that Boston is a very bad boy, but the trouble about it is that we have no control over him. My brother refers to the Act of 1880 : " The city of Boston is also authorized, if the Boston Water Board should be of opinion that the supply of water is sufficient for the purpose, to sell water to the city of Cambridge."

"If the Boston Water Board should be of opinion that the supply of water is sufficient for the purpose." Well, it is pretty plain here that the Boston Water Board is *not* of that opinion ; it is pretty plain they will not be. Extravagant they may be — it is not for me to defend them here ; you have heard the allegation, and you have heard the defence, but whether reasonable or not, whether extravagant or not, there has been so much water used, they say, that they have none for us.

Mr. TORREY. — There is no evidence of that kind in the case.

Mr. HAMMOND. — I am reading from the pamphlet.

Mr. TORREY. — I know ; but you did not read that. The only evidence is that the City of Boston want this water for the Mystic service. They admit that they have enough water on the Sudbury river side ; there is no claim to the contrary.

Mr. HAMMOND. — That is their report of last year. As a matter of fact, they did not have water enough, and were reluctant to let us have it, and we did not get even as far as terms. They simply said, " We are in the same condition that you are, and we cannot let you have any water." That is our condition. I would like to have you point to another municipality in this Commonwealth that is in that condition. Is there no -public exigency here? The last resort has failed, and the Shawsheen river, as though made by Providence for that purpose, appears from the testimony to be the only place to which we can go. It is pure water, it is fit for the purpose, and I ask my friends upon the other side, if they were in Cambridge, what other place they could show us to go to? I ask them now.

Mr. TORREY. — We should look and see, which you have not done at all. That is our position on that.

Mr. HAMMOND. — They acknowledge, I take it, from my friend's answer here, that they do not know now of any place, and they will, upon investigation, find that there is no place except the Shawsheen river.

" Exigency ! " Why, I thank my brother for putting this case upon that ground. If ever a case of exigency was shown, it certainly is shown here. Now, the Shawsheen river is within our grasp ; we can get it. But my friends on the other side say we shall disturb them. If a great exigency exists, it is not very much matter who is to be disturbed ; somebody must be. My brother Stackpole said you could not exercise this right of eminent domain without taking somebody's property. That is what it means.

This case is just like any other case in its main features. They have down there three or four mills. Some of them have been there since King Philip's time. In the Revolutionary war, they had a powder-mill down there. I don't know but they existed prior to the primeval forest that Brother Cowley inquired about here yesterday. But is it not perfectly plain that the water-power on that river is of as little value as the water-power on any river of its size in the Commonwealth? Could we take the same amount of water and disturb fewer people than we shall by taking the Shawsheen river? Is it not perfectly plain that these mill owners do not rely so much upon the water of the Shawsheen river for its power as they do upon its purifying effect upon the goods that they make? This Smith & Dove Manufacturing Company, at Frye village, use no water-power; at the other village they run their engines nine months in the year; and Mr. Bradlee (whose knowledge about his affairs is a little more indefinite than I expected to find it) uses his engine nine months in the year. Mr. Stevens is an exception. But is it not perfectly clear that the people upon that stream have relied more upon steam than upon water for the purpose of carrying their mills for years?

But it comes down to this question, whether you will allow this water to be drunk by the citizens of Cambridge, or whether you will leave it to be used for the purpose of cleansing and bleaching the finished goods of these manufacturers. And how long do they intend to do that? I was a little surprised here at the inconsistency of the defence. What does Andover say here is the main thing she wants that river for? To drain into. The mill owners, I take it, would soon cease to use it for the purpose of washing their flannels after Andover had used it for purposes of sewerage. These men say that they carry their goods to Frye village, which is the last village near the stream, for the purpose of soaking and cleansing them. That is where they do it. That is their testimony. I remember that, because I thought that it was rather curious that our friends upon the other side did not see how inconsistent that was with the claim that Andover village should have the right to drain into the river.

Mr. ——. — Yes, but they would enter their sewer below Smith & Dove's, at Frye village.

Mr. HAMMOND. — They would? I don't know. So this town of Andover, which is so anxious to preserve this water for the purpose of drainage, would pollute the water for the very purpose for which the mills want it, as they say. Now, practically, I don't know. It may be that taking away the water of these mills would force them to go into other business; but the mills would stay there. I have no doubt that the industries upon the banks of that stream have changed many times, and that, although these mills are now used for the manufacture of certain kinds of goods, they can be adapted to the manufacture of other goods. It will be done at a cost, it is true, but not at the cost of taking away all these villages. That is not the way these things work. Show me a single factory village in this Commonwealth that has been depopulated, as they claim this would be, by reason of the fact that the mills which stand there could not be used for the purposes for which they had been heretofore used. Changes are constantly occurring in these mills, and there will be a change here.

Now, as a matter of fact, I believe that the people of Andover will not suffer. Of course, we expect these remarkable claims for damages to mills. The gentleman who estimated his damages at $20,000 for a mill for which he paid $6,500 is a fair specimen of what these mill owners say when they get a claim for damages. If you look at the taxable value of these mills upon the Shawsheen river, you will find that it is a little more than $200,000, — the whole real estate. I tried to get at the valuation of the machinery, but I was unsuccessful. There is not 500 horse-power on that stream used in the town of Andover; not a third of what any one of the large mills of Lowell uses. Why, when you consider the damage which is to be done to people by taking that water, you will see that it is less than would be done upon any other stream of its size in the State; that it is not a growing power, and never has been. And when you consider that, and compare it with the damage which would result to a city like Cambridge from a lack of water, our case seems absolutely irresistible. I challenge my brothers to show us a place where we can go. Will they tell us to go to the Merrimac river? There are mills there. They say they have not investigated. I think that if they knew of any place they would tell us of it. They have told us of one that was not fit, — that was the Concord. Perhaps their ill success in that line determined them not to make any other suggestion.

So I say — for I am not going to argue this question with the fulness that I would before a jury — I say that upon the question of exigency, Cambridge has presented a case here which has been excelled by none ever presented to the Legislature. I have not attended all your hearings, but I believe you have had no other such exigency before you. I say that what we desire to take is the only water we can take that will meet our purpose, and I challenge contradiction upon that. I say that it will do less harm than would be done by taking the same amount of water from any other source, and I challenge contradiction upon that. There is one other feature about it: not only is the Shawsheen now pure, but it is to remain pure as long as any stream will. Go where we want to take the water, and, as I am told by the city engineer, you cannot see a house for miles. The valley is favorable; there is not a spot in the Commonwealth that is so well adapted for the purpose for which we wish to use it.

Now, the exigency being shown, it being evident that we cannot go anywhere else, have I not met my brother Torrey on this matter? And then, is it not time for the Legislature to say that this thing shall be done? Whoever suffers will be paid. That is a question that is not for us. The exigency is shown; public right here is paramount. Less injury, we are satisfied, will be done here than by going anywhere else; but it must be done to meet the public necessity.

I need not say, Mr. Chairman, that I have felt the responsibility of this hearing. It has fallen to my lot many times to speak in behalf of the good old City of Cambridge, but I have never felt more strongly that I wished that an abler hand and a better tongue could be employed in her behalf than I have felt at this hearing. When I reflect upon the consequences to our city from the refusal of the Legislature to grant us this right; when I consider the precarious nature of our water-supply now, and feel that in a year's time it may be lost to us, and think of the time which must elapse, even if you grant this bill, before we can avail ourselves of it, I feel as if we had not awakened to the necessity one moment too soon, but had delayed to the very last moment, and had adopted every expedient, before we came he e and asked you to give us the power still further to exercise the right of eminent domain.

EVIDENCE AND ARGUMENTS

ON

PETITIONS OF CAMBRIDGE AND BOSTON

FOR LEAVE TO TAKE WATER FROM

SHAWSHINE RIVER,

BEFORE THE COMMITTEE ON PUBLIC HEALTH OF THE MASSACHUSETTS LEGISLATURE.

J. W. HAMMOND,
For the City of Cambridge.
A. J. BAILEY,
For the City of Boston.

R. M. MORSE, Jun.,
GEORGE H. POOR,
JOHN R. BULLARD,
NATHAN MORSE,
For the Remonstrants.

BOSTON:
FRANKLIN PRESS: RAND, AVERY, AND COMPANY.
1882.

HEARING.

The CHAIRMAN (Senator HORTON). The parties in interest here so well understand the position of the case, that it is hardly necessary to make even the simple statement I propose to.

Last year the city of Cambridge applied to the Legislature for authority to take the water of the Shawshine River. The city of Boston afterwards put in an application, and the two cities appeared here in a sort of joint capacity, asking for a joint bill; and the city of Cambridge subsequently asked that a joint bill should not be reported, but that a bill might be reported allowing that city to take the water.

The Committee reported to the Legislature leave to withdraw, so far as the city of Boston was concerned, and reported a bill allowing the city of Cambridge to take the water. The Legislature referred the whole subject to the next General Court; and the various petitions and bills of last year have been formally taken from the files, and referred to this Committee.

In addition to that, there is also a new petition this year from the Mayor of Boston for leave to take the water of Shawshine River, and there are several remonstrances from the town of Andover against the same. The whole subject is open, as it was last year.

Is the city of Boston represented here?

Mr. HAMMOND. Mr. Chairman and gentlemen of the Committee, I appear for the petitioners, and I was about to inquire who appears in any capacity here, in order that we may know whom we are to meet.

The CHAIRMAN. The city of Boston understands that this hearing is to be had. If they are not here, it is their own fault. I do not see any reason why we should not go on with the case. Have you made any arrangement, Mr. Hammond, with the city of Boston this year?

Mr. HAMMOND. No, sir: we are untrammelled by any alliances.

Mr. MORSE. I will ask whether the Chairman has a copy of the vote adopted last year, referring these matters to the Legislature of this year, or whether the Chairman can state under what circumstances that vote was passed, whether with reference to the report, "Leave to withdraw," or with reference only to the bill relating to Cambridge?

Mr. BULLARD. I remember what the fact was, because I have referred to the Senate report, which shows that the report of the Committee, "Leave to withdraw," in relation to Boston, was amended by a recommendation that the subject be referred to the next General Court.

Mr. MORSE. I will not trouble the Chairman. I only desired to have the fact clearly understood, how this matter comes before this Committee.

The CHAIRMAN. That is the fact about it. The Legislature referred the whole subject, both the report, "Leave to withdraw," and the bill allowing the city of Cambridge to take the water, to the present Legislature. They were all treated alike.

Mr. HAMMOND. It is the view of the Committee that the question whether Boston shall have the water, or any part of it, is to be heard at the same time with the petition of Cambridge?

The CHAIRMAN. We thought it would be in the interest of economy of time if the Committee heard the petitioners from the city of Cambridge or Boston, we do not care which, and then the other party, and let the remonstrants be heard in opposition to the whole.

Mr. HAMMOND. That is, it is understood that this is to be the beginning of the hearing upon the whole subject?

The CHAIRMAN. Yes, sir: we propose to hear the petitioners. You may settle it between yourselves which shall put in their case first, and then let the remonstrants follow.

Mr. HAMMOND. Now I should like to have the appearances entered here, in order that we may know whom we have to meet.

Mr. POOR. I appear for the town of Andover, and for the Marland Mills, Moses T. Stevens's works. I understand my brother Bullard appears for J. P. Bradlee, of the Ballardvale Mills, and Mr. R. M. Morse, jun., for the Smith & Dove Manufacturing Co. ; and I ought, perhaps, to say that Mr. Nathan Morse is expected also to appear for the town of Andover, but cannot be here to-day.

Mr. BAILEY. Perhaps I ought to say that the position of the city of Boston is not one entirely in opposition to Cambridge. If the Committee see fit to give Cambridge the right to take this water, coupled with permission to the city of Boston to take it also. in such proportions as the Committee shall deem proper, we should not object ; but we should object to Cambridge being granted the right to take this water, excluding Boston. Of course, if the Committee see fit to give the water to Boston, and extend the same privilege to Cambridge, we should not object to that.

The CHAIRMAN. Do you agree to stand or fall together?
Mr. HAMMOND. No, sir, we do not.

OPENING STATEMENT OF J. W. HAMMOND, Esq.

MR. CHAIRMAN AND GENTLEMEN OF THE COMMITTEE. — I appear
here in behalf of the petition of the city of Cambridge ; and, while the
Committee generally may be familiar with the subject, I suppose I
must assume that the question must be gone over *de novo*, as if there
had been no hearing last year.

Perhaps a simple statement of the manner in which Cambridge is
situated now, in reference to water, will be useful in considering the
case.

In the year 1856, or thereabouts, a private corporation was authorized to take water from Fresh Pond, then lying partly in Cambridge
and partly in Belmont, for the purpose of supplying the inhabitants
of Cambridge with water for domestic and other purposes. In 1865
authority was given to Cambridge by the Legislature to purchase
the franchise of that corporation, and, in its municipal capacity, to
supply the inhabitants of Cambridge with water. At that time it
was supposed that the waters of Fresh Pond were entirely adequate
to meet the reasonable necessities of the city for many years to come.
But in 1875 it became apparent that Fresh Pond itself was not
sufficient, and authority was obtained from the Legislature to take
the waters of Spy Pond, a pond situated entirely in Arlington, consisting of about one hundred and sixteen acres, — a shallow pond,
however ; the waters of Little Pond, a pond of about nineteen acres,
situated in Belmont ; and also the waters of Wellington Brook, which
is a stream running into Alewife Brook. Fresh Pond is connected
with the ocean by Alewife Brook, Wellington Brook running into
Alewife Brook. Little Pond also finally comes into Alewife Brook,
and also Spy Pond. It was supposed that this supply would be
ample for the city. It was supposed that the water would be good,
and we should not need any more water for a great while. In 1878–79
the town of Belmont, in which was situated a part of Fresh Pond,
authorized the construction of a large slaughter-house upon the
borders of Fresh Pond. This put the city of Cambridge in a state
of considerable agitation, and a petition was circulated among the
citizens, asking the city to take immediate steps to secure, by purchase or otherwise, sufficient land upon the margin of Fresh Pond to
protect her water-supply from pollution. It was deemed a very
important matter ; and in 1879 a committee was appointed by the
City Council of Cambridge, consisting of the Mayor, the President
of the Water Board, the President of the City Council, the city

engineer, the city physician, and the city solicitor, to thoroughly investigate the subject of the water-supply, and see what steps could be taken to put the matter beyond a peradventure. That committee employed Mr. Chesborough, who must by this time, if not before, be known to this Committee, probably one of the most competent engineers on the whole subject of water-supply of cities in the Union ; especially familiar, by his connection with water-works in this part of the State, with the resources for the supply of water in the eastern part of Massachusetts. They employed that gentleman as a consulting engineer, and they had the full benefit of his judgment and experience upon the matter. He gave it careful attention, made a thorough examination of the whole matter, and made a report to this committee appointed by the City Council. He was an engineering expert. We also had upon the committee Prof. Edward S. Wood, who must be known to the Committee, and who is regarded as one of the most experienced and valuable sanitary investigators. If he were not present to hear what I have to say, perhaps I could speak of him in more complimentary terms. But, in substance, the commission did all that could be done in the way of employing experts, and in the way of getting advice and opinion, to see what it was best for Cambridge to do. They reported to this commission, and this commission reported to the city ; and it is a fact, which I suppose cannot be controverted, that the water of Spy Pond is not suitable for domestic purposes, and we never have used it, and we say it is not safe ever to try to use it ; also, that the water of Little Pond — the nineteen-acre pond — is not suitable, by reason of the situation of the pond, for domestic purposes ; and that Wellington Brook, a small brook upon which many houses are situated, is not suitable, except at certain seasons of the year, — seasons when the ground is frozen, and the snows are melting and running off, substantially without touching the ground or the impurities in the ground. That is to say, that we must give up Spy Pond, we must give up Little Pond, and we must use Wellington Brook only at seasons of the year when the water is running down over frozen ground ; and that is only a few days in the spring of the year, such a day as it is to-day, and such days as we have had within a week or a fortnight. A conduit, however, before this report was made, had been constructed, connecting Fresh Pond with Spy Pond by the way of Little Pond. Little Pond lies between Fresh Pond and Spy Pond, and this conduit connects Fresh Pond and Little Pond ; and then there is another conduit from Little Pond to Spy Pond. Wellington Brook strikes the conduit between Fresh Pond and Little Pond, so that we can take the water of Wellington Brook into Fresh Pond, by means of our conduit, without tapping either of the other ponds; and that is what is done. That, of course, Mr. Chairman, reduced the water-supply of Cambridge to Fresh Pond, and to Wellington Brook at such seasons of the year as the water was suitable for use. It alarmed us; it put us at once to a knowledge of the fact, that all our arrangements for getting any other supply than Fresh Pond furnished, had ended in getting, for a few days in the year, whatever water would run down that small Wellington Brook. Since that report the waters of Little Pond have not been used; we have never used the waters of Spy Pond, and we have done practically this: In the spring of the year, when the waters of Wellington Brook could be safely taken, we have allowed them to be conducted, by means of the conduit, into Fresh Pond, to fill up the pond; and we have drawn from that as a reservoir until the time came again when we could do the same thing.

Now, what is the capacity of Fresh Pond? It is good, all the engineers who have examined it say, for about 1,750,000 gallons a day. We cannot rely upon any more. I need not say to this Committee that the water-supply of a city, like the strength of a chain, is to be measured by its weakest link. It is not the *maximum* supply, but the *minimum* supply, that the cities must reckon upon, when they consider the value of water-supply. We can rely upon Fresh Pond for 1,750,000 gallons a day, and we can rely upon it for no more. The natural water-shed of Fresh Pond has been shut off from the pond by reason of the impurities thereon; so that, while it was originally about twelve hundred acres, it is now only about five hundred acres. It is perfectly clear that it is only a matter of a few years, perhaps of a few months, when the entire water-shed of Fresh Pond, if the water is to be used for domestic purposes, must be shut off from the pond.

Now, Cambridge has a population of rising 52,000. At fifty gallons a day, which all will concede not to be an extravagant estimate, we need more than 2,500,000 gallons per day. That is the actual need, — 750,000 gallons a day, on an economical estimate, more than Fresh Pond can supply us. That is our position to-day, and has been for some years. In order to get this extra 750,000 gallons a day, we are obliged to fill up our pond from the fitful waters of Wellington Brook, and draw upon Fresh Pond as a natural reservoir. That is our condition. If a spring should pass without our being able to fill up the pond from Wellington Brook in the manner which I have described, there would be a water famine in Cambridge : that is indisputable. This shows the necessities of the situation. We need 2,500,000 gallons every day ; we get from Fresh Pond 1,750,000 gallons. We must rely upon Wellington Brook, and whatever surplus water there is in Fresh Pond, for the balance. It is perfectly clear, however, that the capacity of Fresh Pond must constantly decrease, as the water-shed is shut out from the pond, and we shall be eventually reduced, so far as Fresh Pond is concerned, to take such waters as come into it by the deep underground currents, which amount to considerable in the course of a year.

You will bear in mind that we have set our consumption at fifty gallons a day for each inhabitant, which is less than two-thirds the amount of water which is now actually used by Boston; and, if we should require the same amount per inhabitant that Boston uses, we should be in a water famine at once.

The CHAIRMAN. Let me see if I understand you. I understand that your need is 2,500,000 gallons a day, reckoning fifty gallons a day to each inhabitant?

Mr. HAMMOND. Yes, sir: it is over that; it is 2,600,000 gallons.

The CHAIRMAN. And Fresh Pond only furnishes 1,750,000 gallons.

Mr. HAMMOND. That is all; that is its capacity. And, in making that statement, I rely not only upon our own engineer, but I rely upon another engineer, whom all recognize to be an engineer of capacity, who has examined this matter thoroughly; and that is Mr. Crafts, who examined it with reference to a supply for Watertown. My impression is that he put it at only 1,600,000 gallons a day. I have Mr. Crafts's document, which can be referred to by our friends on the other side, if they desire to know any thing about it.

Now, last year, the pond was lowered more than nine feet below its high-water mark, so that the area of the pond, which at high-water mark is about one hundred and ninety acres, was reduced to one hundred and fifty.

Perhaps I ought to explain to you the nature of our water-works to a certain extent. We are obliged to pump our water. We have a stand-pipe system; we have a small reservoir with a stand-pipe. We pump the water from Fresh Pond, the pump-house being upon the borders of the pond. The water is taken, by the suction-pipe of the pump, from a well inside of the building where the pumps are situated. There is a conduit four feet in diameter reaching from that well out into the middle of the pond, and the water comes from the pond into the well through this four-foot conduit. The top of that conduit is nine feet below high-water mark of the pond. Last year the water got below the top of the conduit fourteen inches, so that it would not run into the well from which the pump took the water fast enough for the pumps to pump it, and we had to erect another pump upon the borders of the pond for the purpose of pumping the water into the well, from which it was to be taken by the large pumps for distribution throughout the city. Not only that, but a year ago last August the exigency became so great, that the

City Council, although adjourned for the vacation, were called together by the mayor, by a special message, for the express purpose of considering how to meet what appeared to be an impending water famine; and from fifteen to twenty thousand dollars — I can't give the exact figures — was expended in making a connection by permission of the city of Boston with one of the Boston pipes, by running a pipe across Charles River, over what is called the Brookline Bridge. When the time came, we went to Boston for the purpose of asking her to give us some water. She said she was in as tight a fix as we were, and could not let us have any. I allude to these circumstances, Mr. Chairman, to show to the Committee the exact facts in regard to the manner in which Cambridge is now supplied with water, and the precariousness of the supply of one of the largest cities in the State. I believe you will come to the conclusion, as the Committee did last year, that there is an absolute necessity on the part of Cambridge to look for further water-supply; and I do not believe our friends on the other side will make any contest on that point.

Now, this commission that I have spoken of, not only considered the present supply, but they considered what could be reasonably obtained in the future, and where to go, and what to get. Mr. Chesborough told us, "It will, as I believe, be found best ultimately to abandon the attempt to make and keep all the present sources of supply pure, on account of the great expense and impracticability; and, for an additional supply, to take a part of Shawshine River, or to go to the city of Boston." We find that the city of Boston says that she has not water enough for herself. Looking at the reasonable necessities of Boston, they cannot give us any assurance that they can supply us with water. The only resource open to us in any reasonable way is the water of Shawshine River. That is what we ask for to-day.

The problem has reduced itself to this, after the most thorough investigation that we have been able to make. We desire to take water from the Shawshine River, not to exceed 8,000,000 gallons a day, and conduct it, from a point near where the river crosses the bed of the old Middlesex Canal, to Fresh Pond in Cambridge, from there to be distributed to the inhabitants of Cambridge; or, if Fresh Pond should prove at any time unsuitable for a reservoir, then to take the water to the inhabitants of Cambridge, not through Fresh Pond, but clear of it. The capacity of the Shawshine is conceded by engineers to be, on the average, 20,000,000 gallons a day. It can be relied upon to furnish that supply by making use of such storage facilities as the valley of the river affords. We want to build a dam across the Shawshine, near where it strikes the old bed of the Middlesex Canal, partly in Billerica and partly in Wilmington, and to take about eight hundred acres of land. This blue spot on the map indicates the surface of ground that will be covered with water. This light-pink color indicates the water-shed of the river. The land which we desire to take, you will see, is largely in Billerica; part of it, however, being in Bedford. We desire to have authority to take that land, and construct that dam. The dam will be somewhere about sixteen hundred feet long, and twenty-five feet high. We want to take the water by the bed of the old Middlesex Canal till we get to Winchester, and there leave the bed of the canal, and cross highways and private lands, and get to Cambridge either by way of Fresh Pond or otherwise. This is what we want. We are willing to have it put into our bill that this authority shall not authorize us to lessen the flow of that river to less than 10,000,000 gallons per day.

The CHAIRMAN. Permit me to interrupt you at that point. What is your understanding of the provision of the bill in reference to that matter? Do you propose to store a sufficient quantity of water in that reservoir to enable you to guarantee that the flow of the river shall not be less than 10,000,000 gallons a day at any time?

Mr. HAMMOND. That is just exactly what we propose to do. We believe that this plan which we propose here will be for the mutual benefit of everybody interested in maintaining the flow of that stream. It is a common practice on many streams for mill-owners to store the water. In the western part of the State, where they have quick, rapid streams, through which the water flows in large quantities in the spring, it is a very common thing for the mill-owners to make these reservoirs for the express purpose of storing water. We are willing to have it put into the bill that there shall be at this point where we take this water, — no matter about the subsequent accretions, as the river goes along, by other streams running into it, — that there shall always be, at the lower side of that dam, a stream of water not less than 10,000,000 gallons a day. If the natural supply of the river does not yield it, then it shall come out of the reservoir.

The CHAIRMAN. Even to the extent of draining it?

Mr. HAMMOND. We take that risk. We know what we are about. We have had competent engineers examine that. We do not ask to do any thing in regard to this matter which we do not believe the laws of nature will permit us to do, and the laws of humanity and of health will sanction.

The CHAIRMAN. I asked the question because, notwithstanding the provision in the bill of last year, some question was raised in the Committee on that point.

Mr. HAMMOND. The bill presented last year may not have expressed that as clearly as I have now expressed it. That river is

capable of containing, at its fullest capacity, 2,000,000,000 gallons.
If Cambridge should draw from it 5,000,000 gallons a day, it would
be four hundred days before it would be drained. Of course, it
never would be drained; but you can see from that what allowances
have been made for contingencies. We are willing that that should
be put into the bill: we are able to make that proposition, because
we have investigated the matter thoroughly, and believe it is perfectly
feasible. As a matter of fact, we don't believe that for years to
come we should ever use 8,000,000 gallons. We don't imagine that
the people upon the river would know any thing about it. Still,
we want the right to take 8,000,000 gallons; and this matter
is to be considered as if we were going to take it every day, I
suppose.

. Now, as I was about to say, when the Chairman interrupted me,
we are met here by the town of Andover, and by the mill-owners on
the stream. I most sincerely believe that if the authorities of the
town of Andover would fairly consider the provisions of the bill
which is offered to the Committee, they would see that, so far as the
wants of Cambridge are concerned, Andover by no possibility could
be injured, but would be actually benefited by the fact that there
would be no day in the year when the stream would be as dry as
it sometimes is now. There are days when not more than five or
six million gallons run down that stream. We provide by the bill,
that we will store the water so that there shall be no such dry day as
that; and I think, upon investigation, the authorities of the town
would come to the conclusion that there is no occasion for alarm.
Even if taking the waters of the stream will alarm them, even on
that theory, there is no occasion for alarm in the proposition made
here by the city of Cambridge to-day. I do not understand that
they do find any particular fault with this proposition in itself considered: but they seem to have the feeling there, that they live on
a stream of water the existence of which is vital to the real interests
of the town; and that, no matter where cities may go to get water,
they shall not go to the Shawshine; and that, if Cambridge gets the
right here to take this water, it may be a precedent allowing the use
of it by other cities, and even a larger use by Cambridge if she gets
her hand in. I state their position, as I understand it, fairly. I
understand that to be the reason why they oppose this proposition.
So far as the mill-owners are concerned, until within a day or two I
was hoping that they would come to the conclusion that that dam
is exactly the thing they want; that it would enable them to make a
better use of the waters of that stream than they can make without
it; and that there is nothing in this proposition from Cambridge
which should alarm them, or is detrimental at all to their interests,

but that it would be actually for their interests to have that dam constructed, and in that way to do what is done on many other streams by mill-owners in the Commonwealth. But still they meet us here, and they are to be the best judges of the position they see fit to take in this matter. But I think it will be found, before we get through with this hearing, that, so far as the proposition from Cambridge is concerned, it is a request made to the Legislature for authority to take water by a city which is in strenuous need of water, — a need surpassing that felt by any other municipality in the Commonwealth; to take the water of a stream which is the best water within its reach, and can be got with the least expense ; a stream the taking of the water of which will be less detrimental in a sanitary or business point of view than to take it from any other stream in the Commonwealth of its size. And when the Legislature is granting year after year, almost day after day, when in session, rights to municipalities to take water, we say that you can not and ought not, in reason, to refuse us this privilege.

Mr. Morse. I wish to suggest to the Committee and to my friend, that we ought to have the bill that he proposes to ask from the Committee.

The Chairman. I was going to ask that question, if he had a bill.

Mr. Morse. If the Chairman will permit me, at the last session we went entirely through the hearing, as the Committee will remember, and no bill was presented until after the arguments.

Mr. Hammond. That explains why my brother objected to it.

Mr. Morse. Perhaps it does, and that is the very reason I desire to see it now.

Mr. Hammond. I offer the bill reported by the Committee last year, Senate Doc. No. 211. If sect. 13 is not drawn sufficiently explicit to provide for that 10,000,000 gallons, my brother may draw it to suit himself, provided he does not make us liable for any more.

Mr. Bullard. I would like to inquire of Mr. Hammond whether he has any objection to amending the first section of the bill, as offered last year, so as to provide that the dam which is proposed to be built should be the dam which my brother has indicated on that map? The section, as I understand it now, would allow the erection of a dam at any point in either of those towns, which would be, possibly, a very different matter from the one which is suggested and shown to this Committee.

Mr. Hammond. I am informed by the city engineer that we do not want to agree to furnish the water unless we can have authority to build a dam at that place. The counsel may make it as precise as he chooses.

Mr. BULLARD. And limit it to that place?

Mr. HAMMOND. Yes, sir, substantially. The engineers will do any thing that is reasonable about that.

Mr. BULLARD. Certainly. Practically at that point, I mean.

The CHAIRMAN. Then I understand that you will have a section providing for a dam at that place?

Mr. HAMMOND. Yes, sir: I suppose there would be no objection to that.

Mr. MORSE. I understand that sect. 13 may be amended so that it shall guarantee that at least 10,000,000 gallons a day shall be furnished.

The CHAIRMAN. That is what I understand about that.

Mr. HAMMOND. That there shall be always, so long as we exercise that franchise, a stream of water at the lower side of this dam of not less than 10,000,000 gallons a day. If there is not water enough in the stream, then we will open the reservoir. That is equal to the flow of water over a dam five feet wide, and the water a foot high.

TESTIMONY OF PROFESSOR EDWARD S. WOOD.

Q. (By Mr. HAMMOND.) — You are connected with what institution? A. — Harvard Medical College, in Boston.

Q. — How long have you been connected with it? A. — Since 1871, as a professor.

Q. — You reside in Cambridge? A. — I do.

Q. — Have you had occasion to examine the waters of the Shawshine? A. — I have.

Q. — In what capacity? A. — As one of the medical commissioners of the city of Boston.

Q. — You were appointed when? A. — Appointed by Ex-Mayor Cobb, during his term of service.

Q. — In 1874? A. — About that time.

Q. — Before they took the waters of the Sudbury River? A. — Yes, sir.

Q. — You were upon that commission appointed by the city to see what water Boston should take, or could take? A. — I was.

Q. — Did you have occasion at that time to examine into the matter of the Shawshine? A. — I did.

Q. — Have you been employed by the city of Cambridge to make analyses of the waters of Fresh Pond, Spy Pond, Little Pond, and Wellington Brook? A. — I have, frequently.

Q. — Have you had occasion to consider the purity of the water supply of Cambridge? A. — I have.

Q. — Will you state what your conclusions are about it, with re gard to Fresh Pond, Spy Pond, Little Pond, and Wellington Brook? *A.* — The waters of Spy Pond are totally unfit for domestic use, and they are liable to become very highly contaminated, being surrounded by a very densely populated district, upon one side, at any rate, and containing upon the immediate banks large numbers of market gardens.

Q. — Did you examine the water of Spy Pond, at the request of the city of Cambridge, for the purpose of ascertaining whether the city could use it or not? *A.* — I did examine it for that purpose.

Q. — What report did you make, or what conclusion did you come to? *A.* — I made the report which I have just stated: I advised against its use at any time.

Q. — Did you also make an examination of Little Pond, at the request of the city of Cambridge, for the same purpose? *A.* — I did.

Q. — What did you say about that? *A.* — I made virtually the same report.

Q. — Is that your opinion now? *A.* — It is. That is a small pond: it takes all the surface drainage from very highly cultivated farms in the neighborhood, and at times the water is liable to become impure. At the time when the ground is frozen, a certain amount of surface water can be taken into the conduit from Little Pond. It is a pond of small capacity. The same is true of Wellington Brook. Wellington Brook flows through Belmont, and it picks up a large amount of sewage contamination, even at its head-waters, from the highly cultivated farms there; and in flowing through the town of Belmont, by the Fitchburg Railroad, it picks up a great deal more household sewage, as well as the sewage from a large piggery; and at one time it got a great deal of sewage from a muck-heap connected with the slaughter-house.

Q. — Do you believe that Cambridge can rely upon taking water from Wellington Brook, even when the ground is frozen, for any length of time? *A.* — No, sir.

Q. — And the water of that brook cannot be taken, as I understand you, except when the ground is frozen? *A.* — That is all; taking the flush waters, surface waters.

Q. — Were you employed, also, by a commission appointed by the city of Cambridge in 1879, where Mr. Chesborough was employed as one of the experts? *A.* — Yes, sir.

Q. — Did you make a thorough examination of these matters at that time? *A.* — I did.

Q. — And did you report to the commission? *A.* — I gave a written report to the commission.

Q. — I will ask you whether you made such an investigation as satisfied you as a scientific man of those matters of which you have been speaking? *A.* — Yes, sir; and in addition to that, in regard to Fresh Pond, that there was at that time a necessity for cutting down still further its drainage area, — its collecting area.

Q. — That is, you think that it is necessary to restrict the watershed of Fresh Pond still more, do you? *A.* — It was at that time. Whether that has been done or not, I am not quite sure.

Mr. HAMMOND. Part of it has, and part has not.

Q. — Have you had occasion to make an examination of the subject of water-supply with regard to other towns? *A.* — Yes, sir: a number of cities and towns.

Q. — Name some of them. *A.* — Nahant, Gloucester, Cambridge, Boston, Watertown, are the ones I happen to think of just at this moment.

Q. — Is it your judgment that the waters of the Shawshine are suitable for domestic purposes? *A.* — The stream contains the best water of any stream that I examined at that time.

Q. — Will you say what is your judgment as to the probability of future contamination? *A.* — That was examined at the time by us, and we considered it to be the least dangerous in that respect; that is, that there was less danger of a dense population in future upon the banks of the Shawshine, above that point, than upon the banks of the Sudbury or the Charles above the point of the proposed storage basins; that is, proposed at that time by the city of Boston.

Q. — It is the same point substantially now, I believe? *A.* — Yes, sir.

Cross-Examination.

Q. (By Mr. MORSE.) — Professor Wood, your attention was directed solely, was it not, to ascertaining the comparative purity of the waters of these different streams? *A.* — Both future and present: yes, sir.

Q. — You were not acting in any way as an engineer for the purpose of examining what supply it was possible to take? *A.* — Not at all, sir.

Q. — What year did you make this examination of the Shawshine? *A.* — It was at the time of the medical commission. I have forgotten the exact year, but it was appointed by Mayor Cobb.

Q. — Have you examined the Shawshine since 1874? *A.* — No, sir, I have not since that time. I don't know whether the report went into 1875 or not; but since that investigation I have not.

Q. — Whether the quality of the water is the same now as then, you do not know? *A.* — I do not know, — not by chemical analysis.

Q. — At what point of the river did you examine it? *A.* — I took it from three points, if I remember correctly; I have not had time to look over my old report, or my minutes.

Q. — Do you remember about where those points were? *A.* — One of them was at about the point where the river crosses the Middlesex Canal. I don't remember the exact point; but my impression is that that was one. If my report were here, I could easily point out the place.

Q. — At what season did you make the examination? *A.* — In the summer.

Q. — What time in the summer? *A.* — I think it was in the early fall; possibly earlier than that.

Q. — Well, then, not in the summer? *A.* — Well, it was in the warm weather; if I remember rightly, during my summer vacation, which goes to the last of September. I have not had time to look up the dates, sir: so that I am not clear. It is in the report of the medical commission.

Q. — When last did you examine the Concord River water? *A.* — I don't remember, sir.

Q. — Have you had occasion lately to examine the quality of the Boston water, either from the Sudbury or any of the other supplies? *A.* — I have simply examined one specimen of the Cochituate, or of water coming from the pipes in Boston.

Q. (By Mr. BULLARD.) — Can you tell any thing about these ponds which we find on the map which was prepared for the city of Boston, showing the water-supply? Do you know any thing about the quality of the water in Mead's Pond? *A.* — I do not.

Q. — Do you know any thing about Forest Lake, which was formerly Sandy Pond? *A.* — I do not.

Q. — Or Beaver Pond? *A.* — No, sir: I don't remember that pond.

Q. — You cannot tell me any thing about the territory around those ponds, whether it is open to the objection that it is used for market gardens, or any thing of that sort? *A.* — I cannot. If I went over it, I have forgotten it. It was a good many years ago.

Re-Direct.

Q. (By Mr. HAMMOND.) — When you went over the Shawshine matter, whether you went over it thoroughly or not? *A.* — I went over it the same as I did the Sudbury and the Charles, at the same time, for the purpose of reporting to the city of Boston.

Q. — And made such investigations as you thought you ought to make to satisfy your mind on that question? *A.* — Yes, sir.

Re-Cross.

Q. (By Mr. Poor.) — Did you examine the Concord at that time? *A.* — No, sir, not at that time.

Q. — Subsequently? *A.* — I think I have examined a few specimens of the Concord water ; but I never have inspected it personally, — simply made an analysis of it ; but I cannot recall the time, and I cannot recall the character of the water.

Q. (By Mr. Bullard.) — Have you any reason to suppose that the Shawshine may not ultimately have the same taste that the Boston waters have had this year, I suppose you know, from the sponge? *A.* — I don't know exactly the cause of that spongy taste from my own observation.

Q. — Is there any thing to lead you to suppose that it will not come there? *A.* — Yes, sir.

Q. — What is it? *A.* — Simply because it is less liable to contamination.

Q. — Artificial contamination? *A.* — Yes, sir, that is what I mean.

Q. — If this is a natural contamination from vegetable growth, there is no reason why the Shawshine should not be contaminated as well as the Cochituate, is there? *A.* — With proper care, no, sir : I think there is no more reason.

TESTIMONY OF GEORGE P. CARTER.

Q. (By Mr. Hammond.) — You are President of the Water Board of Cambridge? *A.* — I am.

Q. — And have been for how long a time? *A.* — About eleven years, I think.

Q. — Have you, during that time, had occasion to examine the matter of water-supply? *A.* — I have, sir, many times.

Mr. Hammond. It will shorten this hearing if the gentlemen on the other side will say that they do not intend to contest the fact that we need more water. If they do contest it, I must go on.

Mr. Morse. So far as I am concerned, I admitted that last year, and should be disposed to admit it now.

Q. — Have you also had occasion to consider the whole question of water-supply, as a member of the committee appointed in 1879 by the city of Cambridge? *A.* — I have.

Q. — I will ask you whether, in those various official capacities in which you have acted upon this matter, you have made such investigations as you felt at the time you were bound to make, to make up your mind on the matter? *A.* — I have, very clearly, sir.

Q. — Is the water of Spy Pond used by the city? *A.* — It is not.

Q. — Has it ever been used by the city? *A.* — It has not.

Q. — Will you describe to the Committee the manner in which our water-supply is now used, — how we avail ourselves of it? *A.* — That necessarily will be largely corroborating your opening remarks : it will be going over the same ground. In regard to our supply, it consists mainly of the waters of Fresh Pond. From Fresh Pond we have a conduit extending about four thousand feet, intercepting Wellington Brook, and connecting the supply with Little Pond. We have in former years, at times, used a portion of the water of Little Pond, never that of Spy Pond. The only supply we have in addition to Fresh Pond is what we obtain from Wellington Brook, through a conduit, in the spring of the year, when the ground is frozen, and there are heavy rains, as is usually the case at that season of the year, and melting of the snow, similar to the present condition of things. We are now taking water from Wellington Brook through this conduit, which will give us our only supply through the coming year, as figures which I have here will show beyond any question.

Q. — You take that in the spring of the year ; then do you use the water of Wellington Brook after the ground ceases to be frozen? *A.* — Then we shut the gate, and do not use it again until the season comes round again.

Q. — Why not? *A.* — Because the water is unfit to be used for domestic purposes.

Q. — What is the result of that method of operating on the level of Fresh Pond? *A.* — I have it here. During the last year we have had experience in this matter which presents the case very strongly.

Q. — Well, sir, will you state it in your own way? *A.* — April 5, 1880, the level reached the highest of that year, four feet and one inch above the top of the conduit which conveys the water into the well-room of the engine-house.

Q. — By the way, you heard my description of the manner in which the water is taken from the pond? *A.* — Yes, sir ; and I have a sketch of that matter.

Q. — Was that substantially correct? *A.* — It was. [Sketch shown and explained to the Committee.]

Q. — I suppose that the purpose of having two steam-pumps of the capacity of 5,000,000 gallons each is not for the purpose of pumping 10,000,000 gallons a day, but for the purpose of pumping 5,000,-000, if one gives out? *A.* — For the purpose of reserve.

Q. — Now, Mr. Carter, you may proceed. *A.* — I have said that in 1880, April 5, the level reached the highest point of that year, — four feet and one inch above the top of the conduit. Feb. 9, 1881, it had gradually fallen to that date to one foot and three and one-fourth inches below the top of the conduit. April 18, 1881, it rose to seven feet and one-half inch above the top of the conduit. That, you see, is the effect of the spring rains that we are getting to-day, partially, and the melting of snow. Jan. 25, 1881, it had fallen to two feet and two and seven-eighths inches above the conduit.

Q. — It had got down to only two feet and two and seven-eighths inches above the top of the conduit? A. — Yes, sir. Feb. 23 (that was yesterday) it stood at four feet and six and one-half inches above the conduit.

Q. (By Mr. TIRRELL.) — What does the 16.85 mean on this plan? A. — That is high-water mark.

Mr. HAMMOND. The engineer will explain that. The fact is, as the engineer will state to you, as I understand it, the high-water mark of Fresh Pond is but very little above the high-water mark of the ocean; and, as I understand that line, it is the high-water mark of the ocean. Is that so, Mr. Barbour?

Mr. BARBOUR. Yes, sir.

The CHAIRMAN. We understand that. I think what Mr. Tirrell wanted to know was, whether that 16.85 means the average depth of the pond.

Mr. HAMMOND. Oh, no! that means its height above a certain coping in Charlestown.

WITNESS. I speak entirely in regard to the level of the pond, as relates to the conduit itself. That is easily understood by the Committee. I have not used the city base at all. From April 5, 1880, to Feb. 9, 1881, the loss was five feet four and one-half inches; the rainfall, 22.11 inches. From Feb. 9, 1881, to April 18, 1881, gain, eight feet three and three-fourths inches; rainfall, 16.71 inches. From April 18, 1881, to Jan. 25, 1882, loss, four feet nine and five-eighths inches; rainfall, 25.33 inches. From Jan. 25, 1882, to Feb. 23, 1882, gain, two feet three and five-eighths inches; rainfall, 11.17 inches. Making a total rainfall from April 5, 1880, to Jan. 25, 1882, of 75.31 inches.

Q. — That is a very wet season, is it not? A. — That is a wet season. Now, our mechanical engineer at the engine-house has made, at my request, a statement of the level of the pond weekly from April 5, 1880, until the present day. I will not go over this: it is quite long; but it shows a gradual fall of the pond, a steady loss, from April 5, 1880, to Feb. 9, 1882, — a constant decline, excepting, at times when there was a heavy rainfall, it gained perhaps an inch or half an inch.

Q. — Now, Mr. Carter, I will ask you whether, if you were deprived of the power to draw from Wellington Brook at these times you speak of, the water of Fresh Pond would, in your judgment, last twelve months? A. — No, sir: I should think not.

Q. — Now, does that plan indicate to the eye the changes that you have been speaking about? *A.* — This plan indicates precisely the figures which I have already given the Committee. [Plan shown and explained to the Committee.]

Q. — Now, Mr. Carter, you have stated the manner in which the water is obtained. At any time in 1880 were you obliged to pump water into the well-room from which the pumps took the water for the city? *A.* — We were.

Q. — You may state the circumstances, and what was done. *A.* — When the water reached its lowest level, as indicated upon that plan (we had previously feared that we might be brought to that condition), we had nearly completed our connection with Boston, fearing a water famine, and had also provided an engine placed upon the borders of the pond, with a centrifugal pump, for the purpose of pumping into the conduit should the water get so low that our pumps in the well-room would not reach it.

Q. — Did the water in the well-room get so low that the suction pipes of the pump would not work? *A.* — They did.

Q. — And you therefore used this pump on the borders of the pond for the purpose of pumping into the well-room? *A.* — We commenced pumping the water into the conduit from the centrifugal pump, and pumped it, I think, two days only, when a heavy rain came on.

Q. — Were any other precautions taken by Cambridge, in 1880, to get water, fearing a famine, — any connection made with the pipes of Boston? *A.* — I have already stated that fact.

Q. — What was the expense of that connection? *A.* — That was between $20,000 and $25,000.

Q. — Have you stated, also, that you applied to Boston for the water? *A.* — I have not.

Q. — You may state whether you applied to the city of Boston, and what was said, and what was done. *A.* — Before getting the appropriation for constructing this connection between Boston and Cambridge, we consulted with the Boston Water Board. They said that they would furnish us with water, if we got into a position of dire necessity, although they were losing their water every day: it was growing less and less. Upon that statement we got an appropriation from the City Council, and made this connection as rapidly as possible; and after having completed it, or nearly so, we applied to the city of Boston to let us have water, or to see if they could not furnish us with water. They said that things were different from what they were when we first met them; that they were already pumping into their conduit at the Mystic Works, and were making preparations to pump into the conduit at Cochituate. It seemed to them, therefore, that we ought to do the same before calling upon them; that we should erect an engine, and pump into our conduit. We did so.

Q. (By the CHAIRMAN.) — What year was that? *A.* — That was in 1880.

Q. (By Mr. HAMMOND.) — I will ask you if you remember whether there was a special meeting of the City Council called for the purpose of considering this matter, or not? *A.* — There was. The representation of the Water Board was, that the emergency was such that it was necessary that the matter should be decided upon at once.

Q. (By the CHAIRMAN.) — By your arrangement with the city of Boston, I believe you could draw only from certain sources of supply. The Sudbury was not available for you, was it? *A.* — Yes. So far as the city of Boston was concerned, we could not tell which source would supply that pipe.

Q. — Do you remember what was said on behalf of the city of Boston on that point, if any thing? *A.* — I don't remember what was said in regard to the water.

Q. — What I wanted to know was, what the arrangement with the city of Boston was, whether they were to furnish you water from those two sources, or only from one.

Mr. MORSE. I will remind the Chairman that last year, when the subject was under consideration, the witness was asked that same question, and stated that the connection would be made either with the Sudbury or with the Cochituate.

WITNESS. It may have been the impression upon my memory at that time, perhaps; but I cannot say to-day how that was, whether the Cochituate and Sudbury River waters were united, or which water was to be conveyed in that pipe. It was a pipe running through Beacon Street. They simply had not a supply to give us from any source.

Q. (By Mr. HAMMOND.) — In your examination last year you gave us a statement of the daily supply from 1865 to 1880. I suppose that statement was correct: was it not? *A.* — I believe it to be, sir: it was taken from the records.

Mr. HAMMOND. I should like to put that in. I believe there is no dispute about it: —

"The average daily supply in 1865, as I have stated before. was 1,461,048 gallons. In 1868 (we have no record for 1866 or 1867) it was 1,732,755 gallons; in 1869, 1,677,481 gallons; in 1870, 1,739,869 gallons; in 1871, 1,747,704 gallons; in 1872, 1,626,206 gallons; in 1873, 2,124,884 gallons; in 1874, 2,298,953 gallons; in 1875, 2,718,484 gallons. There was a severe drought that year, and there was more water used than in any other year on the list. In 1876, 2,438,-

564 gallons; in 1877, 2,631,732 gallons; in 1878, 2,257,190 gallons; in 1879, 2,432,386 gallons; in 1880, 2,420,500 gallons."

Q. — What was the average consumption of water last year in the city per inhabitant? *A.* — 46¾ gallons, I think ; that is, including the metred water.

Q. — That includes all the water that is used, does it? *A.* — Yes, sir.

Q. — Has that been about the consumption for two or three years in Cambridge? *A.* — That has been about the consumption for two or three years. I stated to the Committee last year that I thought we had reached the minimum, as far as the consumption *per capita* is concerned.

Q. — I will ask you whether, as a matter of fact, the Water Board have devoted a great deal of attention to the subject of stopping leaks, in order to reduce the consumption? *A.* — They have. I don't know of any other water-works where any thing like the amount of labor is expended in that direction that we give to it. We have felt the necessity of it.

Q. — Now, do you feel at all certain, from what you are told by experts, and from your knowledge of the ground, that you can make use of Wellington Brook, even as you do now, for any length of time? *A.* — I don't think we ought to use it at all now.

Q. — You would not use it if you could avoid it, would you? *A.* — I would not.

Q. — State whether you are careful as to the times when you take that water, — whether you watch it carefully, etc.? *A.* — We do : I remember when our water-level was lowest in the pond, I went up to the Wellington Brook gate with the Superintendent, and there was a large amount of water there, considerably colored, partially from the muck-heaps that have been referred to; and we sat there in the wagon, I should think, fifteen minutes, to determine whether it was best to take that water or not. It did not look in the proper condition to go into our pond ; but the necessity was so great, that I gave the direction to do it, and it was done.

Q. — You would not have done it unless you had felt the necessity, would you? *A.* — No, sir, not by any means.

Q. — Those muck-heaps that have been spoken of were, as I understand it, heaps of muck upon which the slaughter-house in Belmont poured the "soup," as they call it, in which the hogs have been washed? A. — Yes, sir.

Q. — Is there any thing else you desire to say, Mr. Carter, about it? *A.* — I do not think of any special points. It would all tend in the same direction, — of our emergency for a further supply. I don't think that can be questioned by any fair and disinterested mind. The fact is, it is a matter of evidence.

Q. — Whether the inhabitants of Cambridge depend on wells to any great extent, or whether they depend on their water-supply? *A.* — They depend on their water-supply entirely for domestic purposes. I suppose I ought to say something in regard to the supply in connection with the city of Boston.

Q. — Well, sir, state any thing you desire to upon that subject. *A.* — It is not by any means a supply of water. If we could be allowed to take it, it is only a 16-inch pipe, and we tested it one night to see what amount of water we could get from it; and that night, as near as we could estimate, we got 1,500,000 gallons, — that is, at that rate. The gate was only open a short time; but we got at the rate of 1,500,000 in 24 hours. That is only, of course, a supply so far as it goes, in case of a water famine, or a large fire, perhaps, or any thing of that sort.

Q. (By Mr. RAND.) — How many of your water-takers are metred? *A.* — A very small proportion of them. I think we have only about 150 metres. They are mostly manufacturers.

Q. — How many water-takers are there? *A.* — Eight or nine thousand.

Q. (By Dr. WILSON.) — What is the average amount of water consumed by metred water-takers per day? *A.* — I don't recollect the number of gallons. The amount of receipts is a little rising, this last year, $30,000. We furnish it at two cents per one hundred gallons.

Q. — You have no means of knowing how many of the inhabitants use metres? *A.* — It is only the manufacturers that use metres.

Mr. HAMMOND. I understand that the amount of metred water last year was 208,000,000 gallons, out of a total consumption of 902,-000,000 gallons.

Cross-Examination.

Q. (By Mr. MORSE.) — Do all the manufactures use metres? *A.* — They do not.

Q. — Is there any rule in regard to which shall use them, and which shall not? *A.* — There is no rule.

Q. — Who determines it? *A.* — The Water Board.

Q. — Do you determine that with reference to the extent of the use, or what is the principle? *A.* — Not always.

Q. — Is there any definite rule in regard to when metres shall be ordered, and when not? *A.* — There is not: it is left to the judgment of the Board.

Q. — What would it cost to introduce metres generally into the city? *A.* — Well, I suppose a good metre can be bought for about fifteen dollars.

Q. — Have you ever had any estimate made as to the expense of supplying metres for all the water-takers? *A.* — I never have.

Q. — Have you any judgment yourself about it? *A.* — I have not. I never believed in it, and never figured up in reference to that.

Q. — Why do you order a metre in any case? *A.* — We order them for manufacturing purposes in order to ascertain what water they are using, and getting pay for it.

Q. — I understand you do not have any rule in regard to manufacturers, that they shall all have metres? *A.* — Not all of them: there are some very small manufacturers.

Q. — I asked you a moment ago whether you had any rule fixing the use of metres by manufacturers in proportion to the size of their business? *A.* — I answered no.

Q. — Have you made any estimate, or caused any estimate to be made, of the expense of this project of taking the waters of the Shawshine? *A.* — The engineer has made estimates.

Q. — Have you any objection to his giving those to this Committee?

Mr. HAMMOND. You will have them. We are going to put him on next.

Q. — Have you any question that the supply of the city of Boston, if properly managed, is sufficient to furnish what you want in Cambridge? *A.* — I have doubt about the quantity and quality both, sir.

Q. — Well, on the matter of quantity, first. Did not Mr. Chesborough report in this special report that has been referred to, speaking of the supply from the city of Boston, that "such an arrangement could no doubt be made, mutually advantageous, Boston having an abundant supply, not only for the present but for the future"? *A.* — Yes, sir.

Q. — Did you not accept that report as a correct statement? *A.* — I did. I don't know what he would say after the experience of last year, however.

Q. — I am not referring, of course, to the amount of water that the city of Boston may get from its present reservoirs to-day. My question relates rather to what the city can do, availing itself of all its rights under its different statutes. *A.* — You must mean the minimum supply?

Q. — Yes. *A.* — I don't think it would be safe, as Boston is going on, to rely upon it.

Q. — You say "as Boston is going on." My question is this: Suppose that, under some management, the water-supply of Boston could be different from what it is, and that instead of using twice as much, or almost twice as much, per head, as you do in Cambridge, they should use on the average about what you do, and suppose that the city should avail itself of its right to build other reservoirs, and get the benefit of its water-supply, have you any doubt that there would be sufficient to supply Cambridge with a great deal more than you want? *A.*—I should think there would be, with all those additions.

Q.—So that it is a question of management, and not a question of capacity, in regard to the supply of Boston, is it not? *A.*—Not entirely; because, if they showed less waste, they would need still further basins.

Q.—Well, they are building further basins, or providing for them now, are they not? *A.*—I think they are; but a greater objection to me would be the quality of the water: our water is bad enough now.

Q.—We will come to that in a moment; but with regard to the quantity, first: Have you made any inquiry, or caused any to be made by your engineer, as to the capacity of Boston to supply water? *A.*—I don't know that we have.

Q.—But you have a general knowledge of the fact, have you not, that it is sufficient for Boston and for Cambridge, or that it may be made sufficient? *A.*—No, sir, I have not.

Q.—Then we misunderstand each other. I understood you to say that you accepted Mr. Chesborough's report as correct, where he says that Boston has an abundant supply, not only for the present, but for the future. *A.*—I think I have had reason to change my mind about that since that report was made.

Q.—Have you had any examination made by any engineer since Mr. Chesborough made this report for the benefit of the city of Cambridge, which has caused you to change your mind? *A.*—I have not; I have only the facts which we all know of last year.

Q.—What were those? *A.*—That they could not furnish us with any thing.

Q.—They said they couldn't? *A.*—They couldn't. I knew they couldn't.

Q.—The city of Boston claims now that it has not sufficient authority to supply itself with water, but you don't believe that, do you? You must have investigated the subject, of course, and have you not formed an opinion as to whether or not that claim is correct, that Boston needs a further water-supply? *A.*—Yes, sir: I have an opinion that she needs a further water-supply.

Q.—You think so? *A.*—Yes, sir.

Q.—And you mean by that that they have not authority to get water now? *A.*—That I cannot say; I don't know what authority she has.

Q.—Since you laid your sixteen-inch pipe to connect with the main of the Boston water-supply, have you had any negotiations with the Boston Water Board in reference to getting a supply from Boston? *A.* — None whatever.

Q. — And that was a year ago last summer? *A.* — A year ago this time.

Q. — Was that the time that your pipe was laid? *A.* — That was the time our water was lowest, — in February, I think.

Q. — You have not had any negotiations since then? *A.* — No, sir.

Q. — Have you ever brought it to the attention of the city government of Boston? *A.* — We never have.

Q. — Suppose the quality of the Boston water was satisfactory, and that there was a sufficient quantity, have you any doubt that a supply could be obtained by connection with the Boston water-works at much less cost to the city of Cambridge than to take this independent supply from the Shawshine? *A.* — No, sir. I think at the time we talked over that matter, I made up my mind that the cost would be more than it would be to go to the Shawshine.

Q. — The cost would be more? *A.* — Yes, sir.

Q. — How much would it cost to go to the Shawshine? *A.* — The city engineer reports that the expense would be about $600,000.

Q. — That is, the original outlay? *A.* — Yes, sir.

Q. — What original outlay would there be in taking water from the city of Boston beyond the cost of laying the connecting pipe? *A.* — Well, they told us they would have to construct some dams that would cost $400,000 or $500,000, and lay one or two large mains; and the result of it was, that I concluded that it would cost us $500,000 or $600,000.

Q. — Who was the person with whom you negotiated? *A.* — I think it was the president of the Water Board, Mr. Cutter, or it was at a meeting of the Water Board, in their office.

Q. — Are there any figures in existence that were given you by them in reference to what the cost would be? *A.* — I think not; only the statements that they made at the time. They are not very clear in my mind at the present time, only I was satisfied that it would be a very expensive matter.

Q. — Where is this sixteen-inch pipe? *A.* — It runs from Putnam Avenue to Brookline Street, and from there across Brookline Bridge.

Q. — How long is it? *A.* — We laid about three thousand feet.

Q. — What is the size of the main with which you connect in Boston? *A.* — Sixteen inches.

Mr. BARBOUR. Twelve.

WITNESS. It is twelve on the other side.

Q. — How far distant is that twelve-inch pipe from the main pipe? *A.* — Well, I should think it was half a mile.

Q. — Has not a new forty-eight inch pipe been laid in Beacon Street? *A.* — It was laid at that time.

Q. — Why can't you connect with that? *A.* — This pipe did connect with it.

Q. — Then you misunderstand me. My question was, with what size pipe of the Boston supply did your pipe connect? *A.* — I think that was four feet. That was the new pipe.

Q. — Then, when you speak about the quantity of water that you could get through your pipe, you simply mean through a sixteen-inch pipe? *A.* — Through a twelve-inch pipe. It amounts to twelve inches, because we connect with a twelve-inch pipe, of course.

Q. — Of course you could get a much larger pipe to connect with the city main pipe? *A.* — Oh, certainly.

Q. — And that cost would be trifling comparatively? *A.* — Well, we should have to lay a large pipe quite a distance if we undertook that.

Q. — If I understand it, your pipe is connected to-day with the Boston water-supply? *A.* — Yes, sir, it is.

Q. — And you have not any question but what they would give you some water, if they had it, in case of any emergency in Cambridge? *A.* — Give us all they could from that pipe.

Q. — And you could get through that pipe 1,500,000 gallons a day? *A.* — Yes, sir ; and, with certain conditions, we might get more than that. For instance, if our reservoir was entirely empty, we probably should get more then that ; might get double, perhaps. That test was applied when our reservoir, which was the pressure against it, was nearly full.

Q. — Do I understand that the supply which runs through this pipe connected with the Boston main runs to Fresh Pond ; or do you take the water simply into your pipes for distribution? *A.* — We take it into our cistern.

Q. — The water is not conducted to Fresh Pond? *A.* — No, sir.

Q. — Now, in reference to drawing down the water of the pond, I understand that the lowest point which you have ever reached since you introduced the water-supply was last winter, and then you were down fourteen inches below the top of the conduit. *A.* — Fifteen inches and a quarter exactly.

Q. — And the conduit is four feet in diameter? *A.* — Yes, sir.

Q. — Did you make any estimate at that time as to how long it would take to draw out what was left, supposing there was no supply coming in at all? *A.* — Draw out the water where, sir?

Q. — Out of the pond. *A.* — I don't know that I understand your question.

Q. — What I mean is, how long would it have taken you to exhaust

Fresh Pond at that time? *A.* — No, sir: I have not made any calculation. I presume we should have exhausted it if we had not had rains.

Q. — My object was to find out how long, in your judgment, it would have taken. *A.* — We should consume it pretty rapidly when it got to so low a stage as that, the surface area being diminished so much.

Q. — What is the source of supply of Fresh Pond? *A.* — It has not really any of any consequence.

Q. — Well, the water comes from somewhere. *A.* — On the south side we have perhaps a square mile of rain area.

Q. — Are there springs below the pond? *A.* — Well, there used to be a good deal said by my associates and others about springs in the bottom of the pond; but we found, when we got our water very low in the pond, that the springs seemed to give out at the same time: so that the probability is, that we have some water that gets into the pond from the springs when the springs are all full in the vicinity.

Q. — Have you made any examination in reference to getting water, except with regard to the Shawshine, and this supply from Boston? *A.* — You will understand that our commission made an investigation into that matter, which has been referred to by the city solicitor.

Q. — Well, what personally have you learned in regard to it? *A.* — I remember some years ago we came to the Legislature, asking to take the waters of Clematis Brook, as we call it, or Beaver Brook, or something of that kind, in the town of Waltham.

Q. — Have you examined into the matter of the Concord River? *A.* — I have not, sir.

Q. — Have you given it any attention since last winter? *A.* — I have; that is, I have done this: I have requested our engineer to get what information he could about that as a source of water-supply. I never had any faith in it myself.

Q. — Have you had any examination made of the character of the Shawshine water since 1874? *A.* — I have not.

Q. — Then you do not know any thing about its purity to-day? *A.* — I do not. I will have an analysis taken of it, though, before this hearing is over.

Q. — Well, what reason have you to suppose you could take that river, dam it up, and bring the water to Cambridge, and be free from the troubles that the city of Boston has met with in taking the waters of the Sudbury? *A.* — Only from the testimony of experts.

Q. — Those experts thought just as well of the Sudbury before it was taken, didn't they? *A.* — I can't say as to that.

Q. — This trouble in the pond that the city of Boston has found is owing to something growing in the pond, vegetation, or something of that kind, in your judgment, is it not? *A.* — Well, I have not formed any judgment upon that. I am not satisfied with the statements that have been already made.

Q. — No, but I understand you to state to the Committee that one great reason why you should not want to take your supply from Boston, even supposing that all the details could be arranged, is because you would not be satisfied with the quality of the water; but you expect that you can get from the Shawshine River water of a better quality. My object was to see whether you had any reason for that; whether in case you took the water of the Shawshine, and deemed it to be good, you would not be likely to go through the same experience that the city of Boston has? *A.* — My reason for that is the information that I got as to the basin of the river and the ground that it overflows. I know that it must be very different in that respect from the Sudbury River.

Q. — One question more, and I believe I shall have done. You testified that the amount of water which is taken by the manufacturers, which passes through metres, was about a quarter of the entire amount consumed in Cambridge last year? *A.* — No, sir: I made no such statement as that. My statement was, that our receipts show that we get something over $30,000 from them, and that we sell the water for two cents a hundred gallons. That was my statement.

Q. — That was not the statement I refer to. Perhaps I misunderstood you. I understood you to say that the entire amount of water consumed in Cambridge last year was 902,000,000 gallons.

Mr. HAMMOND. I stated that.

Q. — Is not that correct? *A.* — The record will show. I don't know.

Q. — And that the amount that passed through metres was about 200,000,000 gallons. That you stated, didn't you?

Mr. HAMMOND. I stated that.

Q. — Don't you stand by what brother Hammond stated? *A.* — No : I go by the record.

Q. — Haven't you the record at hand, that you can give us? *A.* — I don't think I have. We have records enough of that kind. Mr. Barbour will be put on. We keep a record of about every thing that occurs in the water-supply.

Q. — Assuming, for the purposes of my question, that that is a correct statement by Mr. Hammond, as I suppose we all believe it to be, the real fact is, that the present supply of Cambridge is adequate for the ordinary domestic uses of water? *A.* — I should not say it was. I should not be satisfied with it. I should not be satisfied as to the quantity in future, nor as to the quality at present, in view of the dangers surrounding it.

Q. — Do you know of a single city or town that has ever had any extensive supply of water, that has not had more or less trouble with the quality of the water? Is it not a matter of constant complaint? *A.* — I think I can mention the city of Salem as a place where they never have had any trouble about their water.

Q. — Never had any trouble? *A.* — Never, that I have heard of.

Q. — Any other place? *A.* — The town of Concord.

Q. — That is a small place. I refer to places of any size. Take large cities, either here or elsewhere, and is it not a matter of experience that there have been serious troubles with the quality of the water? *A.* — My recollection is, that I have heard of troubles of that kind in the cities of New York, Boston, and some of our neighboring cities.

Q. — Do you expect that you are going to escape all troubles, and have perfect water, if you take the Shawshine? *A.* — Pretty nearly. Fresh Pond water is of poor quality to-day, and has been.

Q. — That suggests one single question more. A portion of the town of Belmont was annexed to Cambridge within the last year or two? *A.* — Yes, sir.

Q. — For the purpose, mainly, was it not, of giving you control of the nuisances near Fresh Pond? *A.* — Yes, sir, that was one object, that we should not have any more of them on the same territory.

Q. — Have you been able to remove them? *A.* — We have not been able to remove what was placed there before annexation; but we have been able to prevent any more coming there in that vicinity.

Q. — Why don't you remove those that were placed there before annexation? *A.* — I don't know any power to do it, sir.

Q. — Because they have vested rights?

Mr. HAMMOND. Well, brother Morse, it is pretty easy to defend a slaughter-house before a jury.

A. — We could not even get Belmont to withhold permission to erect a slaughter-house, much less to remove one after it has been erected.

Q. — Then I understand you, there are to-day existing nuisances within the territory of Cambridge which pollute the water of Fresh Pond. Is that so? *A.* — I believe there are: yes, sir.

Q. (By Mr. HAMMOND.) — Is the water which you furnish manufacturers used to run wheels, or to put in their boilers, to make steam for their engines? *A.* — It is not used as motive power at all.

Q. — Except as steam? *A.* — Except as steam.

Q. (By Mr. BULLARD.) — Before the water got so low in the pond, was there a record kept, for a short time previous, of the daily fall?

A. — Yes, sir, always; going back to the commencement of our works.

Q. — Does that plan show the daily fall in inches shortly before the lowest point was reached? *A.* — I can't say as to that plan : the city engineer can answer that.

Q. (To Mr. BARBOUR.) — Is that the fact?

Mr. BARBOUR. Yes, sir.

Q. — Don't you know, as a matter of fact, that, as the pond gets low, the water becomes harder and harder? *A.* — Yes, sir.

Q. — What does that indicate to you? *A.* — Well, I have a theory about it : I don't know whether it is correct or not.

Q. — What is that theory? *A.* — That more or less tide-water gets into the pond.

Q. — Not spring-water? *A.* — Not spring-water.

Q. — Does it become brackish? *A.* — It is not brackish.

Q. — Simply hard? *A.* — Hard.

Q. — It cannot be from spring-water coming in? *A.* — I don't know but what it is.

Q. — Don't you know that Boston is ready to lay a main pipe through Cambridge to connect with the Sudbury or the Mystic? *A.* — I think they have.

Q. — If that pipe were laid, would there be any expense involved in taking water from it by the city of Cambridge, except in the matter of laying a larger pipe? *A.* — That is a matter that I was questioned about by Mr. Morse, and I answered his question.

Q. — I did not understand you so. I understood you to be speaking of the connection which you have already made with the Beacon-street pipe. *A.* — No, sir : not when I was alluding to the large expense. I had reference to a former bill that the city of Boston got from the Legislature, allowing them permission to run a large pipe through Old Cambridge, when I was answering Mr. Morse's question.

Q. — You think, then, that if the city of Boston laid a pipe connecting the Sudbury and Mystic supplies, for her own purposes, it would bring an expense upon you of $600,000 to connect with that pipe? *A.* — Five or six hundred thousand dollars, I said.

Q. — Is not that the expense of the whole construction? As I understand the statement by Boston, that pipe would not cost over $300,000 to lay.

Mr. HAMMOND. Then there are additional storage basins to be constructed.

WITNESS. I think Boston at that time wanted eighty per cent of our receipts for water. That is part of the expense, isn't it?

Q. — Don't you think the talk of Boston about not having enough water had a little reference to the price to be secured from you?

Mr. HAMMOND. We think they tried to drive a hard bargain.

Q. (By Mr. BAILEY.) — It was last February that you tried to make an arrangement with Boston? A. — Yes, sir.

Q. — At that time, was not Boston pumping into the Mystic pipe? A. — Yes, sir : I have already so stated.

Q. — And had no water with which to supply you from either source at that time? A. — No, sir.

Q. (By Mr. SMITH.) — You spoke of a certain proportion of your manufactories as being metred. A. — Yes, sir.

Q. — What proportion are not metred? A. — Very small indeed : I cannot tell how small.

Q. — Couldn't you give an idea of the relative number? A. — No, sir. Some of our manufacturers have bored wells for water.

Q. (By Mr. MORSE.) — Have they found water? A. — Oh, yes, in many cases.

Q. — In sufficient supply? A. — In many cases. They have bored artesian wells.

Q. (By Dr. WILSON.) — Did I understand that it is a twelve-inch pipe that connects with the four-foot main on Beacon Street? A. — Our sixteen-inch pipe, that is connected with our general plan for the supply of the city with water, was extended across Brookline Bridge, and connects with a ten-inch pipe in Boston. That ten-inch pipe is about half a mile from its connection with a four-foot pipe.

Q. — So that the 1,500,000 gallons a day that you got for twenty-four hours was what came from a ten-inch pipe? A. — Yes, sir.

Q. — Now, then, would the city of Boston permit you to put in a sixteen-inch pipe in the place of the ten-inch pipe, so that you could get the capacity of a sixteen-inch pipe all the way from the four-foot main to Cambridge? A. — I presume they would be very glad to have us enlarge their pipes ; but then we should not get water enough. One sixteen-inch pipe would not furnish us with water enough.

Q. — I thought that 2,700,000 gallons a day was the maximum amount that you used ; and, if a ten-inch pipe would supply 1,500,000 gallons, I am not an engineer, but I should judge that a sixteen-inch pipe would supply the balance. A. — Our consumption is 2,500,000 a day. That day means about ten hours : we only pump about ten hours.

Q. — If you had a basin for the water to flow into, you could easily regulate that. A. — Yes, sir : we have a basin now.

Q. — Then the question comes up in my mind whether, if the water of Wellington Brook was of good quality, it would be sufficient to supply Cambridge, in addition to Fresh Pond? A. — It would not be safe to rely upon it, from the fact that we can only use it at this season of the year. During the summer, there is some little water. not a great deal, coming from Wellington Brook.

Q. — You could get the water, if it was of good quality, from Wellington Brook all the year round? A. — I don't think we could get a full supply.

Q. — What is it that contaminates Wellington Brook? Is it the surface drainage? Is it any thing that can be remedied? A. — It is the highly-cultivated farms. It is very low. Highly-cultivated farms are on the borders of the brook. and also the drainage of the town of Belmont is put in there; and at this season of the year, we let the first wash go over it before we open the gate. We are supposed to clean out the brook as well as we can before we let the water into the pond.

Q. (By the CHAIRMAN.) — Is there drainage from any houses into the brook? A. — Yes, sir. There is no drainage system: but it is the drainage from houses on the borders of the brook.

Q. (By Dr. WILSON.) — Would it be very expensive to dig trenches to take the drainage from those premises, and carry off the surface drainage that you say now goes into the brook? Would it not be possible to dig channels to take this stuff off? A. — I don't think it is practicable.

Q. (By Dr. HARRIS.) — By building a dam. could you not store any amount of water? I have noticed the small ponds upon that stream, but have not examined them particularly: but it occurs to me at this moment that it might be possible during the winter and spring to reserve a considerable supply of water in Wellington Brook. A. — That is rather an engineering question. I prefer that our engineer should answer that. The fact that our experts have not given us any information upon such a matter as that is a reason why I think we could not adopt it practically.

Q. (By Mr. HAMMOND.) — You stated that 2.500,000 gallons were pumped in ten hours. You mean that the pump goes only about ten hours, and then the water goes up into the reservoir: but it represents what is consumed in twenty-four hours, doesn't it? A. — Yes. sir; we have got a reservoir which contains 5.000,000 gallons, for the supply of water required during the working-hours of the day. We fill up that reservoir during the night.

TESTIMONY OF WILLIAM S. BARBOUR.

Q. (By Mr. HAMMOND.) — You are the city engineer of Cambridge. and have been for how long? A. — Six years.

Q. — You have had occasion. in that capacity, and as a member of the Commission which has been spoken of, to consider the water-supply of Cambridge? A. — I have.

Q. — Mr. Chesborough was a member of the Commission appointed in 1879? *A.* — He was not a member of the Commission, but was employed as an expert.

Q. — Did you consult him? *A.* — I did.

Q. — Did you go to Chicago to see him? *A.* — I did.

Q. — Did he come here? *A.* — Yes, sir, he did.

Q. — Did you and he put your heads together in such a way as to satisfy yourselves, and investigate the question thoroughly? *A.* — We thought we did.

Q. — Have you considered this Shawshine problem? *A.* — Yes, sir.

Q. — What is the capacity of that river? *A.* — The capacity of the river, with full storage, above the point where we propose to build the dam, — that is, near the old Middlesex Canal, — we call 20,500,000 gallons per day.

Q. — Have you made measurements as to the flow of the stream, at various times? *A.* — I have made some.

Q. — How often? *A.* — Well, as often as once a month the last year, and oftener the year previous.

Q. — Was that the capacity, as put down in the report which the engineers made to Boston in 1874? *A.* — I think it was, substantially.

Q. — Your observations corroborate that, do they? *A.* — They do.

Q. — Do you know how large the water-shed is? *A.* — Thirty-four square miles, including the basin.

Q. — What is the character of the water-shed, as to the likelihood of furnishing pure water? *A.* — I think it is well calculated for pure water.

Q. — Now, how large a reservoir do you need there? *A.* — We propose to build there a reservoir covering eight hundred acres, or thereabouts.

Q. — What will be its capacity? *A.* — About 2,000,000,000 gallons.

Q. — Do you believe that Cambridge can safely say that not less than 10,000,000 gallons shall leave that reservoir in any day? *A.* — I think we can do it.

Q. — Have you any doubt about it? *A.* — No, sir.

Q. — What is the length of the dam? *A.* — Sixteen hundred feet.

Q. — And its height? *A.* — The highest point will be twenty-five feet, tapering out on the sides to nothing.

Q. — How do you propose to get the water to Cambridge? *A.* — We propose to get it to Cambridge by laying a pipe along the line of the old Middlesex Canal, until we reach the town of Winchester, near the head of Mystic Pond, and there branch across to Fresh Pond.

Q. — And use the waters then by the way of Fresh Pond? *A.* — Yes, sir.

Q. — You have heard Mr. Carter's statement with regard to the manner in which the waters of Wellington Brook and Fresh Pond are now used : are they true? *A.* — I think they are, substantially ; yes, sir.

Q. — Did you make that plan, showing the rise and fall of the pond? *A.* — I did.

Q. — When the pond is at high-water mark, what is its area? *A.* — About one hundred and eighty-eight acres.

Q. — What was its area when it was at the lowest point? *A.* — About a hundred and fifty.

Q. — Do you feel safe in going down much lower in the pond? Can you tell what kind of water you are going to reach, — whether it will be good or bad? *A.* — We anticipated getting bad water when we were getting near the bottom, and it was rather poorer in quality than it had been before, as we went down.

Q. — Brackish? *A.* — Slightly. Yes, sir.

Q. — As a matter of fact, the surface of Fresh Pond is about on a level with the surface of the ocean, is it not? *A.* — Very nearly. It is a little higher at full pond than mean high tide.

Q. — If there were no artificial obstruction the salt water could come into Fresh Pond, could it not? *A.* — Yes, sir.

Q. — Is it not tradition that it has done so? *A.* — It is supposed that it has been up in there.

Mr. HAMMOND. As a matter of fact, if we look over the legislation passed about the first half of this century, we shall find various statutes which provide for keeping the sea-water out of Fresh Pond. As I understand it, Alewife Brook is very level.

Q. — Now, Mr. Barbour, have you made estimates as to the cost of the construction of the works which it would be necessary to have to take the water in the manner you propose? *A.* — Yes, sir.

Q. — And what is your estimate? *A.* — The estimate which I made last year, and which I think was submitted before this Committee, was $600,000. I think, with the advance in materials at the present time, perhaps we should call it about $700,000.

Q. — What does that include? *A.* — It includes building the dam, with the fixtures, gatehouses, and whatever is necessary ; laying the pipe, purchasing the necessary land for the storage basin, and the right of way.

Q. — Land for the storage basin and right of way, and the cost of the actual physical structures that you have got to build. *A.* — The mechanical structures.

Q. — That does not include mill damages? *A.* — No, sir.

Q. — But every thing else? *A.* — Every thing else I can think of.

Q. — Is the scheme a practicable one, in an engineering point of view? *A.* — It seems so to me.

Q. — Do you know of any other scheme so available for Cambridge to obtain a sufficient water-supply as that? *A.* — I do not.

Cross-Examination.

Q. (By Mr. BULLARD.) — Do you know any thing about those ponds to which I called Professor Wood's attention, — Mead's Pond and Kendall's Pond? What is the objection to using those, and the water-shed that surrounds them, for a water-supply for Cambridge? *A.* — I am not very familiar with those ponds. I only know generally that, previous to my connection with the City Government, all the streams in that vicinity had been examined, and some effort was made to obtain certain ones, and I think without success.

Q. — If those sources would supply a sufficient quantity of water, how would the expense probably compare, as near as you can tell, with the expense of taking water from the Shawshine? *A.* — I have not made any figures, so that I should hardly know how to answer that.

Q. — You can judge something by the distance. *A.* — Generally, I should say, if those were available, I suppose that the expense might be less; but we have considered those streams in Waltham, Belmont, and Watertown out of our reach; they have been granted to other parties.

Q. — Has Mead's Pond been granted? *A.* — Not that I know of.

Q. — Has Forest Lake? *A.* — I can't say as to that.

Q. — Has Beaver Pond? *A.* — I think Kendall's Pond and Clematis Brook, and perhaps Beaver Pond, have been granted.

Q. — The map shows a water-shed of thirty-two square miles for those sources of supply. I think you called the water-shed of the Shawshine thirty-four square miles? *A.* — Yes, sir.

Q. — Then the supply would be sufficient, would it not? *A.* — It would be, if available for us.

Q. — Is not that a subject worthy of consideration by a city like Cambridge? *A.* — I said we considered them out of the question. I knew there had been examinations made of the brooks and ponds in this vicinity previous to my connection with the city government.

Q. — But since your connection, your attention has not been called to them? *A.* — Not specially; no, sir.

Q. — You are the engineer who finally fixed upon the plan that is in Mr. Chesborough's report? *A.* — I fixed upon it in connection with Mr. Chesborough.

Q. — Did Mr. Chesborough make any examination of the sources to which I have called your attention? *A.* — Not that I am aware.

Q. — Then those were not at all considered? *A.* — I think he was generally familiar with what waters were available: he claimed to be so.

Q. — Can you give any reason now why those sources were not hit upon, rather than the Shawshine? *A.* — No more than I have already given you.

Q. — The general idea was, that there was some objection which you did not know, as I understand? *A.* — My understanding was that they had been previously rejected.

Q. — Can you give me any idea of the ground of rejection? *A.* — Because they had been granted, in part, to other towns.

Mr. HAMMOND. They would only give 3,000,000 gallons a day.

Mr. BULLARD. The water-shed is thirty-two square miles, and the water-shed of the Shawshine is thirty-four.

Mr. HAMMOND. I know that; but if you will look at Mr. Crafts' report, you will see that he went into it.

Mr. BULLARD. There are Mr. Crafts' figures upon that map: you can see them now.

Mr. HAMMOND. Here is his report where he went into that, and there were only 3,000,000 gallons a day.

Q. — Have you made any estimate of the damages to the mill-owners on the Shawshine? *A.* — No, sir.

Q. — You have no idea what they might be? *A.* — No, sir.

Q. — Have you any idea how much Cambridge would be justified in expending, to take a river like the Shawshine? What would be your idea of the maximum amount which it would be proper for Cambridge to spend for the purpose of getting a supply of water? *A.* — I think they could safely spend $1,000,000.

Q. — That would be as much as you think would be justifiable? *A.* — Well, I have not been into that very carefully, but I should state that sum, with what information I have.

Q. — Have you personally examined at all into the question of getting a supply from the city of Boston? *A.* — Only in connection with Mr. Carter.

Q. — Do you think, with him, that if the city of Boston should lay a main pipe through your city, connecting the Sudbury and Cochituate supplies with the Mystic supply, as they have already procured the right to do, that, in order to obtain a supply from that pipe, an expense would be brought on Cambridge of $600,000? Do you see how that could possibly be? *A.* — Do I understand you to refer to the mechanical connections?

Q. — What would be the expense, if a pipe ran directly through the city of Cambridge (and, as I understand, it will be very near the centre), of obtaining water from that source? A. — The expense of making the mechanical connections with the pipes would be very small; but that, I do not understand, is the entire expense: it is what we must pay Boston for the water that we use.

Q. — What do you understand you would be obliged to pay? A. — I don't know.

Q. — What do you think would be a fair price to pay? A. — I don't know that.

Q. — Since the last hearing, Mr. Barbour, has there been any effort on the part of Cambridge to re-open negotiations with Boston? A. — No, sir; not that I am aware of.

Q. — Then Cambridge has made no effort to secure a supply from Boston, as Mr. Chesborough suggested it might do, but has simply confined its attention to Shawshine River, which he also recommended? A. — Yes, sir.

Q. — Now, have you any idea what a fair price is between cities for water?

Mr. HAMMOND. That is not the question, what a fair price is: the question is, what Boston would do.

Mr. BULLARD. He says he does not know what Boston would do; and, in the absence of that, I want to get the best information I can on the subject; and that is, what would be a fair price.

A. — I have my idea of a fair price, but Boston's idea would be very different.

Q. — Very likely: but I would like yours, if you have any. A. — I haven't formed any opinion about what we should pay.

Q. — How do you know that Boston would not charge a fair price? A. — Only judging from the negotiations that we had with them, and what they charge other places that they do supply.

Q. — What do they charge other places? Perhaps that will help us a little. A. — I think it is anywhere from sixty to eighty per cent. of the gross receipts of the town.

Q. — With no expense on the city of Boston beyond merely supplying the water; that is, up to the line of communication, wherever that may be? Do you understand that to be so? A. — I don't quite get your question.

Q. — What does Boston furnish for that sixty per cent. of the receipts? A. — Water.

Q. — Simply water — no repairs or piping? Does she furnish the pipes for that? A. — I don't understand that she does.

Q. — Does she incur the first expense of the connection? A. — I can't say as to that.

Q. — What towns or cities have you in mind, when you say that

Boston charges from sixty to eighty per cent. of the receipts? *A.* —
Somerville, Everett, and Chelsea.

Q. — Now, what would be your idea, if the price was to be fixed
by the gallon, of a fair price per hundred gallons, under these circumstances, rather than a percentage? *A.* — I don't think I could answer that question.

Q. — Didn't you have any talk about it at all in your negotiations?
A. — No, not as to the price.

Q. — You seem to have got an idea somehow that Boston is disposed to be unfair. I want to know what you base that idea upon.
A. — The question then was whether we could get water from Boston, or not ; simply whether we could get it.

Q. — Do I understand you that the question of the price was not
at all discussed? *A.* — Yes, sir.

Q. — Then how do you get your idea that Boston would be unfair
in its price? *A.* — From what they charge other cities and towns.

Q. — Simply from that? *A.* — Simply from that.

Q. — You hardly know what their charge includes in that connection ; you are not sure whether it includes pipe, or not? *A.* — I
don't think it does include pipe ; I think the cities own their pipe.

Q. — If it included that, what would be a fair price? *A.* — I
can't say.

Q. — Last year, as I understand your testimony, you knew very
little personally of Concord River, which was at that time urged upon Cambridge as a source of supply? *A.* — I think I said I had
made no examination of it.

Q. — How is it this year? Your attention having been called to it
last year, have you made any further examination? *A.* — I have
made some inquiries in regard to it.

Q. — From whom? *A.* — From those familiar with it.

Q. — From scientific men, or persons who live on the stream? *A.*
— From engineers who are familiar with it.

Q. — What is the result of that examination? *A.* — I am no more
favorably impressed with it as a source of supply than I was last
year.

Q. — On account of the impurity of the water? *A.* — Partly.

Q. — On what other ground? *A.* — And also the difficulty of getting it.

Q. — Is there any water taken for domestic purposes from the Concord River, that you know of now? *A.* — Not below the junction
with the Sudbury, that I am aware of.

Q. (By the Chairman.) — Concord River is a very slow stream, is
it not? *A.* — Yes, sir, below the junction with the Sudbury.

Q. (By Mr. Bullard.) — If it should appear that the interest on the Shawshine outlay would be sufficient to buy an adequate supply of water from Boston for Cambridge, do you see any objection to entering into an arrangement with Boston for that purpose? *A.* — We never thought the interest would be sufficient.

Q. — I say, assuming that the interest on the outlay and on the annual expenses, estimated in that way, would be sufficient to buy an ample supply from Boston, do you see any objection to Cambridge taking the water from Boston? *A.* — I think, at the same price, I should rather take some other water.

Q. — That would be simply on account of the quality, or have you other reasons? *A.* — Well, principally on account of the quality.

Q. — What would be the other objections? *A.* — Taking their works. There is some advantage in having works of our own, and under our own control, I think.

Q. — Have you any doubt that Boston has ample authority now to take sufficient, and more than sufficient, water to supply herself and Cambridge, from what you know? *A.* — I think, if their resources were developed fully, there would be no difficulty in supplying Cambridge, as to quantity.

Q. — But if the consumption in Boston, which, I think, is about 37,000,000 gallons a day, were reduced slightly, of course it would be all that Cambridge would desire ; three or four million gallons a day would be ample? *A.* — There are times when we consume over 6,000,000 ; take it in extreme cold weather, or extreme warm weather, our consumption frequently runs up to 6,000,000 gallons a day.

Q. — That is something that has not been spoken of, I believe. *A.* — No, sir, that was omitted in the other testimony.

Q. — That is, in the winter, because the water is allowed to run from the taps to prevent freezing? *A.* — I presume so ; and in the summer, from the free use of hose.

Q. — I supposed in Cambridge every thing of that sort was prevented. *A.* — We prevent it as much as we can.

Q. (By Mr. Poor.) — Do you know how much water is used in Cambridge for manufacturing purposes, daily? *A.* — The amount of metred water?

Q. — Metred and unmetred, as far as you know? *A.* — I cannot give you any account of the unmetred. The amount of water sold by metre was 208,025,800 gallons.

Q. — Last year? *A.* — Yes, sir.

Q. (By Mr. Hammond.) — Right here, I would like to know if you ever measured the Shawshine when 200,000,000 gallons went by in a day. *A.* — I have.

Q. (By Mr. Poor.) — There is other water used in Cambridge for manufacturing purposes, that is not metred, is there not? *A.* — Yes, sir.

Q. — In building this reservoir of yours, it has been stated that you are willing to allow 10,000,000 gallons a day to run down. Have you ever carefully examined to satisfy yourself that that could be done? *A.* — Yes, sir, I think there is no doubt of it.

Q. — Do you know how much runs down now in the summer time? *A.* — The smallest gauging I have ever made was 8,000,000 gallons.

Q. — At what season of the year was that? *A.* — It was in the dryest part of the year.

Q. — Do you remember just when it was? *A.* — I think it was in July.

Q. — Do you know that to be the dryest part of the year for the Shawshine? *A.* — It may not have been the dryest year. That is the dryest year I happened to gauge.

Q. (By the CHAIRMAN.) — Did you try to get it at the dryest time? *A.* — Yes, sir, I think I did.

Q. (By Mr. POOR.) — You are confident that that reservoir would give you what water you need in Cambridge, besides allowing 10,000,-000 gallons a day to run down? *A.* — Yes, sir.

Q. (By Dr. WILSON.) — What is the entire quantity of water supplied in Cambridge a year, metred and unmetred? *A.* — Something like 902,319,000 gallons.

Q. — How much did you say goes to the metred manufacturing establishments? *A.* — 208,000,000 gallons.

Q. — Now, what proportion of the manufacturing establishments are metred? I don't expect you to tell me exactly, but one-half, or one-quarter, or nine-tenths of them? *A.* — I think our superintendent could answer that better than I can.

Q. — What do you think? *A.* — I should think that the larger part of them were metred, — most of the large establishments.

Q. — You mean five-sixths or three-quarters? *A.* — I should think three-quarters, perhaps.

Q. — At that rate, then, the manufacturing establishments use about 275,000,000 gallons a year, or 250,000,000? *A.* — Yes, sir.

Q. — Would not this Boston water be good enough to use in these manufacturing establishments? *A.* — It might be good quality enough, but I don't see how we could separate the water so that they could have it. I don't know how we could do it without re-piping our city.

Q. — Isn't there any way in which you can keep these nuisances out of Fresh Pond? That is a question that I have not heard answered satisfactorily. I have no doubt that there are a great many polluting substances get in there. The question is, cannot they be kept out? *A.* — I think the city of Cambridge does every thing it is possible to do, to prevent nuisances getting into Fresh Pond. Although we have not succeeded entirely, I think we have made long strides in that direction.

Q. (By Mr. HAMMOND.) — Richardson Pond is one source of nuisance, is it not? *A.* — Yes, sir.

Q. — And that is situated in Belmont? *A.* — Yes, sir.

Q. — It comes down into Fresh Pond by a natural outlet, does it not? *A.* — It does. It drains 122 acres, and a large part of it is highly cultivated. We have no control of it whatever, and have to take the water as it comes.

Q. — Now, as to Cider Mill Pond, — that is situated in Cambridge, is it not? *A.* — It is, now.

Q. — We have stopped that, haven't we? *A.* — We have stopped the outlet of it: yes, sir.

Q. — Now, about Wellington Brook, — have we not done things along the line of that brook to prevent the sewage going in there? *A.* — Yes, sir: we have.

Q. — What have we done? *A.* — We have been the whole length of Wellington Brook, and we have removed privies from the line of the brook, and built cemented brick vaults instead, without any charge to the owners. We have persuaded people, wherever we could, to let us remove the nuisances at our own expense; and have done, we think, all we possibly can in that direction.

Q. — That was within the limits of Belmont? *A.* — That was in Belmont.

Q. — You have gone up there, and asked for permission to do those things? *A.* — We have done them by permission of the owners of the property.

Q. — Can you persuade the farmers up there not to put night-soil on their ground, to raise cabbages? *A.* — I should think not, easily.

Q. — Could you persuade the farmers to let you dig a trench around the pond, to keep the night-soil out of it? Can it be done? *A.* — No, sir: I don't think it is practicable.

Q. (By Dr. INGALLS.) — I understand that nearly all the water you get from Wellington Brook is surface-water? *A.* — Yes, sir.

Q. (By Dr. HARRIS.) — How much lower is the surface of the brook than the land at Mount Auburn? *A.* — I have not got the exact figures, but I should think it might be twenty feet.

Q. — Where is the natural drainage from Mount Auburn? *A.* — The natural drainage from Mount Auburn is towards Charles River.

Q. — Entirely? *A.* — Yes, sir.

Q. — You have improved Fresh Pond a good deal? *A.* — I think we have.

Q. — Can you not go on and improve it still more? *A.* — We intend to do so, but there is not a sufficient supply of water there.

Our plan now is to develop it as a storage basin, and receive an additional supply from some other source.

Q. — Would there not be two-thirds of a supply there? What I am trying to get at is this: whether it would not be cheaper for Cambridge to supply her manufactories by a separate system of supply-pipes, with water that is not sufficiently good for domestic purposes ; and whether there would not be then enough left in Fresh Pond to supply the city? A. — 1 should think not.

Q. (By Mr. Poor.) — Do you consider Fresh Pond a proper storage basin for Shawshine-River water? A. — Yes, sir.

Q. — If it is in such bad condition now, how are you going to improve it, so as to make it safe and desirable as a storage basin? A. — We are trying to take care of Fresh Pond, and to make a suitable basin of it.

Q. — You say you are doing that now? A. — We are doing all we can.

Q. — But you cannot do any more? A. — I think, when the metropolitan system of drainage is constructed, and the intercepting sewers get near Fresh Pond, we shall be able to do more than we can now. Our difficulty has been, that we have had no outlet for sewers. We have blind sewers around Fresh Pond, but no outlet for them. When the metropolitan sewer is constructed we shall have an outlet, and then we shall be able to take care of the pond.

Q. — If you were granted liberty to take the Shawshine, as you ask here, how soon could you use the water? A. — I think, within two or three years.

Q. — Do you think it would be fit for domestic purposes within two or three years? A. — No, sir: not immediately, but after suitable storage.

Q. — How long storage? A. — I think two years after the basin is completed.

Q. (By Dr. Harris.) — Where is the source of this Wellington Brook? A. — The source of Wellington Brook is in Belmont.

Q. — Entirely? A. — And Haverhill.

Q. — Is there any means of damming that, so as to preserve a supply during the winter and spring flow? A. — I think not, sir.

Q. (By Dr. Wilson.) — Why could you not dam Wellington Brook? A. — After we get up where the land is suitable, there is not any thing to dam, — there is no water up there. If you take it down where there is any water, the land is not suitable for storage purposes.

Q. (By Mr. Smith.) — You have spoken about the metropolitan drainage system which is in contemplation. Suppose that goes into operation, what would you think of having a parallel system of water-supply in the same towns? A. — Everywhere, sir?

Q. — I do not say where. There are a number of places where that could be secured. Suppose it could be secured, what would you think of it? *A.* — There would be a good many considerations that would enter into that. I should hardly know how to answer it, without knowing more of the details.

Q. — If Boston should obtain a large supply of water, would you think it desirable that Cambridge, and these other towns and cities immediately surrounding Boston, should co-operate with Boston in this enterprise, rather than to have systems of their own? *A.* — I should suppose that would be considered in its financial aspect, and, if the city of Cambridge thought it was for her interest to join, probably she would.

Q. — I speak of the general interests of the community centred around Boston. Would it be desirable that there should be one common system, rather than have separate systems for each one of those towns which are immediately connected with Boston in the sewerage district? *A.* — I think, under some conditions, it would be better to have one system.

Q. — Then it would not be desirable for Cambridge to go to the additional expense of $600,000, for the purpose of getting a separate system, if the providing of such a system was in the future? *A.* — It would have to be very near for us, — our necessities are very great.

Q. — Could not Boston supply you in the interim, suppose it were ten years hence, with its present means? *A.* — We arranged with Boston last year for that very purpose, but when the time came that we wanted water, they said to us, " We have no water to give you."

Q. (By the CHAIRMAN.) — There is no law which will compel the city of Boston to supply you? *A.* — No, sir; not that I know of.

Adjourned to Tuesday, March 14, at ten o'clock.

SECOND HEARING.

Boston, Wednesday, March 22, 1882.

THE hearing was resumed at ten o'clock A.M.

Cross-Examination of WILLIAM S. BARBOUR, *resumed.*

Q. (By Mr. POOR.) — Mr. Barbour, I want to ask you something about that basin which you have delineated on your map. What is the character of the soil? *A.* — Principally meadow.

Q. — That portion which is colored there to indicate the tract to be covered by the basin, you say is principally meadow? *A.* — Yes, sir.

Q. — How deep would the water be on that meadow? *A.* — The deepest part would be about twenty feet, and running from that to nothing on the sides. As it approaches the hills, of course it runs out.

Q. — What would be the effect of that soil upon water stored there? Do you know any thing about that? *A.* — I suppose it would be the same as it would on any meadow that was flowed.

Q. — Whether or not that would be good water? *A.* — I don't know why it should not be good water.

Q. — Is not water in swamps usually rather inferior in quality? *A.* — In some swamps it is ; not all.

Q. (By Mr. BAILEY.) — Mr. Barbour, what did you estimate would be the expense of putting in such conduits as you may require for Cambridge from that river? *A.* — $700,000. I fixed it at $600,000 last year ; this year, at $100,000 more.

Q. — That is for the whole expense of constructing? *A.* — That is the whole expense.

Q. — Suppose the city of Boston should be granted the right to take water from that river the same as was talked of last year, on the ratio of three-fifths to Boston, and two-fifths to Cambridge, that is, 12,000,000 gallons a day to Boston, and 8,000,000 to Cambridge : what would be the expense of constructing the dams and works then? *A.* — In the talk that we had with the city of Boston, a comparison of estimates was made, and I think we came to the conclusion that the expense to Cambridge would not be very much different to go together or singly.

Q. — That is, the expense would be about $700,000, anyway? *A.* — Yes, sir.

Q. — Have you considered, or do you know that the city of Cambridge has considered, the question of mill damages on that river? *A.* — No, sir, we did not take that into account.

Q. — In that estimate? *A.* — In that estimate.

Q. — But you have considered the question of mill damages? *A.* — I understand that, in all probability, there will be mill damages.

Q. — Whether or not you do not understand that they would be about the same whether the city of Boston came in and took part of the water, or whether both cities took it together? *A.* — I have always thought, if we took it alone, that the mill damages would be less than if we went with Boston.

Q. — That is what you have thought yourself? *A.* — That is my idea of it.

Q. — But you know that others differ from that idea? *A.* — Yes, sir, I presume they do.

Q. — Now, if the city of Boston was allowed to take in that proportion, then Cambridge would have all that she required, would she not? *A.* — Yes, sir, so far as quantity is concerned.

Q. — And you think the expense to Cambridge would be about the same in either case? *A.* — Very nearly.

Q. — Why do you say it would be about the same in either case? *A.* — In building the works for Boston and Cambridge together, there would be more expensive works built; the conduit would have to be of a larger size, and the whole expense would be more than it would for Cambridge alone; but her proportion would probably be about the same amount as would be required to build independent works.

Q. (By Mr. BULLARD.) — Have you been personally a party to any negotiations with Boston to supply Cambridge with water, either last year or this year? *A.* — No, sir.

Q. — Do you know generally what the idea of Boston is as to the value of water? *A.* — I only know, in a general way, as to what they get from other places that they do supply, like Somerville and Everett.

Q. — Have you personally made any estimates of the expense of connecting with Boston for the purpose of supplying Cambridge? I mean, connecting with the new main which is to pass through Harvard Square? *A.* — No, sir.

Q. (By Mr. HAMMOND.) — You were asked whether you have known of any negotiations with Boston with regard to supplying Cambridge with water. Was an application ever made to Boston for water? *A.* — I think there was.

Q. — And what was their reply? *A.* — That they had no water for us.

Mr. BULLARD. I understood Mr. Barbour to say that he did not know any thing about that personally.

Mr. BARBOUR. I said, only in a general way.

Mr. HAMMOND. You asked about *negotiations*. I asked about an *application*.

Mr. BULLARD. I should have gone further, if he had said he knew any thing about it.

Q. — You said, in answer to Mr. Bailey, that you thought the mill damages that Cambridge would have to pay under the bill which we propose would be less than her share of the mill damages that she would have to pay if she went in with Boston?

Mr. BAILEY. No: he did not say any thing of the kind.

Q. — I understood you to say that. Did you say so? A. — I think I said, that, if we took the whole river alone, I thought the damages would be less.

Q. — Will you state why you think so? A. — Because the quantity of water that we want would be quite small for a great many years; and I think that the large storage that we would create in times of freshet would really give to the mills more than what they have now. I think that perhaps some arrangement might be made with the mills by which we could offset in that way, by furnishing them with more water.

Q. — That is, as I understand you, the right to take 8,000,000 gallons a day from the river, in the manner in which it is proposed by this bill to take it, would not injure the mills at all? A. — No, sir: I think it would be a benefit to them.

Q. — Why do you think so? A. — Because, with the large amount of storage that we should have, there would be more surplus water, which would be retained to be let down during dry seasons and dry times. I think the water would be equalized, so that they would really have more water than they do now.

Q. — Have more water when they needed it? A. — Yes, sir.

Q. — I suppose that, on that stream, there are many days when there is much more water there than the mills can use? A. — Yes, sir.

Q. — And your idea would be, as I understand it, that some of that water would be stored, so that it could come down at times when they wanted it? A. — Yes, sir.

Q. — Do your investigations upon that stream lead you to any conclusion as to how small the flow of the river may be on some days? A. — I think I stated last year, that the lowest gauging that I had made myself was 8,000,000 gallons; but I think, from the experiments which have been made in other places, that the extreme dry-weather flow of the river might possibly be reduced to about 5,000,000 gallons — between 5,000,000 and 6,000,000 gallons.

Q. — You have measured it when it was only 8,000,000? A. — Yes, sir.

Q. — When was that? *A.* — That was in 1880, I think.

Q. — Although the route to the Concord River is shorter than the one to the Shawshine, would it be more or less expensive? *A.* — I think it would be more expensive.

Q. — Why? *A.* — Because there are high lands intervening. In order to take it in a straight line, which is the shortest distance, we should have to pump all the water over an elevation of at least one hundred feet: possibly more than that. It would involve pumping all the water we took.

Q. — Twice? *A.* — Yes, sir, twice.

Q. — To get it from Concord River to Fresh Pond, and then to get it from Fresh Pond to the well-room? *A.* — Yes, sir.

Q. — You do not believe the water of Concord River is proper water for domestic purposes? *A.* — I do not.

Q. (By Mr. BAILEY.) — Mr. Barbour, I should like to ask one or two questions in reference to these last questions by brother Hammond. What do you think is the storage capacity of this reservoir which you are proposing to make? *A.* — 2,000,000,000 gallons.

Q. — As I gather from your answers to Mr. Hammond, the only reason for your belief that the mill damages will be less if Cambridge takes the water alone, than they would be if she takes it in connection with Boston, is because you believe that you could make some arrangement with the mill-owners? *A.* — Yes, sir.

Q. (By Mr. HAMMOND.) — Supposing you could not make any arrangement with the mill-owners, the question is whether a bill like that which we propose, allowing at least 10,000,000 gallons to come down there every day, would be as much damage to the mill-owners as it would be if 20,000,000 gallons a day were taken from that stream? *A.* — I think it would be a very important element in the matter of damages.

Q. — It would not be as much damage to them? *A.* — No, sir, I think not. I do not see how it could be.

Q. (By Mr. SMITH.) — I would like to ask you a few questions with regard to that basin. The object, as I understand it, is to get pure water for Cambridge, for domestic purposes? *A.* — Yes, sir.

Q. — How many acres do you propose to cover? *A.* — Eight hundred.

Q. — How far up does that basin run from the dam? *A.* — Four and a half miles, I think.

Q. — About how broad, on the average, would the basin be to cover eight hundred acres? *A.* — I think it is about half a mile wide there; in that vicinity.

Q. — What is the fall from the upper part where you propose to erect the dam? *A.* — Something like twenty feet.

Q. — How high is your dam? *A.* — Twenty-five feet.

Q. — The dam at the centre of the river is twenty-five feet high? *A.* — Yes, sir.

Q. — And sixteen hundred feet long? *A.* — Yes, sir.

Q. — Running out to nothing on each side, you say? *A.* — Yes, sir.

Q. — Now, sir, have you estimated what would be the average depth of water on that four miles? Where there are twenty feet of fall, with a twenty-five-foot dam, what would be the average depth of the water? *A.* — In making my estimates, I call the average depth ten feet.

Q. — The dam being only twenty-five feet high at the centre and running out to nothing on the sides, and the fall being twenty feet in the river, do you think it possible that you could get an average of ten feet in depth? *A.* — Yes, sir, I do.

Q. — How do you make that out? *A.* — On the basis of the levels which I took there, which give me the average. I ran levels the whole length of the river, up and down, and made up my average from the levels actually taken there.

Q. — On the upper half of it, where there is a fall of twenty feet, and a dam twenty-five feet high, what would the depth of water be? *A.* — That would be more shallow, of course, than the lower part. That I believe to be a fair average depth of the basin, from the figures taken. It is quite possible that in improving that basin we should deepen some parts of it. We should remove, probably, some of the muck, which, at certain portions of the meadow, is not very deep. The bed of the river is gravelly.

Q. — I understood you that the basin itself, as a rule, has a mucky, peaty bottom? *A.* — I have no recollection of saying any such thing. I was asked the question, and said it was meadow.

Q. — That means the same thing, don't it? *A.* — No, sir: I should hardly think it did. There is a great variety of meadows.

Q. — Well, what is the character of that bottom? *A.* — The character of the bottom in the meadow, as far as I examined it, is gravelly.

Q. — How deep? *A.* — Not very deep. I think it is one of the best pieces of meadow for flowage that I know, for the purposes of converting it into a basin for the storage of water.

Q. — Have you ever considered the healthiness of that stream, or have you ever studied the healthiness of a stream as affected by flowage? *A.* — No, sir: I don't think that I have made it a special study, any more than in the way of general reading.

Q. — Supposing that this meadow should be flooded in the spring of the year, and should be drawn off so that there should be considerable distance on the sides that would be laid bare, and then flowed again, what would be the effect of that upon the character of the water? *A.* — I do not think it would tend to improve the water any; but I think that is a question that is now mooted. There is quite a difference of opinion as to matters of flowage and its effects.

Q. — You don't pretend to know any thing on that subject? *A.* — I don't pretend to have made a scientific study of that particular point.

Q. (By Mr. REED.) — What effect would it have upon the quality of the water to have dead trees standing in that reservoir which you propose to make? *A.* — In improving this reservoir, we should take out the standing trees. The intention is to take out the standing trees there in improving the meadow.

Q. — Say decaying stumps? *A.* — We intend to take out the stumps.

Q. — Have you made any estimate to determine how many acres of woodland would be flowed? *A.* — My recollection is that there is not a very great extent of woodland upon it.

Q. — Have you taken any measurements to find out how much of the existing meadow is woodland? *A.* — I have not determined the woodland alone.

Q. — You are not aware, then, whether it would be a hundred acres or five acres? *A.* — I know there is some woodland which would be flowed, but the principal part is meadow-land which I speak of.

Q. — In your opinion, you think the principal part of it would be meadow-land, and not woodland? *A.* — Yes, sir.

TESTIMONY OF HIRAM NEVONS.

Q. (By Mr. HAMMOND.) — You are the superintendent of the Cambridge Water-Works? *A.* — Yes, sir.

Q. — And have been for how long a time? *A.* — Five years this spring.

Q. — Mr. Nevons, do you make any attempt to ascertain the leaks in the main pipes? *A.* — Yes, sir.

Q. — To what extent do you do that? *A.* — Well, we generally go through the low territories, the marsh territories, or the filled territories, twice a year.

Q. — How do you do it? *A.* — I take generally about three men with me, and go and shut off a section.

Q. — In the night? *A.* — In the night, yes, sir.

Q. — Why do you prefer the night rather than the day? *A.* — Our object is to take it when all legitimate consumption is supposed to have ceased; people are abed, the factories stopped, and every thing is still and quiet.

Q. — Then, when legitimate consumption is supposed to have stopped, or to be at the lowest ebb, you go at night and shut the gates, for the purpose of ascertaining whether there is any section of the pipe from which more water goes than you think ought to go? *A.* — Yes, sir.

Q. — In that way do you discover leaks? *A.* — Yes, sir, we have. We have not so much this last year as we did years before.

Q. — What was the consumption per head in Cambridge in 1881? *A.* — 46⅔ gallons. It is the same as it was last year; but in the figures of last year we took 50,000 inhabitants as the basis of the calculation : we rather cheated ourselves last year. Our consumption *per capita* should have been less than what our report shows. This year we put it at the actual census.

Q. — How much more water has been pumped in 1881 than in 1880? *A.* — There were 15,000,000 gallons more pumped.

Q. — How many supplies were put in in 1881? *A.* — We put in two hundred.

Q. — How much more metered water was there in 1881 than in 1880? *A.* — There were 37,000,000 gallons more sold by meter.

Q. — You put in two hundred supplies in 1881? *A.* — Yes, sir.

Q. — And you have pumped 37,000,000 gallons more in 1881 than in 1880? *A.* — No, sir : 15,000,000.

Q. — And the metered water has been actually 37,000,000 gallons more than it was in 1880? *A.* — Yes, sir.

Q. — So that the consumption in Cambridge, outside of the metered water, has been actually 22,000,000 gallons less in 1881 than in 1880 : is that so? *A.* — Yes, sir. We claim that we have saved, by stopping leaks, a waste of 22,000,000 gallons over last year.

Q. — For domestic purposes? *A.* — Yes, sir.

Q. — Although you have had, scattered along through the year, two hundred supplies more than you had in 1880? *A.* — Yes, sir.

Q. — That is, you have been more careful, if possible, during 1881, than you were in 1880, about consumption? *A.* — Yes, sir : we have followed out our old plan of inspection.

Q. — Is the water used by manufacturers generally metered? *A.* — All of it.

Q. — With what exceptions, if any? *A.* — Well, I should not say that there were any exceptions. We have some places that might be called factories, such as carriage-manufactories, where the water is not used, except for the men around the buildings.

Q. — They are not factories in the sense of using water for factory purposes, but simply in the sense of employing men who use water? *A.* — Yes, sir.

Q. — Now, Mr. Nevons, how is Fresh Pond filled up during the year? *A.* — We fill it up in the spring by taking the water from Wellington Brook.

Q. — Is there any other method of filling it? *A.* — I don't know of any, sir.

Q. — And what time in the year do you take water from Wellington Brook? *A.* — We endeavor to take it in snow-thaws. We begin along the last of February, when we generally begin to have thaws, and we take it in then.

Q. — When the ground is frozen? *A.* — Yes, sir.

Q. — And a large amount of water is on the surface of the ground? *A.* — Yes, sir.

Q. — And that is taken into the conduit which leads into Fresh Pond, is it? *A.* — Yes, sir.

Q. — Now, if at any time you should be prevented from taking the water of Wellington Brook in that way, do you believe that Fresh Pond would carry you through? *A.* — No, sir. Well, it might carry us through one year.

Q. — But it would go very low, wouldn't it? *A.* — Oh, yes.

Q. — It reduces the area of the pond very much, does it not, when you get down low? *A.* — Yes, sir.

Q. — And then, after the spring is over, Fresh Pond gradually lowers, does it? *A.* — Yes, sir.

Q. — Until you get to the spring again? *A.* — Yes, sir.

Q. — Whether Cambridge is pretty generally supplied with water? I mean by that, whether there are many wells there? *A.* — I do not know of any territory in Cambridge but what is supplied with Fresh Pond water. There are a few houses up in what is called "Dublin."

Q. — There are a few houses that are not supplied with Fresh Pond water, but, as a rule, the houses depend upon Fresh Pond, do they not? *A.* — Yes, sir.

Q. — Speaking generally, there are no wells there that can be used? *A.* — No, sir.

Q. — Or that are used for any purpose? *A.* — I don't know of any, excepting some driven wells for manufactories.

Mr. HAMMOND. My purpose in asking these questions is to show that Cambridge, using 46⅔ gallons per head daily, is not to be compared with some cities which have just had water introduced, where it is not generally used by the inhabitants. That is all. Of course it would not be fair to compare a place like Taunton with Cambridge.

Cross-Examination.

Q. (By Mr. MORSE.) — Is it part of your business to look after the meters? *A.* — Yes, sir.

Q. — Do you determine as to where they shall be put on? *A.* — No, sir, not exactly. That is more the president's duty. I report to the president the particulars in regard to it, and he generally decides.

Q. — What is your rule in regard to the application of meters? *A.* — Well, one is, where we are not able to determine the quantity of water used. If we have any doubt, if we think we cannot get at the facts, we put on a meter to demonstrate : and then, in other cases, people apply for them that are entitled to them.

Q. (By Mr. HAMMOND.) Where they prefer to take the water that way? *A.* — Yes, sir.

Q. (By Mr. MORSE.) — What proportion of your metered customers apply for meters? *A.* — I should think two-thirds of them.

Q. — Then, it is only with reference to one-third that you impose meters? *A.* — No, sir: we intend to put them on to all large consumers, where there is a large quantity of water used. All the large manufactories are metered. There are some of those small factories, such as I spoke of, — carriage-manufactories, for instance, — that are not metered.

Q. — What is the cost of a meter such as you use? *A.* — It is according to what size you mean.

Q. — Are all your meters one make? *A.* — No, sir.

Q. — Whose manufacture do you use? *A.* — We have the Worthington, we have the Union Rotary, and we have the Crown and the Desper. The largest proportion is the Worthington meter.

Q. — Are all the meters made for the same class of customers? Is there any difference, I mean to say, in the size of the meters with reference to different manufacturers? *A.* — It is according to the quantity of water used.

Q. — What I want to get at is, whether each one of those manufacturers makes meters that are suitable for all establishments? *A.* — I don't know about that.

Q. — What determines you, then, in choosing one meter rather than another? *A.* — If we have to go above a two-inch meter, we generally prefer — have so far — the Worthington meter.

Q. — What is the cost of the most expensive meter? *A.* — A four-inch meter costs about three hundred and fifty dollars.

Q. — And the smallest, the cheapest? *A.* — About thirteen dollars.

Q. — What is the average cost of the meters you use in Cambridge? *A.* — Of course that is owing to the size. I never made an average of the sizes, to get at the average price, but I should say somewhere about thirty or thirty-five dollars.

Q. — That takes in, of course, the high-price ones that are used for the manufactories? *A.* — Yes, sir.

Q. — Suppose you take the dwelling-houses alone, what is the average price of a suitable meter? *A.* — I should say, all set up, right through, about eighteen or twenty dollars.

Q. — Suppose, then, you take the manufactories, how will they average? *A.* — I should think about seventy-five dollars.

Q. — Who pays for the meters, according to your system? *A.* — The city of Cambridge. We don't allow anybody to own any meters.

Q. — The city owns them? *A.* — The city owns them, and has full control of them.

Q. — Have meters worked well where you have put them on? *A.* — Yes, sir.

Q. — Have they tended to the reduction of the consumption of water? *A.* — Well, I should not be prepared to say about that. In some cases they have. We have found that they were using water excessively, and allowing water to be wasted about the premises. Of course they stopped that when the meter was put on, and used only what they actually needed.

Q. — That is the natural effect of a meter, — to lead any customer to say that he will not take the water except when he needs it? *A.* — Yes, sir.

Q. — Have you found any practical difficulty in gauging the water by these meters? *A.* — I don't think we have got a meter yet to go into very extensively, or upon which we can rely solely. I think we can accomplish more, so far as our domestic supply is concerned, by inspection. We do not want to complicate the works. Every meter you put on, you complicate the works, and add to the expense.

Q. — How many meters have you on dwelling-houses? *A.* — None at all. We only have 156 meters anyway.

Q. — Then, when you speak of the average price of meters for dwelling-houses, you do not speak from experience, but simply as a matter of estimate? *A.* — Well, I have thought the matter over considerably.

Q. (By Mr. Bullard.) — How do you find meters in the matter of repairs? Are they expensive, or otherwise? *A.* — Very expensive.

Q. — What do you find the average yearly expense? *A.* — I don't know. I could tell at the office; but I have no data with me.

Q. — I only mean generally; that is, take a cheap meter — a thirteen-dollar meter? *A.* — In nine times out of ten, you had better smash it up, and sell it for old junk, than have it repaired.

Q. — What proportion do you have to send to the manufacturers?

A. — Not over four or five out of our 156 during the year. We have a shop where we do some small repairs ourselves; but, if there are any new parts to be supplied, we have to send them to the manufacturers.

Q. — Can you give me a general idea of the expense of taking care of a meter for a year? *A.* — I don't think I could, — not satisfactorily.

Q. — What proportion of your meters do you have in the shop? *A.* — Well, we generally keep four or five in the shop, — spare ones.

Q. — I mean, for the purpose of repairs? *A.* — We don't calculate to keep any there. If a meter wants to be repaired, we send it at once to the manufacturer, and put on one in the place of it. When I say 156 meters, I mean meters that are applied. Of course we have five or six in the shop, in case one gives out, so that we can replace it.

Q. — How long does an average meter go without any repair? *A.* — Well, we have had a Worthington meter go three years. We can't tell when a meter is going to give out.

Q. — You cannot tell us what the average life of a meter is? *A.* — No, sir; and I don't think anybody can.

Q. — After an experience of how many years? *A.* — Five.

Q. — How was the reduction in consumption during the last year, that you speak of, secured? *A.* — Well, this spring, when we went through the main pipes, we found we had not many leaks on the mains, and we put on an inspector to inspect the fixtures of houses, and we found that we accomplished a great deal more than we had any idea we should; that is, we found water-closets, drains, and all sorts of fixtures, that were imperfect, a great many of them fastened up, — water-closets fastened up, tanks fixed so as to run all the time.

Q. — That is, the overflow? *A.* — Yes, sir.

Q. — Do you think that, by a system of inspection, waste would be entirely controlled? *A.* — Well, very closely.

Q. — You prefer that to the meter system? *A.* — I do. I do not believe in complicating the works, as you would have to if you put on meters. It is a big thing when you come to talk of putting a meter on every house, and keeping the management of them.

Q. — Have you thought at all of the district system of meters, for the purpose of aiding inspection? *A.* — Yes, sir: we have something that amounts to just the same thing.

Q. — What is that? *A.* — We have a chronograph; we have a stand-pipe; and we are able to set up this chronograph, and, if our consumption runs up at all, we are able to tell at once.

Q. — Can you tell in what district, or what part of the city, it runs to waste? *A.* — In order to do that, we shut off a certain section, and see what the effect is. We can shut off any section of the city, and, by this chronograph, we can tell just how much is due to that section.

Q. (By Mr. HAMMOND.) — And whether it is more than they ought to have, or not? A. — Yes, sir.

Q. (By Mr. BULLARD.) — What is the gross income from the water? Can you tell me? A. — Yes, sir. It was a hundred and seventy-one thousand dollars this year; a little over that, but that is very close.

Q. — That is, from all sources, metered and unmetered? A. — Yes, sir.

Q. — Can you tell me something about the expense of the department, — whether that is all consumed in expenses? A. — Oh, no! I should rather the President of the Board would answer that.

Mr. HAMMOND. I will put in the Report.

Q. — Is it impossible to take the water of Wellington Brook for the purpose of filling Fresh Pond at any time, except in the spring? A. — I think it is; and I think it is very objectionable to take it even then. I think it is a very serious matter taking it then.

Q. — Do the impurities come from any special source? A. — Well, I don't know how *special* they are. There are objectionable things all along the whole line of the brook to its source.

Q. — Well, is it generally from fertilizers on the top of the ground, or tanneries or slaughter-houses? A. — Well, we have got a slaughter-house there to start with; then we have got piggeries on the line of the brook; we have low land that is highly cultivated; and then all the drainage of the territory lying each side of Concord Avenue.

Q. — What has been your observation of the condition of Fresh Pond, as to the lowest point to which you ever drain it, whether it continued at the lowest point, or whether it seemed to be supplied by springs, for instance? A. — When we get it as low as we did three years ago, we calculate that our consumption is just like dipping so much out of a pail; that we lower it just the quantity we use.

Q. — You had a smaller surface, of course, to draw from? A. — Yes, sir.

Q. — But you think that, practically, you drew out as much of the supply as at any time during the drawing? A. — Yes, sir.

Q. — Then there was nothing gained by the aid of the pond? A. — No, sir. There were a few springs that commenced to flow, as the pond went down, up on the borders; but they soon dried up. As the pond went farther down, they ceased to flow.

Q. — Have you personally had any negotiations with Boston as to a water-supply for Cambridge? A. — No, sir.

Q. — Can you tell us any thing about the expense of making a connection with the Boston main, if it runs through Harvard Square? *A.* — You mean, to connect with our system?

Q. — I mean, if the main should connect with the Sudbury or the Mystic, what would be the expense of connecting that main with Cambridge for the purpose of obtaining a water-supply? *A.* — I understand your question to be, what it would cost to connect their pipes with ours when they went through our territory?

Q. — Exactly. *A.* — I should think it would cost four or five hundred dollars. They cross right under our big mains.

Q. (By Mr. HAMMOND.) — That would not pump it up high enough for us, would it? *A.* — No, sir.

Q. — The water of Cambridge is all pumped by the stand-pipe system, is it not? *A.* — Yes, sir.

Q. — Do you know how high it is pumped? *A.* — It is pumped to an elevation of a hundred and thirty-five feet above the city base.

Q. (By Mr. BULLARD.) — Would not that be high enough to fill Fresh Pond as you do from Wellington Brook? *A.* — Yes, sir.

Q. (By Mr. HAMMOND.) — In saying that it would cost five hundred dollars to connect with the Boston main, you mean simply to join such pipes as you know would be in the vicinity of that main, running in the direction stated? *A.* — Yes, sir: I had in mind the idea that they spoke of two years ago, of crossing by North Avenue. They would cross our two big supply-mains. I meant simply just making a connection there.

Q. — But that would not water the city, would it, making that connection? The pressure would not be sufficient? Or don't you know about that? *A.* — It is my impression that it would be just about equal to our reservoir pressure, — what we call our reservoir pressure now, twenty-eight pounds.

Q. — But that is not equal to our day pressure? *A.* — No, sir: it would not supply the high service.

Q. — I will ask you, to show the Committee how closely we have to watch Wellington Brook, whether you have been up there at times, and stopped the water when it was running in, because you did not think it was safe to let it go any longer? *A.* — Yes, sir, I have.

Q. — Have you let it in when you hesitated whether to do it or not? *A.* — Yes, sir. I shut it off one time when there was a big flow, and reported to President Carter what I had done; and he seemed to doubt my judgment in doing it, and said he would go up with me. He went up there, and deliberated something like half an hour. He said it was almost life or death with us, and he said I better open it; and, if I had not opened it at that time, we should not have filled our pond so full as we did last year by two feet, and consequently it would have been two feet lower this year.

Q. — That is, by opening it, you got in more water? *A.* — Yes, sir : there was a very large flow, and we took in a vast quantity of water.

Q. — You went to the full limit of your daring in doing it? *A.* — Yes, sir : rather more, I think.

Q. (By Mr. Poor.) — Have you any figures showing the average daily waste of water in Cambridge? *A.* — No, sir, I have not. I think that would be a pretty hard thing to determine.

Q. — Have you any knowledge of the waste in the course of a year? *A.* — The only way that I know of to get at that would be to fix some standard rate *per capita*, and get the excess of that, and call that waste.

Q. — There is more or less waste, is there not? *A.* — I think so.

Q. — How does it occur, in your judgment? what is the most prolific source of waste? *A.* — I think it is the house-fixtures.

Q. — Water-closets? *A.* — Yes, water-closets and tanks.

Q. — Do you take any measures to control water-closets? *A.* — Yes, sir.

Q. — To what extent do you take such measures? *A.* — Well, we follow up this house inspection. If we find imperfect fixtures, the occupant is notified to repair within two days. At the end of two or three days, the inspector again visits the premises ; and, if the repairs are not made, the water is shut off.

Q. — You said, a year ago, you thought, if the water-closets alone could be thoroughly controlled, there might be a saving of 150,000 or 200,000 gallons every twenty-four hours. Is your judgment any different now in regard to that? *A.* — I should not take much back-water on that. It may be a little large, but we had found a great deal of trouble with them. We found all sorts of appliances for holding the water-closets open. We have even found a crane fixed on the side of the wall to keep the water running. We found one not over two weeks ago : they would swing that out to hold it up, and have the full size of a half or three-quarter inch pipe running all the time. Come to add thirty or forty of them, you have a vast quantity of water running to waste.

Q. — That waste could be controlled by more thorough inspection, could it not? *A.* — Well, when we visit these places where we find them, we do not ever find them running again ; and then we have a way of putting a stand-pipe on the sidewalk, where we can go in the night, when they don't know any thing about it, and sound the fixtures, and tell them the next day that their water was running.

Q. — How much water is used daily in Cambridge for manufacturing purposes? *A.* — I could not give it to you daily.

Q. — Well, for a year? *A.* — The total amount that we metered last year was 280,000,000 gallons.

Q. — All used for manufacturing? *A.* — Yes, sir: manufacturing, and watering the streets.

TESTIMONY OF DR. HENRY P. WALCOTT.

Q. (By Mr. HAMMOND.) — Doctor, you are now connected with the State Board of Health, Lunacy, and Charity? *A.* — Yes, sir.

Q. — In what capacity? *A.* — Health officer of the Health Department.

Q. — How long have you held that position? *A.* — Two years.

Q. — You reside in Cambridge? *A.* — Yes, sir.

Q. — You are a member of the Board of Health of Cambridge? *A.* — Yes, sir.

Q. — How long have you been a member of that Board? *A.* — Since its organization : four or five years.

Q. — Did you have occasion, as a member of the Committee appointed by Cambridge, to examine into the water-supply of Cambridge, and devote special attention to that subject for a year? *A.* — Yes, sir : as a member of that commission, and as a member of the Board of Health.

Q. — You were a member of the Committee which made this Report which I hold in my hand? *A.* — Yes, sir.

Q. — Now, doctor, in the first place I want to ask you about the contamination of the present sources of our water-supply. *A.* — Beyond Fresh Pond we have no water-supply. The wells are hopelessly bad. The Board of Health investigated that matter : in fact, we have had the matter investigated for the last three years. We have examined between sixty and seventy wells, taking in every case wells of good character, — those wells that were supposed to yield good water, and sought for by people from large districts ; and in no case — except the spring in the Botanic Garden, which comes from some eight or ten acres of uninhabited land — did we find the well-water as good as that of Fresh Pond. As the result of that inquiry we suppressed at least four-fifths of them.

Q. — What is the process of suppressing a well? What do you mean by suppressing a well? *A.* — By recognizing it as one of the things dangerous to health.

Q. — Telling people not to use it? *A.* — Yes, sir.

Q. — That you did not think it was safe to use it? *A.* — Yes, sir.

Q. — Then I understand you to say that you consider Cambridge dependent upon other sources than its wells for water-supply? *A.* — Yes, sir, entirely dependent.

Q. — I will ask you whether you believe that there are wells to any extent used in Cambridge? *A.* — Very few, sir.

Q. — So that our pipes are very generally distributed, are they, throughout the city? *A.* — Yes, sir.

Q. — How about this Wellington Brook? What do you say to that as a source of water-supply? *A.* — Wellington Brook at its source is too polluted as a source of drinking-water, hopelessly polluted. It rises in the near vicinity of dwelling-houses. It is used for the refuse matter of dwelling-houses through its whole course in the first place; and then it flows through market-gardens and cultivated ornamental grounds, and has one or two large piggeries on its course, and winds up with an open drain beneath a slaughter-house. It is only useful during this time of the year, when the ground is frozen.

Q. — Do you believe that it would be safe to use it at any other time? *A.* — I think it would be very unsafe: I don't think it is possible to use it at any other time.

Q. — How is it in regard to the water-shed of Fresh Pond? Is not that largely shut off? *A.* — Yes, sir.

Q. — Why? *A.* — On account of the improvements in the neighborhood, — the improvements or injuries, whichever you call them; the improvements consequent upon building up and occupying all the territory about the pond.

Q. — Now, have you given the subject such attention, doctor, as that you think you are capable of making up your mind whether it is safe even to rely upon Fresh Pond? What do you think about the probability of that being good for any thing? *A.* — I think that the only value of Fresh Pond is as a storage-basin. I think that the condition of things observed subsequently to that report, when the pond was reduced to its lowest point, shows very conclusively the drainage into the pond of a great mass of contamination to the north-east of it. I think that was proved beyond all question. I do not think the city of Cambridge would be justified in reducing Fresh Pond to the level, or within two feet of the level, to which it reduced the pond two years ago.

Q. — You think the effect of it is to draw in from the surrounding country contamination, do you? *A.* — Certainly.

Q. — As the pond goes down, the water from the adjoining country, underground and otherwise, flows more into the pond, does it? *A.* — Yes, sir. The absence of pressure, of course, makes it turn in that direction. That was shown by analysis.

Q. — And in that way the liability to contamination is increased? *A.* — Yes, sir.

Q. — What do you think about the Concord River as a place of water-supply? *A.* — We might possibly get the water for manufacturing purposes: it is out of the question for drinking-water. I do not think it has ever been considered by anybody as suitable for that purpose.

Cross-Examination.

Q. (By Mr. MORSE.) — Have you any objection to using the water-supply of the city of Boston, supposing you were able to do so? *A.* — Yes, sir, personally I have. If it is the same thing as during the three months of last year from September to November, I should object to it very seriously.

Q. — You are familiar with the water that we have here? *A.* — Yes, sir.

Q. — Take it as it runs, don't you think the quality is likely to be as good as the water that would be supplied for Cambridge from any new source? *A.* — No, sir: I think that the Shawshine is a much better source of water-supply than any that Boston has.

Q. — I understand that the difficulties that have been met with in the Sudbury water are incident to the storing in large basins of that kind, the water of any running stream, are they not? *A.* — Yes, sir: I think that has much to do with it; but I would say, go as far back as the origin of the stream, I think the Sudbury is not as good water as the Shawshine.

Q. — When it was taken, it was supposed to be entirely satisfactory, was it not? *A.* — No, sir: it was entirely satisfactory because it furnished an abundance of water. I do not think that the medical commission that decided upon it ever had the opinion that it was the best water.

Q. — Do you understand that, at the time the Sudbury was taken, the Shawshine was considered better? *A.* — Yes, sir: by the medical experts who examined it.

Q. — And yet they did not ask to take the Shawshine at that time, did they? *A.* — No, sir: it did not furnish water enough. They excluded it because it was an insufficient supply.

Q. — At all events, the troubles that have come in the Sudbury since it has been stored up did not exist at the time the water was running in its natural state? *A.* — No, sir.

Q. — Isn't it the judgment of all scientific men that these troubles are largely due to the fact that you store up, in a region such as this, the water of a running stream? Isn't there a growth of vegetation, and a development of troubles, of one kind and another, that is always likely to happen? *A.* — Well, that is an open question, sir. I think it is myself; I think it is incident to storing the water.

Q. — Supposing the Shawshine should be dammed, I do not understand that it is proposed to make any artificial bottom for the reservoir: they propose to use the natural surface of the ground? *A.* — I think it would be the height of folly to use the natural surface of the ground for a basin. That has been shown in every town of the Commonwealth where the experiment has been tried.

Q. — What do you understand is to be done there? *A.* — I don't understand at all what is to be done. I assume that a proper reservoir would be constructed.

Q. — Nothing has been spoken of excepting building a dam, and allowing the water to flow back, and taking out the dead trees? *A.* — Of course I know nothing about the condition of the soil, sir.

Q. (By Mr. BULLARD.) — In regard to the intercepting sewer that may possibly come in the metropolitan district, — I think you were chairman of that committee? *A.* — No, sir: I was a member of that committee.

Q. — Can you tell us whether that would possibly have any effect upon the quality of the water in Wellington Brook ; whether it is not likely that the drainage of Cambridge would be so taken care of that Wellington Brook would become comparatively pure? *A.* — I do not think any system of drainage whatever could improve Wellington Brook.

Q. (By Mr. POOR.) — I understood you to say that this reservoir, as you have heard it described here, would not be a proper one for the storage of water? *A.* — No, sir, I did not say so. I said I did not know any thing about the reservoir. If an artificial bottom were not made, it is possible the soil might not be proper for a basin. I have no knowledge of the district. That is a question that the engineer would be competent to decide.

Q. — What would be proper soil? *A.* — That is also a question for the engineer.

Q. — If it is a swamp in part, and woodland in part, and they should simply cut off the wood, and attempt to flow it, would that be a proper storage-basin? *A.* — That has been tried too often in the Commonwealth to leave any question. It would be utterly improper.

Mr. HAMMOND. I asked Mr. Kingsley, who has been connected with our Water Board for a great many years, to be here to-day ; but this is one of his busy days, and he is not here. I desire to say, that, in arguing the question, I shall call the attention of the Committee to certain portions of the Report of the Special Committee on the water-supply of the city of Cambridge. I will furnish the Committee, or those of you who have not copies, with copies of this Report, made in December, 1879, to the City Council of Cambridge. I would now indicate, if I knew exactly, what portions of the Report I wish to call your attention to, so that the other side might know ; but I should like to have it in as a matter of reference, that either side may refer to in argument. I desire, also, to call the attention of the Committee, in argument, to a report and table showing the consumption of water in different cities, and the receipts for the same, which I find in a book called "Pure Water-Supply," by the Continental Water-Meter Company. It gives the number of gallons per head used in the various cities.

Mr. BAILEY. Will you vouch for the correctness of it?

Mr. HAMMOND. No, sir; but it is a table made up by the water-meter folks, and I suppose it is all right.

The CHAIRMAN. Does it give the extent to which water is taken in various places?

Mr. HAMMOND. I do not suppose it does. It gives the population, the system of supply, the average daily consumption in gallons, the daily consumption *per capita*, the miles of pipe, number of meters in use, number of service-pipes in use, per cent. of service-pipe to meters, total receipts for water, and receipts per million gallons. I should stop here, and will stop here. At the same time I labor under some embarrassment in stopping here, because I understand that the Committee have been out upon certain localities connected with this matter. I do not know what evidence they there got hold of, bearing upon the question, so that it is impossible for me to meet any evidence which you may there have heard or received. I shall be obliged, therefore, Mr. Chairman, to rest my case without knowing in all respects what the evidence is upon — what I cannot call the other side, but what the evidence is upon the question, on one side or the other.

The CHAIRMAN. I think there was not much evidence there. I thought it probable that all parties would be represented there; but we were pretty careful to avoid all talk or argument. We merely took a drive around the locality, without stopping anywhere, and I think no case was prejudiced. It was merely to take a look at the ground.

Mr. HAMMOND. I did not speak for that purpose. I have no doubt that the Committee will consider the question as impartially as though we had all been there. But I only desire to say, that, if there were any facts that were then stated to the Committee, I ought to have an opportunity, if they bear upon the question, to meet them by evidence, if I can. Of course I assume that they would not affect the judgment of the Committee at all.

OPENING STATEMENT BY A. J. BAILEY, ESQ.

Mr. CHAIRMAN AND GENTLEMEN, — As representing the city of Boston, I am here by virtue of the following order, which was passed by the City Council : —

"That the Mayor be requested to petition the Legislature for authority to take Shawshine River as a water-supply."

The reasons why we desire to be allowed to take that river for a water-supply, I will state briefly, and then will call one or two witnesses to more particularly show the needs of the city.

This Committee, or a great majority of them, are well aware that the city has been authorized to take the Sudbury River, and to erect dams for storing the water, for the supply of Boston. It has also been authorized to take, and has taken, and is now using, the Mystic River, or rather the Abbajona River, and the Horn Pond branch of Mystic River. The amount of water which can be furnished by the Sudbury River, when the basins which have been commenced are completed, is about 40,000,000 gallons per day. Of that amount we have the last year consumed 31,000,000 gallons, and that without the four basins on the river being completed : so that it will be seen that the safe limit of the Sudbury River has certainly been reached ; the only question being, whether we shall make, and when we shall make, more basins. There are four more to build, one of which is being constructed now. We can build only three more. These last three basins, which have not been built, it is in contemplation to build only when we shall actually need them ; because, when they are constructed, they will be basins of shallow water, the use of which it is desirable to avoid, if possible.

From the other source of supply, the Mystic, we used last year 7,000,000 gallons a day, and that is about the full capacity of that source. In regard to the Mystic supply, as this Committee is well aware, if we cannot in some way protect its purity, we must of necessity abandon it as a source for the city of Boston. If we abandon it, as it seems likely to us we shall be obliged to, there are but two resources for us, — to construct the remaining basins upon the Sudbury River, build a branch across, and connect with the Mystic supply, which is one way ; or to look elsewhere for other water. If we contemplate the first alternative, to build those additional basins, making connection across with the Mystic, it will cost us half a million dollars to make the connection between the Sudbury River and the Mystic works. It will also cost us at least as much, if not more, than that amount, to construct the three basins ; and, if we construct the three basins for that purpose, we shall not then have the proper quality of water which the city of Boston should have. We shall not have the purity of water that we shall have if we are allowed to take the Shawshine River, and construct basins there. Therefore, taking into consideration the fact that we should have to pay so large an amount for connecting the two supplies, and considering the amount that it will be necessary to expend on the Shawshine River in building basins and paying damages, it seems to us that the latter would be a better and more desirable course to pursue than to take the first alternative. For that reason the city is here, asking for the right to take this water.

Now, we propose to show, or it has already been shown, I might say, by the engineer of the city of Cambridge, that the entire cost of building the dam, and all the works necessary to make this water available to the cities of Cambridge and Boston, would be about seven hundred thousand dollars. We do not desire to take this water, and sell a portion of it to the city of Cambridge ; but we do ask, that, if a bill is given to Cambridge to take a portion of this river, the same right shall also be given to the city of Boston to take a portion for her supply. Last year it was contemplated, in this same connection, that Boston should be allowed to take three-fifths, and Cambridge two-fifths, of the water-supply of the river. With that arrangement we should be perfectly content to-day ; and from the testimony of Mr. Barbour it has also been shown — and therefore I shall not put on any testimony on that point, but I desire to call the attention of the Committee to it now, because some evidence that I may put on may bear upon that — that the city of Cambridge can be supplied with all the water they need from the Shawshine in conjunction with a part for Boston, as cheaply as it can build its own works separately ; so that it can work no injustice, as far as Cambridge is concerned, if we are allowed to take the water-supply of the Shawshine in conjunction with that city.

I will not take up any more time of the Committee at the present moment, but will call one or two witnesses to testify more in detail concerning some of the statements which I have made.

Mr. MORSE. Will you state what is the date of the order which you have read?

Mr. BAILEY. The date of the order is the thirty-first day of January, 1882.

TESTIMONY OF HENRY M. WIGHTMAN.

Q. (By Mr. BAILEY.) — You are the city engineer of the city of Boston? A. — Yes, sir.

Q. — You are the engineer of the Boston Water Board? A. — Yes, sir.

Q. — Will you state to the Committee such reasons as occur to you why the city of Boston desires the Shawshine for the purpose of water-supply, and why it is a necessity that the city should take it? A. — I do not think very much can be added to the statement that was made last year to the Committee, and which appears in print, except this, — that the conditions are somewhat changed since that time. That is, the city of Boston is at present engaged in building one of the sugges.ed basins which it was then contemplated that we should have to build on the Sudbury, in order to supply the southerly portion of the city; and we have commenced the construction of that basin, at quite a large cost, for that section of the city, — which of course reduces the amount which could be used, if any of it could be used, or if it was prudent for us to use it, for the Charlestown supply. The Mystic supply is not sufficient to-day for the amount of water that is required for that section in a dry year, and the Water Board have got to do something to increase the supply on the Mystic. We have been engaged the past year in making experiments on the stoppage of waste; and so far as those have been conducted under the Deacon waste-water meter system, in the Charlestown district, they have been very successful : but the amount that is used in the Charlestown district, as compared with the other portions of the district which are supplied from the Mystic works, is small; and it is very doubtful whether the city has a right (I do not think it has myself, although that is a legal question) to go into other cities and towns that are supplied, and apply the same system there. It will involve making connections with the pipes of those other cities, and also house-to-house inspection, and the enforcement of certain rules and regulations, which I do not think there is any power to carry out in those sections. Consequently the city is in this position : either it must connect the Mystic works with the Sudbury, in order to insure a safe supply, or it must build additional storage-basins on the Mystic, or take the Shawshine. It becomes, then, a question of expediency and cost; and the cost of connecting the Sudbury with the Mystic, with the loss of head, and other objections, is much more than counterbalanced by the advantages of taking the Shawshine, in my opinion. That is, in view of the fact that the city would have to expend as large an amount of money as it would have to do to provide for that additional supply of water, it had very much better spend that money in obtaining a supply from the Shawshine, than on the Sudbury, and in making the connections with the Mystic works. If the Committee wish to go into the question of figures, the figures would be practically about the same as last year, except at that time a division of the $700,000, which was the estimated cost of the Shawshine scheme, was contemplated between Boston and Cambridge, in the proportion of two-fifths for Cambridge and three-fifths for Boston, the supply to be divided in the same proportion. In regard to the cost of the basins on the Sudbury, we have now rather more accurate estimates than we had last year, and they would be increased in amount from the sum stated last year. I think last year I stated to the Committee that in order to build the basins which would equal the Mystic supply would cost $600,000. It would cost according to the present estimates nearer $900,000. These estimates are based upon surveys made the past year in connection with the new basin on the Sudbury. The new basin that we are building will cost $394,000 without the land: it will cost over $400,000 with the land. The additional basins which it would be necessary to make for the Mystic supply would cost about $500,000. That is, one would cost $284,000, and the other $200,000. The pipe to go across would cost more than last year. Iron pipe to-day is worth $43 a ton, and the pipe to make the connection across would cost over half a million of dollars: so that I think the Committee will see that it is a question of dollars and cents, that it is a question of, say, a million of dollars against about $700,000, if we take the whole of the Shawshine, or three-fifths of that amount if we take it with Cambridge. I do not know that I can state any thing more.

Q. — As to the quality of the water that will be got from the remaining basins on the Sudbury, as compared with the water that could be got from the Shawshine? A. — One of the basins on the Sudbury which would be included in that estimate contains a very large amount of what is called shallow flowage. That is to say, the basin that we are building now (I merely state this to illustrate to the Committee) with two hundred and fifty acres, it is expected, will have a capacity of 5,000,000 gallons a day; whereas this other basin, to furnish the same capacity, would flow over eight hundred acres. I think that shows to the Committee what the character of the basin would be, and what quality of water would be derived from it, as compared with the water that we should get from the Shawshine. To get the same amount of water, the shallow flowage of the Shawshine would be very much less.

Q. — I would like to have you state to the Committee what in your judgment the probable result will be, so far as the cost to the city is concerned, so far as the Mystic supply is concerned, whether it will be able to retain that, or not? A. — No, sir, I don't think it would. I have stated that opinion, and the opinion is in print in the evidence last year. I stated to the Committee then that I did not think for a series of years the purity of the Mystic could be maintained. I think that opinion would be indorsed by most scientific experts on that subject. That is, in a valley so densely populated as that will be, I think it is very doubtful whether for a series of years the purity of the water could be maintained, and consequently it would be poor policy for the city of Boston to construct storage-basins on the Mystic. These storage-basins, if constructed at all, would be constructed at the head waters; and the water that was allowed to run down would have to go through districts which would naturally be polluted by a very large population in future, and even in the present.

Cross-Examination.

Q. (By Mr. MORSE.) — Mr. Wightman, I understood you to say last year that you estimated the entire flow from the Shawshine, supposing this dam was built, at 20,000,000 gallons a day? *A.* — Yes, sir, with this one dam.

Q. — Are you contemplating more than one dam? *A.* — In the original survey of the Shawshine River there were sites, I think, for three dams : two certainly.

Q. — Does the plan in regard to the Shawshine contemplate building any other reservoir than the one that Mr. Barbour has described here? *A.* — Not at present.

Q. — Well, at any time do you contemplate another one? *A.* — Yes, sir.

Q. — Where? *A.* — On the upper waters of the Shawshine. I have a plan in my pocket.

Q. — Cannot you show it on that large plan? *A.* — Yes, sir, just as well. The dams are not shown on this plan, but one on Vine Brook, and another at this point here. The dam we propose to build now is just below, at the Middlesex Canal.

Q. — And the next one? *A.* — The next one would be at this point. There is a central dam there now at the mills. The next one would be on Vine Brook.

Q. — Would the city of Boston, then, be contented with a bill which would limit them to the right to construct one dam, — that is, the lower dam? *A.* — I think it would for the present : yes, sir.

Q. — You say that would not give them a sufficient supply, they would want more? *A.* — Yes, sir : as the wants of the district grew, they would want more water.

Q. — This lower dam would give you, you testified last year, 20,000,000 gallons a day? *A.* — Yes, sir : I think so.

Q. — In addition to allowing 10,000,000 to flow down the river? *A.* — I don't remember testifying any thing about 10,000,000 flowing down the river.

Q. — What did you say about that? *A.* — I did not testify last year any thing about 10,000,000 running down the river in addition to the 20,000,000 we took.

Q. — Could you get 20,000,000 gallons a day, from that one dam, besides the 10,000,000 that it is proposed to allow to run down the river? *A.* — I have not investigated that point. We allow anywhere from 1,000,000 to 2,000,000 to flow in the Sudbury ; 1,500,000 is the quantity provided in the bill.

Q. — Is 20,000,000 the amount of your estimate that the cities of Boston and Cambridge would take from that river? *A.* — The building of that one reservoir would render 20,000,000 gallons a day available. Whether the city would take it or not, I don't know.

Q. — That would give you, in the division with Cambridge, 12,-000,000 gallons a day, and Cambridge 8,000,000? A. — Yes, sir.

Mr. HAMMOND. At this point, in order to prevent any misapprehension, Mr. Chairman, I desire to state that Cambridge does not appear here in connection with the petition of Boston at all. I don't know whether I made that clear in my opening.

The CHAIRMAN. I think that is clear to the Committee.

A. — I will say this in answer to your question about allowing 10,000,000 to run. Of course they would let run in the river only what was let out of the dam. The flow otherwise might be nothing.

Q. — Then you do not agree at all to the proposition that has been made on the part of the city of Cambridge, that 10,000,000 gallons a day should flow down the river? A. — No, sir: I should say not.

Q. — In order to get your 20,000,000 gallons, then, you would not allow more than 1,000,000 to run down a day? A. — Well, from 1,000,000 to 1,500,000.

Q. — In other words, if 10,000,000 gallons were to run down a day, there would be left only between 10,000,000 and 11,000,000 to be divided between the city of Boston and the city of Cambridge? A. — That is all.

Q. — And the proportion that the city of Boston would get of that supply, if any thing, would be so small that it would be no object to the city? A. — I think not.

Q. — So that, to make this taking of the Shawshine any object to the city, one of two things must be done : either you must cut off the provision for allowing 10,000,000 gallons to run down a day, or else you must get authority to build more than the lower dam? A. — Yes, sir: I should not think that proposition to allow 10,000,000 gallons a day to run down the river, so far as the city of Boston is concerned, admissible. If the city were required to let 10,000,000 gallons a day run, it is certainly a scheme they would not expend any money upon.

Q. (By Mr. BAILEY.) — Is it possible to build one dam, and enter into a contract to allow 10,000,000 gallons a day to run down the river, and have any thing left for any water-supply for anybody? A. — Yes, sir, with that dam built, it is good for 20,000,000 gallons a day. That is to say, in a dry time.

Q. — For the year round, is it possible to store water enough up there to make it sure that 10,000,000 gallons shall run down that river, and have any thing left for water-supply? A. — It is possible.

Q. (By Mr. MORSE.) — But it would not be a very profitable operation? A. — It would not be a profitable operation for the city : they certainly would not go into it.

Q. (By Mr. Hammond.) — You mean, for the city of Boston? *A.* — I do not think it would be very profitable for any city.

Q. (By Mr. Morse.) — If you were the engineer of the city of Cambridge, you would not advise it, then? *A.* — No, sir, I should not.

Mr. Bailey. I ask that question in this connection: I shall argue to the Committee, that allowing the city of Cambridge to build that dam practically takes all the water, whether Cambridge gets the supply or not.

Mr. Hammond. You are going to argue, that if they build the dam, if Cambridge only takes 8,000,000 gallons a day, the other 12,000,000 will go nowhere?

Q. (By Mr. Morse.) — I understand Mr. Wightman to say, and I will put the question again so that there will be no mistake in regard to that, that he does not think it would be profitable, either for the city of Cambridge or the city of Boston, to take the Shawshine, provided it was to build this one dam and guarantee 10,-000,000 gallons a day to run down there? *A.* — I don't think it would. Of course that is a matter about which each city must judge for itself; but I should not recommend any such scheme to the city of Cambridge, if they should consult me as an engineer.

Q. — Now, with reference to the present capacity of the Boston water-supply. I suppose the Committee generally understand it; but, as there may be some members not familiar with it, I will ask Mr. Wightman to state to the Committee what proportion of the city of Boston is supplied from the Mystic, and what proportion from the Sudbury and Cochituate, and then what other cities or places besides Boston are supplied from the Mystic? *A.* — The Sudbury and Cochituate works now supply the city of Boston entirely, with the exception of the Charlestown district; that is, they supply East Boston now, and have most of the year. The city of Charlestown is supplied from the Mystic, and the cities of Somerville and Chelsea, and the town of Everett.

Q. — You speak of the Sudbury and Cochituate as virtually one system? *A.* — Yes, sir: we call that one system, because we use them together.

Q. — What do you call the total capacity of the two, the Sudbury and Cochituate? *A.* — At present it is about 32,000,000 gallons a day.

Q. — That is what you get from it at present, but that is not the entire storage capacity of the two? *A.* — That is the storage capacity of the two, as at present.

Q. — Suppose you build all the basins you have authority to build, what could you then get? *A.* — 52,000,000 gallons.

Q. — What is the present population that is collected in the district that is supplied by the Cochituate and Sudbury? *A.* — I don't know that exactly, sir. We estimate it at about 340,000, I think, calling 363,000 the entire population of the city.

Q. — What is the average consumption in that district now? *A.* — The average consumption for the last year was something over ninety gallons per head.

Q. — At that rate of ninety gallons per head, for that entire population of 340,000, how much would that be, if you can reckon it readily? *A.* — It is 31,000,000. That is just what the consumption was last year; that is to say, from that source.

Q. — Then you have a capacity there to supply a population of almost double the present population, even at the present rate of consumption, have you not? *A.* — Well, I wish we had; but we have not. I do not know whether I have given you the figures correctly or not.

Q. — You have a total capacity of 52,000,000 gallons? *A.* — Yes: we shall have that total capacity when the storage-basins are all built; but, then, we have not got that now. There is where you confound it.

Q. — I understand it; but you have authority under the statutes to build other basins, have you not? *A.* — Yes, sir: we have authority under the statutes to build other basins. Our present supply is less than 31,000,000.

Q. — What is the objection to building other basins? *A.* — The expense of them, which I gave the Committee, — half a million dollars. It would cost half a million dollars to make the Mystic supply good.

Q. — We are talking about the Sudbury and Cochituate now? *A.* — Exactly: it would be what I say for two basins, — about half a million dollars.

Q. — Well, would half a million dollars, in addition to what has already been expended, enable you to use this entire capacity of 52,000,000 gallons? *A.* — No, sir, it would not.

Q. — How much additional expense will there be? *A.* — That is a question which I have not investigated. The present storage capacity of the Sudbury is 20,000,000 gallons. The basin we are building will give a capacity of 5,000,000 more. The two basins that we might build for half a million dollars would be good for ten millions more, so that would be about 35,000,000 gallons. The other five millions would have to be made up of smaller basins, which would be very undesirable to build, I think. I think it was originally estimated that the river was good for 40,000,000 gallons.

Q. — Have you not, or has not somebody, reported, within this last year, that water enough can be obtained from the Sudbury to supply the city by building additional basins? *A.*—For a certain length of time. Of course I don't know what facts you want to present to the Committee. I will answer any question you put. I was going to suggest, however, that the Sudbury-river conduit was built for 110,000,000 gallons,—intended eventually to take the Charles River.

Q.—We will leave the Sudbury and Cochituate for a moment now, and take the total capacity of the Mystic. How much can you get there? *A.*—I do not think the Mystic supply is good for more than 9,000,000 gallons.

Q.—Didn't you testify last year that it was 17,000,000? *A.*—No, sir: I testified that, with storage, it could be made equal to 17,000,000.

Q.—It could be made capable of yielding 17,000,000 gallons? *A.*—Yes, sir, by storage. I should modify that statement this year, because that statement was based on the estimate that fifteen inches of rainfall could be obtained from the water-shed in a dry year. Recently, actual experience shows us that we cannot rely upon over ten and a half inches : so I should reduce that estimate in that proportion. I don't think that the storage of the Mystic is good for more than about 12,000,000 gallons. That estimate of 17,000,000 was based upon the report of Mr. Francis and Mr. Kirkwood, who investigated the subject very thoroughly, and their estimate was fifteen inches ; but we absolutely did not get over ten and a half on the Sudbury, and not over twelve on the Mystic, in the dry year that we had two years ago.

Q.—How much are you getting from the Mystic? *A.*—We used last year a little over 7,000,000 gallons a day.

Q.—You do not have any doubt that you could double that supply, do you? *A.*—Well, I think it would be difficult to double it, even by building all the storage-basins, and the cost of those basins is very large.

Q.—What will be the cost of the basins on the Mystic? *A.*—They would cost $994,000.

Q.—What was the rate of consumption last year in the Mystic district? *A.*—I think the rate of consumption last year in the Mystic district reached 9,000,000 gallons a day. That, of course, was at a time when the city of Boston was supplied from the Mystic.

Q.—I mean the rate of consumption by each taker on the average? *A.*—Eighty-one gallons.

Q.—Eighty-one gallons in the Mystic district, and ninety in the district supplied from the Cochituate and Sudbury? *A.*—Yes, sir.

Q.—Now, Mr. Wightman, you have no hesitation in saying, have you, that that is a very extravagant consumption of water? *A.* — I think so, sir.

Q. — What proportion of that consumption is waste, in your judgment? *A.* — I think the consumption ought not to exceed sixty gallons per head of population.

Q. — And sixty gallons would be a large estimate, would it not? *A.* — Well, not for an American city.

Q. — Cambridge is an American city, is it not? *A.* — Yes, sir: a small one.

Q. — Why does not a small city use as much per head as a large one? *A.* — Well, perhaps because there are not so many people come into it, so many strangers, in proportion to its size. There are a thousand things that a large city uses water for, that a small one does not.

Q. — That theory was started last year, in regard to the proportion of strangers who come into a small city as compared with a large one. Don't you think as many strangers go to Cambridge in proportion to its size as come to Boston? *A.* — I don't think there are anywhere near so many.

Q. — Have you any figures that will enable you to form a judgment? *A.* — No, sir: that is a matter of judgment. For instance, speaking of a large city, Cambridge has a comparatively small water-front: they use but very little water for shipping; whereas we have a large water-front, and use a very large amount of water for shipping, for public grounds, fountains, etc. Boston has two where Cambridge has one. Urinals, and every thing of that kind, are much more numerous in a large city than a small one.

Q. — Of course I understand that a large city is larger than a small one; but the question is, What data have you to go upon for your assumption that the consumption of water in a large city is larger in proportion to population than in a small city? *A.* — Well, common sense: I think that is about all the judgment that is necessary.

Q. — Let me call your attention, and the attention of the Committee, to some figures that were stated last year. The city of Providence uses twenty-five gallons per inhabitant; the city of Lowell, thirty-three; Fall River, twenty-six; Lawrence, forty-four; Cincinnati, fifty-one; Columbus, forty-three; Cambridge, as has been testified to-day, uses a little over forty-six gallons per inhabitant. *A.* — And the city of Chicago uses one hundred.

Q. — One moment. You have mentioned the city of Chicago. Is it not a fact, that those cities which border on the Great Lakes, like Chicago, and two or three other cities, draw their water from the lake where there is an unlimited supply, and return the water to the lake through their system of sewerage, so that practically there is not any reason why they should put any restraint upon the amount of water consumed? *A.* — No, sir, that is not the fact, because water costs something. For instance, nine-tenths, four-fifths, or two-thirds, whatever the proportion is, of the water used in Boston, is supplied by gravity, whereas in St. Louis and Chicago, especially, every drop of water is pumped, which represents dollars for the gallons that they use or waste: whereas, in this city, it costs nothing but the interest on the cost of the works. After gravity works are built, they can run one hundred gallons a day as cheaply as ten.

Q. — I will ask you, if, in your opinion, sixty gallons per head would be a reasonable consumption for the inhabitants of Boston? *A.* — Yes, sir: I think that the consumption should be reduced to that amount.

Q. — In what way could that reduction be made? *A.* — That is a point I have been considering for the last three months.

Q. — Do you mean to say that you have not considered it until within the last three months? *A.* — No, sir: I have been considering it for years. What I mean is, that, having got through with the trial of the Deacon system, it is a question whether it is advisable for Boston to adopt that system of stopping waste, whether it is better to adopt the meter system, or whether it is better to adopt the system of house-to-house inspection. The Deacon system is extremely effective, and the cost of the meters themselves is small. On the other hand, it involves the changing of all the stop-cocks to the sidewalk, and that involves an expenditure of half a million dollars. To meter the city cannot cost less than a million dollars. Whether any thing intermediate between those two systems, or whether house-to-house inspection, might not accomplish very largely the result desired, is the question I am considering. Some ten or twelve years ago it did accomplish partially the result aimed at; and, although the consumption now has run up to a very large figure, perhaps the same method would accomplish the same thing again. As I say, I have been considering it. It is a pretty large question. It involves an expenditure of a million dollars, you may say, in the end, to carry out such a meter system.

Mr. Morse. Before putting any question, I desire to call the attention of the Committee to a proclamation issued by the Mayor of Boston on the 23d of November, 1881 : —

" *To the Citizens of Boston.*

" The city government has reason to believe that the cause of the impurity of our water has been discovered. It is located, according to the report of the scientist employed to search for it, in Farm Pond alone, and has completely vitiated that body of water. As the water of Sudbury River, the main source of our supply, flows through this pond, it is consequently contaminated, and rendered unfit for use. Until a permanent remedy can be found, we must separate the two waters, and the method proposed is to construct a channel for Sudbury River through Farm Pond. This is being done; and until the work is completed, which will be in about ten days, we shall supply the city with the water from Cochituate Lake, which is good. But the capacity of this lake does not exceed twenty million gallons *per diem*, and the citizens must therefore exercise economy in the use of the water: otherwise we shall be compelled to adulterate it with that which is poor and unfit for use.

"We have been hitherto culpably extravagant in the consumption of water. The average amount, until recently, has been one hundred gallons for each person: it is now eighty-five gallons. No other community indulges such wasteful prodigality. Providence uses only thirty-five gallons, and Fall River twenty-eight. Philadelphia, with its large supply, consumes but sixty gallons.

"If our citizens will be satisfied with what satisfies those elsewhere, and exercise reasonable and considerate care in using the water, Cochituate Lake will supply that portion of the city not supplied by Mystic Pond, with enough for all purposes, until we can draw on Sudbury River. I would therefore earnestly enjoin upon all our citizens to keep constantly in mind what the common safety, convenience, and interest require at this time, and to assist the government in its efforts to supply to all that first necessity, wholesome water.

"There must be no misunderstanding in this matter.

"As I have stated, for a few days the quality of the water will depend upon the quantity used. If you will refrain from waste, it will be good. If you demand more of it than we can supply, we must mix the poor with the good so as to meet the demand. The present action of the citizens, therefore, will determine the character of the water served to them.

"FREDERICK O. PRINCE, *Mayor*."

Cross-Examination.

Q. (By Mr. Morse.) — Mr. Wightman, that proclamation proposes to distribute 20,000,000 gallons a day to that district? *A.* — Yes, sir.

Q. — Was that found to be sufficient? *A.* — No, sir.

Q. — Did they have to mix the bad water with the good? *A.* — Yes, sir.

Q. — How much bad water was used? *A.* — We were supplying the city from the Mystic works as well as the Cochituate works, and in addition to that we had to use bad water. That 20,000,000 gallons was what could be got out of Cochituate Lake for a very short time only: it was the full capacity of the lake.

Q. — Have you any data which you can give as to the amount that was consumed during the few days that followed that proclamation? *A.* — Yes, sir: it was about 28,000,000 gallons. The consumption per day was cut down only 4,000,000 gallons. The balance came from the Mystic, or was taken from the Chestnut Hill reservoir. I had the entire management of the works at that time, and testify by authority.

Q. — You say you have been investigating the Deacon meter? *A.* — It has been on trial in the Charlestown district for a year.

Q. — What is the cost of a meter? *A.* — The meter itself costs $350 set. Each meter will take care of a district varying from 2,000 to 4,000 people.

Q. — A meter is not applied to each building? *A.* — No, sir. It is what is called the "district waste-water system."

Q. — How many of those meters would it be found necessary to use, supposing it was found practicable to use them, in the district that is now supplied by the Cochituate and the Sudbury? *A.* — I have only made an approximate estimate of that; but, according to my estimate, the cost of the meters alone, set, would amount to only $52,000. About one hundred meters would be needed to provide for the water-takers we have now, and the growth of the city.

Q. — I don't suppose you can give an exact statement; but, in round numbers, how much would it cost, in your judgment, to apply the Deacon waste-water system to the district which is now supplied by the Cochituate and the Sudbury? *A.* — It would cost over half a million dollars. I think I have made that statement before.

Q. — What is the amount of reduction that has been effected in the Charlestown district by the use of these meters? *A.* — We have only tried that on the dwelling-house sections; but there we have reduced the consumption to about thirty-five or thirty-six gallons per head, when it was somewhere about fifty in this particular district.

Q. — You have reduced it from fifty to thirty-five gallons a day per head? *A.* — Yes, sir.

Q. — That is a reduction of about thirty-three per cent.? *A.* — Yes, sir. The actual figures are somewhere about thirty-five per cent. reduction in that particular district.

Q. — Are those meters to be used in manufacturing establishments? *A.* — No, sir: we should use the ordinary form of meter for those establishments. We are using them a good deal. The number of meters has been largely increased, and it is the intention to still further increase them.

Q. — How many meters have been put on to the supply from the Sudbury and Cochituate the past year? *A.* — The chairman of the Water Board could answer that better than I; but I think some five or six hundred, — I don't know but more.

Q. — Do you remember the total number now? *A.* — I don't; but I think the total number is in the vicinity of 2,000.

Q. — In that district? *A.* — In the Sudbury and Cochituate district.

Q. — Has the application of the meters that have been put on this year tended to reduce the consumption in those establishments? *A.* — Yes, sir.

Q. — My statement last year, which I suppose I got from the evidence, was, that "in 1880 there were 52,268 water-takers, and 1,097 meters." *A.* — That is about right.

Q. — "The water-takers having increased about eight thousand, and the meters five." *A.* — We have put on about five or six hundred more meters this year.

Mr. CUTTER (chairman of the Water Board). Seven hundred.

Q. — What has been the rule in regard to the use of meters in manufacturing establishments in Boston? Is it left to the water-takers to apply for them, or do the Board prescribe them? *A.* — It is in the discretion, I think, of the Water Registrar. That is a part of the department that I do not have charge of; but, as I understand, the Water Registrar recommends the application of meters to the Board, the Board buy them, and the Water Registrar applies them wherever he sees fit.

Q. — What proportion of the manufacturing establishments in the city use them? *A.* — That is a question I cannot answer.

Q. — You don't know how many manufacturing establishments there are in that district? *A.* — I am not familiar with those figures.

Q. — You have no doubt that under a proper system of meterage the consumption could be very largely reduced? *A.* — I think so; but it would take quite a number of years to do it.

Q. — As I understand you, until within the last two or three months, nothing has been done in regard to applying meters to dwelling-houses in Boston? *A.* — In Boston, no, sir: not that I know of, except for experimental purposes. I do not think it would ever be policy for the city to apply meters to dwelling-houses.

Q. — I refer to the application of the Deacon system? *A.* — Well, no: it is a comparatively new system. It has been tried in Europe with good results. This is the first experiment that has been made in this country.

Q. — Have you any question that, as a matter of expense, it would be cheaper for the city of Boston to use every reasonable expedient to economize its present water-supply than to go out and take additional sources of supply? *A.* — No, sir: I have no doubt that would be a very desirable thing for the city, of course; but I do not think that would obviate the necessity of getting more water.

Q. — Wouldn't you say that, before asking for any more water, they ought to economize their present supply? *A.* — Well, I think they ought to use proper foresight. Taking into consideration how long it will take to stop this waste, and taking into consideration the condition of the Mystic water-supply, it seems to me it is the part of wisdom to seek other sources of supply.

Q. — One thing is certain, is it not, that during the last year, since the attention of the public was called to the great waste of water in Boston, there has been more attention paid to the investigation of meters, and the use of them in Boston, than in any year, or any five years, since the introduction of water into Boston? *A.* — Yes, sir; but that commenced before this trouble that we had with our water.

Q. — Please notice this fact: that in 1880 the whole number of additional meters that was put on in that part of the city of Boston, supplied from the Cochituate and the Sudbury, was five. Now, during the last year, there have been seven hundred put on, as I understand you. *A.* — I think there has been very much more effort made this last year, and I think in the future there will be more and more every year.

Q. — Don't you think that effort has been very largely due to the fact, that during the hearings last winter public attention was called to the great waste of water here? *A.* — I think, if you read the city engineer's reports for the last five years, you would think that constant hammering has had something to do with it.

Q. — I know that you and your predecessors have called attention to it; but I want to know whether the proper authorities had done any thing about it that was effective until last year? *A.* — I don't think they have taken hold of it in the way that it might have been taken hold of until this last year. This last year they made very great effort.

Q. — Then the great public benefit of this hearing last winter was to lead the proper authorities to take measures to stop the waste of water in Boston, was it not? *A.* — It might have tended to that result, sir.

Q. — Now, in regard to the supply of the city of Cambridge: what do you say as to the quality of the Sudbury River? *A.* — Well, the quality of the Sudbury-river water now, I call good. If you depend upon chemical analysis, I don't know what you would call it.

Mr. HAMMOND. I don't think you need spend any time on that. I should not contend that the water taken by the people of Boston — who, perhaps, don't take a great deal of it — is not suitable for Cambridge.

Mr. MORSE. If it is conceded that the citizens of Cambridge would be willing to drink the water usually drank by the citizens of Boston, I will pass that subject.

Mr. HAMMOND. That concession is made — somewhat reluctantly. But if it will tend to shorten this hearing, perhaps it better be made.

Q. — I want to know now, as to what the cost of supplying water to the city of Cambridge would be, so far as the city of Boston is concerned? How much does the city of Boston charge the town of Everett for water? *A.* — That is a thing I am not specially familiar with. I think we take 85 per cent. of the receipts in the cities of Somerville and Chelsea, and the town of Everett. They furnish their own pipes, and we take 85 per cent. of the receipts.

Q. — It is the same price for all those places? *A.* — Yes, sir.

Q. — Have you ever personally had any thing to do with the negotiations with the city authorities of Cambridge in reference to supplying them? *A.* — No, sir. I know that we have a connection through which we can supply them.

Q. — That was made for an emergency, I suppose? *A.* — Yes, sir: that was for an emergency.

Q. — That connection still exists? *A.* — It does.

Q. — How much could the city of Cambridge draw through that pipe now? *A.* — I don't know how much they could draw.

Q. — I mean, how much would flow through there? *A.* — I should think they might get three-quarters of a million or a million gallons a day, perhaps, without much loss of head.

Q. — No more than that? *A.* — No, sir. It is a sixteen-inch pipe.

Q. — Were any terms made in regard to that water? *A.* — No, sir. The city of Cambridge thought they were liable to be short of water, and that connection was made as a precautionary measure to supplement their own supply, in case of accident, or failure of the supply.

Q. — I suppose, if the city of Cambridge should get hard up now, you would not object to that water running through that sixteen-inch pipe? *A.* — I think that we could supply them, perhaps for years, with all the water they would want, in addition to their own supply.

Q. — That is to say, leaving things just as they are at present, you have no doubt you could furnish them with a sufficient supply of water there? *A.* — I think we could, in addition to their own.

Q. (By Mr. BAILEY.) — You don't mean now: you mean when the new reservoir is done? *A.* — Yes, sir: we could now, except when we have a dry time.

Q. (By Mr. HAMMOND.) — You could now when we don't want it most; but when we do want it you couldn't? *A.* — If you took it now, you could save it, because we are wasting 200,000,000 gallons over the dam every day.

Q. (By Mr. MORSE.) — How soon will the new reservoir be done? *A.* — About a year.

Q. — And it would take three years, would it not, to complete this Shawshine system? *A.* — Yes, sir.

Q. — So that in one year you will get your new reservoir, and then you will have sufficient water to supply the city of Cambridge, in addition to what they get from their own supply? *A.* — I think we could.

Q. — Have you any doubt that your Board, or you personally, so far as you have to do with it, would make reasonable terms.with the city of Cambridge? *A.* — Well, sir, the chairman of our Board, I think, had better answer that question himself.

Mr. HAMMOND. I have no doubt that Boston would make terms with us, if she would make any at all, which *she* deems reasonable.

Q. — I simply want to know whether there has been any recent negotiation, to your knowledge, between the respective Water Boards, or the respective city authorities, in reference to fixing any terms on which the city of Cambridge could be supplied from Boston? *A.* — No, sir, I have not. Of course the Water Board would conduct their own business in their own way; but I have not been cognizant of any such negotiation.

Q. — I want to ask you whether you are familiar with the fact, that by the Act of 1875, which authorized the town of Brookline to take the water of Charles River, that town was authorized to sell water to the city of Boston? *A.* — Yes; but, as they only take a million and a half gallons, I don't think they have much to sell, because their consumption has been up to that. It is now 800,000 gallons.

Q. — You don't understand that they are limited to that taking, do you? *A.* — They are, certainly, until they make a new one. Their works are only adapted to that quantity. They have not got works of sufficient capacity to do any more.

Q. — What I want to get at is this: whether, in case of necessity, there is not authority on the part of the town of Brookline to take as much water as they want from Charles River, and authority on the part of the town to sell water to the city of Boston? *A.* — Yes, sir, there is.

Q. — So that that supply is, in a certain sense, accessible to the city of Boston? *A.* — It has no value. It is accessible; but it has no value to the city of Boston.

Q. — Do you mean, on account of the quality of the water? *A.* — No, sir: I mean the quantity. Their works are only large enough for their own supply. If the city of Boston took water from Charles River, it would have to build a dam, and pay damages. It had better take water from the Shawshine. It is a question of cost. The works would cost more money.

Q. — The distance is much less, isn't it? *A.* — It is not much less: it is in a different direction altogether. If we take that water, we have still got to lay pipes across. There is a large expense, — half a million. While the mere taking of the water of the Charles might be the cheapest, when you add the expense of laying the pipes across to it, it is more expensive.

Q. — Still, you would have a much larger supply? *A.* — Yes, sir:

we would have a much larger supply than we want. The Charles was estimated as good for 40,000,000 gallons a day. It would not be any use for the city of Boston to build that dam unless they were going to take the whole river.

Q. (By the CHAIRMAN.) — You said you had no doubt that the city of Boston could supply Cambridge for years to come when the new Sudbury reservoir is completed? *A.* — If they carry out some method of prevention of waste, — yes, sir.

Q. — "For years to come," taking that term as commonly understood, would include some dry years, I suppose? *A.* — Well, if they undertook to supply the city of Cambridge, of course they would go on building additional basins as they were wanted. When this basin is constructed, with a proper use of the water, I do not see any reason why they could not supply the city of Cambridge with 1,000,000 gallons a day; and, by the time they wanted a larger amount, we could build other basins, and supply them.

Q. (By Mr. MORSE.) — A single question more, and that is in reference to your statement to Mr. Bailey, that you thought Boston would give up the Mystic supply. I suppose you referred to contamination from the sewage in that valley? *A.* — Yes, sir ; and the increase of population.

Q. — If a system of sewerage were adopted, either in accordance with the recommendation of the State Board of Health, or any thing else of that general character, which will keep the principal causes of pollution out of the river, that objection would be removed, of course? *A.* — No, sir : it would not be. That objection is, that the population of the valley is increasing very rapidly. The soil itself is becoming objectionable, the drainage of which runs into the pond, independently of any question of sewerage. Any stuff that is thrown upon the ground-surface — sewage, you might call it — of a large population, finds its way into the pond ; and, besides that, the system of sewerage would undoubtedly take quite a large portion of the water that now runs in there. Pure as it is, or pure as it might be, the system of sewerage would intercept a certain portion of the soil-water.

Q. — I thought the city of Boston advocated that sewer on the ground that it would keep its water pure? *A.* — The city of Boston does advocate it. Of course they are urgent to have any system of sewerage adopted that will obviate the necessity of draining the Mystic valley into their water-supply. The Supreme Court have granted an injunction against our discharging where we do discharge, and the only remedy we have is to discharge into the water-supply direct. I suppose that injunction at any time can be enforced when any of the towns who have a right to enforce it are dissatisfied with the city's treatment of the drainage. In that case the city is confronted at once with the danger of contamination of the water-supply. Consequently it is an advocate of drainage as long as it owns the Mystic pumping machinery and works which supply it.

Q. (By Dr. INGALLS.) — You said there was a large quantity of water running to waste now on the Sudbury. Would it not be possible to save that water in Fresh Pond? *A.* — That is just what we do with Lake Cochituate. Lake Cochituate does not fill from its own water-shed, and has not for two years. We fill it from the Sudbury water-shed.

Q. — Then you think that the other reservoir [Fresh Pond] could be filled in the spring, when the water is running away? *A.* — Yes, sir.

Q. (By Mr. BULLARD.) — I understand you to say that it is no longer safe, in your judgment, to estimate fifteen inches as the average rainfall? *A.* — I say that experience has shown that the estimate made by Messrs. Kirkwood and Francis was too high. They assumed fifteen inches as available from the water-shed for storage ; that is, that we could collect it. Experience on the Sudbury and the Mystic shows us that on the Sudbury we collect only about ten and one-half inches, and on the Mystic we collect about twelve inches. That was in the dry year, a year ago.

Q. — What would the water-shed of the Shawshine yield, if the ten and one-half inch rule were applied to that? *A.* — I have not figured it.

Q. — Don't you know that the estimate was made on fifteen inches? *A.* — I don't think it was. I think it was made on twelve inches, the same as the Sudbury. There was but twelve inches that was available in that dry year.

Q. — Is there any reason why the same rule should not be applied to the Shawshine? *A.* — No, sir: I think that twelve inches might be applied to the Shawshine ; but I don't think that fifteen ought to be. I think it would be very much safer to apply ten and a half.

Q. — What do you say is the daily consumption of Charlestown, Somerville, and Chelsea, and the district that Boston supplies with the Mystic? *A.* — That is a variable quantity, depending upon whether we supply East Boston or not; but, taking last year, what we did supply from the Mystic amounted to eighty-one gallons per head.

Q. — What is the difference between that district and the city of Cambridge, which you say is a small city? Why should the consumption of Cambridge be forty-six gallons per head, and that district eighty-one? *A.* — I don't think that is a question that can be answered, except in this way : that the city of Cambridge has given special attention to the question of waste water, and looked after it very carefully.

Q. — That is the very point I wish to make, — whether special attention would not reduce the consumption of the district supplied by the Mystic to the point that has been reached in Cambridge? *A.* — I do not know any reason why it would not, if the city had authority to apply the same process in other sections that it applies in Charlestown. I think it cannot apply the same process.

Q. — What is the difference between European cities like London and Paris, and an American city? *A.* — They do not use water anywhere near so freely. They do not have any water-closet system to the same extent. A very large portion of Paris has not the water-closet system at all. It is not a system, as a system, at all, in Paris. Four-fifths, and I do not know but nine-tenths, is on the vault system. They have no system of sewers in Paris; that is, sewers for the purpose of carrying off sewage. They are now agitating that question; but they have not got any such system yet.

Q. — Is there any other difference that you think of? *A.* — The people do not use so much water. Whether it is because of the climate, or the habits of the people, I do not know; but they do not use the quantity of water that we do in American cities, and neither can they get in some cities the small consumption. In some European cities, — Glasgow, for instance, which is very much nearer Boston in the character of its population than other European cities, — where they have adopted the meter system, and the inspection of all the fixtures that are put in the houses, the consumption is fifty gallons a head. Consequently I do not believe the consumption can be reduced in our city much below sixty.

Q. — Will you tell the Committee briefly what this Deacon meter is? *A.* — The Deacon meter, so called, is not properly a meter: it is a measurer of rates of flow, and not absolute quantities. That is to say, all the water that runs into a certain district is cut off, a meter is put on to the supply-pipe of that district, and that meter is connected with clock-work, and a removable diagram, which shows the rate of consumption all the time, being moved around by clock-work, and recording the rate of consumption. If you put the meter in operation, all the water is running through the meter; if you take off a few of those cards, as you may call them, at night, you can see what the night consumption is. That is a pretty fair indication of how much waste is due to defective fixtures and other causes. Having done that, you commence the system of inspection, which consists in men going round at night, and testing by hearing each one of the stop-cocks, to see if any water is running, and, if it is, it is shut off; and the inspector goes through the entire district in the same way — every stop-cock shut shows on that card — until he has got through the whole district, when he comes back and opens them all. He gives his book to the day inspector after he gets through; and the day inspector goes into each one of the houses where he finds by the record that water was wasted, and takes measures to stop it.

Q. — It is simply a waste-detector? *A.* — A waste-detector. That is about what it is.

Q. — As I understand you, the principal objection to introducing them into Boston is, that it involves moving the stop-cocks to the sidewalk? *A.* — Yes, sir.

Q. — Where are the new stop-cocks put in, as you supply new takers? *A.* — Those are all put on the sidewalk. That practice has been adopted only within the last two years.

Q. — Is not that the better way, independently of any question of the introduction of meters? *A.* — Decidedly.

Q. — And that method will be followed? *A.* — It will be followed in the future.

Q. — How long have the contracts to run, which you have with Somerville, Chelsea, and Everett? *A.* — I think they are contracts that run until they are terminated by the reduction of the water-debt to practically nothing, I suppose.

Q. — The water-debt of Boston? *A.* — The water-debt of the Mystic. But I am not familiar with that. I had the contracts in my office yesterday, and looked them over; but I don't recollect how that is.

Q. — It is not for a fixed term of years? *A.* — I don't think it is for a fixed term of years.

Q. — Is there a fixed rate to consumers in those places? *A.* — You are getting beyond me. I really do not know much about the details of those contracts.

Q. — Your charge is based upon the gross receipts; and of course it is an important matter what those gross receipts are? *A.* — The rates may be more, they cannot be less, than the city rates.

Q. — The rates of Boston? *A.* — Yes, sir.

Q. — Based upon the valuation of the property? *A.* — They probably are the same rates exactly.

Q. — Will you bring up one of those contracts? *A.* — Yes, sir. There are three of the original contracts on my table. I have not had time to read them.

Q. (By Mr. BAILEY.) — Do you know what the amount of loss was, to the city of Boston, by supplying those places from the Mystic, during the past year? *A.* — What do you mean by " loss "?

Q. — What was the cost, over and above the amount of receipts? *A.* — I don't know what it was this year. Last year it was $20,000.

Mr. BAILEY. I understand that it was between $40,000 and $50,000 this year.

Q. (By Mr. HAMMOND.) — Do you think the Shawshine is good for 20,000,000 gallons a day, upon constructing the works which Mr. Barbour proposes to construct? *A.* — I did not hear his testimony, sir.

Q. — It was, substantially, what it was last year. He proposes to have a dam at the same place that was spoken of last year. That is, substantially the same works would be constructed, if Boston were authorized to take the stream? *A.* — Yes, sir.

Q. — You think that, upon constructing those works, 20,000,000 gallons a day could be drawn from the reservoir for the two cities, do you? *A.* — Yes, sir.

Q. — If Cambridge only takes 8,000,000 gallons a day, is there any reason why the other 12,000,000 gallons cannot run down the stream? *A.* — No: I don't know any reason why it cannot.

Q. — Then, why is it not safe enough for Cambridge, if she wants to take only 8,000,000 gallons, to say she will let 10,000,000 gallons a day run down the stream? *A.* — I don't know any reason, except, as I said, it would not be a profitable operation.

Q. — Is there any physical reason why it cannot be done? *A.* — Not the slightest. I don't wish to be understood so.

Q. — Supposing it would not cost Cambridge much more to do it in that way than to go in with Boston, what would be the harm in doing it? *A.* — There would be no harm in doing it, if the city of Cambridge thought so. The cost of construction and damages could not amount to less than $700.000; and I think it would be very foolish for them, if they spend $700,000, to let 10,000,000 gallons a day go down the stream.

Q. — If they don't want to use it? *A.* — If they don't want to use it: yes, sir.

Q. (By Dr. INGALLS.) — Was the loss of $40,000, this last year, on the whole Mystic system, including Charlestown? *A.* — Including Charlestown: yes, sir.

Q. (By Mr. BAILEY.) — Have you any idea what the mill-damages will be on that river? *A.* — No: I don't know. I have an idea, but I should prefer not to answer that question.

Adjourned to Thursday at ten o'clock.

THIRD HEARING.

THURSDAY, March 23, 1882.

THE hearing was resumed at 10.15.

Mr. BAILEY. I expected to put on the chairman of the Boston Water Board this morning; but he is unavoidably absent. The chairman of the Committee on Water, on the part of the Council, Mr. M. S. Greenough, is present; and I will put him on. Mr. Greenough has been chairman of that committee for the past three years, and is perhaps better acquainted than any other man with all the details.

TESTIMONY OF MALCOLM S. GREENOUGH.

Q. (By Mr. BAILEY.) — You are chairman of the Committee on Water, on the part of the Council? A. — Yes, sir.

Q. — How long have you been? A. — This is my third year.

Q. — Will you state to the Committee the result of your experience on that committee, and what the necessities of Boston are which require the use of the Shawshine River? A. — I do not know that I can add very much to what Mr. Wightman stated yesterday; but, after his remarks had been finished, there was so much said about the waste of water that it may perhaps have left an impression on the minds of the Committee that the neglect of the Board, if there has been any, to prevent the waste of water in the districts supplied by the Cochituate and the Sudbury has had something to do with our necessities in regard to the Shawshine on the other branch. Such an impression, if it exists, I think is an entire mistake. I certainly have had a good deal to do with hammering into the Water Board, in the past two years, the necessity of taking some active action in regard to the waste of water, and I feel very much interested in that matter indeed; but it does not affect the needs of Boston on the other branch of its supply. I do not suppose that there can be any question with this Committee that the Mystic system is not sufficient, at the present time, for the demands that are made upon it. There have been various portions of it, in the last few years, that have been quite short of water. Although we have, by the use of the Deacon meter in Charlestown, reduced the consumption over there nearly half a million gallons a day, yet the consumption of water has been more in the last year than it has been at any previous time.

Now, assuming that we must do something over there, the question is, What shall we do? Are we to reduce our consumption, or are we to increase our supply? In the matter of consumption, Boston practically only has control over the Charlestown portion of the Mystic supply. It is doubtful whether we could bring any pressure to bear on Chelsea, Somerville, or Everett, that would be effective. I think it is extremely doubtful whether we can do any thing with those towns at all. But, if we do succeed in reducing the consumption of the Mystic system to some reasonable amount, what have we got when that has been accomplished? That Mystic system is not in a satisfactory condition to-day, and it has not been for years. The gentlemen of this Committee know perfectly well the condition of the Mystic supply, — that it comes through populous towns; it comes through a district which is rapidly becoming more thickly peopled; it comes through towns, two of which have water-supplies and no drainage, so that the water which comes in underneath will gradually become tainted; and every year it brings us into most unpleasant wrangling with gentlemen from neighboring towns, whose views of what is just are diametrically opposed to ours, and with whom we have relations which I should be pleased to change. The Mystic system cannot go on. The Mystic system, in my judgment, has got to be abandoned before any great number of years any way, no matter what we do to-day.

Then, if we are to add to our supply, where do we stand? Are we to increase the basins on the Mystic? I think that would be, obviously, a mistake. The expense of those basins would be very great, and then we should have impure water, as it is to-day; and it is likely to be more impure in the future. If we leave that out of the question, then there are two alternatives left to us, — either to get a new source of supply, or to come across from the Cochituate and Sudbury systems, and connect with the Mystic system. If we were asking you for leave to increase our Sudbury system, you might very well say to us that we are not taking care of what we are getting from the Cochituate and the Sudbury. I admit that at once. If we go on as we are going on at present in Boston, it will not be five years before we shall practically have exhausted that whole supply over there, and shall be looking for something else. If we take hold of the water-supply of the Sudbury, and reduce the consumption to a reasonable amount per head, I do not see why the Cochituate and the Sudbury should not last fifteen years, and perhaps longer. I doubt if it will last any longer than that, because the legitimate increase of consumption in Boston is very large every year. We increased, I think, last year, between three and four million gallons a day; and I do not think we have wasted proportionately any more water than we did the previous year. So that, if we should reduce our Cochituate system and our Sudbury system to a more proper amount, we still have not an unlimited supply there by any means. If we undertake to supply the Mystic system from the Sudbury, we must at once bring up our general system to its full limit of supply, and we shall be obliged to look for another supply on the other side of Boston, at a large expense, in the course of a very few years; and if by expending less money, not over three-quarters of a million, we can get a large additional supply of water on the Mystic side, and can leave the Sudbury system to run for ten or fifteen years, before we have to increase that, certainly that is a reasonable, business-like proposition for the city of Boston to bring before this Committee.

If, as I said before, it were a question of the Sudbury system, I do not think the system of Boston would have a footing here, because we unquestionably can reduce the waste of water in Boston very materially. I trust that before the end of another year we shall have measures under way which will tend materially to that result. But, when the question relates to the Mystic system, it is an entirely different one. I do not think that all the testimony which has been put in here, and all the talk about the waste of water in Boston, really has any bearing upon the position in which Boston stands with reference to the Mystic system.

That is all, gentlemen, that I wish to present to the Committee as the views of the City Council.

Cross-Examination.

Q. (By Mr. Morse.) — One or two questions, Mr. Greenough. I would like to ask you whether you agree generally with Mr. Wightman in the views which he stated yesterday as to what would be a reasonable allowance for consumption here, and also as to the capacity of these different sources of water-supply which the city of Boston has? *A.* — Of course my knowledge of the different sources of supply is derived entirely from Mr. Wightman's statements. In regard to the consumption of water in the city of Boston, I doubt very much whether we could succeed in reducing it below sixty gallons per head of population. I think there would probably be some waste water even then. I do not believe we can reduce it below sixty gallons by any means which it would be advisable for us to adopt. I have had a good deal of talk with Mr. Wightman about that; and, while there are many cities abroad which use less than that, he stated the fact very clearly yesterday, that our position is different from theirs. He said he doubted whether we could get the consumption below sixty gallons a head.

Q. — You would not think it unreasonable to reduce it to sixty gallons? *A.* — I think it could be done, and I think it would pay the city of Boston the expense of doing it.

Q. — Whether you believe there is any difficulty in the authorities of the city of Boston negotiating with their friends in Cambridge, and making an arrangement to supply them with water when the new basin on the Sudbury is finished? *A.* — It seems to me that we could do that cheaper than they could get a supply elsewhere. I can see no reason why we could not sell them certainly the extra quantity of water that they will want.

Q. — You will have enough? *A.* — We shall have enough to supply them for the present. That is, if we can reduce our consumption, as we trust we can, we can sell them all they want.

Q. — There have been no negotiations during the last year about that, have there? *A.* — I think not. I think there were some year before last : I think none this last year.

Q. — Not to go over any of the figures which Mr. Wightman gave, and in regard to which I suppose you would say you depended upon him, do you agree with him in his statement that it would cost about $450,000 to connect the Sudbury and the Mystic? *A.* — He said about $500,000. He said $400,000 was the original estimate. The rise in the cost of iron and labor must have increased that materially.

Q. (By Mr. Bullard.) — Do you remember, as a member of the Council, receiving a communication from the Mayor, about the 25th of last January, calling the attention of the Council to the fact that the city of Cambridge was before the Legislature asking for the Shawshine River? *A.* — Yes, sir.

Q. — Do you remember afterwards making remarks in the Council, of which this purports to be a report : —

"The Committee on Water yesterday gave a hearing to some petitioners who objected to the city making application for authority to take the Shawshine River; but, in spite of the objections urged, the committee concluded to put in this order. The city of Cambridge has asked for the same authority. If Cambridge were willing to leave the Shawshine River alone, I think the city of Boston might be well content to do so, until the question of the drainage of the Mystic valley is settled."

Do you remember that? *A.* — I think I made very similar remarks to those.

Q. — That is still your opinion? *A.* — That is my opinion on that question still ; but, since that time, I have looked into the matter more carefully than I had before, and I find that the position of Boston is stronger than I thought it was.

Q. — What have you discovered, sir, since the 25th of last January, that has led you to change your opinion? *A.* — I do not know that I have discovered any thing.

Mr. Bailey. We take that same ground now, — always have taken it.

Mr. Bullard. You ask for it because Cambridge does?

Mr. Bailey. Not at all.

Mr. Bullard. You would not ask for it if Cambridge didn't.

Mr. Bailey. No, sir. Read the last part, — "until the question of the drainage of the Mystic valley is settled." I say now, if we cannot have the right to protect our Mystic supply, we have got to give it up, and then we shall want the Shawshine. If we can have the right to protect the Mystic supply, we do not want the Shawshine at present. Our position has been the same from the beginning.

Witness. I think we make out a pretty strong case of necessity for the Shawshine, no matter what happens.

Mr. Bullard [reading] : —

"But while it is probable that the Mystic valley is likely to be polluted by drainage, we cannot stand by and see any other corporation come in and take the water of the Shawshine, without making an effort to obtain it. Therefore the committee feel that it is necessary to put in a petition for that supply of water in order to get a standing with the city of Cambridge before the legislative committee."

A. — That was the talk which we had in the Committee on Water the day before that meeting of the Common Council, and it was their views which I presented in the Council. But the last few days I have been looking over the report of the hearing before this Committee last year, and I was surprised to see how strong a case Boston had for wanting that water, whether the Mystic system was disturbed or not.

Q. — I notice in these remarks that you say you gave a hearing to some petitioners who objected to the city making application for authority to take the Shawshine River. What was that hearing? As a matter of fact, was any evidence offered? *A.* — I don't think there was any evidence. I think you are aware who the petitioners were, and what hearing they had.

Mr. Bullard. I am quite as well aware as you are that no hearing was ever given. It was said that the last meeting of the Council, at which it would be possible to get that order in, was to be held the next day ; and therefore the committee declined to give any hearing.

Witness. That is not my recollection at all, sir.

Q. — I understand you to say, as a matter of fact, that there was no hearing? *A.* — I don't say any thing of the kind. You had an opportunity to put in any evidence that you wanted to put in, and you did not put in any.

Q. — There was no evidence put in, then? *A.* — There was none offered by you. That was your business, not ours.

Q. — Was anybody there who testified? *A.* — You did not choose to put anybody on.

Q. — Was there anybody there who testified? *A.* — No, sir. There was a hearing given, and the committee heard what you had to say.

Q. — At that meeting didn't you hear Mr. Cutter, the chairman of your Water Board, make a statement as to what had happened during the year, by reason of which it was necessary for Boston to come a second time for this supply, when it had been refused by the same committee the year before? Is not that so? *A.* — Yes, sir.

Q. — And then your committee sustained the commissioners without going into a hearing at all? *A.* — The position of our committee was this : The Water Board had sent in a communication previously, asking us to petition the Legislature for the Shawshine. Before the petition was put in, the people whom you represented remonstrated against it, and asked for a hearing. The Committee on Water gave you a hearing, and asked you what you had to say about it. You said you had nothing to say about it until the Water Board had considered the case. We said that was none of your business : we wanted to hear what you had to say about it. You declined to put any testimony in, and we then went on with our business without consulting you. You had an opportunity to put in any evidence that you wanted to.

Q. — How much notice did we have of that hearing? *A.* — I don't remember. I think you said that you only had one day's notice.

Q. — You gave the notice yourself of that hearing, didn't you? *A.* — To whom?

Q. — To me, in the street? *A.* — Yes, I think I did.

Q. — It was a notice of twenty-four hours of an important hearing ; and, when we got there, were we not told that we could not have any further time than could be given that afternoon? *A.* — That was obviously the case. The order had got to go in the next day. The reason the thing was hurried in that way was, that I had supposed we had a standing to come up here, without putting in another petition.

Q. (By the CHAIRMAN.) — I would like to ask you a question ; and you may answer it, or not, just as you like. Does the city of Boston have the impression that the city of Cambridge wants to get this Act in order to make better terms with Boston for the water? *A.* — I should be unable to answer that question. I have heard rumors of that kind in the air.

Q. — Really, to be frank about it, is not that about all there is to it? *A.* — No, sir, not exactly. We do not want to be coming up here every year asking for this thing ; and we would be content to stand still for a little while until we see how that metropolitan drainage system is coming out down there in the Mystic valley. If we can drain that valley properly, I think that the Mystic system, or at least a portion of it, can very properly be maintained. If we cannot, we have got to let that whole system go. If other people would let the Shawshine River alone for a year or two, we would be content to sit still and look at it. If Cambridge comes here and asks for it, we propose to show that we have as good a claim to that river, and want it as much as she does. I do not know what Cambridge may have in her mind in asking for the Shawshine River, I am sure.

Q. (By Mr. SMITH.) — If I understand you rightly, you think that neither Cambridge nor Boston wants it just now? A. — I don't think we should build the dam just now.

Q. (By Mr. CHAMBERLAIN.) — You said you did not think Cambridge wanted it now? A. — No, sir: I did not mean to say that. It seems to me, without professing to know Cambridge's business better than she does, that Cambridge could get along for a short time by calling on Boston.

Q. — Are you pretty conversant with the feeling of Cambridge in regard to this matter? A. — No, sir: only from what I have heard up here, and from having read the testimony. I heard what Mr. Barbour had to say. I know how Cambridge stands pretty well about the matter.

Q. (By Mr. BULLARD.) — As I understand Mr. Bailey's statement, you are the only representative of the Boston water management who is to be here to-day. The Water Board consists of Mr. Cutter, Mr. Stanwood, and Mr. Thompson, neither of whom is expected to be here. That being so, I would like to ask you whether you can explain this language, which seems to be rather remarkable, in the report of the Water Board to the city of Boston. The city having applied for leave to take the Shawshine, the Board say, "The petition was refused by the Legislature for reasons not necessary to discuss here"? A. — You do not expect that I am going to back up every thing the water commissioners say, do you?

Q. — Do you know what those reasons were supposed to be? That is the report of your water commissioners. You are the only representative of the Boston water management who is here to-day, or will be here, as I understand it. I should have asked Mr. Cutter if he were here. Do you understand what that means? Do you know what the reasons were that it was "unnecessary to discuss"? If you don't know, that is the end of it. If you do know what it means, I would like to have you explain to the Committee. That is all. A. — No, sir: I don't know what it means, unless simply that they do not care to go into it at length.

Q. (By Mr. HAMMOND.) — Does Boston want to use any part of the Shawshine River? *A.* — When?

Q. — At any time. *A.* — I should think it did, most decidedly.

Q. — When? *A.* — I should think we would want it in the course of a few years anyhow.

Q. — How long? *A.* — I should say it would be impossible for the Mystic system, no matter what is done to it, to last for more than eight or ten years.

Q. — If the Mystic system does not stand, they may need it in eight or ten years? *A.* — We shall need it in that time anyhow. It may be that we shall want to use it very much sooner than that.

Q. — You will then want to use that part of it which Cambridge wants to use now? *A.* — You mean the whole river?

Q. — Cambridge asks for 8,000,000 gallons a day. Does Boston expect in ten years to want the whole river? *A.* — I don't know that I quite gather your question. Do you mean, in ten years from now shall we want the whole supply of the river?

Q. — Do you expect to need the whole supply of the river in ten years from now, or simply 12,000,000 gallons a day? *A.* — I should think 12,000,000 would be enough for that Mystic system.

Q. — How, then, is the petition of Cambridge for 8,000,000 inconsistent with the possible wants of Boston in ten years?

Mr. BAILEY. That is not for him to settle; that is for the Committee to settle. We do not object to that.

Mr. HAMMOND. I want to know what your position is.

Mr. BAILEY. I do not care to tell you.

Mr. HAMMOND. I think it is important to see how Boston stands to-day on this matter.

Mr. BAILEY. I have made the statement that we do not object to your taking 8,000,000 to-day. We are willing to join you in taking the river, and divide the water between us, you to have two-fifths, and we will take three-fifths. That is my statement.

Mr. HAMMOND. That you do not object to our taking 8,000,000?

Mr. BAILEY. Not at all.

Mr. HAMMOND. And you do not object to our taking 8,000,000, whether the Committee give you the right to take 12,000,000 or not?

Mr. BAILEY. We do not have any thing to say about that. That is for the Committee to settle.

Mr. HAMMOND. I would like to have an understanding about this matter. If Boston takes the position that she is willing that Cambridge should have 8,000,000 gallons a day, that is one thing. If she takes the position that she is not willing that we should have the 8,000,000, unless she can have at the same time 12,000,000, that is another thing. I should like to know which position she takes.

Mr. BAILEY. She takes neither. I state it now just as I stated it in the beginning. So far as the action of the Committee on the Cambridge petition is concerned, it is none of our business; but, if it is proposed to allow the use of that river for the purposes of water-supply, then we are interested. And when I come to the argument I shall take this position: that, if you give the right to Cambridge to take it, you are giving them all the supply there is there; that the damages to the mill-owners, whether Cambridge takes 8,000,000 gallons a day or the whole river, will be the same. Therefore, in passing whatever bill you do pass, you pass a bill giving away the entire water-supply of the Shawshine River. If you give the city of Cambridge the right to take 8,000,000 gallons a day, you practically give them the whole river. Therefore, if the river is to be given for domestic purposes to any municipality, the city of Boston says it has got to look after its own interests. We are not antagonizing Cambridge at all. We simply show the needs of Boston so far as regards the Shawshine River, and then leave the Committee to decide between us.

Mr. HAMMOND. My brother is generally pretty clear; but I do not quite get the exact position that he proposes to take in the argument. If I understand, him it is this: he intends to argue, that, if you give Cambridge 8,000,000 gallons a day, as Cambridge asks, the mill-owners will get just as much damages from the city for that taking as they would if we took the whole river, which I do not see concerns him at all; and also that the water would be appropriated so that Boston could not get the remaining 12,000,000, which is not true as a matter of fact.

Mr. BAILEY. I think it is.

Mr. HAMMOND. I do not believe that my brother intends to oppose Cambridge here on any such flimsy foundation as that.

Mr. BAILEY. I say again, I am not opposing Cambridge at all. I don't want you to state that I am here opposing Cambridge.

Mr. HAMMOND. Will my brother say whether Boston would oppose a bill before this Committee or elsewhere giving Cambridge only 8,000,000 gallons, which did not give Boston any thing?

Mr. MORSE. That is not the form of bill which you have submitted, — a bill allowing you to take 8,000,000 gallons from the river.

Mr. HAMMOND. It allows us to take only 8,000,000 gallons.

Mr. MORSE. I beg your pardon. That may be the inference which you draw from it; but that is not the language of the bill. The bill is to take the Shawshine River.

Mr. HAMMOND. Not exceeding 8,000,000 gallons a day.

Mr. BAILEY. No, sir. You will not find that provision in the bill.

Mr. HAMMOND. The bill provides that we may take not exceeding 8,000,000 gallons a day. If it has got any more than that in it, it got in without my knowing it. I cannot find out what position the city of Boston takes here.

Mr. BAILEY. I do not propose that you shall find out, until the proper time comes.

Mr. HAMMOND. I don't suppose you do.

Mr. BAILEY. I don't usually give away my hand at the beginning of the game.

Mr. HAMMOND. My remarks have brought my brother to this point at least, that he does not intend to let us know where he stands. I will call the attention of the Committee to the first section of the bill, which provides that we shall take not exceeding 8,000,-000 gallons. I am perfectly frank in stating the position of Cambridge here; but I cannot get my brother to state his position.

Mr. BAILEY. I think I have stated, to the satisfaction of the Committee, the position of the city of Boston. Brother Hammond is trying to get out of me whether I propose to oppose Cambridge if she gets this bill. I don't propose to tell him whether I shall or not. The Committee know we want authority to take that river; and the Committee know, from what I have said, that we are willing to join with Cambridge in taking the river, and divide the water on the basis that has been stated. I am not going to tell him what I shall do in case the action of the Committee is one way or the other.

Mr. HAMMOND. I know.

Mr. BAILEY. Then why do you ask me?

Mr. HAMMOND. I wanted to see if you would own up. I did not ask you to find out: I asked you to see what you would say.

Q. — If I understand you, the granting to Cambridge of a right to take 8,000,000 gallons a day would not be inconsistent with what you conceive may be the wants of Boston ten years from now. Is that so? A. — I should not want Cambridge to have control of the river now.

Q. — Why not? A. — I think it might be harder for us to get our 12,000,000 gallons by and by.

Q. — Why? A. — I should think that might possibly be so, without going into the reasons.

Q. — Then, the substance of it is, that if Cambridge would mildly submit to the situation, and crawl up to the Boston Water Board, and ask for some water when she wants it, Boston would be content? That is the substance of it, isn't it? A. — I don't know as I should have expressed it in just that way.

Q. — No: but that is the idea, isn't it? A. — That is not the way I should put it exactly: no, sir.

Q. — Will you put it in your own way? *A.* — You mean in regard to your obtaining a supply from Boston?

Q. — Will you put that idea which I did not exactly express?

Mr. BAILEY. No, don't put that idea: put your own idea.

Q. — I stated my question, perhaps, in rather forcible language, but I thought clearly enough for you to understand it; and your reply was, that that did not exactly express your idea. Now, I would like to have you express the idea which I came pretty near expressing. *A.* — I don't propose to express the idea which you expressed; but I should say, that if Cambridge were desirous of increasing her water-supply from Boston, and addressed a communication to the Mayor of Boston, which would be referred to the Committee on Water and the Water Board, it would be extremely probable that some arrangement could be made between Cambridge and Boston by which Boston would supply Cambridge, on liberal terms, with all the water she needs.

Q. — For how long a time? *A.* — I do not see why they should not give it for a long time.

Q. — What! when you are going to need the Shawshine? *A.* — I think we should be able to supply Cambridge with a million gallons a day.

Q. — Notwithstanding you need the Shawshine? *A.* — If we undertook to do it, we should use the Sudbury. There is plenty of water over there.

Q. — Suppose the Mystic to be gone in five or ten years, or Boston to be in such a condition that she wants the Shawshine, and supposing she could not get it: how could she supply Cambridge then? *A.* — Then she would have to go somewhere to increase her supply to the extent of the million or two million gallons that Cambridge would take.

Q. — Then there is no certainty that we can rely upon Boston for five years if the Mystic is gone? *A.* — I think a contract could be made that would last more than five years.

Q. — I can't understand how, when, in five or ten years from now, Boston will want 12,000,000 gallons a day from the Shawshine for its own consumption. *A.* — On the Mystic system.

Q. — I don't care where it is. *A.* — It makes a great deal of difference.

Q. — I don't care any thing about that, whether it is the Mystic or otherwise. You will want 12,000,000 gallons a day from the Shawshine when the Mystic is gone, to supplement that system, as I understand? *A.* — The Mystic system.

Q. — To take the place of it when it is gone, if it ever goes? *A.* — Yes, sir.

Q. — You say you can furnish Cambridge from the other sources of supply, whether you get the Shawshine or not? *A.* — I think we can : yes, sir.

Q. — And that you would be inclined to do that, rather than to supply the people who are now supplied by the Mystic? *A.* — Yes, sir.

Q. — Although you have contracts with those people to supply them? *A.* — Yes, sir.

Q. (By Mr. Morse.) — I do not understand, Mr. Greenough, that you mean to say that you would violate your contracts, but simply, upon the expiration of those contracts, you would not go on? Having agreed to supply customers with water, you don't mean to say that you are going to break your contracts? *A.* — No, sir : not at all. We shall continue our supply to the Mystic people from the Shawshine, or whatever water we can get there. That has nothing to do with Cambridge. Those people are supplied with Mystic water. I do not see any reason why we cannot supply Cambridge from the Sudbury, which is an entirely different thing.

Q. (By Mr. Hammond.) — The Sudbury is equal to how much — 40,000,000 a day? *A.* — 52,000,000.

Q. — As I understand it, if the Mystic should give out, and you were obliged to make a connection between the Sudbury and the Mystic works, you think you might be able to supply Cambridge also : are you prepared to say that? *A.* — Well, I should hesitate to say that, if we were obliged to abandon the Mystic, and fall back upon the Sudbury supply.

Q. — That is what I supposed. Your idea is, that if the Mystic is gone, and you cannot get the Shawshine as a substitute for that, it would not be safe to make any contracts? *A.* — I should think, in that case, we had better attend to our own business, and supply our own customers. If we can get the Shawshine River to supplement the Mystic system, I see no reason why we cannot supply Cambridge.

Q. — But, if you cannot get it, you cannot say, as at present advised, what you would do? *A.* — I cannot.

Q. (By Mr. Bailey.) — I get the impression from what you say, that after the new basin is completed, whether we get the Shawshine or not, we can supply Cambridge? *A.* — We can supply Cambridge at present unquestionably, — until we abandon the Mystic at any rate.

Q. (By Mr. Hammond.) — It is pretty certain, in your mind, that you will abandon the Mystic in five or ten years? *A.* — By and by I think we shall have to : say in ten years.

Q. — In calculating upon so important a matter as a water-supply for the city of Boston, would you consider it safe to rely upon the Mystic for more than five or ten years? *A.* — I think not.

Q. — See if I understand it: suppose the Mystic gives out, and you do not get the Shawshine, and your only sources of supply are the Sudbury and the Cochituate, you would not then feel inclined to make any extended contract with Cambridge to furnish her with water? That is, as at present advised, you would not say that that would be done? *A.* — Of course, if we undertook to supply Cambridge with water for any definite period, if we found we had not water enough, we should have to go on sooner than we expect, and increase our water-supply. I think you only use about 2,000,000 gallons a day there, and you can get about a million and a half from Fresh Pond anyhow. We could supply you with the balance that you want from Boston without affecting our position very seriously.

Q. — Suppose Fresh Pond to give out, and that we should need three, four, or five million gallons a day, as we shall in a few years from now? *A.* — Then, if we were driven off from the Mystic, we should have to go to the Charles sooner than we anticipate. It seems to me, without professing to know much about it, that we can sell you water fully as cheap as you can get it elsewhere; and at present I see no reason why we should not do so.

Q. (By Dr. HARRIS.) — I would like to ask one question in reference to some testimony put in yesterday. If I understood Mr. Wightman correctly, he said, if Cambridge would store water, he thought an abundant supply might be stored in the spring to last them the whole season. I want to know whether Cambridge can store water. *A.* — That I don't know, sir.

Q. — He said that there is enough water that runs over the dam of the Sudbury in the spring of the year to give an abundant supply? *A.* — During the spring freshets, there is a great deal of water going over the dam of the Sudbury. 200,000,000 gallons a day were running away there a few weeks ago when I was there, and about the same quantity has been running away since. That water runs to waste. If Cambridge had any means of storing that water, we could give them all the water they want at present.

Q. — I understand you to say that this Mystic supply will probably cease in about ten years, whatever may be done to purify the water? *A.* — Of course, in making that remark, I am dependent upon the opinion of other people; but at the same time it must be obvious to anybody who goes up there, that the water-supply is not in a satisfactory condition; that a great portion of the water comes from a rather thickly settled district, which is growing; that the neighborhood of some of those tanneries to the upper ponds is certainly not advantageous to the ponds, to say the least. Whether the stuff that comes from those tanneries is all kept out of the ponds, I should think was somewhat doubtful from what I saw. Then I understand that Woburn and Winchester both have water-supplies, and no sewerage system, and the drainage in those towns must affect the ground, and in the course of time must affect the water that comes from the ground. The district is growing so rapidly, that I doubt very much whether it is possible to keep that water pure any considerable length of time. I said ten years as a mere limit of time. It may be fifteen, it may be twenty, it may be five. If we are driven to the position that we cannot economically look after the drainage of the Mystic district, then the question will be brought upon us much more forcibly than it has been.

Q. — It is a fact, is it not, that the water from the Mystic reservoir is not nearly so good at the present time, or was not in '80 and 81, as it was in '75, notwithstanding you have protected it by the sewer you have made there? *A.* — No, sir: I do not understand that to be the fact.

Q. — It has been so stated in the papers, has it not? *A.* — I don't think it has been so stated by any representative of Boston. That may be the position of gentlemen who wish to empty sewage into the Mystic; but I do not think Boston has ever made that statement.

Q. — No: but I know it was stated very broadly and generally, that the supply was even better in '75 than the Cochituate; and I believe it has been stated as a fact, that in '80 and '81 it was not as good? *A.* — I do not think that is true at all.

Mr. BAILEY. It is better, and has been better, for the last two years.

Q. (By Mr. CHAMBERLAIN.) — What is your opinion of the water of the Mystic now, as compared with five years ago? Is it better or worse? *A.* — There is no question that it is better.

Q. — It is better? *A.* — I have no doubt of it.

Q. — Then it is improving? *A.* — Of course it is better now than it was when they emptied all that sewage into it which now goes into the Mystic sewer.

Q. (By Mr. SMITH.) — If I understand you, you think it is possible and probable that the Mystic system may give out in about ten years; and that the Sudbury system will supply Boston, and Cambridge perchance, for fifteen years? *A.* — If the Mystic system is supplemented, I should think so.

Q. — Now, I want to ask you this question: whether you have any other source of supply for the city of Boston or the city of Cambridge, on the Mystic system, than the Shawshine River, after all these sources give out? *A.* — Of course: the Charles still remains for us to apply for. If we should come in here fifteen years from now, and show that we were saving our water in Boston, and spending it economically, I suppose the Legislature would allow us to spend a million dollars for the Charles.

Q. — Is it policy for the city of Boston to take up all these little rivers that are in its immediate vicinity, as it needs them, rather than to go to some larger river, where it can get a supply for all time? *A.* — That is a question which I should hardly like to answer directly, yes or no. At the time that the Sudbury River was taken, an investigation was made, as I think you very likely know, of the different sources of water-supply from which it would be possible for Boston to draw its water. I suppose you have in your mind the Merrimack, the Concord, and Lake Winnipesaukee, or some of those other schemes which have been brought forward. From what I have read on the subject only, of course, I should judge that the city of Boston acted wisely in taking the Sudbury River. I have only the report of the commission to refer to on that matter; but I should think it would be extremely doubtful, and more than doubtful, whether it was policy for the city of Boston to look to the Merrimack River, to go no further than that.

Q. — Don't you think it would be wise to look beyond fifteen years? It is anticipated that Boston is going to grow very rapidly, and to be a very large city. My question leads to this, whether Boston is to be supplied with water after fifteen years, or not? You do not say, of course, that the Shawshine River, which yields, at the best estimate, only 20,000,000 gallons daily, would last Boston very long if that were to be depended upon for the increase of its population? *A.* — I should think that 20,000,000 gallons or 12,000,000 gallons a day ought to last the population dependent upon the Mystic system a good while.

Q. — I was looking forward fifteen years. *A.* — I do not see why it should not last even that length of time.

Q. — Supposing at the end of fifteen years your Sudbury-river system gives out, that your Mystic system has given out before that, and that all the additional population of Boston will be dependent upon some other source of supply than those which you now have, even if you take the Shawshine River to supply the lack of your Mystic system: what is going to be done then? Don't you look beyond fifteen years in your Water Board? *A.* — Certainly, sir.

Q. — What are you going to do then? *A.* — As I said, they will apply for the Charles. The Charles will give 50,000,000 gallons a day. The conduit has been built in view of the intention, at some time, of applying for the Charles.

Q. — Why don't you apply for it now, instead of going for this little river? *A.* — In the first place, the expense would be very much greater.

Q. — You say you will ultimately have to go for Charles River: why don't you go now? *A.* — We have not got the money that we want to spend now. Fifteen years from now two million dollars may not seem so large an amount as it does now for the city of Boston to pay.

Q. — You put it into bonds, don't you? You don't pay the debt: you only pay the interest, and you get that from the water-takers? *A.* — We do not get the interest out of the water-takers. We get it on one side of the city; we don't on the other.

Q. (By Dr. CAMPBELL.) — What would it cost to go to the Charles? *A.* — My impression is, that the Charles would cost between two and three million dollars; but I don't know.

Q. (By Mr. SMITH.) — Should you regard this as a suitable basin for storing water for domestic uses, unless it was thoroughly cleaned out by removing all the mud and peat now lying on the bottom? *A.* — No, sir: I think that ought to be done.

Q. — What would you estimate the expense of cleaning out a bottom of that character, over an area of eight hundred acres? *A.* — That would depend upon the thickness of the soil.

Q. — Suppose it was from one to six feet deep? *A.* — I should think, if it was six feet deep, it would cost a great deal of money.

Q. — Does anybody know that it is not six feet deep? *A.* — I don't know: it may be twenty. The engineers, of course, are the persons to whom the Committee on Water go for information of that kind. If they recommend that as a proper place for storing water, the Committee on Water are bound to take their opinion. I should object to making a basin there unless the muck was removed.

Q. — We will suppose (it may not be true) that it is from one foot to six feet deep, over that eight hundred acres: what should you think would be the cost of removing that, so as to make a suitable basin? *A.* — If it was a foot thick, I should suppose it would cost from fifty to one hundred thousand dollars. If it were six feet deep, it would cost a great deal more; of course not six times that, but it would cost a great deal more.

Q. — You would not think you could get it removed for less than half a million dollars, would you? *A.* — Yes, sir: I think we could get it removed for less than that.

Q. (By Mr. BULLARD.) — Has this paper which I will read been referred to your committee, and do you expect to have a hearing at some time on it?

" *To the Honorable the City Council of the City of Boston.*

" The undersigned, citizens of Boston, general taxpayers, and largely interested as *special*-tax payers in the form of *water-rates*, respectfully represent, that, according to the reports of the Water Board and its engineers, an enormous amount of water is wasted, — estimated to be more than one-half of all that is brought to the city; and believing, that, by the use of proper means, a very arge proportion of this waste may be prevented, thus obviating the immediate necessity for any further increase of the water-debt for costly extensions and additional supplies, we hereby protest against the proposed costly schemes for obtaining new sources of supply, and building new high-service works, and recommend, instead thereof, that measures be taken to reduce the waste, thus insuring a much-needed reduction in our water-rates.

"THE BOSTON & ALBANY R.R. CO., by J. A. RUMRILL, *Vice-President.*
OLD COLONY R.R. CO., by C. F. CHOATE, *President.*
N. Y. & N. E. R.R. CO., by J. H. WILSON, *President.*
STANDARD SUGAR REFINERY, by J. B. THOMAS, *President.*
CONTINENTAL SUGAR REFINERY, by DAVID TOWNSEND, *Treasurer.*
BAY STATE SUGAR REFINERY, F. G. TENNEY, *Treasurer.*
NASH, SPAULDING, & CO.
BOSTON & MAINE R.R. CO., N. G. WHITE, *President.*
FITCHBURG R.R. CO., M. D. BENSON, *Treasurer.*
EASTERN R.R. CO., N. G. CHAPIN, *Treasurer.*
BOSTON & LOWELL R.R. CO., E. A. BARTLETT, *Treasurer.*
BAY STATE IRON CO., J. AVERY RICHARDS, *Treasurer.*
METROPOLITAN R.R. CO., C. A. RICHARDS, *President.*
CHAS. L. THAYER.
A. A. FOLSOM, *Superintendent B. & P. R.R.*
SOUTH BOSTON IRON CO , WM. P. HUNT.
BOSTON SUGAR REFINING CO., L. P. HOWLAND.
N. D. WHITNEY.
RICE, KENDALL, & CO.
WM. E. COFFIN & CO.
NORWAY STEEL & IRON WORKS, NAYLOR & Co.
OTIS NORCROSS."

A. — Yes, sir: we expect to give a hearing on that subject.

Q. — Whenever they want it? *A.* — No: when we get ready. The committee are considering that subject very carefully.

Q. (By Mr. CHAMBERLAIN.) — Do these great corporations use arge quantities of water? *A.* — Yes, sir: I believe they do. They are all of them metered. I don't think they understand the question, or they would not have signed that paper.

Mr. BULLARD. Otis Norcross was a member of the Water Board for a great many years, and ought to know something about it.

WITNESS. That does not follow. I don't want the impression left by Mr. Bullard's remarks that the Committee on Water are shirking that matter at all. The Committee on Water know what they are about. They are investigating some subjects on their own account, which they propose to get information about before they let these gentlemen have their say. I think we know something about that matter now ; but I don't suppose this Committee cares to hear any thing about it.

Q. (By Mr. MORSE.) — Will you state the date of that petition? *A.* — The paper is not dated. It was just about election time last year, in November, so that it was impossible for the Committee to give those people a hearing last year.

Mr. BAILEY. That is all that the city of Boston desires to put in. I will put in some figures which show the rainfalls for the last six or eight years.

RAINFALL FROM 1872 TO 1881.

Year.	Inches.
1872	52.73
1873	46.81
1874	38.73
1875	51.
1876	47.65
1877	44.68
1878	54.53
1879	38.
1880	35.22
1881	47.53

OPENING STATEMENT OF GEORGE H. POOR, ESQ.

MR. CHAIRMAN AND GENTLEMEN, — The town of Andover, and the mill-owners there, appear here in opposition to these petitioners. We think we shall be able to show to the Committee that there are very substantial reasons against yielding any portion of the Shawshine River. I will state that my brother Morse also appears for the town, and will be heard from in due time.

The Shawshine River, from the earliest days of the history of Andover, has been of very great importance and value to the town; in fact, it has been the very foundation of the prosperity of the town. Without the river, Andover would never have been heard of. It not only furnishes power for the mills, but supplies water for the many other uses for which it is required in manufacturing; and, upon the use that has been made of it in times past, the success that has attended the efforts of the manufacturers there has been largely dependent. Even our schools are indebted for their very existence to it. The town, as you know, is on the lower waters of the Shawshine, and within a few miles of the Merrimack. All the substantial manufacturing on the stream is within the limits of Andover. There are four dams and four manufacturing villages there. I shall ask the attention of the Committee, somewhat in detail, to those villages; and I can do it the more briefly, because so many of you recently visited the locality, and saw the mills and villages along the river. Perhaps it would be well to take them in their order, as we go down the stream: therefore I will begin at Ballardvale.

That village has a population of about seven hundred, three

churches, a hall, library, and two or three stores. The only industry of any importance is the mill of Capt. Bradlee, which furnishes employment to two hundred persons, and practically supports the whole village. Every other industry of any magnitude that has ever started there has failed, leaving Mr. Bradlee's mill the sole reliance of that population. That mill-property, real and personal, was assessed, last year, at $117,000. Some forty or more families of operatives own their houses. These were assessed at $27,000, averaging about $675 each. That mill-privilege is a very ancient one, having existed from about the year 1750.

Proceeding two miles down the stream, we come to Abbott Village, close by the Andover railroad-station, where are the upper Flax Mills of the Smith & Dove Manufacturing Company. That corporation employs, at that point, two hundred or two hundred and twenty-five hands. That privilege is a more ancient one still, a fulling-mill having been set up there as early as 1690.

Then, half a mile below that, we come to Marland Village, where are the Marland Mills, owned by Moses T. Stevens; and there are employed a hundred and fifty hands in the manufacture of flannels and dress-goods. That manufacturing property is assessed at $96,900. That privilege is also a very ancient one, having been used about the year 1700; and it was there that Judge Phillips, the founder of Phillips Academy, laid the foundation of that fortune which he afterwards expended in founding schools, and in blessing our community, which has reason to be proud of the school now in existence there.

The next privilege on the stream is Frye Village. Here is mill-property assessed at about $30,000, occupied by the Smith & Dove Manufacturing Company, which I have before named, for a portion of their works, and employing a hundred and twenty-five operatives. That privilege was used in 1718. You see these are all very ancient mill-privileges.

Now, the total assessed valuation of the Smith & Dove Manufacturing property, real and personal, was $164,700 last year. So that we have a total of four manufacturing establishments, with property taxed at over $400,000, employing seven hundred hands, and directly supporting more than two thousand of our people. In fact, it may be safely claimed that about one-half of the population of Andover depends upon the manufacturing interests which I have named. They are the substantial business of the town; and without them Andover would be, to a great extent, depopulated. Therefore, you must see that by the diversion of the Shawshine River and the closing of these mills we should lose taxable property to a great extent, — we should lose population, opportunities for employment, and should greatly increase the rate of taxation for those who remain.

These facts and figures are perhaps material merely in a business view; but there is a sanitary aspect of this question to which I desire to call your attention. The Shawshine enters Andover about a mile and a half above Ballardvale, and runs through the town, six or seven miles, towards the Merrimack; and three-quarters, I think I may safely state, of our population is in the valley or on the adjacent slopes. The natural drainage of the town is into this stream. Numerous small brooks enter the stream through the villages, and convey into it no inconsiderable amount of sewage, in the course of a year. This causes no trouble, because there is sufficient water to carry it off. If the dams were removed, a large area of flats, and low, muddy land, which is now flowed at all seasons of the year, would be exposed to the sun; and it is hardly necessary for me to suggest to this Committee what would be the dangers to the health of Andover resulting from that. Too many of you are physicians to require any suggestion of that sort; but we apprehend that the danger would be very great, and we shall show you what the effect is upon the public health of the valley when the water gets low, as it sometimes does now, in dry seasons.

Again, we claim that we may need this water for our own supply. Andover is considering the subject of water-supply, and a committee of the town has it in charge. That committee was instructed by the town, at the last annual meeting, to apply to the General Court for the Shawshine. We could take from that river what water we want for the limited number of people who would use it, perhaps 3,000 or 4,000, without material injury to the other interests on the stream. We need it, moreover, for drainage. We have no system of drainage, which is our misfortune; but that subject is under consideration, and is a necessity which is forcing itself upon our attention very urgently. In short, gentlemen, we have got to have a system of drainage; and, if we have it, for topographical reasons we must drain into the Shawshine: it is impossible to discharge the sewage anywhere else. If we pour it into the river below Frye Village, and the water is not diverted, it will go off without any trouble to anybody. Therefore, it does seem, from priority, that we ought to have rights in that river superior to these people who come here asking for that water which is absolutely essential to our prosperity and our health.

Again, we claim that the Shawshine is of value to our schools. Phillips Academy, Abbot Academy, the venerable Theological Seminary, have an interest in the Shawshine most assuredly. Thousands of students for generations have resorted to it for recreation, and we hope they may continue to do so for years to come. So we may well ask you, gentlemen, to pause and consider our claims to this stream before giving any of it to these petitioners.

I think I will not take up any more of your time in opening the matter. My brother Morse will close it, and will show you what may be deduced from the testimony which we shall offer here.

Mr. BAILEY. — Let me ask you just one question. Is Frye Village on the river?

Mr. POOR. — It is the last privilege on the river. It is a little settlement by itself.

TESTIMONY OF CHARLES GREEN.

Q. (By Mr. POOR.) — You are one of the selectmen and assessors of Andover? A. — Yes, sir.

Q. — For how many years have you been? A. — Seven years.

Q. — Native of the town, and have lived there all your life? A. — Yes, sir.

Q. — Familiar with the localities I have described, with the villages, etc.? A. — Yes, sir.

Q. — What proportion of the inhabitants of Andover, in your opinion, live in the Shawshine valley and on the slopes adjoining? A. — I should say from two-thirds to three-fourths of the population of Andover reside on the slopes of the valley.

Q. — Are you familiar with Ballardvale? A. — I am.

Q. — Do you live there? A. — I do.

Q. — The population of Ballardvale is about how much? A. — Very near seven hundred.

Q. — What is the principal business there? A. — Capt. Bradlee's mills form the principal business. Within a year or two, one or two enterprises have been started there; but his is the principal business of the village.

Q. — Those other enterprises are small, are they not? A. — Yes, sir.

Q. — Did I correctly state the value of Capt. Bradlee's property there, as assessed last year, at $117,000? A. — Yes, sir: I think that was the assessment made last year.

Q. — And the houses of the operatives, $27,000: is that correct? A. — I think those are the figures that we made: yes, sir.

Q. — How much real estate is there, in your judgment, besides that of Capt. Bradlee and his operatives, in that village of Ballardvale, that may be said to be part of that village? A. — As near as I can estimate, about $200,000.

Q. — In all, including Capt. Bradlee's and the others that have been named? A. — Yes, sir.

Q. — Now, you know about the valuation below there. Is the valuation of the Smith & Dove Company stated correctly at $164,700?

A. — What you stated this morning I think is correct, according to our books.

Q. — The figures, then, that I have stated are generally correct?
A. — Yes, sir.

Q. — What, in your judgment, would be the consequences, in regard to Ballardvale, if Capt. Bradlee's mill were deprived of water?
A. — It would be the ruin of Ballardvale, as far as any manufacturing business is concerned there.

Q. — What would be the consequences to the other villages if those mills were deprived of water? *A.* — I should suppose they would all be affected in the same manner.

Q. — Would the business be driven away? *A.* — I should judge so.

Q. — What would become of the property of the operatives who were compelled to leave? Would it not be practically confiscated?
A. — It would be very much depreciated in value, certainly.

Q. — And that would be true not only of the property of the operatives, but of all the other real estate in the valley, would it not?
A. — It would be true of all the property in the vicinity of the river.

Q. — How would it affect the whole town, take it away from the river? Would it depreciate the value of property outside of the valley? *A.* — I should judge it would, certainly.

Q. — Would it not materially increase the rate of taxation? *A.* — If the running expenses of the town were as much as they are now, a great deal of the property would be depreciated, and of course the rate of taxation would be proportionately increased.

Cross-Examination.

Q. (By Mr. HAMMOND.) — What is your business? *A.* — I am a storekeeper in Ballardvale: that is my business; and I am also one of the selectmen and assessors of Andover.

Q. — I suppose the substance of your views about it is, that, if that mill in Ballardvale should be shut up, it would be a pretty disastrous thing there, wouldn't it? *A.* — Yes, sir: it must be.

Q. — Whether taking half a million gallons of water a day from the Shawshine would shut it up, you don't know, do you? *A.* — No, sir: I can't say as to that.

TESTIMONY OF WILLIAM S. JENKINS.

Q. (By Mr. POOR.) — You are one of the committee of the town of Andover to oppose the taking of the Shawshine River? *A.* — I am, sir.

Q. — Are you a native and life-long resident of Andover? *A.* — I am.

Q. — Have you been chairman of the Board of Selectmen and Assessors for years? *A.* — I was for a few years ; but I am not at the present time.

Q. — What is the sentiment in Andover in relation to this Shawshine question? *A.* — Well, sir, the sentiment, as far as I know, would be all one way, and that would be that it would be a very disastrous and bad thing for the town of Andover and all its interests.

Q. — You know about the business that is carried on there. Are the mills the principal business of the town? *A.* — The mills, taking it within the limits of the town, including the four villages that have been spoken of, are, in my estimation, the leading business. The prosperity of the town depends, and has depended from its earliest day, as I see it, upon the industries on the river.

Q. — There are a good many smaller industries, — tradespeople and others : how would they be affected if the manufacturing business were driven away from Andover? *A.* — Very materially.

Q. — They would be injured? *A.* — They would be injured directly and indirectly.

Q. — And what would be the effect upon the value of property in the valley? *A.* — That, of course, would be in proportion, so far as the factories were stopped from want of motive-power, or from any other cause.

Q. — Suppose they were entirely driven away, what would be the effect? *A.* — It would be a desolate valley largely, so far as the cultivation of the soil is concerned. I would say here, without the question being asked me, so far as our little business of building is concerned, it would affect us nearly one-half the number of men employed in the town of Andover.

Q. — That is, your firm of Abbott & Jenkins? *A.* — Yes, sir, so far as building is concerned, — repairs of buildings, etc. These several corporations furnish that amount.

Cross-Examination.

Q. (By Mr. Hammond.) — Your business, sir, is what? *A.* — Building.

Q. — And you think, if these mills should stop work, that those consequences would follow that you have described? *A.* — I do, sir.

Q. — And the sentiment of Andover against this thing arises from their belief that the mills would be stopped by the bill which Cambridge offers here, does it? *A.* — I don't get your question exactly.

Q. — You believe, that, if Cambridge has a right to take not exceeding 8,000,000 gallons of water a day from the Shawshine, the mills would be obliged to stop, do you? *A.* — No, sir : I don't believe that, because I don't know it.

A. — Well, have you any belief about it at all? *A.* — No, sir: only so far as practically to be shown by experience. I do not claim to have any knowledge in that direction.

Q. — What do you say now, standing there, as to the probability of the mills stopping if Cambridge has a right to take not exceeding 8,000,000 gallons of water a day from the Shawshine River, and is obliged to let 10,000,000 gallons run down there? *A.* — I don't know any thing about it. I have no means of knowing.

Q. — Do you remonstrate, then, against this matter without knowing any thing about what its consequences would be, or having any belief about it? *A.* — I believe, if the mills should stop, the consequences would follow that I have stated; but so far as taking a certain quantity of water is concerned, to stop or not to stop, I have no knowledge of it.

Q. — You would not be opposed to this if the result of this bill was not to stop the mills, would you? *A.* — Yes, sir.

Q. — Why? *A.* — Because I believe that if the water, or any portion of it, was taken from that stream, it would, in a dry season, make it still drier, and leave the bottom uncovered with water, which must be injurious, in my judgment.

Q. — Do you know whether the practical operation of this bill is to do that or not? *A.* — No, sir.

Q. — Have you any belief about it? *A.* — Yes, sir: I have a belief.

Q. — Well, what is it? *A.* — That, if you take any portion of the water, it would affect the stream so much in a dry season as to work to the disadvantage of people living upon the river.

Q. — But suppose the bill compels the city of Cambridge to allow more water to come down that stream every day than now comes down many days in the year: would that change your views about it? *A.* — That is a supposition.

Q. — Would it change your views if that was true? *A.* — Compelling water to run down hill is a very easy matter: you have only to allow it to run. I don't know as there would be any compulsion about it if it was allowed to run.

Q. — I ask you if it would change your views any if you knew that this bill compels the city of Cambridge to so regulate that water as not to let less go down there than 10,000,000 gallons a day, whereas now there are many days when not so much goes down there? Would it change your views any if that was the effect of the bill? *A.* — It would depend upon how certain you could make that.

Q. — Suppose it could be made certain to your mind: would it have any tendency to change your views? would it affect your position on this bill? *A.* — I don't know that it would; that is, so far as probability goes. You put in the probability and supposition, and not the fact.

Q. — Do you know how low down the flow of the river sometimes is in a dry time? *A.* — No, sir: I don't know that. I do know that it is very small.

Q. — Are there not many people up in Andover in just your condition, — who are opposed to the bill, and do not know any thing about it? *A.* — Very likely.

Q. (By Mr. BAILEY.) — Are you familiar with the construction of those mills there? *A.* — No, sir: I won't say that I am familiar with the construction, not so much so as to place it on strong ground.

Q. — You said just now that you knew that the river was sometimes mighty low? *A.* — Yes, sir: *very low*. I guess I didn't say " mighty." I think I said *very low*.

Q. — At those times, have the mills shut down when the stream was so low? *A.* — Well, I think the mill-owners can tell you better than I can about that.

Q. — Haven't you lived there all your life, and don't you know? *A.* — I don't know.

Q. — Don't you know whether the mills are closed there on account of the lowness of the stream or not? *A.* — I know, by remarks that have been made, that certain portions of the mills have to be shut down when the water is low.

Q. — Don't you know that they are run by steam when the water is low? *A.* — They have engines there, and have steam-power.

TESTIMONY OF COL. GEORGE RIPLEY.

Q. (By Mr. POOR.) — You are a resident of Andover? *A.* — Yes, sir.

Q. — And one of the committee to oppose the taking of Shawshine River? *A.* — I am: yes, sir.

Q. — What, in your opinion, would be the injurious effect of such taking upon Andover? *A.* — I think it would have a very serious effect upon the population and prosperity of the villages especially. I think it would have a very injurious effect upon the town as a whole every way.

Q. — Diminution of values, etc.? *A.* — I should think that that would necessarily follow.

Q. — Public health? *A.* — I should think the public health would be very likely to suffer. I should think that the uncovering of the flats by taking away the water would have a very serious effect upon the health of the community.

Q. — Are you one of the trustees of Abbot Academy? *A.* — Yes, sir.

Q. — Would that institution be injured, in your opinion, by diverting the water of the Shawshine? *A.* — I think it would, if, as I suppose would be the case, the health of the community was affected very seriously.

Q. — Would not the attractiveness of the town be injured if the Shawshine were materially diminished or diverted? *A.* — I think it would.

Cross-Examination.

Q. (By Mr. HAMMOND.) — What is your business? *A.* — I am president of a bank.

Q. — Have you ever been engaged in any engineering operations? *A.* — Never, sir.

Q. — Do you know what the flow of the Shawshine is now in a dry time? *A.* — I do not, sir.

Q. — Do you think it would hurt it any to make it flow more in a dry day than it does now? *A.* — I don't think that would injure it any, if you make more flow down there in a year than now flows.

Q. — That does not answer my question. Do you think it would hurt the town any to make it flow more in a dry day than it does now? *A.* — No, sir: I don't think that would be any injury. I don't think it would hurt it on that day: on the contrary, it would improve it on that day.

Q. — Then your academy would be better off on those days, would it not? *A.* — No, sir: I don't think it would. I don't think it would have any effect on that institution: it might on the manufacturing.

Q. — Do you know how much water in a time of freshet frequently goes down that stream, — to what limit it goes? *A.* — No, sir: if you mean how many gallons, I am utterly ignorant.

Q. — I suppose the substance of what you mean to say is (not to carry this out any further), that, if the Legislature should grant to anybody the right to diminish the flow of that stream in such a way as to leave the flats bare and to stop the mills, it would be disastrous upon the town? That is what you mean, isn't it? *A.* — Yes, sir.

TESTIMONY OF JOHN L. SMITH.

Q. (By Mr. POOR.) — You are a resident of Andover? *A.* — Yes, sir. .

Q. — Trader there? *A.* — Yes, sir.

Q. — One of the committee to oppose the taking of Shawshine River? *A.* — I am.

Q. — What is the sentiment of Andover as to that taking?

Mr. HAMMOND. You need not ask that question. I will assume that every man is opposed to it.

Mr. POOR. That is true, — every man, woman, and child.

Mr. HAMMOND. They don't know any thing about it : that is the trouble.

Q. — What would be the effect upon the town of Andover if the waters of the Shawshine were diverted or materially diminished? *A.* — Well, if it caused any stoppage of the mills, — that is the foundation of all our industries there, — it would materially affect the town.

Q. — Would it injure any business outside of the mills? *A.* — It certainly would.

Q. — Your own business, for instance, as storekeeper, trader, — how would it affect that? *A.* — If those mills were closed, it would ruin half of our trade, or more than half.

Q. — Is not the same true of numerous other traders, shoemakers, blacksmiths, and no end of minor interests? *A.* — I should think it would affect all the industries in the town about the same.

Cross-Examination.

Q. (By Mr. HAMMOND.) — Your business is trader? *A.* — Yes, sir.

Q. — Retail trader? *A.* — Yes, sir.

Q. — In what? *A.* — General country store.

Q. — If the people left the town, you would not have so much trade as you would have if they remained there, would you? *A.* — Certainly not.

Q. — Have you examined this bill that is asked for by Cambridge? *A.* — I have seen it.

Q. — Do you know what its effect would be upon the water? *A.* — Not exactly, sir : I have an idea what it might be.

Q. — What is your idea? *A.* — My idea is, that, if Cambridge gets part of the water, next year she will want it all.

Q. — I don't want your idea as to what may happen next year; but I want your idea as to what this bill will do. *A.* — I cannot tell you.

Q. — Are you on this committee of the town to oppose this bill? *A.* — Yes, sir.

Q. — But you don't know what the effect would be? *A.* — Well, I cannot tell, sir : that would have to be demonstrated.

Q. — You never have had it demonstrated? *A.* — No, sir.

Q. — What is your belief about it? *A.* — I believe, that, if more water can run in a dry time than runs now, it would be beneficial.

Q. — Will it hurt you in any other time except a dry time? *A.* — I should presume that they would want more than 10,000,000 gallons to run there in a dry time.

Q. — Of course you have not examined that as an engineer, have you? *A.* — No, sir; but I have an idea like this: that, if the manufacturers have to put in steam-power now to supplement the water-power, when you reduce that at all, it is an injury to those corporations to that extent.

Q. — I suppose you have lived on the banks of the stream for a number of years, or near there, so that you have observed it frequently? *A.* — I have lived there for the greater part of the time for thirty-eight years.

Q. — I suppose that stream is like any other stream: it has its freshets and its dry times? *A.* — Yes, sir, certainly.

Q. — As you are here to oppose this bill, I should like to ask you what your belief is as to the effect of the bill, — not some other bill, but as to the effect of the bill which Cambridge proposes here upon that stream? *A.* — I cannot tell about that bill.

Q. — Haven't you any belief about it? *A.* — I have a belief like this: that, if the Legislature of Massachusetts would give us an equal supply of water the whole year round, and give us all we wanted, it would be a very good thing.

Q. — Do you know whether this bill will do that or not? *A.* — I have no idea that you can manufacture water.

Q. — Did it ever strike you that there was any such thing as equalizing the water of a stream? *A.* — Yes, sir.

Q. — Don't you know that frequently, in other portions of the State, dams are constructed for the express purpose of keeping the water back in times of freshet, in order that it may go down in dry times? *A.* — Well, sir, if the city of Cambridge would build a reservoir that should be under the control of the manufacturers of Andover, I think it would be an excellent thing.

Q. — You do not answer my question. Don't you know that, on many streams, they do store water for the sake of using it in dry times? *A.* — Yes, sir, I am aware of that fact.

Q. — Do you think that the people of Andover who are opposed to this bill know just as much about it as you do? *A.* — I hope they know more about it.

Q. — Do you think they do? *A.* — I presume they all have an opinion.

Q. — Is not this the fact: that the view has been spread around in that town, that, if Cambridge is granted a right to take what she asks to have by this bill, it will ruin the place by stopping the mills, and all that sort of thing? *A.* — I think the people of Andover feel thus:

that, if any of the water is granted to Cambridge, there is no guaranty that some other town, or Cambridge itself, will not come along in a year or two, and want the rest of the water to sell to Boston, instead of using it. I do not think that Cambridge or any other city will spend money to get any more water than they want to use if they can dispose of it to advantage.

Q. — You think that the opposition of Andover to this petition is partly on the theory that Cambridge wants to sell this water to Boston? *A.* — I can't tell you what the idea of the people of Andover is as to this case. I don't know what Cambridge may do.

Q. — To your knowledge, has there been any information given to the people of Andover about what Cambridge wants definitely? *A.* — Well, I presume some know. They have read the reports of the testimony and the bill that is proposed.

Q. — You have heard these two gentlemen, Mr. Jenkins and Col. Ripley, testify here. Do you think they are fair specimens of the knowledge on the part of Andover citizens as to this bill? *A.* — I cannot tell, sir.

Q. (By Mr. BAILEY.) — Supposing, sir, that the Shawshine was reduced to such a stream as 10,000,000 gallons would make the year round, would it be any worse, in your judgment, for the interests of the town, if they took the whole? *A.* — I should say it would be very injurious. I don't know what the result would be ; but I should say that it would impair the manufacturing industries. The only thing that would induce any manufacturer to remain there would be securing the water-privilege.

Q. — In your judgment would it not be just about as bad to reduce the stream to a mere thread, such as 10,000,000 gallons a day would make, as to take the whole thing? *A.* — It would not be as bad, but it would be bad. It would ruin the industries of the town.

Q. (By Mr. MORSE.) — I suppose that what you and the other gentlemen from Andover mean is, that you have not gone into an exact calculation, so that you are able to say precisely how much water is going to be left in the stream if that quantity is taken ; but you oppose any taking because you believe that is the entering wedge to take it all? *A.* — That is my opinion, and I believe that is the general opinion of people in the town.

TESTIMONY OF JOSEPH A. SMART.

Q. (By Mr. POOR.) — You are secretary of the Merrimack Insurance Company at Andover? *A.* — Yes, sir.

Q. — You live in the valley of the Shawshine? *A.* — Yes, sir.

Q. — And have always lived there? *A.* — Yes, sir.

Q. — What, in your judgment, would be the effect of diverting the water of the Shawshine upon the health of the people in that locality, judging from your experience? *A.* — Well, if they take all of it, or most of it, so as to leave the mud bare in the summer months, I think it would be bad for the health of the people.

Q — Have you known the water to be drawn down somewhat low in summer, so as to leave the mud bare? *A.* — Yes, sir.

Q. — Have you known of any increase of sickness on such occasions? *A.* — I have heard it reported that the people thought there was more sickness ; and in passing through the village, as I have had occasion to do several times, I have noticed a very offensive odor.

Q. — Proceeding from the river, in your judgment, or the riverbed? *A.* — Yes, sir, undoubtedly.

Q. — You are acquainted with most of the people in Abbott Village and thereabouts? *A.* — Yes, sir.

Q. — Do you know any families or operatives who own their homes there? *A.* — Yes, sir.

Mr. HAMMOND. I don't think it is necessary to spend any time upon that : to show that some of the operatives own their homes there, and that if they have to leave them, it would be a damage to them.

Mr. POOR. You concede that they would lose their homes, do you?

Mr. HAMMOND. No : I concede, that, if the mills stopped, they would have to leave their homes, and it would be a damage to them. There is no use in spending any time upon that.

Cross-Examination.

Q. (By Mr. HAMMOND.) — You have seen a time there when there were flats there that smelt badly? *A.* — Yes, sir.

Q. — Where were the flats? *A.* — In the mill-pond, and below the pond.

Q. — At what village? *A.* — Abbott Village : that is where I live.

Q. — That is the second one ; that is next to Ballardvale? *A.* — Yes, sir.

Q. — About how far from it? *A.* — I believe it is called two miles and a quarter.

Q. — There is a dam there? *A.* — At Abbott Village, yes, sir.

Q. — And these flats were below the dam? *A.* — No, sir.

Q. — Above the dam? *A.* — Above the dam. The principal flats were above the dam.

Q. — Have you noticed that frequently? *A.* — When the pond has been drawn off. It has not been drawn off more than perhaps half a dozen times within my remembrance, for repairs of the dam.

Q. — Then the flats you speak of are flats that are usually covered with water when the water flows over the dam? *A.* — Yes, sir.

Q. — But when they dry off, and all the water from the mill-pond goes by that dam, then those flats smell badly? *A.* — Yes, sir.

Q. — What do they draw it off for? *A.* — For repairs of the dam, usually.

Q. — Whenever they want to repair the dam, and expose the flats, then they smell bad? *A.* — Yes, sir: whenever the flats are exposed, then they smell badly.

Q. — And you think you have known cases of disease to arise every time they have been wicked enough to do that? *A.* — When they had to make quite extensive repairs on the dam, and the flats were bare quite a while, it was said that during that period sickness increased considerably.

Q. — When was that? *A.* — I think it was a year or two ago.

Q. — Does Andover put any sewage into that stream? *A.* — None that I know of, except what runs in from the brooks that run into the stream. They have no sewerage system.

Q. — Brooks above or below Abbott Village? *A.* — Both, sir.

Mr. Morse. Mr. Poor stated in his opening that there was no general system of sewerage. If individuals should drain their sewage in there, it would be a different thing.

Q. — There are streams that run into the Shawshine above this dam and these flats? *A.* — Yes, sir.

Q. — And those streams carry sewage into the Shawshine? *A.* — Yes, sir.

Q. — To what extent? *A.* — I don't know how much.

Q. — And that is done by the citizens of Andover, is it? *A.* — It must be so, of course.

Q. — And they are the folks who are opposed to having any of that water taken, because it will make the flats smell bad, are they? *A.* — They are the people.

TESTIMONY OF JAMES HOWARTH.

Q. (By Mr. Poor.) — You are a physician in Andover? *A.* — Yes, sir.

Q. — Been in practice there thirty years or more? *A.* — Some thirty years.

Q. — Live near the Shawshine? *A.* — Within a few rods.

Q. — Will you state what your observation of the Shawshine has been at stages of low water, and what would be the probable effect if there should be permanent low water there? *A.* — I may premise what I have to say by saying that Andover has been our family home the greater part of the time since 1819, and that I have practised medicine there as a visiting physician for something over thirty years. Our family were once engaged in the manufacturing business, near our present residence; and our residence is on the eastern bank of the Shawshine, — well, at a guess, from eight to ten rods from the edge of the river, and probably twenty-five, thirty, or forty feet higher than the surface of the river. During the earlier period, — say from 1820 to 1845 or 1850, — in the dry season of the year, the water was usually very shallow, so that the mills did not have a full supply of water, and at that time, not using steam, they had to run part of the time; and during the dry time the odor from the Shawshine was very marked and nauseating. I remember at the mill that our family used to operate (being the only stone mill on the stream, it was called "the stone mill"), that, on going down into the finishing-room, in the basement, the fishy and lamper-eel odor of that water was so strong as to make many people sick at the stomach, — nauseate them; and, among others, myself. About the period that I have named, the health of the Shawshine valley was very markedly below what it is at the present time. Since the present companies have arranged to have a reserve supply of water, the public health has been better, and the average flow of water has been more in the dry season; but still there have been seasons when there has been a lack of a sufficient quantity of water to prevent the bad odor that I have referred to. A good deal of the water of the river is top-drainings, — drainings from the swamps; and when that water is low it is very highly colored and highly charged with organic matter; and, from my personal knowledge of it, I should dislike very much to use it for drinking. When there has been a rainy season and a free flow of water, the color has of course been better, and there has been less organic matter in the water; and, the shallow parts of the bank having been covered with water at those seasons, the odor of the water has been very much better. I can remember, in my own family, when the people in the house objected, in a dry time, to using the Shawshine for washing, on account of the strong odor that it had. Up to about 1850, — I don't remember exactly the date, but up to the time that the manufacturing companies made a storage basin for their water (Foster's Pond, or whatever it was), — up to that time, the health of the Shawshine valley had been very seriously affected by the river, by shallows, and by the exhalations from the Shawshine River. During that time malarious forms of fever in that district of country were prevalent. Some seasons, whole families of children were swept off by diseases which, as a physician, I and others connected with influences from the river. Since the reserve of water has been in existence, the average flow in the Shawshine has been very much increased and better; but every year it fails in a dry time more or less. I remember, last summer and the summer before, there were times when the odor of the water was perceptible. Cholera infantum, diarrhœa, dysentery, typhoidal forms of fever, where there was evidently a connection with the state of the blood, blood-poisoning, were much more prevalent than they are now. I should say that the public health of the Shawshine valley is at least fifty per cent. better now than it was at the period I have referred to, when there was a lack of water.

Q. — How is it now, when the water is low, as it sometimes is? A. — Well, it has a bad effect; but there is a better average supply of water in a dry season now than there used to be, and consequently an improved state of health. As drinking-water it would be quite an addition; but I do not think it would be an improvement on any water I ever saw in the State.

Q. — If the waters of the Shawshine are diverted, and this mud exposed, and a mere ditch left there, what would be the effect upon the health of Andover or of the valley? A. — If there were less water flowing, and more exposure of flats, the public health would decline to the extent I have named. In fact, if we had to return to the state of things that once existed there, I should want to sell out: I should not want to live in my present dwelling. I should consider it objectionable to live so near the Shawshine River as I do.

Cross-Examination.

Q. (By Mr. HAMMOND.) — Are you a practising physician? A. — I am retired now. I do office business. My health broke down some years ago, and, having cardiac difficulties, I have avoided general practice; but I do an office business, and treat disease now.

Q. — I understand you to say, that from your recollection, up to 1845 or 1846, the health of the valley was not good? A. — Not good, — no: during the season of the year when there was a lack of water in the Shawshine.

Q. — You lived there upon the bank of the river how many years while the health of the valley was as bad as that? A. — It has been our family residence since 1819.

Q. — From 1819 to 1845 it was a sickly place? A. — Well, as a physician, I cannot testify during the whole of that time; but I know, since there was more water there, the public health has improved. There has been less sickness, less fatal cases, than there were before.

Q. — Then there was what you call an equalization of the flow of water, and the sewage has been carried off?

Mr. POOR. If you will pardon me, I will state, as I do not think there is anybody here who can do it as accurately as I can, that Foster's Basin, which has been referred to, is a basin of sixty or seventy acres about a mile east of Ballardvale, which was made in 1847 or 1848. It is a very shallow basin, where water is caught and stored in the spring, and kept closed up until July or August, when it is particularly needed for the stream ; and then it is all run out in the course of five or six weeks, and the basin is good for nothing afterwards.

Q. — If I understand you, in 1845 or 1846, or thereabouts, measures were taken by which Foster's Pond — a shallow basin, as described by Mr. Poor — was let out, and the water allowed to flow down into the Shawshine in a dry time? *A.* — Yes, sir.

Q. — That made all this improvement that you speak of? *A.* — Yes, sir.

Q. — Did it ever occur to you, that, if some other ponds should be served in the same way, it would make a great improvement? *A.* — An increased flow of water would improve it right away.

Q. — That is what you want, — more flow of water in a dry time? *A.* — Exactly. I admit it right off.

TESTIMONY OF JOHN C. PENNINGTON.

Q. (By Mr Poor.) — You are a practising physician in Andover? *A.* — Yes, sir.

Q. — Have you paid any attention to the subject of drainage there? *A.* — I have not made any close investigation of it : I have noticed it since I have been there.

Q. — Is it true that the natural drainage of the town is into the Shawshine? *A.* — It is. That is the only source of drainage.

Q. — Are there numerous brooks that pour into the Shawshine, bringing more or less drainage from the villages? *A.* — There are.

Q. — What, in your judgment, would be the effect upon the public health of Andover if the water in the Shawshine was materially diminished? *A.* — I think, if the total amount of water that passes through the valley of the Shawshine in the course of the year were diminished, it would be likely to have an injurious effect upon the health of the community. The stream is a slow one, almost stagnant a large portion of the year ; and if Cambridge takes this water-supply, and allows say 10,000.000 gallons to remain, it must take that supply largely out of the water which comes in the spring. Unless we increase the rapidity of the stream, and carry off the accumulations of refuse, large quantities would remain there, and lie exposed in the summer, drying on the flats ; and there would be likely to be unhealthy emanations from the water, even if the flats were not dried in the sun.

Cross-Examination.

Q. (By Mr. HAMMOND.) — Do I understand you to say that you are a practising physician? *A.* — I am a practising physician.

Q. — In Andover? *A.* — In Andover.

Q. — And have been for how long? *A.* — Two and a half years.

Q. — Did you practise anywhere else before you settled there? *A.* — I have been in practice seven years.

Q. — Are you on the Board of Health there? *A.* — I am not.

Q. — Have you devoted any special attention to this subject? *A.* — I do not know exactly what you mean by "special attention" to it. I have not had any occasion to make a special study of it by any means.

Q. — I don't mean that; but have you had occasion, in any public capacity, to consider the effect of the Shawshine as it is at present upon the inhabitants in that vicinity? *A.* — No, I cannot say that I have.

Q. — Can you state what investigation you have made into this question? *A.* — I have lived for two years and a half where I could see the river. I have lived in the town long enough to have observed the general effect of drainage in the town and the facilities for drainage there, and I can reason from analogy and from the effect of similar procedures elsewhere.

Q. — What do you mean by "similar procedures"? *A.* — From the effect of taking away the use of water-courses for drainage purposes ; from the effect of allowing fresh-water ponds to dry and become low at different seasons of the year; and from information on the subject. which every medical man has, which are well-known facts.

Q. — That is to say, you have lived upon the bank of the Shawshine, and, as a physician, have more or less studied into the question of the effects of the drying of flats? *A.* — Yes ; but I claim no special knowledge in regard to it.

Q. — Can you give me any definite information as to the amount of drainage and sewage matter which now goes into the Shawshine from the citizens of Andover? *A.* — No, sir, I cannot: a great deal less than there ought to be, for there ought to be an efficient system of drainage in the town, which there is not yet, but which I think there must be if the town continues to grow.

Q. — What would be your idea as to the disposition of its sewage? Where would you put it? *A.* — Well, I think, if the town continues to grow, that the drainage must be put into the Shawshine, as that is the only means of removing our drainage in the future.

Q. — Notwithstanding the fact that the flats may be dry in the summer? *A.* — I have understood that you do not contemplate leaving the flats dry.

Q. — You don't answer my question. The question is not what I contemplate, but what happens on the river in summer. *A.* — The flats do not lie dry every summer.

Q. — Don't they frequently become dry? *A.* — Not to any great extent, I think.

Q. — Suppose that this bill provides for keeping the flats covered at seasons of the year when they would be otherwise dry, would there be any objection to that? *A.* — On that point there would be no objection. There would be objection on another point, I think.

Q. — What is it? *A.* — That is, the total amount of the water flowing through that stream in a year would be diminished ; and thereby these matters that would have been carried out by the force of the current would be allowed to accumulate.

Q. — That is exactly what I was asking you about. Have you investigated that subject? *A.* — I consider that self-evident. I don't think it requires any evidence to prove that, where there is a freshet, the refuse matter will be carried away by it.

Q. — Have you investigated this matter to such an extent that you can give an opinion as to whether the Shawshine River, assuming that it sometimes runs as low as 8,000,000 gallons a day, and sometimes as high as 200,000,000 gallons a day, can be deprived of any of that water without injury to the inhabitants of Andover? *A.* — You wish to ask if I can affirm that no water can be taken off under those circumstances without injury?

Q. — Yes. *A.* — I cannot make that affirmation.

TESTIMONY OF PROFESSOR J. W. CHURCHILL.

Q. (By Mr. POOR.) — You are a resident of Andover, professor? *A.* — Yes, sir.

Q. — What, in your view, would be the injury to Andover if the waters of the Shawshine were diverted? *A.* — My general opinion would be that the manufacturing interests would suffer. I can't see how the public health could avoid being impaired ; and the future public improvements of the town, so far as a general public system of sewerage is concerned, would be very seriously impaired, because the river is the natural scavenger. That, of course, is something problematical, but by no means unlikely.

Q. — That would affect the whole of the thickly settled portion of the town, would it not? *A.* — Yes, sir.

Q. — And the schools? *A.* — The schools. It would affect what we term "the hill," as well as the lower portions of the town, where the manufacturing interests are concentrated.

Cross-Examination.

Q. (By Mr. Hammond.) — Professor Churchill, you are connected with what institution? A. — The Theological Seminary.

Q. — As elocutionist? A. — Yes, sir; and I discharge the other collateral duties devolving upon any one who occupies a chair in the seminary.

Q. — You are on that branch of learning, I suppose? A. — Yes, sir.

Q. — You have given special attention to that, and that is in substance your duty there? A. — Yes, sir.

Q. — How long have you resided in Andover? A. — My residence there has been about twelve years. I have been in the place much longer as a student.

Q. — I suppose you have no more knowledge on this matter than could be obtained by any intelligent citizen residing there, have you? A. — Probably not.

Q. (By Mr. Smith.) — What, in your opinion, is the prevalent feeling among the intelligent portion of the citizens of Andover in regard to taking any portion of that river? A. — The opinion is decidedly opposed to it. I don't know an exception.

Q. — There is a feeling that it would be an injury to the town? A. — A great injury.

Q. — In all its interests? A. — Yes, sir.

Q. (By Mr. Hammond.) — Will you give the ground on which that feeling is based? A. — Those which I just stated to Mr. Poor: in the first place, the injury to the manufacturing interests; in the second place, the injury to the public health; in the third place, the injury to the not-at-all unlikely public improvements in the way of sewerage. The river, as I say, is the natural scavenger of the town.

Q. — Those are the grounds, are they? A. — Yes, sir, chiefly, as I understand them.

Q. — Do you know how many of them are applicable to this bill which Cambridge proposes? A. — No, sir. The specific nature of the bill I do not know.

Q. — Nor do you know what its effect would be? A. — No, sir.

Q. — So far as you know, the intelligent people of Andover do not know any more about it than you do? A. — I would not affirm that. I presume there are a great many who know more about it than I do.

TESTIMONY OF PROFESSOR EDWARDS PARK.

Q. (By Mr. Poor.) — Will you state to the Committee what, in your judgment, would be the injury to Andover and to the schools of

Andover if the Shawshine was diverted or materially diminished in its flow? *A.* — I think the injury to the Andover schools would be very great. I am connected with the Abbot Academy, a school for young ladies, and I have been also for forty-five years connected with the Theological Seminary; and I think the Shawshine is a great attraction to Andover. It attracts students to Andover. It is a beautiful river; there are very many beautiful prospects connected with it; and it is a favorite resort of the four hundred students who are very often connected with the institutions. They need the relaxation connected with walking, bathing, and boating. They suffer from want of relaxation, and I think it would be an injury to the health of the students of the institutions. I think the Andover schools — Phillips Academy, the Theological Seminary, and the Abbot Academy — have been essentially aided by the families that have been drawn to Andover by the Shawshine River. I think the influence of the Shawshine River can be well illustrated by the very fact of the origin of the academy. Judge Phillips had a powder-mill and a paper-mill upon the Shawshine River. These two mills attracted the Phillips family to Andover, and attracted other families connected with them. It led to the foundation of the Phillips Academy, which celebrated its centennial three years ago. It led to the foundation of the Theological Seminary, which has been in existence seventy-three years. It led to the foundation of the Abbot Academy, which celebrated its semi-centennial two years ago. I think that it ought to be considered that ancient institutions, a hundred years old, seventy-five years old, fifty years old, are too precious to be interfered with by the wants of manufacturers in the vicinity; and it seems to me, if the Shawshine River is now diverted from its course, no one knows what the result would be. I think it would be like letting out water: nobody knows what comes after it has once started. My opinion is, that a diversion of the water of the Shawshine would diminish the attractiveness of Andover, and would thus injure the schools, which are too precious to be injured by any such project; and it would be injurious to the health of the students. I was a member of the Theological Seminary three years, and I know that all the students found a walk along the banks or a bath in the river very conducive to their health. I believe there is considerable boating on the river. Any thing that diminishes the flow of the water will injure all these interests.

Q. — Is it not a fact that most of our public institutions in Andover may be traced in their origin directly to the Shawshine through the manufacturers? *A.* — Yes, sir.

Q. — That is, they were founded by gifts from manufacturers? *A.* — Certainly.

Q. — That is true of the Free Church, is it not, in a large measure? *A.* — Yes, sir.

Q. — And of the Episcopal Church? *A.* — Yes, sir.

Q. — And of the Memorial Hall? *A.* — Yes, sir.

Q. — And of your noble library building on the hill? *A.* — Yes, sir.

Q. — Which, I think, was given by Smith & Dove, was it not? *A.* — Yes, sir.

Q. — At an expense of sixty thousand dollars? *A.* — Seventy thousand dollars. Ten thousand dollars has been added since by Mr. Dove.

Q. — And the Punchard School: seventy-five thousand dollars were given by one of the proprietors of the Marland Mills toward it? *A.* — Yes, sir; and the chapel, which is a very elegant chapel, could not have been what it is now, had it not been for that firm of Smith & Dove. They gave the memorial windows and the organ. And I would say that the indigent students have been relieved times without number by the families connected with those establishments. There are very many indigent students connected with those schools, who come from the far West and from the South; and without the families who are attracted to Andover by these manufacturing establishments these students would suffer very much. The charities given by these families have been secret: they cannot be exposed. I could easily, I suppose, if I devoted my attention to it, call up over a hundred thousand dollars given to our institution by families connected with those factories; but the amount of money given to private individuals, suffering students, cannot be computed. And any thing which would induce those families to leave the place would be, I would not exactly say fatal to the institutions, but I think it would be fatal to their prominence. It would be impossible for them to maintain the position which they now do.

Cross-Examination.

Q. (By Mr. HAMMOND.) — Your position on this bill, as I understand it, is, that it would have a disastrous effect upon the interests of Andover, by reason of diminishing the waters of the Shawshine, — is that so? *A.* — During the whole year, yes, sir. I think that the institutions, I think that the agreeableness of the river, the attractiveness of the river, are very much promoted by what nature has done for it. I don't think that any regular mechanical flow of a certain number of gallons a day would conduce to the beauty or to the attractiveness of the river.

Q. — Have you made any such investigation as to speak with any more authority upon that matter than any other gentleman of intelligence? *A.* — No, sir: I would not say that I had made any particular investigations.

Q. — Did you live on the banks of the Shawshine before 1845? *A.* — I began to live on Seminary Hill in the year 1828, and continued there until '31, then went there again in '36, and have lived there since.

Q. — That institution got along pretty well, while you were connected with it, during those serious times described by the doctor who was here, didn't it? *A.* — Well, sir, I must rely very considerably upon the testimony of Dr. Kimball, who is now deceased, and whose judgment was very excellent. He considered that when the water was low in the Shawshine the health of the students at the seminaries was affected.

Q. — Did not Dr. Kimball die recently? *A.* — Yes, sir.

Mr. MORSE. His testimony is in the printed report.

Mr. HAMMOND. I am perfectly willing that Dr. Kimball's testimony should go in.

WITNESS. I have not read his testimony : only I know his opinion from what I have heard him say.

Q. — Have you examined the proposition made here by Cambridge sufficiently, so that you are at all sure that you can see what its effect would be upon the Shawshine River? *A.* — Well, I wouldn't say that I am absolutely certain. It is nothing that can be demonstrated ; but we must act upon probabilities. I think that the probabilities are that the health and beauty of the town would be injured.

Q. — You proceed upon the assumption, do you not, that the water would be substantially taken by the city? *A.* — Well, sir, I am sorry to say I do think that would be ultimately the result. I think this is the letting out ; it is the first beginning of the flow.

Q. — Then, in judging of this proceeding, and giving this gloomy statement of the result, you are influenced by what you think may be done hereafter by the Legislature? *A.* — Not altogether, but partially, perhaps.

Q. (By Mr. SMITH.) — Professor, I would like to ask you one question upon this very subject, as you may not have given your attention to the amount of water that it is proposed to allow to flow, — 10,000,000 gallons daily. It has been testified before this Committee that this 10,000,000 gallons daily is equivalent to the flow over a dam five feet long and a foot deep, so that it would be equivalent to a river ten feet wide and half a foot in depth. What sort of a river would the Shawshine be during the whole season, half a foot deep and ten feet wide? *A.* — I think it would be just about this : between the health-giving influences of walking along a river made by nature, and walking along a small canal, I think the difference is just as great as can well be conceived. It is something in the poetry of the thing, in the taste of the thing. Although we cannot measure taste by the gallon, yet I think we can easily see that the attractiveness of such a mechanical canal would be far less than the beauties of a river flowing at its own sweet will.

Q. (By Mr. HAMMOND.) — One other question I want to ask you, professor: Do students bathe there now? *A.* — Yes, sir, certainly. I am sorry to say I do not know how frequently the theological students bathe there: but I know the Phillips Academy students, who number about two hundred, bathe in it, and I have no doubt that the theological students do also.

WILLIAM S. JENKINS. *Recalled.*

Q. (By Mr. POOR.) — Are you a member of the town committee on water-supply and drainage? *A.* — Yes, sir.

Q. — And are you taking measures looking to a water-supply? *A.* — Yes, sir, that was the vote of the town at the last annual meeting. Previous to that, two years ago, the committee of which I am a member looked for water for fire purposes. We found ourselves minus water in case of fire. We have a steamer, and some small reservoirs, which are only available in the thickly settled part of the town. A committee, as I have said, was raised for the purpose of ascertaining whether a supply of water could not be obtained in some other way. The town voted at its last annual meeting, in March, the sum of five hundred dollars, I think it was, for the purpose of making surveys, to see in what way we can provide ourselves with water for fire purposes, and also including the matter of a system of drainage. I would state here, as far as the main street of Andover is concerned, which is the most thickly populated part of the town for a mile or more, that it is largely destitute of drainage, except in the gutters in the street, which we find becoming offensive, and very difficult to manage, except we get a system of sewerage, which we must make in the near future, and deliver it into the river at some point probably below the manufacturing establishments.

Q. — That would be below the settled portion of the town? *A.* — Below the settled portion of the town, as well as the manufacturing establishments.

Q. — And where there is a considerable amount of water, if there is any anywhere? *A.* — Where there is always, and especially in the spring of the year, considerable water. The Merrimack sets back, and forms quite a stream at all times.

Q. — Let me ask you about the water-supply, if the Shawshine is not the most available source for Andover? *A.* — So far as I can see, without any surveys, taking into account the distance, I should say that the Shawshine River was the nearest point and the surest point of supply.

Q. — And if these petitioners are correct, it is good enough for us, isn't it? *A.* — Yes, sir.

Q. (By Mr. CHAMBERLAIN.) — I understand you to say that the gutters on the street are foul. What fouls them, on an elevation like that of Andover? *A.* — The drainage from sinks, and the overflow from cesspools, soil-pipes, etc.

Q. — Soil-pipes where? *A.* — Soil-pipes that would come from the use of bath-rooms.

Q. — You think the gutters in Andover are foul from that source? *A.* — No, sir: I do not say that. I say that is the only source at present that we have, and we are considering the question of sewerage. The town is becoming populous.

Q. — I understood you to say, sir, that those gutters were foul now from surface drainage? *A.* — I say it is the only source by which we can drain at all, on account of the location of the street, and the buildings upon the street. The main street runs up and down the hill.

Q. — Allow me to ask you, are the gutters now foul by that drainage? *A.* — As a general thing, no, sir. The town desires to guard against their being foul by taking measures to secure surveys, and adopting a system of sewerage.

Q. (By Mr. SMITH.) — I would like to ask you one question in regard to this matter of the town taking action about securing water. Was this action previous to the application of the city of Cambridge? *A.* — I have stated here — perhaps you may not have noticed — that a committee was appointed, of which I was a member, more than two years ago, it may be three years ago, for that purpose. That committee is still in existence and pursuing the same course, only more so.

Q. (By Mr. HAMMOND.) — You had a committee appointed about three years ago? *A.* — Yes, sir.

Q. — Under what vote? *A.* — Under a vote of the town.

Q. — How did it read? *A.* — I can't tell you, sir, just how it reads.

Q. — Well, substantially? *A.* — Substantially, it was for a supply of water for fire purposes.

Q. — Has there been any other vote since? *A.* — Yes, sir.

Q. — What was that substantially? *A.* — That we engage surveyors to make surveys for the purpose of developing the water that may be used.

Q. — For what purposes? *A.* — Getting water for fire purposes and all others.

Q. — The vote said so substantially, did it? *A.* — I can't tell you how it reads.

Q. — When was this second vote passed? *A.* — The second vote, as far as concerns making the survey, was passed the first Monday in March, I think.

Q. — Why didn't you do any thing about that two years ago? *A.* — Well, sir, I think we did do something.

Q. (By Mr. Poor.) — Isn't it a fact that you have been experimenting with a sort of reservoir upon the hill for the last two or three years? *A.* — Yes, sir: the town has expended money to develop a certain portion of high land for a basin to hold water. That was expressly for fire purposes.

Q. (By Mr. Hammond.) — That is to say, under this first vote for fire purposes, the only thing the committee did, or ever have done, up to the second vote, was to try to develop some water elsewhere than from the Shawshine? You did not look to the Shawshine at all? *A.* — No, sir, not at that time.

Q. — And you have not looked at all to the Shawshine for water for fire purposes until since this petition came in from Cambridge? *A.* — I think not.

Q. — Now you understand that, when you do drain, you will drain below Frye Village, don't you? *A.* — I don't know what the town may do, but that has been my idea.

Q. — In order to keep the drainage from the river immediately in front of the villages, I suppose? *A.* — In order to deliver it below a point where there might possibly be an objection.

Q. — When you get your system of drainage, the effect of that would be to take from the river all the drainage which now goes into it from the town of Andover above Frye Village, wouldn't it? *A.* — Well, I don't know as I could say that exactly, that it would take it *all;* but it would take the principal part: it would lessen the amount of drainage which now goes in there.

Q. (By Mr. Bailey.) — You don't mean to tell this Committee that any considerable number of thinking men in Andover contemplate the taking of the water of the Shawshine for domestic purposes? *A.* — I think we shall want it within a short time, from the fact that the river is the nearest point, and the most available point. We have no pond within a reasonable distance.

Q. — Do you think that is one objection to our getting it? *A.* — That would come in as an objection, of course.

Q. (By Mr. Smith.) — One object that the town has in view is to take water for the extinguishment of fires. That was the purpose of the first vote, three years ago; and they wished also to provide for ordinary domestic purposes, and to look forward to the future wants of the town. You think the future wants of the town are being taken into consideration, do you not? *A.* — It is very apparent to any individual here who knows the town of Andover, or who does not know it, that a town of that size, sooner or later, must provide for sewerage ; and sewerage without water, as we all know, would not be practicable.

Mr. Poor. That closes the evidence for the town of Andover ; and for the Marland Mills, I should be content to rest the case of the proprietor, Mr. Stevens, upon the evidence of last year. My brother Bullard will make whatever statement he may deem desirable for the manufacturers : I shall say nothing on that subject. Perhaps that will come in at the next hearing.

Mr. Morse. Perhaps it will be convenient to state now, in order to save the Committee some time, and to save us time and expense, that we propose, with the permission of the Committee, to place before them copies of the printed Report of last year. I desire to call special attention to the testimony of Mr. George H. Torr (p. 99), and George W. W. Dove (p. 109 and p. 131), who testified in regard to the use made of the Shawshine by the Smith & Dove Manufacturing Company. I will not detain the Committee at this time by reading from the Report, but I shall desire to call their attention to it in argument. These gentlemen, I assume, do not desire to change their statements from last year, and it will probably save time to put them in in that shape.

Adjourned to Friday at ten o'clock.

FOURTH HEARING.

Boston, Friday, March 24, 1882.

The hearing was resumed at ten o'clock.

STATEMENT OF BROOKS T. BATCHELLER.

Mr. Chairman and Gentlemen, — I appear here as one of a committee of the town of Lexington. I do not know exactly what I should say. There seem to be two parties courting this old lady, the Shawshine, and I don't know which has got the inside track. But we want to be protected against any thing arising in a distant day, like Wellington Brook poisoning the Cambridge water. We think we have a prior claim to drain into that river our surface drainage or underground drainage : we have no other way. Lexington is a small town, with no large taxpayers ; and the people who own real estate in the vicinity of this Shawshine top-dress their land, as they term it. They draw out night-soil and other manures from the city, when they come in with produce, and top-dress their land ; and, in a measure, unless the water runs itself pure, of course that would impregnate it, and render it unfit for domestic purposes. But we think, if Cambridge is allowed to take this water, we have a prior claim to drainage. We, of course, should be careful : we don't wish to do any thing to pollute the water. If they could show to this Committee that it was a public necessity to take the water at this time, it would be another question. I don't say but they may ; and we want to get ready against that time. We have a little amendment to sect. 13 of the Act which they have put in ; and, if that can be accepted, we have nothing more to say. But we do protest against being brought into any unfortunate connection with this matter. If they get the right to take this river, they will probably send a commission up there, and put an injunction upon our draining into it. Our people are putting in bath-rooms more and more ; some good houses are now being erected ; and there is some drainage, also, into Vine Brook. There is not any thing very offensive goes into the river now, because the quantity put in is not large ; but it will increase more and more. Lexington is going to grow : it is a very healthy town to live in, and we wish to be protected.

Q. (By the Chairman.) — Your point is, that the farmers in your town wish to top-dress their land, and you think the stream might be polluted by surface drainage? *A.*— Yes, sir: it is right in the centre of the town, near the Massachusetts House, and near our churches, and near the most populous part of the town; and it is a very fine place to drain into, because there is a great fall, and it goes to the Shawshine, that runs very full in the spring, and carries off every thing that is offensive. If we can be protected against any interference with our rights, if this water is taken, we have nothing to say. There are three or four small streams, but they all tend towards Bedford, northward, and into the Shawshine; and we want to be protected against any thing arising in the future by which we may be brought to grief by this thing. We think we have a prior claim to drainage; and we think, if they want to take the water, they should take it at their risk, not ours. I was born within four or five miles of the Shawshine, and drove a stage along there by the old Middlesex Canal a good many years, and know all about that river. The stream is one that runs very quick; and a good deal of water can be saved in the spring, if proper means are taken to save it. We think it is no more than justice, no more than right, that we should be protected. We do not want to deprive anybody of water, if it is a public necessity to take it: if we can be protected, that is all we want. If it is a public necessity for Cambridge or Boston, or both together, to take that water, I do not know why they ought not to have it; but they have not shown it exactly, in my judgment. They did not show it last year, and I do not think they have now. I have this amendment, which I should like to put in, if there is no objection by counsel on the other side :—

"Nor shall the inhabitants of said towns be prevented from using such river or its tributaries to carry off the drainage of said towns, whether the same flow from fields under cultivation or elsewhere, or from the use of its waters for the purpose of generating steam for manufacturing."

Q. (By Mr. HAMMOND.) — You want the Legislature, in giving the water of the river to a city for domestic purposes, to provide that the adjoining towns may drain into the water that that city is to drink? *A.*— We have rights there, and you have none yet.

Q.— That is your proposition? *A.*— Yes, sir.

Mr. HAMMOND. We should object to that.

Q.— I understand you to say that you are familiar with the valley of the Shawshine? *A.*— Somewhat. I have lived in Billerica: that is my native town.

Q.— It is a rapid, quick-rising stream? *A.*— Very.

Q.— By that you mean, I take it, that the freshets, when there are freshets, suddenly appear and suddenly disappear? *A.*— Mr.

Hammond, there is a great water-shed to the Shawshine; and when there is a rise, I have noticed, in passing over the road in old staging days, in coming down from Lowell, it would rise, between the afternoon and the next morning, high enough to come right over the road : and where your folks propose to make the first reservoir, at the old Middlesex Canal, — I think it must be in Billerica, or Wellington. or very near the line, — there is a great fall all the way down.

Q. — It rises and falls very rapidly? *A.* — Yes, sir : in the spring, after heavy rains.

Q. — So that in the spring-time there must be a large amount of water that is wasted? *A.* — That is so.

Q. — So far as that is concerned, if the flow could be equalized, to that extent, at least, it would be an improvement to the mill-powers upon the stream, would it not, Mr. Batcheller? *A.* — I am not posted much on mill-powers or those things. Those people in Andover know their own affairs; but I know there is a great lot of water runs to waste, — there is no doubt about that.

Q. — Now, I understand your difficulty to be in regard to the drainage of the town of Lexington; but I should like to ask you, as a fair-minded man, if you would be willing, if your town wanted water. to provide that the place where you took the water from should be used as a sewer for some other town? *A.* — Well. I know what the way of the world is. They say, " The devil take the hindmost !" " Get all you can !"

Q. — I ask you, as a fair-minded man, if you would be willing to recognize that right in a bill? *A.* — Well, lawyers know more about such tricks than I do anyway.

Q. — Is it a trick to put such a thing into a bill? *A.* — Yes, sir, it is, to take away rights which we have from nature : that is the amount of it.

Q. — Is it a trick to put into a bill, which is intended to give another city water, the right to put the drainage of a town into it? *A.* — You are the best judge of those tricks.

Q. — Are you willing to answer that question? *A.* — State it plainly, and I will try to answer it, sir.

Q. — If Lexington were here desiring to take the water of the Shawshine, should you be willing to have a provision in the bill that the towns above you should have a right to drain all sorts of things that they had occasion to have drainage for into the very water that Lexington was to drink? *A.* — Lexington should have a right to take the water, and we propose to take it if we can get it in a proper way.

Q. — Do you think that is an answer to my question, Mr. Batcheller? *A.* — If I was on a law case, I should want to beat. " Success," you know they say, " is a public duty."

Q. — If that is the only answer you have to give to my question, I will leave it there. *A.* — I think that is about as good an answer as I can give.

Q. (By Mr. BAILEY.) — Do you know any thing about the number of millions of gallons that run in that river at the lowest season of the year? *A.* — I can't tell you, Mr. Bailey. All I know about the stream is from looking at it daily for about twenty years.

Q. — What is the ordinary character of the stream during the summer months? *A.* — When it is a very dry time it is pretty well down, I can tell you.

Q. — How much of the year is it "pretty well down"? *A.* — The spring rains bring it up always. During the spring rains it flows right over the meadow. It don't stay up long, because there is so much fall to it.

Q. — Ordinarily it runs down to a very small stream? *A.* — Yes, sir.

Q. (By Mr. POOR.) — You say you were born in Billerica? *A.* — I was.

Q. — Are you familiar with this locality where the city of Cambridge proposes to make a basin? *A.* — I am familiar with the territory where the old Middlesex Canal was, where the aqueduct crosses it on the edge of Billerica.

Q. — Are you familiar with the stream above there? *A.* — Somewhat.

Q. — What is the nature of the soil there? *A.* — It is colored.

Q. — Where it goes through the low meadow, is there much mud and muck there? *A.* — I should think so: I have never tried it. Without any experience, you know, I could not tell.

Q. — Are there woods there? *A.* — Some.

Q. — How deep should you say the soil was there, if you know any thing about it? *A.* — That would be guesswork. I can't tell you what the subsoil is.

Q. — Do the meadows spread out some distance on each side of the stream? *A.* — In some places they do, and then in other places the hills come in quite up to the edge of the stream. There isn't much top-dressing round there in Billerica, unless it has been done since I have been familiar with it. It is a good many years since the old canal was built, and some years since the railroad went over it. In old staging times, forty years ago, I used to go over there every day one way or the other. That makes a nice embankment. Just fill up where the canal was, and then you have got a nice chance for a reservoir.

Q. (By Mr. HAMMOND.) — Do you know whether the bed of the stream is gravelly or not? *A.* — It is, near where the aqueduct crosses.

Q. — Do you know how it is elsewhere? *A.* — No: I have never followed it.

Q. — Wherever you have seen it, it appears to be gravelly? *A.* — It does.

Q. — You never have made any other investigations about it than a man would ordinarily make who lived in that vicinity? *A.* — No, sir: I never have had occasion to.

Q. (By Mr. Poor.) — How deep is the stream where the aqueduct crosses? *A.* — It is pretty deep. The aqueduct is some twenty-five feet above the stream. When there is a freshet it goes up seven or eight feet, and runs very rapidly under the aqueduct.

Q. — How deep is the stream at ordinary water up there? *A.* — I never explored it up there.

Q. — Three or four feet, or more, should you think? *A.* — I should think it was as much as that in some places. There are places where it falls, where there are shallows, and where it runs down to a gravelly bottom. Then there are other places where there is a very muddy bottom, and the water stands.

Q. — How deep is it at that point? *A.* — Some fifteen or twenty feet where it passes under the aqueduct, or more, perhaps, in a time of freshet; but it is a very small stream in summer. You can run across it there easy enough. The banks are high there.

Q. — The banks adjoining the meadows are muddy, are they? *A.* — Yes, sir.

TESTIMONY OF EBENEZER BAKER.

Q. (By Mr. Poor.) — You are a member of the House from Billerica? *A.* — Yes, sir.

Q. — Are you familiar with the Shawshine and its course from Billerica? *A.* — Yes, sir.

Q. — Do you know where Cambridge proposes to build a storage-basin? *A.* — Yes, sir.

Q. — What is the nature of the soil there? *A.* — In a great many places the meadow is very narrow : the hills come right down pretty close to the river. Then it will spread out. In some places it is not more than twice the width of this room ; then again it will be a quarter of a mile wide.

Q. — Where it is narrow, what is the character of the soil? *A.* — It is harder.

Q. — Is there muck? *A.* — There is muck where you get out into the meadows, where it is pretty near a quarter of a mile wide.

Q. — Where the bottom is muddy, how deep is it? *A.* — It is from one foot to six feet. You can run a rake's tail into it the whole length.

Q. — Are there trees and bushes there? *A.* — Yes, sir, more or less bushes ; and, when you get a basin there, of course you are going to flow a good deal of the meadow and the upland, which is covered more or less with wood and bushes. There is not much wood grows on the meadow that they mow.

Q. — From your acquaintance with the locality, would you wish to drink water stored on it? *A.* — If I could get it out of the river, I should not object to it ; but when you come to talk of flowing that mud, with all that vegetation on it, I should think it would be pretty poor water. Take it in the dry time, it is a very small river : there are a good many places where a man could jump across it. My boys, when they were going to get hay, would take a rake, and jump right across the river.

Q. — Along that basin, which extends for four miles? *A.* — Yes, sir. I have known the land there for twenty years. I used to go fishing there when I was a boy. In some places the mud is very deep, especially on the wide meadow, which you call the basin. It is almost always muddy. Where the banks come down, where the meadow is narrow, and where there is wood growing, you will find hard bottom. The bottom of the meadow is muddy a good distance over it.

Q. (By Mr. Smith.) — If a dam was built at the Middlesex Canal, and the water was thrown back by that dam, would the water come up on the banks, or flow over the meadows? *A.* — It would flow the meadows, and go up partly on the high land ; but mainly it would go on to the meadows. In some places it is quite wide there.

Q. — On the meadows? *A.* — Yes, sir, very wide. In other places, as I told you before, where the hills come down on each side, it is narrow.

Q. — Where would you think the great amount of that water would be gathered? Would it be on the high land, or would it be in the meadows? *A.* — It would be in the meadows.

Q. — The larger portion of the land covered would be meadow? *A.* — Yes, sir.

Q. — And the mud on this meadow, you say, is from one to six feet deep? *A.* — Yes, sir : in a great many places deeper.

Q. — Deeper than six feet? *A.* — Yes, sir.

Cross-Examination.

Q. (By Mr. Hammond.) — What is your business? *A.* — I am a butcher in Billerica.

Q. — How long have you been a butcher? *A.* — I have been a butcher about fifteen years, and four years I worked for another man.

Q. — Have you an establishment on the banks of the Shawshine? *A.* — No, sir ; I am up in the Centre.

Q. — You have nothing to do with the Shawshine? *A.* — No, sir: I own land on the Shawshine.

Q. — Where is that land? *A.* — It lies on the south side of the Boston and Lowell Railroad.

Q. — Is it a part of the land which would be covered by the reservoir? *A.* — Yes, sir.

Q. — Have you ever made any surveys there to ascertain the depth of the water, etc.? *A.* — No, sir, I have not at all.

Q. — The bed of the Shawshine, so far as you know, is gravelly, isn't it? *A.* — From the best of my knowledge, — and I have been up and down the river a great many times, — I should not think over a quarter part of the bottom for four miles could be called gravelly.

Q. — What is the rest? *A.* — I think it is mud.

Q. — How deep? *A.* — I never measured it.

Q. — You could put a rake-handle in there, and get across, couldn't you? *A.* — Yes, sir, in some places you can.

Q. — If I understand your idea, it is that if they should flow that water over there, and leave the trees and mud just as they are now, you think it would be bad water? *A.* — I should not want to drink it.

Q. — Suppose they were going to improve it, and take the mud and trees out, what would you say then? *A.* — I don't know, I am sure, what the effect would be.

TESTIMONY OF JOSEPH WHITNEY.

Q. (By Mr. Bullard.) — You reside in Cambridge? *A.* — I do.

Q. — And have resided there for some years? *A.* — I have.

Q. — How long? *A.* — Most of my entire life.

Q. — Been city treasurer? *A.* — I have.

Q. — Have you at various times given attention to the matter of water-supply, and the leakage of water, and subjects of that sort? *A.* — I have, a good deal, first and last.

Q. — Will you tell us, briefly, what your experience has been in the matter of detecting and stopping leaks? *A.* — Well, I commenced about fifteen years ago, I think it was. At East Cambridge there was a great loss of pressure and head, and I made some observations which showed me it was occasioned by leaks entirely; and, as I found leaks one after another, and stopped them, I found that the head was very materially increased, and that the consumption was very much reduced.

Q. — And the inspection then instituted has been kept up? *A.* — Very largely since that, so that the result is our low consumption to-day.

Q. — Have you ever made any investigation in Boston on that subject? *A.* — I did several years ago.

Q. — What was the result of that? What did you do, and what did you find? *A.* — Well, I made a house-to-house inspection, and I found, as near as I can recollect now, about six thousand leaks on the house-fixtures. It is very difficult to tell how much water was saved by that; but my estimate was, that it would be about five hundred gallons to each case of leakage.

Q. — Five hundred gallons in how long? *A.* — In twenty-four hours: five hundred gallons daily.

Q. — Where did you find the leaks? *A.* — In water-closets, and from imperfect fixtures through the houses in the city of Boston. In Cambridge I found them very largely in our supply-pipes, and some quite large leaks in our mains.

Q. — How large a force did you have in Boston to aid you in detecting those leaks, and how long did it take? *A.* — I had to go through the houses. I did not complete the examination that I wished to make. We were about five months. I had an average of about six men. This was in the year 1873, I think.

Cross-Examination.

Q. (By Mr. HAMMOND.) — You were educated as a civil engineer, I believe? *A.* — Yes, sir.

Q. — Were engaged in that profession practically for some years? *A.* — I was.

Q — And afterwards became city treasurer of Cambridge? *A.* — Yes.

Q. — And, as I understand it, your taste has led you, notwithstanding you were in the office of the city treasuryship there, to investigate questions of water-supply? *A.* — That is true. It was a very interesting subject to me.

Q. — And on your own account, by permission of the water authorities of Cambridge, you commenced your investigation in a part of Cambridge about fifteen years ago? *A.* — Yes, sir.

Q. — And you succeeded in stopping many leaks, did you not? *A.* — I did, so that it increased the head very materially.

Q. — And, as I understand it, you invented, or put in practical operation there, a self-registering machine, by which every morning you could tell how much water had been consumed in the night, and at what hours of the night, and showing also the varying changes in every minute of the night? *A.* — We could not determine by that gauge the amount of water consumed; but we could determine at every moment of the day what pressure was relieved of the true pressure, the normal pressure, what it should have been.

Q. — It aided you in ascertaining where the leaks were, to a certain extent? *A.* — To a certain extent. I recollect one particular case: there was a break in a four-inch pipe, and my gauge indicated a very great loss of pressure when I came into the office in the morning. I could not account for it. I told our superintendent there must certainly be a leak. He made quite a careful examination, and, when he returned, said there could not be any leak. He said the pressure seemed to be very good everywhere else. That ran along eleven days. I could not get my pressure on my gauge at all; and at last some of the subordinate men closed some of the gates in some sections, and at last they struck upon this particular point, and stopped this leak, and my gauge went up at once to its normal pressure.

Q. — Do you know what the trouble was in that section? *A.* — They dug down, and found that a four-inch pipe had been broken off, so that one edge was below the other.

Q. — In that way, by looking at section after section, you were able to detect many leaks, and then, of course, to repair them, were you not? *A.* — Yes, sir.

Q. — That method of examination resulted in reducing the consumption? *A.* — Unquestionably.

Q. — And it is your belief to-day, is it not, that that system is practically carried out that you inaugurated there? *A.* — Certainly.

Q. — And by that means we get the low consumption in the city? *A.* — I have no doubt of it at all: so that we have the lowest consumption of any place in the country almost.

Q. — Have you any doubt that the inspection in Cambridge is as rigid, constant, and severe as anywhere? *A.* — I think it is more so.

Q. — Did your experience in operating there upon those pipes show that there were many leaks in large supply-pipes in the streets? *A.* — Certainly it did.

Q. — Caused by sinking of the ground? *A.* — At times.

Q. — What other ways? *A.* — Well, almost entirely by sinking of the ground. Sometimes, of course, it might be owing to an imperfect pipe; but as a general thing, where the mains are leaking, the occasion is a settling of the ground.

Q. — Sometimes, I suppose, the break would be near a sewer, and the water would run into the sewer, and never make its appearance above ground, so that you would never have detected the leak from any external manifestations on the surface of the ground: is that true? *A.* — Yes, sir: that was exactly the case in the instance about which I just told you, where that four-inch pipe broke. The settling of the ground also broke the sewer, and left an opening in the sewer, so that the water had been flowing there eleven days, and never would have come to the surface. That is the class of leaks you have to look for, because, if water comes to the surface, you don't need to look for it: you know where it is. But my experience has shown me that there is a certain percentage of leaks where there is blind drainage. It may be five or ten per cent.; but, unless those are watched carefully, they accumulate, and in the course of a few years it gets up to an enormous amount.

Q. (By Mr. BAILEY.) — Do you know any thing about the Deacon system of inspection? *A.* — I do not, except by reading. I understand the working of it.

Q. — It is something similar to what you have been describing, is it not? *A.* — Yes, sir: except in Cambridge we shut off a section, and leave one gate partially open, and then we hear the water flowing, instead of reading it on the register, as they do here in Boston.

Q. (By Mr. RAND.) — What was your connection with the city of Boston? Did they employ you? *A.* — They employed me: yes, sir.

Q. — In what year was it? *A.* — I think it was in August, 1873.

Mr. RAND. Does an account of Mr. Whitney's experiments appear in any report?

Mr. BAILEY. I don't know.

(Subsequently a Report of the Cochituate Water Board for 1874 was put in, which contains a reference to Mr. Whitney's experiments.)

Q. (By Mr. HAMMOND.) — How long were you city treasurer of Cambridge? *A.* — Twenty years.

Q. — Ending when? *A.* — Ending in 1878.

Q. — So that at the time you were employed by Boston, and all the time you were operating in Cambridge, you were also city treasurer there? *A.* — Yes, sir.

Q. — What you did, you did out of love and enthusiasm for the science, as much as any thing? *A.* — Yes, sir.

Q. — Were you ever paid for what you did in Cambridge? *A.* — I never was: no, sir.

TESTIMONY OF J. P. BRADLEE.

Q. (By Mr. BULLARD.) — You are proprietor of the Ballardvale Mills? *A.* — Yes, sir.

Q. — How long have you been proprietor of those mills? *A.* — I have been connected with them over forty years.

Q. — You are a citizen of Boston, and always have been? *A.* — Yes, sir.

Q. — How long has your mill been on that stream? *A.* — The Act of incorporation was obtained in 1836: the mill was built prior to that time.

Q. — Now, will you tell us generally about the village which has grown up there?

Mr. HAMMOND. I suppose the Committee have seen it: I don't think you need to spend any time upon that.

Mr. BULLARD. I don't propose to spend any great length of time upon it. I simply wish to draw the attention of the Committee to the unusual character of the class of people who are there for a factory village, and to the fact that their interests are bound up in the presence and success of the mill.

The CHAIRMAN. You might very briefly examine him upon that point, — not at any great length.

Mr. HAMMOND. I will concede that it is a very happy New England factory village.

Mr. BULLARD. Do you concede all that I claim?

The CHAIRMAN. Do you concede that the general prosperity of the village depends upon that factory?

Mr. HAMMOND. Yes, sir: I will concede, that, if that factory should be compelled to shut down, it would be a great disaster to the village.

The CHAIRMAN. Possibly ruin to the village?

Mr. HAMMOND. Well, "ruin" is a comparative term. The major premiss we concede; the minor we do not.

The CHAIRMAN [to Mr. BULLARD]. You might ask a few questions.

Mr. BULLARD. The point is, that this is not an average factory village.

Q. — I will ask you, Mr. Bradlee, in regard to the inhabitants of that village, the churches, and what methods of culture and amusement have been provided for the people there? *A.* — Well, sir, I have got a very nice piece of property up there, employing about 180 or 200 people. The annual product of the mill is about $400,000. I have got a very happy community there, indeed; and they feel that if I were obliged to go away from there, with the specialty which I have, — which is making white flannels, for which I must have plenty of water, and must have it good, and must have it at a high pressure if I can get it, — it would be a great injury to them. I have taken particular pains to make the village a contented and happy one. I have a large hall, which is free to them for all purposes for which they want it. Lectures are delivered there every winter. I have a library, and have provided for their amusement a bowling-alley and a pool-table, with strict regulations, so as to keep them on holidays and other days from going to other places. I think I have got a factory village there that is not excelled by any other in the State to my knowledge; and I should feel very bad if it should be disturbed by having the water taken away, so that I should be obliged to abandon my specialty there. Ever since 1852 I have had exclusive control of it. It was originated by Mr. Marland in 1836. He got into trouble and left. and since then I have had charge of it. I have had charge of it since 1852, the year he left. The charter was given up in 1866, and since then it has been an individual enterprise of my own.

Q. — Did you say there were three churches there? *A.* — Yes, sir: there is a Catholic church, an Orthodox church, and a Methodist church.

Q. — Are there any inhabitants there who are not either directly or indirectly dependent for their prosperity upon the mill? *A.* — There are very few that are not dependent upon the mill. There is a small concern there which makes leather bottoms for chairs. There is another man who has hired a small place to make pottery. Prior to the establishment of these enterprises, all other things failed. But these, as I say, are very small industries; and, if I should stop, the main industry of that village would be gone. I was sorry, when I heard that the Committee had gone up to Andover, that they did not give me an opportunity to show the mill. It would have been a pleasure and a pride to me if I could have had these gentlemen go up and see it. because I believe they would think more of it than they will from any description which I can give of it.

Q. — I understand you to say that the product of the mill is between $400,000 and $500,000 a year? *A.* — Yes, sir: it has been as high as $500,000. That was when prices were high. I try to get it about $400,000.

Q. — Is this a sample card of your goods? *A.* — Yes, sir: that is a sample of our regular make.

Q. — Is that a sample of the yarn? *A.* — That is a sample of the yarn that we made for the Centennial.

Mr. BULLARD. In a pound of this yarn, there are 44,000 yards, or twenty-four miles. In other words, a pound of that material would reach from where we are sitting to the mills.

Q. — Now, Mr. Bradlee, do you use a very large part of the water of the Shawshine for scouring and cleaning? *A.* — We use considerable. I cannot say that we use the whole of it for that purpose.

Q. — Is the first process, after the wool leaves the bales, scouring? *A.* — Yes, sir.

Q. — How thoroughly is that done? *A.* — It is done to get the wool as clean as we can possibly get it, — get the grease out of it: that requires a large quantity of pure water, and a head so as to give force to the water.

Q. — In your scouring-box you require force to rinse the wool? *A.* — Yes, sir: the wool is put into liquor, and then we take it out from there and put it into cold water, and we want a head there to get that liquor out.

Q. — And the expedition with which the wool is scoured depends entirely upon the force of the water, does it not? *A.* — Yes, sir.

Q. — If it were necessary to do without force, it would take an immensely long time, would it not, to clean the wool? *A.* — Yes, sir.

Q. — After the goods are made, are they scoured again? *A.* — Yes, sir.

Q. — How thoroughly is that done? *A.* — They are passed through two rollers, to get them as clean as they can be made.

Q. — Those pieces are sixty yards long, are they? *A.* — That is the length of the roll. The baling pieces are thirty yards.

Q. — Those are put over a drum and run through water for the purpose of washing? *A.* — Yes, sir.

Q. — Do you know how long a piece is left in the suds? *A.* — I cannot tell you. The whole operation of fitting the goods for market, after they are manufactured, takes just about a day. After scouring, they are bleached with brimstone, in a stove-house, we call it that gives them their whiteness.

Cross-Examination.

Q. (By Mr. Hammond.) — You have owned this place ever since 1852? *A.* — Well, as I said, in 1866 I got the title to it. I said I had had the sole management of it since 1852. That was under the corporation. The charter was given up, and the fee came to me.

Q. — Now there is no corporation, and you are the owner? *A.* — The individual owner, sir: it is an individual enterprise.

Q. — What are your rights, if you are willing to tell us, as you understand them, as to the water-power there? *A.* — We have got a dam there, and we flow back to a certain extent. We have a right of flowage, and all the water that comes in there is ours.

Q. — You have a right to retain that water up to a certain point? *A.* — Yes, sir: up to the height of my dam.

Q. — And then you must allow the rest to run down? *A.* — I never let it run over the dam if I can help it; but, when there is plenty of water, it runs over the dam, and that dam affects the people above me.

Q. — I don't understand how. *A.* — When we flow it, we have to pay for it.

Q. — You have a right to flow to the height of your dam? *A.* — Yes, sir: to a certain mark in the mill, right at the head of the dam.

Q. — But all other water you have no right to stop: it goes by to the mill-owners below? *A.* — Yes, sir.

Q. — Have you a pretty large mill-pond there? *A.* — It is a pretty good size: yes, sir.

Q. — How large? *A.* — I don't know, sir.

Q. — What is the busiest season with you in manufacturing? *A.* — We manufacture the year round, sir. The busy season for selling is along in May and June. Then we have to manufacture for the fall.

Q. — Your manufacture goes along pretty nearly even? *A.* — Yes, sir: we make light goods for spring, and a little heavier, coarser goods for fall.

Q. — You don't manufacture upon orders: you keep a stock? *A.* — We keep manufacturing to supply the market.

Q. — When the river is low, are you not troubled sometimes about water? *A.* — Yes, sir: we have been, for scouring purposes. I explained it last year.

Q. — As I understand it, you use the water for the generation of steam in your mill? *A.* — Yes, sir.

Q. — And for water-power in your mill? *A.* — Yes, sir.

Q. — And also for scouring purposes? *A.* — Yes, sir.

Q. — And the peculiar value of the water is for scouring purposes? *A.* — Well, I should say, if I did not have the water to scour, I could not finish my goods.

Q. — So I understand; but you think that the superior quality of your goods is due to the fact that you have the Shawshine water to clean them with? *A.* — Well, I can't say that it is that particular water; but it is very good water, and, the way it is situated now, I have the control of it. There is nothing above us to hurt us at all.

Q. — If this bill which Cambridge proposes provides that more water shall go down stream in a dry time than now goes, it would not hurt you in a dry time, would it? *A.* — Well, I don't know, sir: it is an experiment.

Q. — I do not propose to use your answer, if we should get a bill and go to a jury on the question of damages. *A.* — I understand; I want the gentlemen to understand that I am here objecting to this thing, not on account of dollars and cents. I have a personal feeling in relation to this property. I do not think there is money enough to induce me voluntarily to sell the property.

Q. — That is as I understand it; but I want you to understand that you can answer the questions that I put to you freely, as bearing simply on the question as to how much we shall hurt you, in this hearing alone. I do not think it would be fair to take whatever you may say here anywhere else. Now, you have times when you do not have water enough? *A.* — There have been such times. In 1880 there was such a time.

Q. — How was it in 1880? *A.* — That was a very dry time. As I explained last year, when the water began to get low, I started one engine for half the mill, and then went to the other side and started

that. It was a bad way of doing it. I generally had water enough
to do my scouring ; but there were a few days when we scoured one
day, and washed the next day. Now, to show you about that stream,
if you want to get at that point, I will say that in 1879, which was
a rainy season, I stopped for some repairs the Fourth of July week ;
and for four weeks out of that year, say, I was repairing. That left
eleven months that the mill was in operation. During that time I
only ran that big engine eleven days. In 1880, which was a dry
season, I had to run that same engine nine months. Last year I ran
it six months. Last year was a better year for water than 1880.

Q. — And those six months. I suppose, were in the summer-time
or early fall? A. — Well, say early fall. Then we have, outside of
what comes in the Shawshine, what we call Foster's Pond, that we
reserve in a dry season. We do not touch that water until we absolutely need it, and then we let it down by degrees : that will last us,
the way we manage it, six or eight weeks.

Q. — That is a small pond, isn't it? A. — I don't know how
many acres. Somebody said here it was sixty. I never saw much
about it.

Q. — So that you have actually adopted on the stream the practice
of storing the water in Foster's Pond, and that ekes out your supply
in a dry time? A. — Yes, sir.

Q. — If storage should be adopted upon the same scheme above
there, and the water allowed to pass out in a dry time, that would be a
benefit to you in those times, wouldn't it? A. — It depends entirely
on the result. It is an experiment. I can't say what the effect would
be, because you might not let it out at the proper height : it might
flow more sluggish. I cannot tell what the practical effect of that
section of your bill would be.

Q. — Can you tell why the flowing of the water from that reservoir
should not have the same effect that the overflow of water from Foster's Pond does? A. — Well, flowage coming from a big pond there
of eight hundred acres would spread, probably, over the meadows,
and we probably should not get the full effect of that water. Foster's
Pond is very near us : the water comes down in a brook. We do not
have to let the water go on to the meadows at all.

Q. — You cannot give me any answer why there should be any
different effect, only you are not sure that that would be the effect?
A. — Yes, sir : that is the story. I am afraid of it. We are well
enough off as we are. We don't want to try experiments. I am
willing to take the natural flow of the stream.

Q. — Do you know what the other mills do with reference to storing
water? A. — I don't trouble myself much about what other people
are doing.

Q. — You have some knowledge of the fact that other mill-owners piece out their water in the same way that you do? *A.* — By reservoirs; but they control the reservoirs.

Q. — I am speaking now of the physical effect of it, not of the control of it. Ten million gallons of water a day, going out of a reservoir owned and controlled by the city of Cambridge, would do the same thing that 10,000,000 gallons going out of the same reservoir owned by anybody else would do? *A.* — Yes, sir: ought to. It depends upon how you get it out.

Q. — Suppose it goes out in the same way? *A.* — What do you mean by going out in the same way?

Q. — What I mean is, is the ownership of the reservoir at all material on the question whether 10,000,000 gallons running from one place to another place is going to have the same effect? *A.* — Suppose you put it this way : You have a reservoir, and have 10,000,000 gallons a day going out of it, and suppose there was a brook, or something that would bring that down directly to me, and it did not have to go over the meadows, then I should get the full effect of those 10.000,000 gallons.

Q. — And you don't know that you would not in the other case, under the plan proposed by the city of Cambridge? *A.* — I cannot tell : I am a little apprehensive.

Q. — But, if you were satisfied that that would be so, that would take away, to a great extent, your opposition to this bill proposed by Cambridge, wouldn't it? *A.* — If it was demonstrated to me that it would do me no harm, and give me all the water that I want for scouring, that would be one thing. I cannot see how you can demonstrate it until the injury is done.

Q. — I want to ask you another thing. There are times when water runs over your dam in large quantities? *A.* — Yes, sir.

Q. — When you really cannot use in your mill profitably all the water that goes by? Isn't that so? *A.* — Yes, sir.

Q. — To what extent is that so? *A.* — I really don't know.

Q. — That is principally in the spring of the year? *A.* — In the spring of the year : yes, sir. Take, for instance, this spring or last spring, but this spring particularly, after the heavy snows that we have had, there was a superabundance of water there ; and I was obliged to stop on account of back-water.

Q. — I suppose the mills are so arranged there that, except in freshets, there is no trouble about back-water? *A.* — No, sir : no trouble at all.

Q. — The stream is a quick stream, — rises and falls rapidly? *A.* — Yes, sir. Take, for instance, such a rain as we had Friday. We shut down Saturday afternoon, and Monday morning we found that, although we might have had to run a little steam on Friday or Thursday, we could shut off that engine by Monday noon. There is a great water-shed where you propose going.

Q. — What is your steam-power? *A.* — Engines.

Q. — What power have you? *A.* — I have got one engine of one hundred and the other thirty horse-power.

Q. — One hundred and thirty horse-power in all? *A.* — One hundred and thirty horse-power.

Q. — What do you estimate your water-power at when your dam is full? *A.* — I never estimated it at all.

Q. — Will this one hundred and thirty horse-power do what the water will do? *A.* — It drags hard when we do that. The engines are tributary to the water.

Q. — Haven't you ever had an estimate made by any engineer of what your water-power was? *A.* — No, sir: all the estimate I ever had was, when I put in that one hundred horse-power engine some years ago, the party who made it up at Fitchburg told me that that would do all I wanted it to do auxiliary to the water. That is all I know.

Q. — Have you ever run your mill at any one time entirely by steam? *A.* — Yes, sir.

Q. — With those two engines? *A.* — With those two engines.

Q. — And they did what your water-power does, although not so well? *A.* — Oh, no. If the water was taken away from us, and we had to run that mill by steam entirely, I presume I should have to have larger engines.

Q. — During the past year you have run six months both engines? *A.* — One engine. The large one was run six months, and the small one — which is on the other side of the river, and runs a small mill — was run three weeks.

Q. — I suppose, to come right down to it, there would be no difficulty about running that mill by steam ; but the particular value that you attach to that water is its purity for washing purposes? *A.* — Yes, sir.

Q. — And, if Lexington should want to drain into it, you would not like it, would you? *A.* — Probably, Lexington being so far off, it might get purified before it got down to me.

Q. — But it would be a benefit to you if somebody should put up a dam, one of whose main objects would be to keep the water pure, wouldn't it? *A.* — I should think so.

Q. (By Mr. MORSE.) — Suppose you got the benefit of the entire 10,000,000 gallons that they propose to let down from that reservoir : have you any idea how much of that you would be able to let down for the people below you, after you got through with it? *A.* — I think there would be difficulty there, because our pond would not be more than half full if the reservoir was there. I think it would be a cause of trouble between me and the men below me, where it would raise a question, and a very serious question, I think. Naturally, I should keep all the water I got, you know, to run the whole year; and they would get what ran through my wheels. If I should keep it back unnecessarily, it might cause some trouble between me and my next-door neighbor. That is something, you know, that you cannot tell about until it is demonstrated; and, when it is demonstrated, the child is born, and you cannot help yourself.

Q. (By Mr. HAMMOND.) — Would it be any worse than it is now? A. — They get all the water now when we run.

Q. — Exactly. What I want to get at is, would 10,000,000 gallons that come out of that reservoir act any differently after it got down to your mill than 10,000,000 gallons coming from any other place when it got down there? A. — I don't think it would have the same effect exactly, whether it came from Lexington or the Sudbury River.

Q. (By Mr. SMITH.) — If I understand you, the business in which you are now engaged would be destroyed unless you can have sufficient water to do the cleansing of your goods? A. — Yes, sir, most decidedly.

Q. — If your business should be destroyed, you would leave? A. — Yes, sir.

Q. — And if you should leave, and your mills are to be run by steam, what do you think would be the prospect of any other company going in and taking the property there, and manufacturing any class of goods by steam, judging from the fact that is before your eyes there with regard to the great works of the file manufacturing corporation? A. — Well, the file-works have been lying there dead, I don't know how many years. I don't know when the company failed: they failed two or three times; and everybody that has been in there failed, and everybody that had any thing to do with it.

Q. — They had no water-power? A. — They had no water-power but a little brook that comes down there.

Q. — How much did that establishment cost? A. — Over a million dollars.

Q. — How much was it sold for at auction? A. — The real estate, I think, was sold for $25,000 or $28,000.

Q. — And yet, with that great depreciation, you say that nobody has been found willing to go in there to manufacture any class of goods by steam? A. — Yes, sir. It is not fitted for a woollen or cotton mill. It might be arranged for a cotton-mill; but nobody who knew any thing about the cotton business would ever start a cotton-mill there. A machine-shop might go there; but that has been tried, and failed.

Q. — What I wish to get at is this: if any manufacturing interest at Ballardvale has to depend entirely upon steam, according to your experience in the past, whether there is any prospect that a company would start up to keep the property? *A.* — Well, sir, I don't know what other people might do. I know what I would do: I would not start one up there.

Q. — I want to ask you one other question with regard to the character of your work-people. Do you ever have any strikes? *A.* — No, sir.

Q. — Never have had one? *A.* — No, sir.

Q. — Are your work-people to an unusual degree permanent? Do they make homes there, build homes? *A.* — Yes, sir.

Q. — What proportion of your people are people that have continued in your employ for years, and have little homes of their own? *A.* — I cannot exactly answer that. Right along in one row there are four or five widows whose husbands used to work in our mill, and there are some below; but generally, after persons come there, if they are good workmen and thrifty, they put up houses of their own, and stay there. I have got some men now that I cannot discharge because nobody else would want them, they have got so old. I have spinners there that I am paying men's wages, nine shillings a day, when I might put in boys for $1 or $1.25 a day. These men are not strong enough to operate a "jack" in the old-fashioned way, where the man had to run it up by hand; but now we have an operator that runs the jacks up, and all the workman has to do is to put on the spools, and, if a thread breaks, mend it. We do not intend to crowd our people at all: we want them to be good, tidy people, and make a good community for themselves. I have done every thing in my power to have it so.

Q. — You have aimed to have a good class of people there, to have them thrifty, and induce them to make little homes of their own, and you have succeeded? *A.* — Yes, sir. As I said before, I have provided all the amusements for them that are reasonable and right. In the winter season I have lectures, ten during the winter. I have run an adult school for two years. I found that some of the boys who had been in our primary district school some years ago were lacking in education; and I started up a primary school for men, women, and children, two years ago. The first year it was very largely attended; this last year not quite so well, — the new was rubbed off of it. That is the story of that village there; and, as I said before, I should have been very happy to have had you gentlemen see it.

Q. (By the CHAIRMAN.) — I understand that you pay the expenses of this school? *A.* — Yes, sir: they are not called upon for a dollar. As far as the library is concerned, if they abuse a book, their names are taken off of the list, and they cannot have another.

Q. (By Mr. HAMMOND.) — If you were manufacturing anywhere else, you would do the same thing, wouldn't you? *A.* — I don't know : it would depend upon where I located myself.

Q. — Do you think that the prosperity of that village is any greater than would be the prosperity of any other country village that had such management as yours? *A.* — I think that the prosperity of any village depends upon the management. They are so near Boston, being within twenty miles, that I can slip up there almost any day : that is a great thing. If I had to go to some place away from a large city, where nobody would be likely to come in a few years, and take the water away, it would make a great difference. I should not want to go to such a place : I would not go.

Q. — What I want to get at is, whether that factory village is any better than any village of New England where such a factory is situated? *A.* — I don't want to blow my own horn too much.

Q. — I have no doubt you would say that it is. Now, what I want to know is, whether you do not think that it is largely due to your own individual management? *A.* — I think the success of any mill is largely due to the parties that run it.

Q. — Now, I should like to inquire about this file-factory. I did not see that : where is it? *A.* — It is right at the depot, between my mills and the railroad. I am sorry to say I have seen it a great many years.

Q. — It went down when? *A.* — Ten years ago, I should think.

Q. — What made it go down? *A.* — Bad management.

Q. — Anybody take the water of the river away from them? *A.* — No, sir : they had no rights in the river. They started there with steam-power.

Q. (By Mr. BAILEY.) — Did you ever have any estimate made of the amount of water that you require in your mill? *A.* — No, sir.

Q. — Nor the amount that you use? *A.* — No, sir : we take things as we find them, and do the best we can with them.

Q. — About how much of the year are you in want of water now? *A.* — I told you how much I had to run that engine.

Q. — Did you have water enough for your flannels at that time? *A.* — I don't think we stopped more than a few days. We did the scouring one day, and the finishing the other.

Q. (By Mr. BULLARD.) — What is the proportion of your product of white flannels to the whole product of the country, as near as you can estimate? *A.* — The only other person who makes the same class of goods that I do is Mr. Gilbert, up at Ware. I understand he is running three sets on those goods. He has thirty sets of machinery, running on dress goods and other things ; but mine is a specialty.

Q. — You make, probably, what proportion of the entire product of the country? Is it four-fifths? *A.* — I think I make three-fifths certainly. Mr. Gilbert has made flannels for a great many years, and he makes them now because he simply wants to keep in the market; but his other goods have been doing better for him.

Q. — I suppose, if the reservoir that Cambridge proposes to make could be entirely under your control in regard to letting out the water, you would look at it in a different light? *A.* — Yes, sir: I should, decidedly.

Q. — But you think, that, if it was not under your control, it might create trouble between you and the mill-owners below you? *A.* — If the mill-owners could have the control of the water, how it should go up and down, that would make a difference.

Q. (By Mr. SMITH.) — You say, if the water of the river is taken away, you could not manufacture your present class of goods. Supposing you should run the factory on cotton goods, or any other class of common goods, that would not require so much cleansing, and use steam for power instead of water? *A.* — I think we should have trouble in finishing our goods.

Q. — That is not the point I am particularly aiming at. I want to know what prospect there would be of your competing successfully, in running the factory on cotton, for instance, with the manufacturers in Lowell and Lawrence, who run by water? *A.* — We could not compete, sir.

Q. — And the small margin of profit which is made ordinarily on those goods would be lost on account of the increased expense of manufacture by the use of steam? *A.* — Yes, sir.

Q. — So that you think that if you were obliged to give up because you could not use this water, and some other party should go into the manufacture by steam, they would probably succeed about as well as the file-factory? *A.* — Just about.

Q. (By Mr. HAMMOND.) — Below you is what village? *A.* — The Smith & Dove Company Mill, they call it: Abbott Village, I think.

Q. — What is the first one below you? *A.* — That is Abbott Village; that is the Smith & Dove Company.

Q. — They run by steam partly? *A.* — Yes, sir: they have to do the same as we do.

Q. — Do you know to what extent? *A.* — I don't know: they testified last year to what extent.

Q. — Who is below them? *A.* — Mr. Stevens.

Q. — He has steam? *A.* — Yes, sir.

Q. — What is that mill? *A.* — That is a flannel-mill; but he makes colored goods.

Q. — What is Smith & Dove's business? *A.* — They manufacture flax.

Q. — Who is below Stevens? *A.* — John Smith: the Smith & Dove Company run it. They have got a small village there.

Q. — Frye Village? *A.* — Frye Village, yes, sir: just below Stevens.

Q. — They run partly by steam? *A.* — Yes, sir: they have put in steam in case of a dry time.

Q. — Can you give the amount of horse-power of those various mills in those four villages? *A.* — No, sir.

Q. — Do you believe that it equals five hundred? *A.* — I have no idea about it at all.

TESTIMONY OF JAMES R. REED.

Q. (By Mr. Poor.) — Are you familiar with the locality of this proposed basin in Billerica? *A.* — Yes, sir: I am quite familiar with all the meadow-land along the stream.

Q. — Will you state what your observations have been? *A.* — In the first place, as a boy, I was very often fishing. I was brought up at my grandmother's, and used to go up and down the stream a good deal fishing, and to a certain extent keep it up now; and I should say that the stream through that region, much of it, certainly, has a very slight fall, and that anywhere along there, where the brook flows through the meadow, if the water at the brook should be raised eight or ten feet above the present level of the brook, it would flow back over the meadows into the woods on the other side. The meadow there is from twenty to fifty rods wide, I should think, with woodland on the other side of it. There are one or two little streams running in with a very slight fall, and they run quite a ways back. Any attempt at damming that water there would inevitably throw it back into the woods. The bottom there, as far as I have noticed it, is muddy. There are only one or two places where the bottom is hard enough to wade upon. In other places it is soft mud. I do not know a place there where it would be safe to try to cross the stream. A man would sink six or eight inches, perhaps more, into the mud.

Q. — How deep is the mud generally, Mr. Reed, if you know? *A.* — The mud in the meadow seems to be pretty deep. There are three little streams that I had in my mind, that run into this river, and the bottom of their channels would be a foot or a foot and a half below the top of the meadow. The bottom of these brooks is mud, not sand or gravel.

Q. — You say the bottom of the Shawshine itself in most places is muddy? *A.* — Yes, sir.

Q. — How deep is the Shawshine in that proposed basin, as it now is? *A.* — There are two or three holes, as the boys call them, where

the water is from six to perhaps twelve feet deep ; but, as a rule, the
water below the top of the bank wouldn't average over three feet. I
don't think it would average as much as that below the top of the
bank.

Q. — How wide is the stream? A. — Perhaps, on an average,
fifteen or twenty feet through the reservoir : I am speaking of this
country now just through the reservoir. Above, it is not very much
different.: the stream does not seem to be much wider after Vine
Brook enters it than before.

Q. — Do you think that would be a fit place for the storage of
water for domestic uses? A. — I think the persons who put it there
would have to incur a great expense in taking out the trees that are
there. I don't know how badly it would affect the water if the stumps
were left in it. There would be a very large area of country that
would have to be stumped over : I cannot say how large. As it is, I
know the flat land runs back after it gets to the woods.

Q. (By Mr. Smith.) — What is your employment? A. — I am a
lawyer in Boston ; but I live in Lexington, and was brought up in
that region.

Q. — Can you make any rough estimate of what it would cost to
take out and cart off that muck and mud? A. — No, sir : I don't
know any thing about that. I can only tell what I have observed along
there. I have always been in the habit of going up and down the
river, especially as a young fellow.

Cross-Examination.

Q. (By Mr. Hammond.) Mr. Reed, you are a lawyer? A. —
Yes, sir.

Q. — You have caught trout on that stream? A. — I have : yes,
sir, — a good many.

Q. — The water appears to be pretty good for that sort of fish to be
in? A. — It is very good water. The upper branches of the Shawshine are very pure water, except Vine Brook : that is not.

Q. — Suppose you wanted to know whether it is practicable to
build a reservoir there in the manner contemplated by the city of
Cambridge, would you rely upon your own judgment as a lawyer,
aided by what you have observed when catching trout on that stream,
or would you rely upon the surveys of an engineer, and his opinion
in regard to the matter? A. — Certainly not. I am merely giving
you what I know about the character of the river.

Q. — I suppose you would not say that the taking out of the mud
would hurt the water any? A. — I would not.

Q. — As to the expense or the practicability of taking out the mud,
I suppose, as a lawyer, you know nothing? A. — I know nothing
whatever.

TESTIMONY OF NATHANIEL H. CRAFTS.

Q. (By Mr. BULLARD.) — You reside in Boston? *A.* — Yes, sir.

Q. — What is your occupation? *A.* — Civil engineer.

Q. — How long have you been a civil engineer? *A.* — Since 1850.

Q. — Were you at one time the engineer of the city of Boston? *A.* — Yes, sir : for nine years, about.

Q. — Have you given special attention to the subject of water-supply? *A.* — I have.

Q. — During the time you were the engineer of the city and since? *A.* — Yes, sir.

Q. — Now, will you tell us what the resources of Boston are in the matter of water-supply; that is, how many gallons can she get, in your opinion, from the sources which have already been granted to her, by a proper development of those sources? *A.* — You mean to include the Mystic as well as the Sudbury and Cochituate?

Q. — Certainly, sir. *A.* — My recollection is, from the size of the basins and the average yield that may be expected from them when all the storage-basins are completed, that Boston ought to have, on both sides, somewhere about 60,000,000 gallons a day.

Q. (By the CHAIRMAN.) — That is, when all the reservoirs are completed? *A.* — Yes, sir : the Sudbury basin, together with the new basin that is now being built, I reckon as good, the driest year, for 40,000,000 gallons. That is a low estimate.

Q. — What is your estimate of the Mystic? *A.* — The Mystic has no large storage capacity. At the present time its capacity should be the same, according to its area, as the other basins. The area of the Mystic, I think, is about twenty-seven square miles.

Q. — Properly developed, it would yield about 17,000,000 gallons a day? *A.* — Yes, sir.

Q. — And then the Cochituate, is that usually reckoned at about 18,000,000? *A.* — It is put down at 12,000,000 in dry weather ; but it has been found good for 16,000,000 or 18,000,000. Those figures are given for a dry year.

Q. — Allowing 40,000,000 for the Sudbury, 17,000,000 for the Mystic, and only 12,000,000 for the Cochituate, would make a supply of 69,000,000? *A.* — Then it was 70,000,000.

Q. (By the CHAIRMAN.) — We may change the 60,000,000 to 70,000,000? *A.* — Yes, sir.

Q. — The present population of Boston is estimated at 360,000, is it not? *A.* — 362,000, I believe.

Q. — That includes a part of the Mystic district? *A.* — That includes Charlestown.

Q. — In your judgment, what is a proper water-supply for a city for all purposes? *A.* — My judgment is, from forty-five to fifty gallons.

Q. — Per head, each day? *A.* — Yes, sir.

Q. — Is there any reason why the Mystic system should be considered as a separate system entirely from the Cochituate and Sudbury system? *A.* — None at all, that I see. That is, I presume you mean, is there any reason why the population now supplied by the Mystic cannot be supplied from the other side as well?

Q. — I mean this: there has been an effort made here to make it appear, that, if any thing happens to the Mystic as a source of supply, a new source must be found; for instance, from the Shawshine. My question is, whether there is any reason why the Mystic, the Sudbury, and the Cochituate should not be united, so that there should be one system for the entire city? *A.* — There is no difficulty in the way: it would be merely a matter of the expense of making the connection.

Q. — Has that subject been considered by the officials of Boston, to your knowledge? *A.* — It has been considered so far as to secure an Act of the Legislature authorizing such connection to be made.

Q. — Do you remember what estimate Mr. Davis made as to the expense of that connection? *A.* — I think it was $340,000 for a pipe large enough to supply the city of Cambridge. I have forgotten what the size of the pipe was now.

Q. — That, of course, would be somewhat lessened by the fact that there is a sixteen-inch pipe now which connects with Cambridge, to furnish part of their supply? *A.* — Yes, sir.

Q. — The $340,000 was for pipe that would be employed to connect the two systems, and also be employed to furnish the city of Cambridge with a sufficient supply of water? *A.* — So it was understood.

Q. — In your judgment, is there any reason why Boston should not undertake to indefinitely supply the city of Cambridge with water? *A.* — I see none.

Q. — How much water would flow through the sixteen-inch pipe which is now connected with the Cambridge system, leaving it connected in the manner in which it now is? *A.* — That depends upon how the water is delivered. That pipe connects with the Cambridge distribution. Under the ordinary flow of water in pipes, it ought to be good for 2,000,000 gallons in twenty-four hours.

Q. — Do you understand that that is a sixteen-inch pipe? *A.* — I understood the pipe that crosses the bridge to be a sixteen-inch pipe.

Mr. HAMMOND. It connects with a twelve-inch pipe on the Boston side.

WITNESS. That makes a difference, of course. A twelve-inch pipe is good for about 1,000,000 gallons a day.

Q. — How near the twelve-inch pipe in Boston, with which it is now connected, is there a larger pipe? *A.* — I cannot tell you. The large pipe, the new main, is laid in Beacon Street. This twelve-inch pipe, I take it, is a branch from that, running over as far as the bridge. I don't know what the distance is : probably it may be half a mile.

Q. — Suppose that pipe, Mr. Crafts, were emptied into Fresh Pond, instead of connected with the Cambridge system ; that is, suppose that all the water which could run through it to the level of Fresh Pond, which is practically the level of the sea, as I understand it, were allowed to run through, — what would the supply be ; that is, approximately? *A.* — That would be about double. It would be increased by the increased pressure, being delivered at a lower level. In the one case, the water would be delivered with a head of thirty feet ; and, in the other case, with a head of one hundred and twenty feet. Those differences would just about double the supply. That is, if it was a sixteen-inch pipe, it would deliver, under one hundred and twenty feet head, about 4,000,000 gallons in twenty-four hours.

Q. — Have you made any figures showing what the water-shed of the Shawshine basin, as proposed by Cambridge, would yield on the basis of Mr. Wightman's estimate of ten and one-half inches of rainfall during the year? *A.* — Yes, sir : the basin is estimated as furnishing about 20,000,000 gallons a day ; but, if that were based upon a rainfall of twelve inches, the yield from that basin would be 19,482.000 gallons per day. If the rainfall were reduced to ten and one-half inches, the amount would be 17,047,000. Then, if 1,500,000 gallons a day were allowed to flow down the stream, as was proposed last year, it would leave the net capacity of the basin in a dry year 15,500,000. In that case, if Cambridge took 8,000,000, there would be 7,500,000 left for Boston.

Q. — Could you give us some idea of the size of a stream, running as it would naturally run in the Shawshine River, of 10,000,000 gallons a day? *A.* — That would have to be based upon a variety of assumptions.

Q. — Well, assume that it were running through Mr. Bradlee's flumes, which I believe are about fifteen feet wide altogether, how great a depth would there be? *A.* — I think perhaps a fairer way to consider that would be to consider it as an open canal, or raceway, and to assume a velocity of flow which is common in rivers of that kind, which would be a surface velocity of two feet a second. Under those conditions, if the water were running five or six inches deep, the channel would have to be fifteen feet five inches wide. That would be the size of a stream flowing 10,000,000 gallons a day, supposing the velocity of it to be two feet per second. Of course, if the depth were increased to one foot, the width would be decreased to

7.71. I think it is fair, however, to say, that the natural flow of the stream would not correspond with that condition, owing to the fact of the frequency of dams on the stream. The fact that the whole stream is a series of mill-ponds makes the flow, of course, very unequal. Sometimes it is large, and sometimes it amounts to nothing. The water is comparatively still; but I could see no other way to give the Committee or the gentlemen an idea of what the volume of water would be, than to assume a canal of a certain size, a certain depth of water, and a certain velocity of run.

Q. (By Mr. SMITH.) — Do you make any allowance, Mr. Crafts, for the feeding of the stream, for the absorption of water by the banks of the stream, and for evaporation? A. — No, sir.

Q. — Would not that amount to considerable in warm weather? A. — The evaporation from water-surfaces? yes, sir.

Q. — Take the bed of a river where there has been but little water flowing in the spring, and the banks of a stream, as that stream flows along, does not the stream itself have to be fed, to some extent, by the water that flows through it? A. — It is always so, I believe.

Q. — The evaporation and feeding of the stream would detract, then, somewhat from your calculation? A. — I think that the feeding of the stream would exceed the evaporation; and, taking the two things together, they would verify the statement.

Q. (By Mr. BULLARD.) — Would the storing of this body of water in such a reservoir tend to make the quality of the water better or worse? A. — It would probably tend to the discoloration of the water for a time, — to a loss in the purity of color. It depends upon how the basin is constructed, I suppose. If the dam were built so as simply to overflow the soil in its present condition, and much of that soil is peaty or boggy, and covered with leaves, the water would be discolored for a number of years.

Cross-Examination.

Q. (By Mr. HAMMOND.) — Have you looked into Mr. Barbour's plans on this matter at all? A. — I have examined this plan here. I have not seen all his plans.

Q. — Is there any thing impracticable about it, that you can see, considering it now simply as a water-supply for the city of Cambridge? A. — Oh, no.

Q. — Have you paid any attention to Mr. Barbour's estimates as to the cost of construction? A. — I have looked over his estimate on the dam. I think we agree very nearly upon that. The other parts of the work I have seen no details of whatever.

Q. — Well, from such parts of the plan as you have examined, would you, or not, have confidence in Mr. Barbour's judgment about the other parts? *A.* — I should, certainly; and the only point I have in my mind is as to the allowance that should be made for clearing the basin. To what extent that would be necessary I don't think that either of us know.

Q. — Would you suppose that a city about to erect a reservoir for the purpose of supplying water to its inhabitants to drink would erect one that would make the water any worse than it was before, if it could help it? *A.* — I should suppose not.

Q. — From your knowledge of that basin, is there any difficulty in storing water there for drinking purposes, as well as in any other basin that you would be likely to find? *A.* — I am not familiar with the basin at all.

Q. — The storing of water in basins is a common method of supplying cities, is it not? *A.* — I do not know why it should be any different from the other river-basins in Massachusetts.

Q. — Can you indicate to the Committee how fast two feet a second is by the movement of your hand? *A.* — I don't know that I could any better than you or any member of the Committee.

Q. — If 10,000,000 gallons of water should go by Mr. Bradlee's mill, it would make a stream fifteen and a half feet wide and six inches deep, running two feet a second? *A.* — Yes, sir.

Q. — That is a good deal more than goes by there now sometimes, isn't it? *A.* — I don't know: I never have made any gaugings there.

Q. — Do you know what the dry-weather flow of the Shawshine is? *A.* — I don't.

Q. — Have you any doubt, from such investigations as you have made, and from the information that you have, that it is frequently less than 10,000,000 gallons a day at Mr. Bradlee's mill, — that is, in dry times? *A.* — I can't say as to his mill. At the point where you propose to take the water, I should suppose, in an extremely dry time, it would be as low as five or six millions.

Q. — And, of course, in an ordinarily dry season, there would be many times when it would not be equal to 10,000,000 gallons there, would there not? *A.* — Very few, I think.

Q. — Now, between the point where we should let out the 10,000,000 gallons and Mr. Bradlee's mill, what is the distance? *A.* — I should think it was between four and five miles.

Mr. HAMMOND. Our engineer says, as the stream runs, it is six and a quarter miles.

WITNESS. I merely judge by the proportions [looking at the plan].

Q. — Now, between those two points, water comes into the Shawshine from the water-shed and small streams and ponds, I suppose? *A.* — Certainly.

Q. — And you say, that, in an extremely dry time, you have no doubt that there are days when no more than five or six million gallons go by the point where we propose to let out 10,000,000 gallons? *A.* — I say, in a very extremely dry year. Perhaps I ought to state that that is not based upon any observations in that valley.

Q. — But from your general knowledge? *A.* — From observations made in other river valleys as to the flow of water, and considering the extremely dry-weather flow.

Q. — You wrote this pamphlet for the town of Watertown that I hold in my hand, did you not? *A.* — Yes, sir.

Q. — And you have actually devoted a good deal of time to the consideration of this question in this vicinity, have you not, as a practical engineer, for the purpose of telling people what to do? *A.* — Yes, sir.

Mr. HAMMOND. This pamphlet was written in 1874; and I desire to call the attention of the Committee to the remarkable accuracy of Mr. Crafts's estimate about the supply that would be needed in Cambridge.

Q. — In 1874 you estimated that in 1880 Cambridge would have 51,514 inhabitants, as I see by this table. The census shows that that estimate is within two or three hundred of the actual number of inhabitants. You made an estimate that Cambridge, at fifty gallons a head, would require 2,575,000 gallons of water a day? *A.* — Yes, sir.

Mr. HAMMOND. That is almost exactly our consumption for 1881. It is remarkably near. Now, the table goes on and gives the estimated quantity which Cambridge will require up as far as 1925 at fifty gallons a day per head, and at sixty gallons a day per head. Of course the estimated part of it is simply the population: the rest is a mere matter of multiplication.

Q. — Have you had any reason to change your views as to that table since 1874, when you prepared it? *A.* — You mean, in regard to the estimate of population?

Q. — In regard to what Cambridge would require for water-supply, if we are going to have new railroads, and all that. *A.* — No, I have had no occasion to change it.

Mr. HAMMOND. In the year 1890, which is only eight years from now, Mr. Chairman, this estimate calls for 3,848,000 gallons per day for Cambridge, at fifty gallons a head. This table is contained on the twenty-ninth page of Mr. Crafts's report to the committee appointed by the town of Watertown on the subject of water-supply and drainage, and I should like to say that I will allude to that table in the argument. I do not care to put it in, because it is simply a matter of figures.

Q. — Do you think it is safe for a city situated as Cambridge is to rely upon a supply of less than fifty gallons per head a day? What I mean to ask you is this: if it was your duty to look for a water-supply for Cambridge, would you deem it safe to rely upon a source which would yield less than fifty gallons per head a day? *A.* — No, sir.

Q. — I suppose, practically, it would be one of those questions where you would hardly think it safe to rely upon less than sixty gallons, would you? *A.* — I think it is best to be on the safe side. In seeking for a source of supply, I think it is very undesirable to have a source which is just equivalent to the requirements: it is better to have a large surplus.,

Q. — That is not practically the way that such questions are considered by municipalities, is it? *A.* — No, sir.

Q. — As I understand you, you see no practical difficulties here in allowing 10,000,000 gallons to flow from that reservoir every day under the plan of Cambridge? *A.* — No.

Q. — Is it not frequently the case that dams are constructed upon streams by mill-owners themselves, for the purpose of equalizing the flow? *A.* — I presume it is.

Q. — Don't you know, as an engineer, that it is, and haven't you ever had occasion to do it? *A.* — Yes, sir, it is. I never have had occasion to do it.

Q. — Can you tell us the amount of available water-power there is on that stream for those four villages? *A.* — I have never made any estimates. I don't know what the fall is.

Q. — Have you been down there to look at it enough so that you could give a sort of rough estimate? *A.* — I haven't made an estimate that I should have any confidence in as to the water-power.

Q. — I suppose there are mills in Lowell where they have fifteen hundred horse-power, are there not? *A.* — Yes, sir.

Mr. HAMMOND. I don't know but my friends on the other side will concede that the water-power probably does not exceed five hundred horse-power in those four villages. I think that was about the substance of the testimony last year. At least, I made that statement in my argument, and I know I never make any statement in argument, especially when the evidence is before those to whom I am talking, which would not be sustained by the evidence. I have not examined that evidence, though, recently. I will ask my friends if they know what the water-power is?

Mr. MORSE. I do not.

Mr. HAMMOND. Do you, Mr. Poor?

Mr. POOR. I do not.

Q. — Do you know, Mr. Crafts, anybody who does know what the water-power is on this stream? *A.* — I do not.

Q. — What is one horse-power? How do engineers describe it? *A.* — Why, it is a power that is sufficient to raise 33,000 pounds one foot high in one minute.

Q. — You were asked about the discoloration of the water by storage. You have no reason to believe, I suppose, that the storage of that water would make it less clear than it is now, — I mean, if the basin is properly prepared? *A.* — If the basin is properly prepared, — no, sir. If it is merely flowed, as they do in building reservoirs for mill purposes, I think the water would be discolored.

Q. — But any such measures as you would recommend, as an engineer, to be taken in building a reservoir for water to be used for drinking purposes, would not be likely to make the water any less pure than it is now? *A.* — No, sir.

Q. (By Mr. MORSE.) — Would you recommend the city of Cambridge to-day to build this basin, and carry out the plans necessary to connect that river with Fresh Pond, and then permit 10,000,000 gallons a day to flow down from that? Do you think it would be a wise way to provide water for Cambridge, — I mean, wise from an economical point of view? *A.* — I don't know that I understand your question.

Q. — Well, I mean, taking all the conditions that you understand to exist to-day, — taking the need of Cambridge for an additional water-supply; taking the opportunity, such as you understand it to be, for Cambridge to get water from Boston; and then taking the fact that they can, if they get this bill, build the dam that is proposed by Mr. Barbour, and then, having built it, they are to guarantee that 10,000,000 gallons shall run down from it, and they are to have the benefit of the balance, — I want to know whether or not you would recommend it to the city of Cambridge to-day as a wise expenditure, taking every thing you have heard into account? *A.* — Looking at it in this way, I should think, if the city of Cambridge could secure a supply of 8,000,000 gallons a day of good, pure water, at an expense of $700,000, it would be a good investment: it would be a desirable thing.

Q. — You do not understand that $700,000 covers the entire expense, do you? *A.* — That has been reported.

Q. — That is the engineering expense, as I understand: it makes no allowance for mill damages, or any other damages that may be claimed. *A.* — I do not understand that the letting down of 10,000,000 gallons has any thing to do with the estimate of cost.

Q. — No. I understand Mr. Barbour to say that he assumes that it would cost $700,000 to do the necessary work upon the land, build the dam, and lay the pipes to connect the reservoir with Fresh Pond. *A.* — Yes.

Q. — And that does not include any allowance for damages to be paid the mill-owners, or anybody else who is affected? *A.* — I understand that to be so.

Q. — Now, taking into account that uncertain element, which must be some amount, and may be a very large amount, — taking that into consideration, and considering the opportunity, which you understand exists, for making an arrangement with the city of Boston for water, would you advise the city of Cambridge to enter upon this plan of taking the Shawshine? *A.* — I have the same views which I had last year upon that point, — that, in my judgment, it is for the best interest of the city of Cambridge to take her supply of water from Boston.

Q. — Then, of the two plans, supposing that either was feasible, looking at the question, and taking every thing into account, you would recommend taking water from Boston rather than from the Shawshine? *A.* — Yes, sir.

Q. — Have you any doubt that water could be obtained cheaper from Boston than it could be by this plan from the Shawshine? *A.* — It depends entirely upon what sort of a contract could be made. Equitably, I think they could be furnished cheaper by the city of Boston than they can get it from the Shawshine.

Q. — That is what I mean. I mean, assuming that the city of Boston will sell water at what would be a fair rate, taking into account the actual expense? *A.* — I think a rate could be adjusted that would be equitable to both parties, that would be a benefit to Boston, and cheaper for Cambridge ; but that would be entirely different from the contracts which Boston already has in existence with other places.

Mr. BAILEY. Which Boston did not make.

Q. — Let me suggest this to you : Supposing both cities desired to deal with the matter fairly, as I have no doubt they would, but should not be able to agree upon the terms, have you any doubt that competent men could be found who would be able to arbitrate upon that question, and fix some rate which it would be advisable for Cambridge to pay, rather than to take water from the Shawshine? *A.* — I have no doubt of it.

Q. (By Mr. BAILEY.) — In the estimate which you gave of the cost of the connection between the Sudbury and the Mystic systems, you took, as I understand, the estimates of Mr. Davis? *A.* — Yes, sir.

Q. — You have not considered, have you, the increased cost of iron and labor, at the present time, over what it was then? *A.* — No, sir : I did not give that estimate as the present cost.

Q. — You do not see any reason to differ from Mr. Wightman when he says that the cost at the present time would be about half a million? *A.* — I think the difference in the price of iron at the present time amounts to something like thirteen dollars a ton, — about thirty-three per cent. more than at that time.

Q. — About a third more than it was then? *A.* — Yes, sir.

Q. — Then you do not see any reason to differ from Mr. Wightman as to the cost at the present time? *A.* — I thought it was a large estimate when he made it at the time ; but I have not gone into any figures. Probably it would be between four and five hundred thousand dollars.

Q. — You base your estimates of the water-shed, or of the storage capacity of the Sudbury system, the Mystic system, and the Shawshine system, upon the surveys made by the Boston Water Department, I suppose? *A.* — Certainly.

Q. — And, as I understand, you differ from Mr. Wightman's estimate in this way, — you make the storage capacity of the Sudbury and the Mystic more than Mr. Wightman does, and the storage capacity of the Shawshine less, basing them both on the same surveys, do you not? *A.* — No, sir : I merely give the statement of the Shawshine on Mr. Wightman's last figures, based on the dry year of 1880. The other estimates are estimates which are considered safe for an ordinary dry year.

Q. — So that you and Mr. Wightman both start with the same figures, on the same basis, in making your estimates, do you not? *A.* — Yes, sir.

Q. — And in one case, in the case of the Sudbury and the Mystic, you make the storage capacity more than he does, and in the case of the Shawshine you make it less than he does, do you not? *A.* — I have not compared my figures with his. I gave them just as I have them here.

Q. — You give the Sudbury as 69,000,000, and he makes it 64,000,000 or 66,000,000? *A.* — Yes, sir.

Q. — You make the Shawshine 15,000,000, and he makes it 20,000,000? *A.* — Yes, sir.

Q. — Now, sir, whether, in your judgment, it would be more economical, and a better business arrangement, for Cambridge and Boston both to take that river, than it would be for Cambridge alone to take what she asks for? *A.* — No, sir : I don't think it would.

Q. — Well, sir, will you give your reasons why you do not? *A.* — I do not think it is policy for either of them to take it.

Q. — I am not putting that question : I am supposing that either of them is to take it. If the river is to be taken at all, would it not be better for the two cities to take the whole, and pay for it on the basis of three-fifths for Boston, and two-fifths for Cambridge, than it would be for either of them alone to take part of it? *A.* — It may be better, as a matter of dollars and cents, as between the two parties.

Q. — Is it not better, then, that the two cities should take it together, in that proportion, than that Cambridge should take it alone, as she asks to do by this bill? *A.* — Of course it is.

Q. (By Dr. HODGKINS.) — Have you made any estimate about the cost of excavating the basin of this reservoir? *A.* — No, sir: I have no means of knowing how much should be excavated.

Q. — It is reported here that the mud is from one to five feet deep over a large part of this surface. That would all have to be removed, or ought to be, ought it not? *A.* — I should say that all the peat would need to be removed. Generally, in such basins as that, all the cleaning up that is done is cutting down the trees and bushes, taking out the stumps, and removing all the objectionable soil and vegetable matter. Clean earth or loam is not objectionable.

Q. — You would take off all the turf? *A.* — Yes, sir.

Q. — Over that whole 800 acres, that would be quite an expensive piece of business, wouldn't it? *A.* — Yes, sir, it would.

Q. — Have you made any estimate of the cost? *A.* — No, sir.

Q. — Could you give any idea of what the cost would be of removing the turf and stumps from such a surface as that? *A.* — I should not want to give an estimate on that.

Q. — Well, can you give us simply an approximation? *A.* — I think it might cost $150,000 to $200,000.

Q. (By Dr. INGALLS.) — What is it worth a foot to remove such material? *A.* — That depends upon circumstances. I should say twenty-five cents, perhaps less, if there is a favorable place for depositing it. In some instances, this material is of value. I know, when we built the Chestnut-hill Reservoir, we took the soil off to the depth of five feet out of the small basin. A large part of that was carried off by farmers, who came there during the winter with their teams, and took it off for their own use in compost-heaps.

Q. (By Mr. HAMMOND.) — I understood you to say that you thought if Boston would sell Cambridge water upon an equitable basis, it would be cheaper for Cambridge to pay Boston than to go to the Shawshine? *A.* — Yes, sir.

Q. — Suppose Boston will not do that, what could Cambridge do? *A.* — They must get a supply somewhere.

Q. — Well, where? *A.* — The Shawshine is one very good source.

Q. — Would you recommend the city of Cambridge to go there? *A.* — Not without further examination; not without looking at some other sources, perhaps.

Q. — But, as at present advised, the Shawshine is as proper and practicable a place as any, is it not? *A.* — So far as the quality of the water is concerned, and the quantity.

Q. — You also stated that you thought the contracts which Boston made with other cities were not equitable, as I understood you? *A.* — I think they are not equitable.

Q. — Now, suppose you were looking out for a water-supply for Cambridge, and suppose you were aware of the fact that the authorities of Boston had a notion that their water was a little short, and from what knowledge you have of them generally, would you advise the city of Cambridge to rely for a water-supply on a contract that she could make with Boston, or would you advise her to go on her own hook? *A.* — I think she could make an arrangement with Boston that would be reasonable and just to both parties, and to the advantage of both parties.

Q. — Well, suppose she thinks she cannot? *A.* — I think I have answered that question before. If she cannot, she must go somewhere else.

Mr. MORSE. Not if she *thinks* she cannot.

Q. (By Mr. BAILEY.) — What are these contracts that Boston has made with other parties that are not equitable? *A.* — I think they are inequitable as to the amount which the parties pay.

Q. — With what cities has she made contracts? *A.* — Chelsea, for instance. I speak of the Mystic contracts.

Q. — I want to know what contracts Boston has made with other parties that you do not consider equitable. You give Boston the name of being inequitable in regard to contracts for supplying water to other places. I want to know what you base your opinion upon. *A.* — I know of no contracts which the city of Boston has made. I merely refer to the contracts which the city of Boston inherited.

Q. — Then you have no reason to judge that Boston is not ready to make an equitable contract with the city of Cambridge? *A.* — I have no reason to think so.

Q. — Don't you know that Boston has tried to have those contracts modified, and the other parties would not agree to it? *A.* — I never heard of that.

Q. — Now, do you know this : that during the dry season of last year, or the year before last, when there was such a terrible want of water, the city of Boston supplied the Jamaica Pond Aqueduct Corporation on terms that were perfectly satisfactory to them and to the people there? *A.* — I heard so.

Q. — There was never any complaint from anybody about that, was there? *A.* — I have had no occasion to hear of any.

Q. (By Mr. HAMMOND.) — Is not the president of the Aqueduct Company one of the Water Commissioners of Boston? *A.* — No, sir.

Q. — Well, one of the leading officers there? *A.* — I believe one of the Water Board is interested in some way in Jamaica Pond.

Q. (By Mr. BAILEY.) — Will you tell us how? You say you *believe* he is.

Mr. MORSE. I know, I regret to state, that one of the members of the Water Board is a large stockholder in the Jamaica Pond Corporation.

Q. — Was not this contract with the Jamaica Pond Aqueduct Company made with the approval of the city government of the city of Boston? *A.* — Yes, sir.

Mr. HAMMOND. On the recommendation of the Water Commissioners.

Mr. MORSE. I want to explain what I said. I agree with brother Bailey entirely in believing that the city of Boston would make an equitable contract with the city of Cambridge or anybody else ; but I also wish to say, in reference to this action towards the Jamaica Pond Aqueduct Company, that I do not understand that it was under any vote of the City Council, but was a private arrangement between the Water Board and that company, and that one of the members of the Board is a large stockholder in that company.

The CHAIRMAN. With the approval of the committee to whom the city government delegated its power beforehand?

Mr. BAILEY. Yes, sir.

Mr. MORSE. I presume so. I do not want to make any imputation that it was not authorized.

Mr. BAILEY. That is the only contract that the city of Boston has ever made with any outside parties to supply them with water.

TESTIMONY OF GEORGE H. TORR.

Q. (By Mr. MORSE.) — You are the treasurer of the Smith & Dove Manufacturing Company? *A.* — I am.

Q. — Which has two mills upon the Shawshine River? *A.* — Four mills : two mill-privileges.

Q. — They have two villages there? *A.* — Yes, sir.

Q: — The business of that company is flax-spinning? *A.* — Yes, sir.

Q. — It is a very old establishment, is it not? *A.* — Yes, sir : they have been spinning flax there since 1835 ; and the same parties have carried on the manufacture of machinery since 1824.

Q. — You testified last year that you required three or four million gallons of water a day for bleaching purposes? *A.* — I testified that we were using two millions a day at Frye Village.

Q. — My question was, as I have it here in the report, " Then you would need at least four million gallons a day at those two places for bleaching purposes alone?'' and your reply was, '' Yes, sir.'' *A.* — I do not claim that we need more than two millions for bleaching purposes at Frye Village. We are not bleaching at the other village.

Q. — The special question that I want to ask you is this : you have heard the statement here of the proposition of the city of Cambridge to let 10,000,000 gallons a day run over the dam. I want to know what your judgment is as to the amount of that water that you would get at your mills? *A.* — I am not able to say in regard to that. I think that a great proportion of it would be soaked away and evaporated in dry weather.

Q. — Would you get at your mills any thing like 10,000,000 gallons a day? *A.* — I have no idea that we would.

Q. — How, in your opinion, would 10,000,000 gallons a day compare with the dry-weather flow of that stream? *A.* — I don't think it is any larger, except in extraordinary cases. I understand that Mr. Hammond claims that this reservoir is going to be a great benefit to Andover, because it is going to insure that the river shall never flow less than 10,000,000 gallons a day at that dam ; but I think the benefit will be very small, because it is very seldom it falls below that, — only in extraordinary years.

Q. — What do you estimate to be the ordinary dry-weather flow of that stream? *A.* — I never had it measured : I don't know. This opinion that I have in regard to it, I have made up from the figures given to the Committee by Mr. Carter and Mr. Barbour.

Q. — Have you made some figures from what has been stated here to this Committee? *A.* — Yes, sir. I will say that Mr. Carter stated in his evidence before the Committee last year, that the year 1880 was an extraordinary year ; that their pond went lower then than ever before. He also said that the rainfall of that year was 33.31 inches, and that the average rainfall is 48 inches, — that is, the average rainfall is 44 per cent. larger than the rainfall of 1880. Now, I understand Mr. Barbour to say in his testimony this year, that the lowest measurement he found at any time in 1880 at the place of their proposed dam was 8,000,000 gallons. Now, add 44 per cent. to that, and you get 11,500,000 as the extreme lowest point in an average year. Mr. Barbour also says in his testimony last year that he found the flow in July to be from 10,000,000 to 12,000,000. That was an extremely dry year. Add 44 per cent. to that, which I think is a proper allowance to make for an extraordinary season, to bring it up to an average season, and it would give a flow at the corresponding season, in an average year, of from 14,400,000, I think it is, up to 17,000,000, at that season of the year.

Q. — In other words, you would assume that the dry-weather flow there exceeds rather than falls below the amount of 10,000,000 that they propose to let flow down the river? *A.* — I would, except in an extreme year, which would come once in twenty or thirty years. That is, if it fell below 10,000,000 in an ordinary year, it would be only for a very short time.

Q. (By the CHAIRMAN.) — Do you remember what time that measurement was made in 1880? *A.* — I think it was in June. That was the lowest he found during the year, and he made measurements every month. For these reasons, I think that the guaranty of 10,000,000 gallons a day is not worth any thing to Andover practically, — that we should have so little use for it, that practically it would not amount to any thing.

Cross-Examination.

Q. (By Mr. HAMMOND.) — Mr. Torr, as I understand your figuring, you have found the lowest flow that Mr. Barbour reports, and then you have made a sum in what we boys used to call the Rule of Three, — as the whole rainfall for that year is to the average rainfall, so was that measurement on that day in July to the same day in July of an average year? That is about the principle you have gone on, isn't it? *A.* — I assume that the flow of the river depends entirely upon the rainfall; that, if there was no rainfall, there would be no river there. When there is a heavy rainfall, there is a large river. Therefore I infer that the proper way to bring that up to an average year would be to add the percentage of rainfall on an average year to the percentage of that year. It would have a direct effect upon the river, of course. In that way I undertake to bring the river to the average flow in an average year.

Q. — All that rainfall might have been early that year? *A.* — Neither Mr. Carter nor Mr. Barbour states that. We have only the figures of that year.

Q. — You have used some of this water for bleaching purposes? *A.* — We have : yes.

Q. — Will you state the size of the basin in which you bleach? *A.* — We bleach in tubs. The washing is what we use water for mostly, washing the chemicals out.

Q. — You wash where? *A.* — In running water, in a trough.

Q. — How does the water get into the trough? *A.* — It goes through an aperture in the bulkhead of the mill.

Q. — How large? *A.* — I never have measured that; but I think it is about a foot square, and some foot and a half or so below the head. We also have a pipe, a three or four inch pipe, with a head of some four or five feet, if I remember correctly. I am not positive about these measurements, never having had my attention called particularly to them. Mr. Dove's testimony was given in that respect last year. I think Mr. Dove was in error in stating that the head was one foot. I think he told me afterwards that it was one foot to the top of the hole. The head would be an average to the middle of the hole.

Q. — How do you get at those 2,000,000 gallons a day that you say you use for bleaching purposes? *A.* — I get that from information that I picked up. about the works there. I never measured the hole myself.

Q. — How do you fix on 2 and six ciphers instead of any other number of ciphers? *A.* — Because I suppose that is about the number of gallons that run through that hole.

Q. — Can you tell me the precise calculation? *A.* — I can make a calculation based on the evidence given this year. They tell us that 10,000,000 gallons a day are equal to the flow over a dam a foot high and five feet wide. Cut off a section of that, of a foot, and you have a flow of 2,000,000 gallons, with no head except a six-inch head, — a flow of a foot deep over the top of the dam.

Q. — How much is your water-power? *A.* — I don't know. At our lower mills the fall is six feet; at the upper mills the fall is thirteen feet. The same water would give us double power at the upper mills.

Q. — Have you never made an estimate of your water-power? *A.* — I have not.

Q. — Have you put in steam? *A.* — We have put in steam to assist the water.

Q. — In both mills? *A.* — Yes, sir.

Q. — What horse-power have you by steam? *A.* — We have at the upper village about 150 horse-power.

Q. — Will that run the mill? *A.* — I think that has run the mill a short time ; but I am not sure that all the machinery was on.

Q. — You appear to have a mathematical turn of mind : can you tell me if you ever made up your own mind in any respect as to the amount of water-power you have there in those two mills? *A.* — No, sir, I have not. I never have had any occasion to figure it up. I am busy about other things.

Q. — Didn't you have occasion to figure it up when you put in steam? *A.* — That was put in before I went there.

Q. — How much have you used steam during the last year? *A.* — I am not able to say. In an extraordinary dry year we run steam nine months to assist the water. Sometimes we have run steam only one or two months. We run steam only a very few months last year.

Q. — Mr. Bradlee says he has run steam six months this last year :

do you think you have run it that length of time? *A.* — I don't know how much we have run it.

Q. — Can you give us any idea about it? *A.* — No, I cannot. I only know that we run it nine months once in an extraordinary year, and we have run it as low as three months.

Q. — Did I understand you to say that you use the water now for bleaching? *A.* — Not at Abbott Village. We use the water at Frye Village for bleaching.

Q. (By Mr. BAILEY.) — In ordinary dry seasons do you supplement the use of water with the steam-engine at all? *A.* — We supplement the water at Frye Village at nearly all times with the steam-engine, except in the spring, when the water is high. At Abbott Village we put on the engine so as to keep the water at the top of the dam.

Q. — Then, do I interpret the course of your answers correctly when I think that you regard diminishing the water of your stream to 10,000,000 gallons a day as substantially the same as taking the whole thing? *A.* — It would not be worth much. It would be reducing it below what it is now a great deal. Instead of its being, as Mr. Hammond claims, a benefit to the stream, I think, except in the driest seasons, it would reduce it more than it is now.

Q. (By Mr. HAMMOND.) — Do you know any other stream that has less water at its mouth than four or five miles up? *A.* — I suppose all streams have less water at their mouths, because it is continually evaporating.

Q. — Rivers grow smaller as they go towards the sea? *A.* — They would, if no springs came in.

Q. — Do you believe that there would be less water in the river at Frye Village than ten miles up the stream? *A.* — I believe, in a very dry season, when the banks of the river are partially exposed, the water would soak away in the banks of the river to a great extent.

Q. — Will you please answer my question, whether you think there would be any less water at Frye Village than there would be at that reservoir? *A.* — I will say this: that I think that giving 10,000,000 gallons in a little stream, and letting Capt. Bradlee wash in it, and Mr. Stevens wash in it, by the time we could use it, it wouldn't be worth much to us. It would be like a dirty tub of water.

Q. — Do you decline to answer my question? *A.* — I think the water would be smaller at Frye Village than above, because there are no small brooks coming in.

Q. — Your observation is, that the nearer you get to the mouth of a river, the less water there is? *A.* — Where there are no brooks coming in.

STATEMENT OF CHARLES H. CLARK.

I have a mill at Bedford, on the Shawshine, for grinding corn and sawing lumber, and a cider-mill ; and I would say that it is a farming section there where I am located, and the farmers feel, that, if that mill-privilege were destroyed, they would have to go a great distance to mill, and would have to pay more to get their work done, which, I think, is very true, — that they would have to do one or the other of those things. I believe that is all I have to say.

Q. (By Mr. Hammond.) — Is your mill included in the territory that it is proposed to take for a reservoir? A. — I don't know exactly : I should think not. A question might arise there, if I was allowed to run. There is considerable refuse matter that goes into the stream now.

Q. — From the cider-mill? A. — From the cider-mill and saw-mill, and my house and stable. The banks are quite steep, so that it has no chance to soak into the ground before it goes into the stream ; and, furthermore, in the course of the year, there are thousands of horses there, that are standing from one hour to two hours, and their droppings, of course, go directly into the stream.

Q. (By Dr. Hodgkins.) — The sawdust, of course, could be kept out? A. — It is mainly kept out; but still there is a great deal that works in. In the cider-mill, some years, there is a large amount of apple-pomace, which goes directly into the stream. I consider it a great convenience to dispose of it in that way.

Q. — Yes ; but you could keep it out, of course? A. — I could, by going to a large expense for carrying it away.

Q. — It is not worth any thing to put on land, I suppose? A. — No, sir.

TESTIMONY OF CHESTER W. KINGSLEY.

Q. (By Mr. Hammond.) — You are a member of the present Legislature? A. — Yes, sir.

Q. — And for many years were president of the Water Board in Cambridge? A. — Yes, sir.

Q. — And are now connected with it? A. — Yes, sir.

Q. — As such you have had occasion, I suppose, to observe the capacity of Fresh Pond, have you not? A. — Yes, sir.

Q. — Will you tell the Committee what you have observed in regard to that? A. — There have been various theories in regard to the capacity of Fresh Pond since the pond was bought by the city. I would say that I have been connected with the Water Board ever since the city owned the pond, which is now seventeen years. It was at first supposed that the pond was unlimited in its sources of supply ;

that it would be impossible for us to pump it down after we reached a certain point. But the experience of years has dispelled that idea. Another theory was, that there was an underground connection between Fresh Pond and Spy Pond and Little Pond. That was disproved by the fact that we could pump Fresh Pond down five or six feet without affecting the other ponds, showing conclusively that there was no such connection. In the extremely dry year, 1880, when we became so much alarmed, the capacity of our water-works was very thoroughly tested, and calculations were made, which are very brief; and perhaps I cannot put them before you any better than just to read the report that was made at the end of the year on this very point, — the capacity of Fresh Pond to supply water in a dry time, — and, as these calculations were made carefully, and by measurements, they are reliable, I think : —

		GALLONS.
Whole amount of water pumped during the year		886,898,400
Deduct amount pumped in March, 31 days	67,757,400	
Deduct amount pumped in April, 30 days	65,006,700	
Deduct amount pumped in May, 31 days	87,130,800	
Deduct gain in these months, 1¾ inches at 4,000,000 gallons per inch .	7,000,000	
		226,894,900

Showing the amount of water furnished by the conduit south of Wellington Brook, filter basin, and pond, in 274 days, to be		660,003,500
Deduct amount received from conduit south of Wellington Brook, 274 days, at 500,000 gallons per day, as ascertained by city engineer,	137,000,000	
Deduct amount received from the filter basin, 63 days, at 400,000 gallons per day, measured as above	25,200,000	
		162,200,000

And we have the amount of water furnished by the pond during the 274 days to be, 497,803,500
We have found that the level of the pond was reduced during the year 3.75 feet, or 45 inches. Deduct now 45 inches at 3,500,000 gallons per inch (the area of the pond being much reduced) 157,500,000
And we get at nearly the amount of water furnished by the pond from springs and ground-flow, being the unseen sources of supply of water to the pond . . . 340,303,500

This amount is equal to 1,241,984 gallons per day. We think this falling-off in the pond-supply is clearly accounted for by the falling-off in the rainfall the past two years.

The foregoing calculations take in the supply for the whole year, and show the pond capacity for 274 days. Some have entertained the idea, that, as we lowered the pond-level by pumping out of it, we should reach a point where the inflow would equal our wants, and the pond would go no lower. We wish now to present a statement which we think proves that, so far as we have gone, exactly the contrary of this is true, and that the lower we pump the pond, the more the supply to the pond from unseen sources diminishes.

	FEET.
We find that on the last of November the pond stood below high-water mark . .	8.33
On the last of August it stood at	6.79
Showing loss in the pond in three months to be	1.54
or about 18½ inches.	

GALLONS.

Whole amount of water pumped during the months of September, October, and November was 214,007,900
Deduct from this 30 days from conduit south of Wellington Brook at
500,000 gallons 15,000,000
Also 61 days' supply from the conduit including the filter basin at
900,000 gallons 54,900,000
Also deduct 18½ inches of water, being the loss in the pond-level at
3,500,000 gallons 64,750,000
—————— 134,650,000

And we have, as the amount furnished by the pond the last three months, only . 79,357,900

This is equal to 872,065 gallons daily, showing a significant falling off, which should command most careful consideration.

These calculations show, that as the pond was lowered, and as we pumped it down, the amount of water which came into it from unseen sources constantly decreased, and grew less and less, until, in the last three months of 1880, the supply was only 872,065 gallons a day, while our demand is 2,500,000 gallons a day.

Q. (By Mr. SMITH.) — From your knowledge of legislatures, city governments, and water-works, supposing Cambridge to take the Shawshine River at an expense of $700,000 or $1,000,000, under a bill agreeing to let Andover have 10,000,000 gallons a day, more or less, and then you should find that the amount you obtained, for some cause, either the giving out of your pond, as you seem to imply that it may ultimately give out, or the annexation of a neighboring city was not sufficient, and you should come to the Legislature and ask that you might have the other 10,000,000 gallons, in your judgment, would you get it? A. — I don't know exactly how I could answer that question. It involves a great many considerations that are problematical.

Q. — Do you think you would be likely to get it? A. — Generally, I should say this, that I think the Legislature of Massachusetts would grant any people, who were suffering for the want of water to drink, any water within their reach before it might be used for any other purpose.

Q. — That is, you would not think it probable that this guaranty in the bill would have any effect on the action of the Legislature under those circumstances? A. — I do not see how this bill can go any further than the provisions of this bill.

Q. — For this year, you mean? A. — I don't see how it can.

Q. — So that, in your judgment, Andover would be under a constant menace of losing the whole of this water, provided Cambridge gets a bill of the character which is here presented? A. — In my judgment, Andover would be a great deal better off if this right is given to Cambridge, than she is now; and she will be under no more menace with this bill than without it, because I have not any doubt

that the river will be granted if anybody wants it at some future time,
whether Cambridge gets it or not.

Q. — Do you think anybody would be as likely to want it, if they
had not spent $1,000,000, as if they had? *A.* — No, sir : that is the
reason I think Andover better let us have it.

Q. — Have the whole of it ultimately? *A.* — No, sir : I think the
bill will be a decided benefit to Andover, and to the individual mill-
owners.

Q. — That is, you mean if it could be fixed so that Andover should
perpetually have this 10,000,000 gallons daily, it would be better for
Andover? *A.* — I don't know how it can be fixed except by the
Legislature, and one Legislature cannot bind another ; and what the
next Legislature may do, I do not know.

Q. — That is all you mean, I take it. You don't mean that it
would be better for Andover to have you get 8,000,000 gallons now,
and then next year get 10,000,000, and the third year get 15,000,000,
and so on, until you get the whole? You don't mean that that would
be better for Andover? *A.* — If I understand Mr. Crafts's estimates,
— and I believe they are as reliable as any estimates can be, —
Cambridge will not need 15,000,000 gallons a day any time in this
century.

Q. — Unless your pond fails, or you annex territory? *A.* — I am
a great deal more afraid of being annexed, than I am of annexing
anybody, as far as Cambridge is concerned. That is so far off that I
do not take that into account.

Q. — You would not think it unwise for Andover to look a little
ahead? *A.* — No, sir : that is the reason why I think the interests of
Andover and Cambridge are identical. Perhaps the next party that
came along would not be satisfied with 8,000,000 gallons : they might
want 20,000,000.

Adjourned to Tuesday, March 28.

FIFTH HEARING.

Boston, March 28, 1882.

The hearing was resumed at ten o'clock.

Mr. Hammond. Before we proceed to the arguments, I think I ought to state, for the benefit of all concerned, that I had some desire to make this thirteenth section as plain and explicit as it can be, and I have thought it best to insert a new section, called "Sect. 13," in this language : —

"Sect. 13. The city of Cambridge shall cause a running stream of at least ten millions of gallons a day, for each and every day in the year, to flow in said river at the lowest dam which it may construct and maintain, in pursuance of this Act, so long as it shall draw water from said river under this Act. The Supreme Judicial Court, sitting in equity for either of the counties of Suffolk or Middlesex, shall have jurisdiction, on complaint of any person aggrieved by the failure of said city to observe the obligations of this section, to compel such observance by injunction or otherwise, and to give any other suitable equitable relief."

That section, in this language, is satisfactory, as I understand, to my brother upon the other side, so far as expressing the idea that we shall be liable for 10,000,000 gallons a day. Of course, the *idea* is not satisfactory to them ; but they make no objection to the language, as I understand it.

Then I propose to re-number sect. 13, and call it sect. 14.

"Sect. 14. Nothing contained in this Act shall be so construed as to prevent the inhabitants of the towns of Billerica, Wilmington, Burlington, Bedford, and Lexington from taking from said river, or its tributaries, so much of the water thereby granted as shall be necessary for extinguishing fires, and for all ordinary domestic household purposes, and for the generation of steam."

I may say that I have adopted the language of the counsel for the mill-owners, in draughting that section, in every other respect than this : I have not given to them an action of tort for damages against Cambridge in case she fails to carry out the provisions of the bill. I would agree to such a section at once, if the opposition of the mill-owners would be removed thereby : but I agree to give them a remedy in equity ; and, when the section concludes with " any other suitable equitable relief," we put ourselves in a court of equity in regard to this matter, and, if they think money is better than any thing else, they have a right to decree it. I only do this because I stated at the opening, that I would allow the other side to express that idea in their own language, and I have done so ; that is their language.

Mr. MORSE. Perhaps it would be best, as long as brother Hammond has suggested this change, to submit at this time to the Committee a section which I handed to him some time ago, as expressing what I thought would protect the mill-owners, if any bill was to be passed giving the city of Cambridge the right to take this water. I mean, protect the mill-owners, so far as, I assume, from the legislation of last year, the Committee would be disposed to protect them. The section which I hand to the Committee is as follows: —

"SECT. 13. Said city shall permit the inhabitants of the towns of Billerica, Wilmington, Burlington, Bedford, and Lexington to take from the Shawshine River so much of the water hereby granted as shall be necessary for extinguishing fires, for all ordinary domestic household purposes, and for the generation of steam. It shall also cause a running stream of at least ten million gallons a day, for each and every day in the year, to flow in said river at the lowest dam which it may construct and maintain, in pursuance of this Act. The Supreme Judicial Court, sitting in equity for either of the counties of Suffolk or Middlesex, shall have jurisdiction, on complaint of any person aggrieved by the failure of said city to observe the obligations of this section, to compel such observance by injunction or otherwise, and to give any other suitable equitable relief; or such aggrieved person may maintain an action of tort against said city for the recovery of his damages."

This differs from the section which brother Hammond read, in the fact that it leaves the provision in regard to the towns of Billerica, Wilmington, Burlington, Bedford, and Lexington in the thirteenth section, and further, it provides that any person who is injured by the failure of the city of Cambridge to send down the amount of water that is guaranteed here, 10,000,000 gallons a day, shall be entitled to bring an action of tort for damages. In other words, it provides a remedy in damages for a person who does not get the water that the city says shall come to him.

Mr. HAMMOND. I will ask you, if you don't think that a court of equity could, if it chose, give damages, if it thinks that the proper relief that the party should have?

Mr. MORSE. I think very likely it could; but I don't propose that the mill-owners shall be shut up to that form of action. I want to provide that they may be entitled to bring their action at law.

Mr. HAMMOND. Do you think they would be shut up to that form of action, brother Morse, anyway?

Mr. MORSE. No. I understand, that, if the city of Cambridge should get a bill embodying this section, the mill-owners would have the right to have their damages assessed, in the first instance, of course, by petition, which they would file in the ordinary way; but this bill is designed to give something beyond that, — a guaranty, that, if the water is taken, 10,000,000 gallons a day shall flow down. I wanted to make it perfectly clear that any person who failed to get his proper proportion of that water might maintain an action against the city for damages. I assumed, from what was said by brother Hammond in the opening of this case, that, in case the Committee should decide to grant a bill to the city of Cambridge, I might put into it a section drawn in the strictest way, guaranteeing the preservation of this right to the people below the reservoir. I do not advocate the bill, or consent to the bill, with this section. It is only that, if any bill must be reported, I contend that such a section as that is absolutely necessary.

CLOSING ARGUMENT OF JOHN R. BULLARD, ESQ., FOR THE REMONSTRANTS.

Mr. Chairman, and Gentlemen of the Committee, — I do not personally attach any importance to the discussion of a single section of this bill, because I do not entertain for a moment the thought that this Committee will report any bill, although I am aware that they, or another Committee, reported one in favor of Cambridge last year. But it seems to me that the facts which have been shown this year make a different case ; and I say, without hesitation, that I do not believe this Committee will report a bill in favor of either city.

The controversy to which you have listened all too patiently, is simply a contest between two cities for position. Andover and its mill-owners, with their valuable rights, — rights which have been vested and unselfishly enjoyed for generations, — are the victims. Neither city needs *this* water. One, at least, does not in sincerity ask for it ; and, if there were need, both could be better supplied elsewhere. Before you will advise the Legislature to exercise the extreme right of eminent domain, you will, I am sure, insist, as keepers of the legislative conscience, in this matter, upon being satisfied of two things : first, that there is a public exigency, — that is, a pressing need for legislative interference ; and, secondly, that the way proposed by the petitioners to meet that need, if not the only possible way, is at least the best, taken as a whole, and followed, so far as human foresight can follow it, to its ultimate results. The wishes of the petitioners are not to afford even a *prima facie* case. You have a duty of which they know nothing, and for which they care nothing : it is the duty of protecting property already acquired, and rights already vested.

As Engineer Wightman told us the other day, Boston is a large city, and Cambridge is a small city ; but if cities, large or small, come here without a just cause, they must go away empty-handed. Boston, gentlemen, is a large city, so large that a thousand years before Christ, King Solomon foresaw her condition when he said (as at least one of you will remember), "The horse-leech hath two daughters, crying continually, 'Give, give.' There be three things that are not satisfied, yea, four things that say not, 'It is enough;'" and among them he named "the earth that is not filled with water," evidently referring to the dry and thirsty soil of the tri-mountain city, which, although it has had poured upon it successively the waters of Jamaica Pond, Lake Cochituate, the Mystic, and the Sudbury, does not say, "It is enough," but still cries, "Give, give!"

Mr. BAILEY. Was that the time your mill-owners acquired their rights in the river?

Mr. BULLARD. Earlier than that, sir.

Now, gentlemen, the question arises, What is a proper water-supply for a city? and on that there is no great conflict of opinion. Everybody agrees that Boston is using at least twice her proper supply. I have here a table made up by Mr. Crafts showing the average supply of fourteen different cities; and among those cities are Philadelphia, St. Louis, Cleveland, Milwaukee, Fall River, and Providence. Cambridge is put down in it at fifty-five gallons per head, which is nearly ten gallons more than she is using to-day; and the average of that table shows forty-four gallons to be a fair supply. Mr. Davis, city registrar of Boston, says that forty gallons is a liberal supply; and, as you remember, it has been shown in evidence that some years ago the members of the Boston Water Board, by the careful use of meters upon their own houses for a year, found that they were using but twenty-five gallons for each member of their families a day. So it is not difficult to come to the conclusion that Boston is using largely in excess of her needs. She has to-day a supply of nearly a hundred gallons per day for each and every inhabitant. She has sources of supply granted to her by the Legislature which can be developed up to seventy millions of gallons a day, which, at forty-five gallons to each inhabitant, would be ample for a population of a million and a half. It is dangerous to grant cities an unlimited supply of water. Mr. Parry, in a little book published in England, puts it so forcibly that you will pardon me if I read his language : —

"The introduction of water from a new source yielding a supply by gravitation greatly beyond the immediate demand has in almost every instance led to carelessness on the part of water-works managers, and extravagance on the part of consumers. The delivery of the Loch Katrine water into Glasgow affords an example of this. The consumption in Glasgow rose to such an alarming extent soon after the Loch Katrine water was brought into the city that attempts were made to check the waste; but the prevailing feeling that there was a practically inexhaustible lake to draw upon prevented the enforcement of suitable regulations. The present consumption in Glasgow is at the rate of fifty gallons per head per day [which is there considered an enormous use].

"There have been similar experiences in many American cities. In New

York the engineer who designed the Croton aqueduct estimated the requirements for a liberal supply thirty years ago at twenty-five gallons per head. The actual consumption at present is about seventy-five gallons per head. That most of this is wasted, has been proved by observations on the discharge from the reservoirs at hours when very little water is being consumed for any useful purpose.

"The volume of water flowing into New York from the Croton aqueduct is enough to supply more than double the present population at the rate per head originally estimated; but the consumption which now obtains is so excessive that the aqueduct cannot convey sufficient water to satisfy it. New schemes for procuring additional supplies are now under consideration, and measures for suppressing waste are receiving serious attention.

"In Boston the consumption per head per day was twenty-three gallons in 1849, and fifty gallons in 1870. It has now risen to sixty-two. In 1873 the Boston water engineers made some observations to determine the rate of waste by measuring the water flowing out of the Beacon-hill Reservoir between midnight and three A.M. in a district containing about 60,000 inhabitants. At the beginning of the experiment 'the consumption was found to be somewhat irregular; but between one and three o'clock it was remarkably uniform, showing that the draught was not due to irregular opening and shutting of cocks, but to a continuous flow at almost unvarying outlets.' In other words, it was due to continuous waste. . . .

"That all American cities are not equally extravagant in the consumption of water is shown by the city of Providence, where, notwithstanding that waterworks have been constructed which are capable of supplying about five times the quantity now delivered, the total daily supply is only twenty-one gallons per inhabitant. This includes an unusually large supply per head to manufacturers; and water is said to be liberally used for all purposes.

"The consequences of neglect and wasteful habits are most seriously felt when available sources approach exhaustion, and the expenditure of a large amount for additional supplies has to be faced. By this time the number of defective appliances has become so great, and the interests by any proposal to condemn existing arrangements have become so numerous and powerful, that it is often found to be easier to obtain powers to carry out a scheme for a further supply, involving a large outlay, than it is to obtain and put into operation powers to interdict the use of wasteful fittings."

This, gentlemen, is exactly the position in which Boston finds herself to-day. She finds it easier to come here and ask for new supplies, easier to expend immense sums of money for them, than to do what it has been admitted here she could do, — stop her waste. The experiment of which Mr. Greenough spoke in Charlestown, by which consumption was reduced to thirty-five gallons per head, shows that Boston to-day has an ample supply of water for generations to come.

Mr. BAILEY. Did he say thirty-five gallons per head?

Mr. BULLARD. That is what I understood him to say.

Mr. BAILEY. He said they had saved 400,000 gallons a day: that is all.

Mr. BULLARD. If Boston should adopt the Deacon system, which is simply a system for the detection of waste, — by which the night inspector is enabled to report at the central office the exact location of a leak, and the day inspector can go and stop it, — it is perfectly manifest, that, without even going to the Charles River, the water of which can be conveyed to the city by conduits already made, and which, as Mr. Greenough testified, would furnish 50,000,000 gallons a day, and could be had at an expense of $2,000,000, — without going to that source, I say, which is at her very door, Boston has an ample supply for generations to come.

But, gentlemen, does Boston come here in good faith? If she asks in good faith for the Shawshine River, where are her Water Commissioners? *They* could not, perhaps, plead ignorance on questions affecting the water-supply of the city. Why is she represented here by her engineer, who is popularly supposed to be a man whose office it is to make under-estimates on public works, and to build monuments to his own greatness, but to know nothing especially as to the water-supply; and by the young chairman of the Committee on Water, who is certainly more frank and truthful in his statements than discreet? Gentlemen, the Water Board are not here, in the language of that remarkable report which they made to the confiding citizens of Boston after their rebuff of last year, " for reasons which it is not necessary to discuss here;" but their absence means something, just as the remonstrance at City Hall, signed by millions of property, protesting against a further expenditure of the public funds for new supplies, means something. It means, gentlemen, that Boston is here simply because Cambridge is here; and that is demonstrated by the communication of her mayor to the City Council, in which he asks that action be taken because Cambridge has petitioned for the Shawshine River; by the remarks of the chairman of the Water Committee in the Council, who plainly said, that, if Cambridge would let the Shawshine alone, Boston would also; and by the whole course of the evidence before you. Boston does not ask for the Shawshine River in good faith: she does not want it.

I understand that the present city solicitor admits before you that Boston does not want the Shawshine, except in the possible contingency of the abandonment of the Mystic supply. Is any one here so foolish as to believe that the Mystic supply will ever be abandoned? In the Council last August the present city solicitor said, " I believe that the Mystic water is as good to-day as the Cochituate is. It is as good water as I want to drink."

Mr. BAILEY. It is better now.

Mr. BULLARD. That was true then, it is true now, and it will always be true,· as this Committee knows. If it should be negligently allowed to be polluted so that it must be abandoned as a supply, the system is not necessarily a different system from the Cochituate and the Sudbury: it is simply to-day a different system, because it was constructed by a different city. Every argument is in favor of a union of those two systems; and whether Boston gets the Shawshine or not, whether the Mystic supply is abandoned or not, the Cochituate and the Mystic systems will one day be united.

Cambridge has a more meritorious case; but Cambridge's case is put here upon an exceptionally dry year, such a year as is given once only to a generation to see, — the year of 1880. By the adoption of the same means of preventing waste to which I have alluded in reference to Boston, Cambridge could easily reduce her consumption to a point at which her supply would be ample for years to come. Before she will be allowed to go twenty miles away, and interfere with and harass the owners of valuable rights already vested, she will be forced to use the water which is now at her very door. She must open the gate which she has placed to prevent its flowing into her mains. To-day Boston is able and willing to furnish her a supply. The pipe is laid through which she could easily throw into Fresh Pond 4,000.000 gallons each day, if Cambridge is willing to take the water, as she proposes to take it from the Shawshine, without head. If she prefers to have water with a head from Boston, she can have 2,000,000 gallons a day without difficulty. But, further than that, legislation has already been secured by which a main forty-eight inches in diameter is to run directly through Harvard Square.

Now, gentlemen, the answer to Cambridge's petition is too plain for argument or comment: she must get her water from Boston, not only in the interest of Andover, but for her own interest. The "burdensome" contracts now existing between Boston and neighboring cities have been alluded to here. Mr. Wightman promised to produce one of those contracts here; but, for some reason, it is not forthcoming. But I do not understand that these contracts necessarily put an expenditure of 85 per cent. of her gross receipts upon the city which takes water from Boston. On the other hand, I understand that they provide a sliding-scale, on which the rate is from 50 to 60 per cent. when the income of the purchasing city has reached $50,000; and, if that be so, Cambridge would have to pay but 50 per cent. of her receipts to Boston, even on the basis of these contracts. But, be that as it may, the contracts are repudiated by Boston. She did not make them. She professes to stand ready to-day to make a fair contract with Cambridge: I believe she is ready to do so. Of her ability to supply Cambridge with its comparatively small demand, there can be no question; and if Boston should refuse to make a fair price, on an application from Cambridge, — which has not been made since the last hearing, no communication having been had between Boston and Cambridge on the subject during the past year, — I say, if Boston should refuse, let Cambridge come before you, gentlemen, with a solicitor of only half the ability of my brother, with such a cause as that, and none of us can doubt what the result would be.

CLOSING ARGUMENT OF HON. R. M. MORSE, JUN.

MR. CHAIRMAN AND GENTLEMEN, — My first acquaintance with this subject was as counsel for the Smith & Dove Manufacturing Company, one of the large establishments interested in the use of the water of the Shawshine; but, since this hearing began, I have been asked, in connection with my brother Poor, to represent also the town and people of Andover in their objection to the passage of any bill such as is contemplated. I desire, therefore, to add, to what has been said in remonstrance against this petition, the expression of the views of both these parties.

It is clearly proved here that Cambridge needs some additional supply of water; for, even granting that a greater reduction can be made from the amount now consumed, it is undoubtedly true that the supply has been well and economically managed: and, taking into account the chances that are liable to occur, the dry seasons, and various emergencies, it is no more than the dictate of a proper prudence to make further provision for the future. I did not question that point last year, and I shall not do so now. On the contrary, I am entirely ready to concede the propriety of the action of that city in reference to the need of an additional water-supply. But I submit that it is also clearly proved that Boston has an adequate supply of water, not only for her present needs, but for those of a generation to come; not only for her own population, but for the population which is embraced within the district which, sooner or later, may become part of the city itself, — a district which includes Chelsea, Everett, and Somerville (at present supplied by it), and Cambridge also.

Last year the facts, as they were presented to the Committee, stood very differently from what they do now. The city of Boston had not then determined to build an additional basin upon the Sudbury, and the engineer and other officials of the city spoke with some hesitation as to the extent of their water-supply; but as the appropriation has been made for building this fourth basin, and the work has been begun, the engineer now comes here and speaks with entire confidence as to the amount of water the city is to have. I have some figures showing the capacity of the different basins, to which I ask the attention of the Committee. They are as follows: —

	GALLONS.
Reservoir No. 1 has a capacity of	288,400,000
Reservoir No. 2 " "	479,700,000
Reservoir No. 3 " "	1,074,200,000
Reservoir No. 4 " "	1,100,000,000
Lake Cochituate, above top of conduit	1,508,000,000

GALLONS.

Farm Pond	130,000,000
Chestnut-hill Reservoir	557,000,000
Mystic Lake	380,000,000
Making a total of	5,517,300,000

If the basins on the Sudbury and Cochituate alone should be filled, as I assume that they are filled, or will be filled in the spring, and no rain should fall thereafter, there is a quantity sufficient to furnish a daily supply, for one hundred days, of 52,000,000 gallons, which is at the rate of over sixty gallons per head for a population of 850,000. In addition to this is the supply from the reservoirs upon the Mystic. Mr. Wightman said that the capacity of those reservoirs was 7,000,000 gallons a day, but that there was a storage capacity on the river of 17,000,000 gallons daily. From the Cochituate and Sudbury the daily supply, when their reservoirs are completed, will be 52,000,000 gallons daily. That alone, at sixty gallons per head, is enough for a population of 850,000.

Further, there is an important fact as to the quantity of water that is wasted over the dams. My brother Bullard has called your attention to the fact that 1880 was an exceptionally dry year; yet in that year, according to the Report of the City Engineer of Boston, there were wasted over the dams of the Sudbury 11,290,000,000 gallons, — equal to a daily supply of 30,847,000 gallons for a year. During that year, by the same Report, the quantity of water that went to waste upon the Sudbury was twice as much as was actually used. That is the statement of the engineer, — *the quantity of water that went to waste upon the Sudbury was twice as much as was actually used.* Now, in the presence of such figures as these, it is perfectly evident that the supply from that river is practically without limit. It is also clear that the city of Cambridge may get what it wants from Boston, in one of two or three ways : it may take it through the pipe now laid ; or, as my brother Bullard has pointed out, from the main that it is proposed to lay through Harvard Square ; or by some temporary connection in the spring, by which the waste water from the Sudbury shall be used to fill up a reservoir, such as the city may perhaps construct to receive it.

Chap. 126 of the Acts of 1880 contains, in sect. 6, the following provision : —

" The city of Boston is also authorized, if the Boston Water Board shall be of opinion that the supply of water is sufficient for the purpose, to sell water to the city of Cambridge, when conducted through the main pipes laid by virtue of the provisions of sect. 2 of this Act, upon such terms as may be agreed upon by the City Council of the city of Cambridge and said Boston Water Board."

There is an ample supply of water for the population of Boston and of the places I have named for at least a generation to come. At the end of that time some further and larger supply must be looked for. undoubtedly, or probably; but, when that time comes, the need will be for something more than the Shawshine can satisfy. There is no difficulty to-day in making a fair arrangement between the city of Cambridge and the city of Boston. Every Boston official who has appeared at this hearing — the city solicitor, of course, will state it with much more authority than I — recognizes that that city is in a condition to supply Cambridge, and is willing to do so. The real trouble is. that the city of Cambridge has made no application for it. It is rather extraordinary that, with the needs that it is said that city has, and which I agree that she has, her Water Board, so efficient and attentive in every other direction, should have allowed a year to go by without communicating in some way, formally or informally, with the city authorities of Boston. They admit that the water is good enough for them; they admit that Boston can furnish it, provided only a reasonable charge is made, at a less price than it would cost them to go elsewhere and take a new supply. And yet it is a fact, that no communication of any kind has been had with the Boston Water Board or any Boston officials during the last year. It seems to me that. under these circumstances, with a supply right at their hand which is ample, which the parties who hold it are perfectly willing to dispose of at a reasonable price, before the city of Cambridge is authorized to do an act so serious in its consequences as the taking of the Shawshine, it should be told to make application to the city of Boston. I agree that if that application should be made, but met with a refusal, or with a proposal of terms that manifestly are unreasonable. a different case would be presented. But no harm can possibly be done by allowing the matter to rest another year, in order that that application may be made.

The question seems to me to be so entirely free from doubt, that it hardly seems necessary, as it was last year. to discuss at length the reasons why the Shawshine should not be touched, even if there were need for some special provision for Cambridge. Yet, as I cannot anticipate what may be urged in behalf of the city of Cambridge, and as possibly a different view may prevail in regard to the propriety of remitting Cambridge to a negotiation with Boston, I ask the attention of the Committee to the reasons why the Shawshine should not be taken, as contemplated by this bill, under any circumstances.

I may say, in the first place, that the bill has been put into a shape as plausible and tempting as any bill with such an object could probably be put. The amendment that was suggested in behalf of the mill-owners has not been adopted in terms; but I assume that it or its equivalent would be adopted in any bill authorizing Cambridge to take the river. At the same time I believe that a bill authorizing a part of a river to be taken must be treated as if it authorized the whole river to be taken, provided that the river is a small one; if its capacity, I mean, be limited. Of course, if you were dealing with the Charles or the Merrimack, it would be quite a different thing; but when you are disposing of a stream that is confessedly a small one, where the supply, never large, must vary considerably from year to year, you will see that you cannot grant any part of it without making it difficult, if not impossible, to refuse ultimately the appropriation of the whole. At a subsequent session Cambridge would very likely come in and say that upon careful investigation it was found that the yield of the river was not as great as was anticipated, or that the expense of taking the property and building the works was out of proportion to the amount of water that would be received, or that for some other reason it was necessary to amend the Act and increase the proportionate part of the river which the city might take. I do not propose to argue the question, therefore, as if the Shawshine were to be left a stream of running water: I do not believe that it will be so left. The entire river will ultimately be taken.

Looking at the matter in that view, the Committee will observe that the first — perhaps the Committee may think the least important — interests that are affected here are those of the manufacturers. But consider who these manufacturers are, and what they represent. They are not merely the aggregation of property that manufacturing establishments frequently are: they are the centres of a very wide and a very valuable influence, which has pervaded Andover and the community round about. It would be difficult to find in this Commonwealth a set of men who have done more for the right development of the best interests of her people than the manufacturers who have grown up by the banks of the Shawshine. You have at Ballardvale a community of six hundred inhabitants, all dependent upon the woollen-mills of Capt. Bradlee. You have, as the reports of the assessors show, forty-one of the operatives there owning, in their own right, some $27,300 worth of real estate, — an average of $666 to each. I mention that, not because the amount of property is large, but because it indicates the thrifty character of the people employed there. You have at Abbott Village, where one of the establishments of the Smith & Dove Company is, a community of four to five hundred inhabitants. At Marland Village, where Moses T. Stevens has a woollen-mill, there are four hundred inhabitants. At Frye Village, the place of the other manufacturing establishment of the Smith & Dove Company, there are several hundred inhabitants.

In the villages other than Ballardvale I find that there are forty-seven of the operatives who own $53.900 worth of real estate, an average of $1,147 each, — additional evidence of the character of the operatives.

Now, gentlemen, those manufacturing establishments are of very large and national reputation. They are not maintained at Andover because the water-power of the Shawshine is remarkable; for it appears here that the power at times is insufficient, and they have to supplement it with steam. But they were first established, and they are now maintained there, principally because the water being very pure is of special value for scouring and bleaching purposes in making the fine quality of goods which they turn out. Their reputation is identified with Andover. The Ballardvale flannels of Capt. Bradlee, and the Andover shoe-threads and Andover twines made by the Smith & Dove Company, are known all over the country. It is easy to say that you can compensate these manufacturers with damages for the water-power or even the pure water you take away; but the payment of damages to them will not enable them to continue their business in Andover. Practically their work would be ended. They could not go anywhere else. and build up under another name the reputation which years of honest, intelligent, and generous conduct have given them here. My brother may say that this bill guarantees these manufacturers sufficient water for the purposes for which they really need it. I have already argued to the Committee that, whatever may be its form, if you once grant any bill that permits a portion of the river to be taken. it will be a precedent under which the rest of it will be taken hereafter ; that, therefore, although it is true that, if 10.000,000 gallons of water a day were allowed to flow down, there would be enough for the manufacturers to use for the purposes we have named, yet it is also true that if this right is once granted no such stream will run for any considerable time.

Another important point in connection with the manufacturers is this : that, if a bill should be passed authorizing the taking of only a portion of the river, the manufacturers are so convinced that it would be an entering wedge for the taking of the whole stream, that it would discourage or restrain them from making any improvements upon, or development of, their property. What manufacturer in Andover is going to lay out money for the increase of his business, if he believes. as they all do believe, that, if the right now asked for is granted to Cambridge, the whole river must ultimately be taken ?

I must not forget to remind you that these manufacturers have not only built up successful establishments, which have given the place a national reputation, and that they have not only achieved fortune for themselves, and prosperity and happiness for the large number of peo-

ple dependent upon their business, but, further, that they have been
great benefactors to their community; and the literary and theological institutions of Andover, which give distinction to the town wherever its name is known, are the splendid fruit of her manufactures,
as the manufactures of the town are the product of the Shawshine.

Leaving the case, however, so far as it may be looked at from the
side of the manufacturers, and those immediately connected with
them; disregarding, if you please, the effect, however serious it may
be, upon their interests, — I beg you to consider the fact, as testified
here by the officials of Andover, that the river is essential to its health
and safety. It is the natural drainage of that district; it is there,
not by accident, but by design; it conducts away the water that runs
upon the surface, and is a necessary part of the physical structure of
the region. You cannot destroy a stream of that kind, planted there
by Nature, without producing some serious consequences. Again,
with reference to material uses, the water is needed for the domestic
purposes of the people of Andover. It can be used for a supply
against fire, and a committee of the town have the matter in hand,
and are now considering what arrangements, if any, can be made,
which will enable them to supply their modest requirements, and, at
the same time, not disturb the general character of the stream. For
these reasons, — because it is a reasonable necessity of the people of
Andover, because they have the first claim upon it if it is to be appropriated by anybody for water-supply, I submit to the Committee
that nothing ought to be done to preclude the town of Andover from
hereafter utilizing it.

There is still another point which I may fairly touch upon even in
so prosaic a discussion as this has been. Professor Park alluded to
the sentimental considerations which are involved in this proposed
taking of the Shawshine. He spoke of the tender associations which
the people of Andover, and those who have frequented the town, have
had with this little river, and of the influence it must have on those
who shall hereafter know it. For generations the citizens and students have enjoyed its beauties, and become attached 'to it as an
important feature of the landscape: they have walked by its banks,
and sailed on its waters. It cannot be destroyed without a rude dis-
turbance of very precious memories. For, indeed, it is not large
rivers alone which are endeared to the people who live by them and
use them; and the memory of the little mountain torrent or meadow
stream to which the youth was attached is as potent as that of some
great wonder of nature. The Thames at Oxford, and even where it
flows under the proud keep of Windsor, is no larger than the Shawshine, yet the boys at Eton and the students of the ancient university
who have rowed upon it, and strolled along its winding course, would

rightly think it an unnecessary profanation of it if anybody should propose, in order to accomplish some purpose of utility, to divert its waters, or confine their flow to a twelve-inch pipe, or even a little canal. It seems almost as if great literary institutions existed only on the banks of running streams. There is hardly a college of eminence in the world which does not have its river near at hand. The great university of Heidelberg is situated upon the little river Neckar, a smaller stream, most of the year, than the Shawshine. It comes down out of the Black Forest into the plains to give life and beauty and health to the little town. The students of that university would feel it as great a deprivation and sacrilege that the Neckar should be destroyed, as would the mighty German nation in losing the noble Rhine. Now, Mr. Chairman, although it is true that in this country we are less regardful of preserving the picturesque features of our natural scenery, and are more ready to sacrifice its beauties to the demands of practical and material uses, yet, after all, memory, imagination, and good taste upon such a question as this will each assert claims that cannot be entirely overlooked. You know, that in old times, next to the sun and the host of heaven, the rivers were regarded as their most beneficent gods. They were the source of all blessings, fertile fields, golden harvests, happy homes. All the protection that a grateful people could give them was exerted to keep them from harm. It was a touching indication of the natural yearning for one's native streams, the little rivers associated with earlier years, that, when Naaman the Syrian was enjoined to wash in the waters of the Jordan, he was prompted to reply, " Are not Abana and Pharpar, rivers of Damascus, more excellent than all the waters of Israel?" Indeed, when you consider what this little Shawshine has been to the people of Andover, how it is connected and identified with their interests, and woven into their history, and how it has been the source of their prosperity and happiness, you feel that their regard and affection for it, and their intense longing to preserve it for generations to come, are perfectly natural, and that it should remain as the tutelary divinity of their homes.

CLOSING ARGUMENT OF A. J. BAILEY, ESQ., CITY SOLICITOR, FOR THE CITY OF BOSTON.

Mr. CHAIRMAN AND GENTLEMEN, — The pathetic appeal of my brother Morse not to compel the town of Andover to give up its beautiful Jordan, and his great distress as to what will become of the factory operatives, remind me of the reply of Ruth. When Naomi was leaving the land of Moab, poor and destitute, she took leave of her two daughters-in-law, Ruth and Orpah, and told them that she was so poor they ought not to follow her, but should stay in their own land. So brother Morse, speaking for Andover, says that they are so poor there on that river that they hope we will let it alone, and stay where we are; but I have to reply to him, in the words of Ruth, " Entreat me not to leave thee, or to return from following after thee; for whither thou goest I will go, and where thou lodgest I will lodge; thy people shall be my people [thy river shall be our river], and thy God my God."

Now, Mr. Chairman, bearing in mind that the city of Boston has been so clearly shown here, first, not to be acting in good faith, and, secondly, to have all the water it wants, it would certainly seem to be the proper thing for Boston to gather up its papers, and retire from this room. Nevertheless, so persuaded am I that this is not exactly a fair representation of the facts in the case as they have been shown to this Committee, that I shall take some few minutes in trying to impress upon your minds both that the city of Boston is in earnest and acting in good faith in asking for this river, and that she has not sufficient water to meet the daily wants that are pressing upon her.

The Committee will bear in mind that the city of Boston is in this position: one section of it, bounded by Charles River and the harbor, is supplied by the Sudbury and the Cochituate systems; the other, bounded by the Mystic River and the Charles River, is supplied by what is called the Mystic system. We are exactly in the position that you would be, Mr. Chairman, if you had two houses in different parts of the city, and had laid in coal to supply the furnace of one of those houses for two years, and had laid in coal for one year to supply the other house. The coal in the house in which you had laid in a store for one winter is nearly exhausted, and you must look to see where you will get more coal to keep your house warm. As a prudent man, would you for one moment consider that the sensible thing for you to do would be to go to the other house, in the other portion of the town, where you had laid in two years' supply, and bring an extra year's supply to the first house at the same cost that it would be to you to buy the same amount of coal at the coal-yard? Or would you consider that the sensible thing for you to do would be to buy the additional amount of coal that you want, and leave the year's supply in the house where it is? That is exactly the position in which the city of Boston is to-day. Granted that, so far as the Cochituate and Sudbury systems are concerned, we have sufficient water for the present, — we have sufficient there, probably, for years to come. — I do not question that for one moment; but when you come to the other house, the Mystic system, what do you find? You find that the capacity of that system at the present time is seven millions of gallons a day. That is the entire capacity of that system as it stands; and we have shown that last year, and the year before, we drew upon it for even more than that, at the risk of depriving every person who took water from that system of his supply at a moment's notice, because we had to pump water from that pond into the conduit which supplied the consumers.

Now, with reference to the peculiar situation of the Mystic, no persons can be better aware than yourselves of the innumerable difficulties that surround the use of the Mystic water. There are those tanneries upon the banks of the brooks which at one time contaminated it to such an extent that we contemplated giving it up, and should have done so if we could possibly have gone elsewhere for water. Then we built the Mystic sewer, by which we were able to take care of the sewage which polluted that water; and we have put it into the condition in which it is to-day, — the purest water that comes into Boston. But, having done that, the danger stares us in the face to-day of being compelled to give up that sewer, in which event the sewage will go back into the river, and we shall be compelled, of course, to abandon it. Then where have we got to go? There are but two courses left open to us if we give up that system, or even if we do not, because we have only just sufficient water there for to-day. Brother Morse has alluded to the fact that we can build two dams, which will increase the supply to seventeen millions of gallons a day. Is it sensible for the city of Boston, constantly increasing in population as it is, to build dams upon a river which there is such imminent danger of our being compelled to abandon? Is that a thing which any reasonable man would ask us to do? I do not think the Committee would listen for a moment to a proposition to oblige us to do that.

Then, to carry out the illustration which I suggested, there is this question before us: Shall we carry a pipe across, and connect the Sudbury and Mystic systems, at a cost of $500,000, and also involve ourselves in an expenditure of $500,000 or $600,000 more, making a round million, to supply us from the storage for the future supply of another section of the city, instead of taking that same amount of money and obtaining a supply from the Shawshine valley? There are, I say, only two courses left to us, — either to carry the Sudbury system across to the Mystic, and build those additional basins; or to take the same, or even a less amount of money, and buy an abundant supply of good water farther on, leaving our storage for the parties for whom we intended it. I submit that there can be but one answer to that question: that the only practical way for the city of Boston to do is to go to the Shawshine River.

Now, then, as I said before, that system was used to its full capacity last summer. This is not disputed by anybody; and I ask, Does not that show a necessity for a supply from the Shawshine greater even than the city of Cambridge has shown, when they show that they have not been in danger of a water famine but one year, and that two years ago? This last year they do not complain that they have not had plenty of water; but we show that this very last year we took every available gallon that could be had. I say that shows a public exigency for taking this water such as Cambridge, strong as is the case that she has made, has not shown.

Therefore Boston is here in good faith, and because she needs this water, and not because Cambridge is here. Perhaps we might struggle along a year or two more just as we are; but we have that danger staring us in the face. It will take two or three years for us to get this water, even if we begin now, and meanwhile we shall be in continual fear of being deprived of water from the Mystic.

Supposing the city of Cambridge is allowed to take this water, then certainly Boston ought to be allowed to take it with her. It is claimed here by the counsel for the remonstrants, and it is conceded also by the counsel for the city of Cambridge, that the taking of even 8,000,000 gallons is practically to take the whole river; that the damages, if there are any, done to the mills on the stream, will be just as great as if the whole river was taken. That, I understand, is conceded by both sides. And, furthermore, it is conceded by the counsel for the city of Cambridge, that the same works will have to be built for Cambridge that will have to be built for the two cities. Now, the city of Cambridge only wants two-fifths of this water: she only wants 8,000,000 gallons a day. That being the case, is it not better for all parties, for the city of Cambridge and the city of Boston, inasmuch as both want the water, that only two-fifths of the burden of paying the mill damages and the cost of building the dams and laying the conduit should be imposed upon Cambridge, instead of the whole amount, which she would have to pay if she took it alone?

Now, to look once more at the question, so far as the interests of Boston alone are concerned, supposing the city of Cambridge is given the right to take this water. If they take any portion of the river, I contend that they will have to pay all the mill damages, and it may cost them $1,000,000. Then supposing Boston, some time in the future, comes here and asks for that water, and the exigency can be shown to be so great that the right will be granted to the city to take the portion that she asks for now, what will be the result? The result will be that we shall be brought into contention with the city of Cambridge as to the amount we shall pay for the balance of that water, for which they will have paid. Now the two cities are substantially agreed. I do not think they will say to-day that they occupy any different position here from that which they did last year: that they are willing, if the Committee think best, that a bill should be granted, giving the city of Boston the right to take three-fifths, or 12,000,000 gallons a day, — they to be allowed to take the other 8,000,000. Whereas, if the time goes by, and they take all this expense upon themselves, we cannot tell what the position of the two cities will be then, with reference to the possibility of making any kind of an agreement.

Therefore, I say, taking the whole matter into consideration, the fact that Boston needs this water just as much as Cambridge does; the fact that to-day they are perfectly united as to the amount of water which each requires, and the proportion of cost which each shall pay for it; and the fact that in future years we cannot tell the exact position which the two cities will occupy, — I say, that, if any bill is granted, it should be granted to both cities. And my judgment is, from the testimony that has been put in here, that both cities should be granted a bill.

CLOSING ARGUMENT OF J. W. HAMMOND, ESQ., CITY SOLICITOR, FOR THE CITY OF CAMBRIDGE.

MR. CHAIRMAN, AND GENTLEMEN OF THE COMMITTEE, — I desire to call your attention to the precise question before you. I am not sure that I can bring you back from Heidelberg, and the other countries to which your attention has been called by my brother Morse; but I should like to suggest to you that the simple question before you is, whether Cambridge shall have the right to take eight millions of gallons of water per day from the Shawshine River, here in Massachusetts, to-day, or as soon as we can make the necessary arrangements. If I thought I could excel my brothers in scriptural quotations, I would attempt: it but I do not feel quite sure of success, and I am not exactly certain that such quotations have any logical or special bearing on this case. What Cambridge desires to do is to take a certain quantity of water, not exceeding eight millions of gallons a day, from the Shawshine River, at a point in Billerica near the old bed of the Middlesex Canal, for the purpose of distributing it to its inhabitants for domestic purposes, and for the generation of steam. She desires to do that because she believes that to be the only way in which she can get what everybody concedes she absolutely needs. She comes to the Legislature for certain authority, because without that authority she cannot do it; and the only question for you to consider is whether, as legislators for the State, you believe that request of hers to be proper, and that it should be granted.

What is the present condition of Cambridge? Why, it is conceded upon the other side that our water-supply is extremely limited. Even their own engineer concedes that no community is safe in looking for a supply of less than fifty gallons a head *per diem*. You have seen the plan which has been introduced, showing the manner in which the surface of the pond from which we draw is lowered every year. We can fill up Fresh Pond only from Wellington Brook. Fresh Pond itself gives only one and three-quarters millions of gallons a day, and we need two and a half millions every day. Where do we get the remainder? We get it from Wellington Brook. And what is the character of Wellington Brook? Some year or two ago the city of Cambridge had Wellington Brook examined by the best engineering and sanitary experts to be obtained, and this was the report. I read from Professor Wood's report, which is found on pp. 35 and 36 of the " Report of the Special Committee on the Water-Supply of Cambridge : " —

" Before reaching the Belmont railroad-station, it [Wellington Brook] receives a large amount of drainage, direct and indirect, from buildings near the bank. Formerly the sewage from the privies and sinks was discharged directly into the brook, the privies in many instances being built over the brook. These were moved back as far as possible, and brick vaults provided for the inhabitants by the Water Board, so that, at the present time, the *privy* drainage in this district is indirect. A considerable amount of house-drainage, however, still goes directly into the brook. After leaving the railroad-track, it enters the lowlands, which are highly cultivated and manured, partly with night-soil. In its flow through these market-gardens it necessarily takes up a large amount of animal matter, especially after a heavy rain. How much of this is human depends largely upon the amount of night-soil used as manure, which varies according to circumstances.

" A short distance from Brighton Street it receives the drainage from Richardson's piggery, about which so much has been said in the various Water Board reports. Formerly the drainage from this piggery was received into the brook by an open ditch, which has been filled up, and a dyke built, so that it is now obliged to flow over the meadow or soak through the soil before entering the brook. ' After a heavy rain, however, the water rises high enough to overflow this dike; and for the time at least this attempt to divert the drainage of the piggery is rendered abortive.' "

Professor Wood goes on to speak of the slaughter-house in that vicinity, and the muck-heap connected with it, and says, —

" This muck-heap is situated on the top of a gravel bank, west of the slaughter-house, between it and Wellington Brook. During the warm weather, when the ground is not frozen, the muck will absorb very large quantities of soup, so that if the muck-heap is properly taken care of, there is no danger of pollution of the water of the brook or of the subsoil. In the winter, however, the soup cannot be absorbed, and must flow down the hillside to Wellington Brook."

That is the stream from which Cambridge is compelled to take water with which to fill Fresh Pond. The investigations then made showed conclusively that it was safe to take the water of Wellington Brook into Fresh Pond only during the spring freshets, and when the ground is frozen. At such times we fill up Fresh Pond if there is water enough, and then shut off Wellington Brook for the rest of the year.

Year after year we go on in that way, filling up in the spring, and using what the pond will give us, drawing the pond down constantly until the next spring rains enable us to fill it up.

Now, that is not a safe and substantial water-supply for a city. Our brothers concede it. Consider practically what is the exigency there. Do you remember the picture which was given you here of the president of the Water Board and the superintendent of the water-works standing upon the bank of Wellington Brook, hesitating whether to take the flow of that brook or not? On the one side, a sense of responsibility as to the character of the flow, whether it was safe; on the other side, urging them on, the absolute necessity for taking it, almost whether safe or not. Does any other municipality present to you a case like that, where the public authorities, acting under the most delicate and responsible sense of their duty, are driven by necessity to consider such a question? And, moreover, are you not satisfied that our inspection is as close as it can be made? They tell us here about twenty-five or thirty gallons a day per head. I do not know how long the water-works of the city of Providence have existed; but I do know that the most complete, persistent, and active inspection is made of the Cambridge water-works, — an inspection started by a man, years ago, interested in it by reason of his enthusiasm in the subject, and kept up since by the absolute necessities of the case.

I dwell on this, gentlemen, because I want you to see how Cambridge is situated. I want you to brush away the cobwebs introduced by the respondents into this case, and consider the subject as it stands to-day, — the actual situation of Cambridge. Its Board of Health has closed its wells, so that it must rely for its water upon its aqueduct, or it must be depopulated. I venture to say, and I say it without fear of contradiction, — especially do I so say it when my brothers upon the other side, active and keen as they are, have not been able to give us any particular advice on this subject, — I say, I do not believe that there is a city in the civilized world whose water-supply is more precarious than that of Cambridge to-day, as to quantity and as to quality; and the members of the Water Board do not feel that they perform their duty without constantly urging the city to seek further for a supply. The exigency is absolute.

Now, my brothers make but one reply to this, so far as the exigency is concerned. They tell us that we are situated near Boston, and that we can take water from Boston. Well, I want to argue this question fairly, Mr. Chairman and gentlemen, and I want to call your attention to the exact situation. You sit here, not as representatives of any particular locality, nor as prejudiced by the supposed interests of any particular locality, but to represent the State, to legislate for " the greatest good of the greatest number." Have I not then a right to assume, that, in the consideration of the problem, you will give your fair, and, in so far as human nature will permit, your unbiassed judgment, on our petition? We are a municipality, one of the largest in the State, and in absolute need of water; able to get it if you will give us a chance; willing to expend the necessary money, and presenting a practicable plan. We come here before you with a plan which is approved by the only engineer who is introduced upon the other side, and within our means, anxious to get that water, and we come to you for legislative permission to carry out this plan. And what is the reply upon the other side? Why, they say, " Cambridge is not very badly off. She has got a rich neighbor that has water enough, and she ought to go and see if she cannot trade with that neighbor before she undertakes to set up on her own account." Well, gentlemen, I do not know how long you have served in this business of legislation; but I venture to say that you never heard that answer given before to a municipality coming here for water. Suppose, for instance, that we do go to Boston; suppose I take my brother Bullard's book, from which he read, and I stand up with as much solemnity as he did, if that is possible, and read to the president of the Boston Water Board the remarks which he read from the European author who says that we should not have more than twenty-five or thirty gallons of water per head, and I say, " You have got plenty of water; you can let us have it just as well as not." Suppose I take my brother Morse's statement which he has read here, and show the Board absolutely, by figures, that they have got water enough for us; suppose I allude to the basins and reservoirs they may build; suppose I believe all I say; and suppose they do, but will not admit it: what would be their answer? You heard from the chairman of the Committee on Water of the Boston City Council how he treated that petition which was read here, which had been presented to his committee. He said he was going to give those petitioners a hearing when he got ready; that Boston did not want any advice about taking care of its water. In my judgment, the water of Boston is wasted; in my judgment, it always will be wasted, pretty nearly as much as it is now, and there never will be a time, so long as certain influences in Boston can prevent it, in which the consumption will be very much below what it is now. Now, are you going to turn us away on some supposed theory as to the duty of the city of Boston to supply us? It is said on the other side that Boston is willing and anxious to furnish us with this supply. That does not appear. They say, on the other side, that we should have made efforts to get water from Boston this last year. The only time we ever did apply to them to get water, they told us they had not got it, and they intimated something about eighty-five per cent. of the receipts, — that the contracts they had required the payment of eighty-five per cent. of the receipts; and it was pretty plain that Boston — the good old Puritanic city of Boston — had not lost its Puritanic shrewdness.

Now, can you safely calculate upon the fairness of the city of Boston in this matter? Is it a sufficient answer for the Legislature to say to a municipality, in the stress in which Cambridge is, "Boston, we think, will be fair: we do not know, but we think Boston will be fair with you, and do what is right." Look at the history of Boston on this water question. They have contracts now where they take eighty-five per cent. of the receipts. The city solicitor comes here, and says that Boston wants to reduce that price. Why in the world cannot Boston reduce it? He has not given us any reason. If they think eighty-five per cent. is too much, and say to those cities and towns that they will take fifty per cent., I do not believe that concession will be refused.

Mr. BAILEY. Do you know who paid for the pipes, and every thing of that kind?

Mr. HAMMOND. I cannot say any thing about that; but the only contracts they have require the payment of eighty-five per cent. of the gross receipts. But call it fifty per cent., if you please, and see what the figures are. The water receipts in Cambridge in 1881 were $171,-135. Suppose that Boston furnished that water, and charged only fifty per cent. of the receipts. One-half of $171,135 is, in round numbers, $85,000. That is, if Boston furnished us with the water which we now use, and charged us only fifty per cent. of our water receipts, which is the lowest price, as it is conceded on the other side, that even benevolent Boston would ever be willing to make a contract for, the charge would be $85,000.

Mr. MORSE. Don't you expect to use your own supply also?

Mr. HAMMOND. I am speaking now with regard to the supply which we can get from Boston; and I am speaking of it by way of comparison, on the question whether we had not better get our

8,000,000 gallons from the Shawshine. Now, suppose we take 8,000,000 gallons — the quantity that we ask to take — from the Shawshine: that would be sixteen-fifths of 2,500,000, the amount we now use. For that 8,000,000 we would have to pay Boston $272,000 a year. That is equal to the interest of about $5,500,000 at five per cent. per annum. And this, remember, is only on the basis of paying fifty per cent. of the receipts. I ask this Committee whether the Water Board of Cambridge would be justified in making a contract with Boston upon any such terms as have been suggested here; whether it is not altogether better for them, in a pecuniary point of view, to go to the Shawshine? We can take the waters of the Shawshine, and take 8,000,000 gallons a day, and it will cost us, we will say, a round million dollars. (You may think it will cost more, but we will put it at that.) That loan can be floated — I am liberal here with figures — at five per cent., to say the least: so that the interest upon the expense of getting the water of the Shawshine is $50,000 a year only for 8,000,000 gallons. Is it wise to provide that Cambridge shall pay from $85,000 now to $272,000 by-and-by, rather than to incur an expenditure which will cost them only, at the outside, $50,000 or $60,000 a year? Is it not your duty here, as members of this Committee, to consider whether you will impose upon Cambridge, on any such flimsy arguments as we have heard upon the other side, such an additional expense as that for water? And I am not speaking now of the fact that we ought to control our own works. It is absolutely demonstrable that it is much cheaper for us to take the water of the Shawshine than to go to Boston, even if Boston is disposed to make more favorable contracts with us than she has ever made with anybody else.

Mr. Morse. She has never made any contracts with anybody else.

Mr. Hammond. I know you say that; but the moment we go to the president of the Water Board and say, " We want 8,000,000 gallons a day: how much will you charge?" he says, " We are charging those folks over there eighty-five per cent. of the receipts."

Mr. Bailey. The Water Board are not the parties to whom you should go. The city government are the only parties who have power to make terms with you. The Water Board have no power to sell you a dollar's worth.

Mr. Hammond. Does anybody in this world suppose that the city government of Boston would do any thing different in regard to this matter of the disposal of water than the Water Board should suggest?

Mr. Bailey. They do it every year.

Mr. Hammond. Now, my brother Morse, with his lynx eye, has discovered a statute, chap. 126 of the year 1880, which he thinks will solve this problem. I should like to analyze that statute a little.

In the first place, the city of Boston, by sect. 6, is authorized, "if the Boston Water Board shall be of opinion that the supply of water is sufficient for the purpose, to sell water to the city of Cambridge, when conducted through the main pipes laid by virtue of the provisions of sect. 2 of this Act." "*If the Water Board is of opinion that the supply of water is sufficient for the purpose.*"

Now, you may not have the idea that the Water Board of Boston are careful enough about the water-supply ; but it is pretty plain that it is their judgment which is to control this matter, even under that statute. You may think they have poor judgment ; but their judgment, whether good or poor, is to determine whether, after the Mystic is connected with the Sudbury, Cambridge can have any water from the connecting pipe. The city government of Boston can have nothing to do with it without the sanction of the Water Board. Are you going to say to us substantially, "Gentlemen, you are in a hard stress over there in Cambridge : it is a pretty hard case ; no mistake about that. We don't quite see what you can do, except to go to the Boston Water Board, and get down on your knees before them, and see if you can convince them that they have got water enough for you." It is on that ground that we shall be turned from this State House, if we are turned at all, — on that ground, and on none other. But the beauty about this is, that it is perfectly clear that Boston does not even mean to build that main, if she can help it. The first section of the Act authorizes a main pipe to be laid in Beacon Street, which has been done. The second section authorizes the construction of a main pipe, which shall connect the two systems through Cambridge. And then the last section says, —

"This Act shall take effect upon its acceptance by the City Council of the city of Boston ; but the powers conferred by sect. 1 of this Act may be exercised without any obligation on the part of said city to exercise the powers conferred by sect. 2."

That is, they may construct one without the other ; and they have constructed one, and not the other. Cambridge can neither construct the other, nor compel Boston to construct it.

Now, is it fair, when you see a municipality in the stress in which Cambridge is, to make her rely upon the good-will of an adjoining city for a supply of water? Is it the principle on which you should legislate? I am now assuming that we should hurt Andover. Is it, I repeat, the principle on which you should legislate?

Now, Mr. Chairman, and gentlemen of the Committee, I have been endeavoring to show you, by figures, that it is absolutely more economical for Cambridge to get water from the Shawshine than to go to Boston. I have shown you that it is not safe to rely upon Boston ;

that she must look out for herself first. I believe you are satisfied
that it is not right to turn us away, and leave us to the mercies of a
more powerful neighbor. And now I ask your attention to the
precise proposition which is before you.

This bill concerns the water of a small stream. My friends upon
the other side have argued with remarkable ability — I had no idea
that a sentimental idea could be brought out so clearly until I heard
my brother Morse — their theory that the passage of this bill is going
to shut down those mills and ruin Andover. Why, as I thought
over the lugubrious prophecies that were made by the witnesses from
Andover, and scanned the sombre features of my brother Poor, I was
reminded of the familiar lines of Goldsmith : —

> " Sweet, smiling village, loveliest of the lawn !
> Thy sports are fled, and all thy charms withdrawn.
> Amidst thy bowers the tyrant's hand is seen,
> And desolation saddens all the green.
> One only master grasps the whole domain,
> And half a tillage stints thy smiling plain. •
> Nor more thy glassy brook reflects the day,
> But choked with sedges works its weary way.''

I could not understand how the people of Andover had got into
such a frame of mind ; but I remembered that for generations their
theology has been somewhat gloomy. They have been educated,
year after year, and generation after generation, to have the most
lively anxiety *for the future. Not present works*, but *faith*, is that
on which the people of Andover rely ; and, the more serious their
view of the future, the happier they believe that future will actually
be. No other community could have got into such a frame of mind
on this question as they have. Why, their anxiety about the future
makes me think of Mrs. Toodles, who, you remember, bought a
second-hand sign. She was a great buyer at auctions, and she
bought a sign with the name Thompson upon it, spelled with a " p.''
Her husband remonstrated with her for buying such a thing, and she
replied, " We may have a child. That child may be a daughter, and
that daughter may marry a man by the name of Thompson, who
spells his name with a ' p ; ' and that sign will be just the thing.''

Now, Andover makes the objection to this bill, not that it of itself
is bad, — and I desire to call attention to this fact, — but that it is
" the entering wedge,'' as it was expressed here by one witness ;
and that phrase has been echoed and re-echoed through this chamber
ever since in the evidence and in the arguments. I asked the mill-
owners, Mr. Bradlee, for instance, — a very estimable man, who has
apparently done a good deal for his operatives, — " Mr. Bradlee, do
you believe we shall hurt you ?'' — " I don't know,'' said he : " it is

an experiment." Is there any doubt in your minds that that Theological Seminary will still exist; that the students will have the same
opportunities to bathe they have had heretofore; that they can walk
upon the banks of that stream with all the sentimentality which their
education will leave in them, with the gloomy feelings which their
theology creates? Do we hurt their stream? See what my brother
Morse last year said, who always has an appearance of candor in
whatever he says. I read from his argument on p. 151 of the
report of the hearing of last year, —

"Nobody objects to having the water taken from any of these rivers in the
spring. There is great waste, of course, from all rivers at that season of the
year. But you are to look at the minimum supply; you are to look at the minimum quantity that runs through the river, and say whether or not an application that seeks to take that away is not practically an application to take the
entire river.

"The Committee are so familiar with this class of questions that I need not
dwell upon it. I merely suggest to them that where a small river, which furnishes only a limited amount of water, is to be drawn upon to supply a certain
amount, like 8,000,000 gallons a day, it is, practically, to be exhausted at the
most critical time."

We propose to take it only when it would otherwise be wasted,
and actually to increase the flow in a dry time.

Is not the opposition of Andover here the most ill-founded and unreasonable opposition that you have had to any project before this
Committee? I put that question to you in all sincerity. Do they
know what they are opposing? Why, I asked the town committee,
as the other side brought them out one after another, "Have you
looked at this proposition of Cambridge?" Well, no, they hadn't.
"Do you know what you are opposing?" Well, no, they didn't.
Is not that a fair statement of their evidence? "Why do you oppose
it?" "Because we feel that it is an entering wedge." In the mind
of Andover, the sanctity of that theological institution permeates
every drop of water that goes by it! I had the honor to say, when
I opened the hearing before this Committee, that I really believed,
that, if the mill-owners of Andover would consider carefully the proposition of Cambridge, they would come to the conclusion that, instead
of hurting them, we were absolutely benefiting them; but, Mr.
Chairman, they "fear the Greeks, even bearing gifts." They do not
know what to say to it. Their own engineer, Mr. Crafts, says our
plan is perfectly practicable, that more water will go down that stream
every day of the year than now frequently goes down there. I am
informed that when you were at Andover the other day the water
was going to waste over the dams. What this bill proposes to do is
to preserve that pure water which is thus running to waste over those

dams, and save it in the reservoir, to give a portion of it to the city
of Cambridge, and to give the mill-owners of Andover actually more
of it when they need it than they have now. Is not that a fair statement of the proposition? If, Mr. Chairman, you need any general
principle upon which to legislate here, I ask you to consider the one
grand principle of economy, which has built up this State. From
the sands of Cape Cod to the cliffs of Berkshire this State is dotted
with houses, — pleasant homes, — made possible only by the most
severe economy. There is water running to waste within the limits
of the Commonwealth, as pure water as flows anywhere within its
borders. He is a good legislator who saves and puts to a better use
that which exists in his own State, under his own jurisdiction. Can
we not save and use that water, and hurt nobody? Is it not plain to
you that we can? that our whole plan is that of economy in the use
of the water? I do not believe that the quantity of water which
Cambridge will use for years to come will be any thing like that
which now goes to waste over that dam. My brother Morse speaks
of the purity of the water. What can be better for those mill-owners
than to have a municipality on that stream which is interested in the
preservation of the purity of the water? Bear in mind that gentleman from Lexington, who said that that town desired to drain into
this stream, and presented an amendment to this bill for the purpose
of preserving that right. Is it not better to put a powerful municipality on that stream, prepared by all means which the law has given
it to protect the purity of its water? Will it make the flannels any
less pure that are manufactured by this Ballardvale mill, to have
above it a reservoir from which water is drawn by a city? Are not
these considerations which you may legitimately take into account?

My idea about this theory of " an entering wedge " is, that, if this
bill is passed, the question of taking the water of the Shawshine will
be substantially settled for all time, because the Legislature will
recognize, by the passage of this bill, the importance of letting
10,000,000 gallons a day run down there, so that the effect will be
to keep everybody else off more than if no bill had been passed.

So I say, in substance, that the proposition which we make here, to
take the water of the Shawshine River, is a proposition to equalize
its flow, so that the mills and the town will get more water when they
need it than they get now. We say that 10,000,000 gallons a
day shall go down; we agree that it shall; we are bound that it
shall; we submit ourselves to a court of equity if it does not. How
much is 10,000,000 gallons a day? What will run constantly
over a dam five feet wide and one foot high. It will put more mill-
power upon that stream. The mill-power now is not equal to five
hundred horse-power. It is not one third as much as exists in one of

those mills at Lawrence. I grant you that that is a small consideration, if it is the power upon which a community lives; but it is not
the water-power that carries these mills. Mr. Bradlee's mill was run
nine months year before last by steam, six months last year. The
other mill-owners have not been on the stand; but it is fair to assume
that they run no less by steam than his mill does. Not as motive-
power do they need this water, nor do they chiefly use it as such.
They use it chiefly for washing their goods, and desire to have the
discharge equalized; and I believe that the mill-owners themselves,
if they considered their own interests, would do exactly what we are
going to do there, as far as the dam is concerned. Of course they
would want all the water; but it would equalize the flow, and be better
for them. Why, what have they done with that little pond called
Foster's Pond? The stream is so small that they have actually done
with Foster's Pond what we desire to do for them upon the river.
Mr. Bradlee says the fact that Cambridge is to have control of it is
the main thing that troubles him. *Cambridge is not to have control
of it.* That is where he is mistaken. This Legislature, by passing
that law, places Cambridge under an obligation to give those who are
aggrieved the right to enforce that guaranty. Cambridge is under
the law, and Mr. Bradlee will not find his dam within the power of
Cambridge: he will find it under the power of the law, where every
other right in this Commonwealth ought to be.

It is stated here that Boston has a pipe connected with Cambridge
by which we can now take 4,000,000 gallons a day into Fresh Pond,
and 2,000,000 gallons a day into our pipes. That is not true, and it
was not so stated by the engineer. We can draw through that pipe,
the engineer stated. about 1,000,000 gallons a day.

Mr. BULLARD. That is because there is a twelve-inch connection.
My statement was as to the capacity of the sixteen-inch pipe, as
laid, not as connected.

Mr. HAMMOND. I only desired to allude to that mistake, and not
to go over the argument again with regard to Boston. Almost any
honorable man, and I know my brother Bullard is an honorable man,
would say that it was not well to open that gate until Boston gave
us permission.

I say then, Mr. Chairman, in substance, — I do not care to go
over this to any further extent, — that Cambridge is in serious stress
for water; that she comes to the State for the right to get water;
and that it is unprecedented and unfair to compel her to go, as her
only resource, to a municipality where all the bargains in existence
show that it will be much more expensive to take water from Boston
than to go to the Shawshine; that the Shawshine is the only other
place we can go to; that we do not hurt, but actually help, that

community, as the bill is now drawn; and that all these gloomy remarks have their origin in an entire misconception of the purpose of this bill. And I ask you as legislators, legislating as well for the economical use of whatever there is within the limits of this State as for the greatest benefit of the greatest number, to give us this bill.